Killer Cities

Theory, Culture & Society

Theory, Culture & Society caters for the resurgence of interest in culture within contemporary social science and the humanities. Building on the heritage of classical social theory, the book series examines ways in which this tradition has been reshaped by a new generation of theorists. It also publishes theoretically informed analyses of everyday life, popular culture, and new intellectual movements.

EDITOR: Mike Featherstone, *Goldsmiths, University of London*

SERIES EDITORIAL BOARD

David Beer, *University of York*
Nicholas Gane, *University of Warwick*
Scott Lash, *University of Oxford*

The Theory, Culture & Society book series, the journals *Theory, Culture & Society* and *Body & Society*, the TCS website and related conferences, workshops, and other activities now operate from Goldsmiths, University of London. For further details please contact:

e-mail: tcs@sagepub.co.uk
web: http://tcs.sagepub.com/

Recent volumes include:

From Being to Living: a Euro-Chinese Lexicon of Thought
Michael Richardson & Krzysztof Fijalkowski

After Capital
Couze Venn

Understanding the Chinese City
Li Shiqiao

French Post-War Social Theory
Derek Robbins

The Body and Social Theory, Third Edition
Chris Shilling

The Tourist Gaze 3.0
John Urry and Jonas Larsen

Consumer Culture and Postmodernism, Second Edition
Mike Featherstone

The Body and Society, Third Edition
Bryan S. Turner

Formations of Class & Gender
Beverley Skeggs

The Consumer Society, Revised Edition
Jean Baudrillard

Nigel Thrift

Killer Cities

Los Angeles | London | New Delhi
Singapore | Washington DC | Melbourne

Los Angeles | London | New Delhi
Singapore | Washington DC | Melbourne

SAGE Publications Ltd
1 Oliver's Yard
55 City Road
London EC1Y 1SP

SAGE Publications Inc.
2455 Teller Road
Thousand Oaks, California 91320

SAGE Publications India Pvt Ltd
B 1/I 1 Mohan Cooperative Industrial Area
Mathura Road
New Delhi 110 044

SAGE Publications Asia-Pacific Pte Ltd
3 Church Street
#10-04 Samsung Hub
Singapore 049483

Editor: Natalie Aguilera
Assistant editor: Eve Williams
Production editor: Katherine Haw
Proofreader: Camille Bramall
Indexer: Charmian Parkin
Marketing manager: George Kimble
Cover design: Wendy Scott
Typeset by: KnowledgeWorks Global Ltd.

© Nigel Thrift 2021

First published 2021

Apart from any fair dealing for the purposes of research or private study, or criticism or review, as permitted under the Copyright, Designs and Patents Act, 1988, this publication may not be reproduced, stored or transmitted in any form, or by any means, without the prior permission in writing of the publisher, or in the case of reprographic reproduction, in accordance with the terms of licences issued by the Copyright Licensing Agency. Enquiries concerning reproduction outside those terms should be sent to the publisher.

Library of Congress Control Number: 2020940187

British Library Cataloguing in Publication data

A catalogue record for this book is available from the British Library

ISBN 978-1-5297-5182-6
ISBN 978-1-5297-5183-3 (pbk)

For Fagan

The glacier knocks in the cupboard,
The desert sighs in the bed,
And the crack in the tea-cup opens
A lane to the land of the dead.
                      W.H. Auden (1937) 'As I Walked Out One Evening'

Contents

About the Author ... viii
Preface and Acknowledgements ... ix

1 An Uncommon Humanity ... 1

PART I: CITIES ... 13
2 The Urban World ... 15

PART II: LIFE ... 37
3 Thinking Animals ... 39
4 Animals Thinking ... 53

PART III: DEATH ... 67
5 The Animal City ... 69
6 The City of Surplus Death ... 92
7 Not Meat But Still Dead ... 116
8 But Some Animals Do Adapt to the City ... 130

PART IV: A NEW SETTLEMENT ... 145
9 Dreaming More Human Cities 1 ... 147
10 Dreaming More Human Cities 2 ... 167
11 There Is Another World But It Is This One ... 189

References ... 203
Index ... 239

About the Author

Nigel Thrift is the Chair of the UK Committee on Radioactive Waste Management as well as a Visiting Professor at Oxford University and Tsinghua University and an Emeritus Professor at the University of Bristol. He was the Executive Director of Schwarzman Scholars. Before he held that position, he was the Vice-Chancellor of the University of Warwick and before that a Pro-Vice-Chancellor of the University of Oxford. He has also held positions at Bristol University, ANU, Leeds University and Cambridge University as well as visiting positions at NUS, the University of Vienna, Macquarie University, and Institutes of Advanced Study in Sweden and the Netherlands. His research spans a broad range of interests, including international finance; cities and political life; non-representational theory and performance; affective politics; repair and maintenance; digital life; and the history of timekeeping.

Preface and Acknowledgements

Cities are often considered to be one of the high points of human civilization. I am not so sure. It might be better to think of them as an amalgam, containing both hope and despair. Rather like Miró, who chose two very different works of art, Velásquez's Las Meninas and Goya's Dog, as the works he most admired in the Prado, so we might argue that cities currently contain spaces glowing with an easy power and privilege, like Las Meninas, mixed with spaces which seem to announce both a premonition of doom and a final burst of defiance, so brilliantly marked out by Goya as a dog facing the imminent prospect of inundation by forces unknown[1]. But neither depiction, however extraordinary it may be, inspires much confidence in our collective future. So we have to find another way. No wonder that Picasso wanted to refigure Las Meninas[2]. Heaven knows what he would have done with Goya's dog: perhaps it is there somewhere in the sufferings of the horse in Guernica.

Cities are often depicted as the safe havens of human civilization, as the places where the best outweighs the worst. They are certainly where much that can be counted as positive about the human endeavour has flourished. But against that record of success needs to be set a rather different reckoning. Cities have also been the scenes of the most extraordinary levels of violence and barbarity. Not surprisingly, given the different ways in which statistics on violence are gathered, it is not possible to give any kind of exact accounting. But the evidence is there in the historical record, however approximate it might sometimes be. Furthermore, as societies have become more urbanized, so more and more violence has tended to occur within city bounds rather than without.

Direct human-on-human violence is just one kind of harm, however, and it may even be declining (Pinker, 2012). But there are many other kinds of violence done by cities. To begin with, there is all of the silent and not-so-silent violence done to humans that arises from being exposed to 'ordinary' urban living conditions, from road deaths to pollution. Then, on the underside of this underside, there is all of the violence done to the other beings we inhabit the city with, some of it undoubtedly purposeful, some collateral. Finally, there is the violence done to the very fabric of the planet.

This book takes a slightly different tack from many studies in that it focuses on the violence done not just in but by the city. Why? Because cities are killers. They really are. Hence the title of this book and the opening stanza plundered from the poem by a lovelorn, even despairing, W.H. Auden.

Preface and Acknowledgements

But it doesn't have to be like this. We shouldn't have to keep making a stocktake of death in which, as Shelley famously wrote of London, the city 'vomits its wrecks and still howls on for more'[3]. It should be possible to produce a state of affairs where the killing in and by cities decreases substantially and cities chime with cycles of life and death that are not 'natural' – never that – but are at least proportionate. Getting to this ecliptic might be hard, but, as I hope to show, it isn't impossible. I will argue that we can instigate new forms of wakefulness that can lead to new ways of living in cities which will allow the city to stand on its own feet instead of fecklessly treading on the feet of others. After all, our hopes must now rely on a future where the very cities that have caused so many of our problems must now become the key to our salvation. We need a new covenant with other beings which is not just an exercise in ethical principles but a simple matter of survival.

This book, like its subject matter, is a hybrid – part social theory, part polemic, part primer for taking practical action. It might seem to be about denaturing 'nature', 'society', 'human' and even the 'city'. But it is not just an attempt to move beyond one-sided categories like these, categories which have produced something like an epistemic lock-in. That has become a relatively familiar pursuit. It is also meant to provide the beginnings of a pragmatics which will allow us to reach a clearing where, when we speak, all kinds of entities, and not just humans, can speak back – not just at us but with us. In other words, it is an encouragement to rebuild the city as something truly spacious. The city becomes both a set of tasks and duties to be performed and the domain of new forms of responsibility. New freedoms, yes, but also new forms of obligation.

This wasn't a book I expected to write. But it became a book I had to write. That said, it is neither a eulogy nor a panegyric. Nor is it yet another stentorian proclamation following on in the wake of so many other proclamations which have signally failed to reveal their own undersides. Rather, it is an attempt to hail the world differently. After all, when we teach our children their first lessons in manners, greeting someone properly is usually the start. In that sense, this book is simply trying to craft new means of saying 'hello'.

I have tried to underscore what I write by providing appropriate references and footnotes, hopefully not in too wooden a manner[4]. There is a reason for this profusion of 'evidence'. I want to get away from a certain style of social theory which blithely pronounces on what the world is like as though it is somehow offering an authoritative account. It doesn't, and it can't. There is far too much going on to offer more than a preliminary sketch. The world is not one thing, nor can it be read as being one thing, like an instruction manual. So social theory has to be both confident but also hesitant. By the way, I don't think that is a contradiction in terms.

This is a book that has taken a number of years to, if not complete, at least get as right as it ever will be. The original draft of the manuscript was 147,000 words, the result of including not only animals – now very much the book's main focus – but also plants and a new breed of electronic sentients within its pages. Things were getting out of control. Wisely, the referees recommended a crash diet, even though that also meant saying goodbye to the history of early urbanism, the current rethinking of domestication, what hunter-gatherer societies can and can't teach us, and what *is* distinctive about human beings. I still miss them, though.

Getting to the end of a book like this requires a number of votes of thanks. I owe a particular debt to Ash Amin and Noel Castree for parsing the manuscript in detail. I want to acknowledge Josh Dorman for kindly giving permission to use one of his excellent works of art for the cover. I want to thank participants at a 2016 public lecture at the University of Melbourne for their tolerance of a really very drafty recounting of the main themes of this book. Equally, I would like to extend my thanks to participants at the Symposium to honour Peter Sloterdijk on the occasion of his 70th birthday for listening to a more developed but still drafty – though not quite as drafty – recounting of some of those same themes in Karlsruhe in 2017. With the permission of Suhrkamp Verlag, which published the papers from this Symposium, I draw on some of this talk in revised form in parts of Chapters 3, 5, 6 and 11. Finally, I offer my thanks to the class of Master's students at Schwarzman College in Tsinghua University for their forbearance in sitting through a 2018 Cities course which relied on some of the material on which this book is based without looking too bored. They reminded me that my generation failed to stop the planet suffering from a bad case of urban rot and decay. Now they must somehow turn the tables on the legacy of death and destruction we have left them to deal with.

Extract from Adele Brand *The Hidden World of the Fox*. Reprinted by permission of HarperCollins Publishers Ltd © (2019) (Adele Brand)

Notes

1. As depicted on one of the walls of his house outside Madrid and then brought to the Prado. Of course, the dog could also be interpreted as a sign of the human condition, though the looming conflagration has now been brought about by humanity itself.
2. As he did in a series of variations started in 1957. It is worth noting that the mastiff in Las Meninas is transformed into a portrait of Lump, Picasso's pet dachshund, in 15 out of the 44 Las Meninas studies.
3. Even as 'in its depth' he also finds 'treasure' (Percy Bysshe Shelley, Letter to Maria Gisbourne, 1820; http://spenserians.cath.vt.edu/TextRecord.php?action=GET&textsid=36326 (accessed June 17, 2020).
4. My work has been criticized for being too keen to fill up the page with references, however I think it is incumbent on writers to document why they are willing to make particular statements. I have read too much social theory which blithely asserts the primacy of its account of the world on the basis of not much except other social theoretical accounts and a kind of theoretical puritanism. Fine, but with this tendency comes the risk of writing 'phiction'. Equally, my work has been criticized for being too theoretically heterogeneous whereas what it is actually trying to do is let different accounts bump up against each other, taking the best from each, rather than instigating another beautifully honed system. The world is not Copernican. It's lots of things. Traffic calming is fine. Stop signs are not.

1
An Uncommon Humanity

Introduction

Why is it that nature writing has reappeared in such profusion just as the planet becomes city? Is it because nature is being extinguished or occluded rather than tended and guarded? Is it because we have internalized guilt about the state of the planet and now need to externalize it? Is it because we know there is a disturbance in the ether which is going to become much more than just a vague sense of foreboding? All of these things and more, I'm sure. But the question I want to answer is somewhat different. It is this. Is it because we are struggling to comprehend a world that we have made and unmade because the categories we use not only no longer apply but are actively damaging? In particular, I want to argue that the very foundations of the category we call 'human' have been unsettled as we confront the limits of what we understand as thinking, and very likely that sense of certainty about what's what will never return in its most confidently species-centric form in which theory is still often made manifest (Cavell et al., 2008). After all, 'Dogs are not surrogates for theory […]; they are not here just to think with. They are here to live with' (Haraway, 2003: 298).

As Robert Macfarlane (2015a) does wild swimming, as Charles Foster (2016) tries in vain to become beast, as Helen Macdonald (2014) engages with a raptor, they are not naively trying to recreate a natural realm where 'wild' is a primal quality. They are all of them knowing about the artifice of what they attempt and about the perils of anthropomorphism (Daston and Mitman, 2005). But equally, there is a longing for a different kind of relationship with the denizens of the Earth – one of respect, even of obligation, one of giving life back, one of connection and coexistence – and a corresponding anxiety about the sick state of the planet and its cities which is in itself an orientation towards the world.

And that is surely right. In a world in which cities rely on energy sources which cast a dirty pall over the earth, in which cities produce waste in profusion, in which cities stain the oceans with their detritus and in which cities exist only on the back of the death, often in pain and agony, of perhaps as many as 72 billion land animals killed for meat each year[1] as well as goodness knows how many wild animals and aquatic dwellers[2], there is an obvious disjuncture between a narrative of cities as the greatest of humankind's achievements, innovative hotbeds full to the brim with youthful creativity, and their parallel existence as the climax predators on the planet. Rather than portraying them as some kind of eighth wonder of the world, cities can just as easily be likened to a set of hive beings which resemble nothing so much as a poisonous disease, a planetary plague[3] in which the pathogen is human beings rather than bacteria or viruses. Switching metaphors, perhaps instead they should be likened to a composite group of tyrannosaurs rampaging around the globe, roaring[4] loudly as they go and carelessly trampling on everything that should be held dear. In other words, cities provide endless stimulation to being but at the cost of endless damage to its fabric. They express a longing for humanity, but only by meting out destruction.

That is a judgement only made worse by the fact that so many supposedly human characteristics are turning out to be shared by the many entities with which they cohabit cities, the animals that act as entertainment, unfree labour or simply as fodder, from the humble canine, whether carried in a bag or simply scavenging as a commensal, to the mule or donkey or horse, who did so much to bring cities into being, to the lobster or crab awaiting their turn to die in some supposedly sophisticated restaurant. Yet what seemed like the triumph of human cognition – the justification for these practices – seems neither as distinctive as once it was nor as triumphant as once it might have seemed[5]. The examples of sophisticated animal cognition are now legion and they must give pause to even the most ardent of human speciesists. The spirits of Dürer's hare, Stubbs' two leopards, Delacroix's two tigers, Hughes' caged jaguar (Oswald, 2014), Berger's (2009 [1980]) skittish roundelay of mice, Hogarth's pug Trump or even Traylor's dogs stare out at us and, each of them in their different ways, see us and find us wanting, find that we have closed down horizons and instituted a terrible babbling silence[6].

Indeed, at the risk of being labelled a misanthropist, humanity itself can sometimes seem more like a barbarian horde of 'inhumanity', as much a war machine as a moment of enlightenment, as much an epidemic as a cure. This is a narrow and cramped humanity at work. But, unlike other aggressive diseases, this is a plague that could choose to stop before it runs out of fuel. And that braking process would need to start with cities.

Redefining the City and Humanity

So can the city join with an expanded and inclusive definition of humanity which no longer sets us apart and so end the age of a self-imposed and aggressive loneliness? Can we create, instead, a network of solidarity with non human beings, a retooled set of *obligations*, a different set of voltages, if you like, in the name of a broader understanding of reality that both includes and overcomes the notion of species and, at the same time, offers new consolations? I want to try to answer questions like these by arguing that the city can be a vital element of an expanded and mutually inclusive definition of humanity[7], rather than the vision of the city that has become engrained in many cultures which makes no room for animals except as adjuncts to the human. In other words, I want to redefine not just what it means to be human but what can be counted as human. My approach is not 'antihumanist', therefore. Rather, it is humanist, but understanding human in an expanded sense. Not more than human. More human. *All* in the family.

Usually, a project like this is associated with some kind of expansion and recalibration of our relationship with the planet and that ambition is revealed by cognomens like 'Terran' or 'Earthling', which are meant to signify new forms of humanity which stand for all of the peoples of the earth (Danowski and Viveiros de Castro, 2017; Latour, 2017)[8]. My purpose in tying this expansion and recalibration to the city is both the same and different. I certainly want to rethink where humanity begins and ends. But I also want to get down and dirty, so to speak, by outlining, sometimes in graphic detail, the costs we bear day on day by not making this move – by marking the actual death toll, the real *work* of subtraction and calculated disappearance, the contemporary version of the harvesting of souls that is taking place here – and here – and here, right under our noses[9]. If you like, I want to draw up the charge sheet against the contemporary city so that we can have a proper trial, even though the verdict will be messy. The sentence may be indeterminate but hopefully it will result in a new definition of community service, one that includes the whole community and not just one portion of it.

Whatever the nature of the case for the prosecution, this act of redefinition of humanity is no pipedream. What legitimately thinks and is allowed to constitute 'we' has always been a fractured quantity and it has changed many times over the course of history: 'the human ... is not now and never was itself' (Wolfe, 2003: xiii). It has never been as clear-cut as it has sometimes been portrayed. For example, it may be that Cartesianism cemented a view of animals as radically distinct from humans in the eighteenth century (though this is a deeply contentious statement which, at best, relays only a part of the story; Riskin, 2018). But there were many other competing intellectual currents which thought of the human as far less distinct (Wolfe, 2015). After all, this was also the point in time when Linnaeus classified humans with other primates – and even with bats (Tague, 2015). But whatever may have been the case in the past, we now know that there is not one righteous pathway to mental complexity, to what counts as thinking, or to what constitutes consciousness. 'We' can cover a multitude of different manifestations of being and thinking.

Just looking at the history of how many human beings were defined as outside 'we' only underlines the point about who thinks. Thus, until quite recently in the historical record of more than a few cultures, enslaved people were regarded by many 'men' as being outside the pale of thinking humanity[10]. So were women. So were colonial peoples. So were indigenous peoples. So were a multitude of different ethnicities who could be fashioned as barbarians or worse. So were all kinds of people who were regarded as disabled. The list goes on and the weight of rejection of the right to life and the ability to forge an identity still continues even now, as the figures for domestic and racist violence show only too well. In each of these cases, an appeal to a biological fiction of the nonhuman 'brute' is often used to uphold numerous forms of human – all-too-human – oppression: each of these rejects from the world of 'really human' humans was able to be subjected to barbarous violence and brutality in the name of civilization (Mbembe, 2019). As the other to thinking humanity, this *logic of disposability* meant that they could be legitimately controlled through force – and cast down each time they made a break for freedom. In a horrible inversion, humanity was defined by inhumanity and, correspondingly, life on the planet by the degree to which it benefited this skewed and twisted definition of the human[11].

But the record is not just a dark one, though it can sometimes feel like it. This habit of thinking about the world as inclusion by dint of exclusion is by no means the only available option. Different peoples have thought about the world in different ways from this rejectionist bloodline and that provides an opportunity to regroup. There are plentiful resources to draw upon, not so much a static archive of other realities as a constantly evolving inventory of experiments with thinking the world which reveal the cracks in how it is thought and the possibilities of thinking it differently. The asymptomatic becomes symptomatic, in other words. Perhaps we can sniff out new more inclusive ideas about how we might go about thinking about thinking, and thinking the other, thereby holding out the promise of opening up and capturing new worlds[12]. As just one example, many writers and artists have used speculations about how animals think and act to inform their work on recasting human thinking, from anthropologists like Claude Lévi-Strauss, alighting on birds as a both a motif and an ambition to think differently, to painters of animal destinies like Franz Marc, to contemporary installation/video artists like Heather Phillipson. Each of them wants to produce a model of kinship with animals which sets aside claims to the automatic superiority of the category of human, which understands that 'the "human" is only ever meaningful in relation to the "non-human"' (Fudge, 2002b: 10), and which risks setting out new typologies and characterizations. Animals serve not as food but as food for thought (Wróbel, 2015). If you don't take them into account, you miss the whole point of reimagining the planet.

We can be more radical than any self-declared radical if we take more note of these different ways of constructing what we think of as thought – not as simply the beliefs or mental states brewed up by psychologism, or the kind of austere logicism that wants to believe that everything can be rendered down into a set of neat propositions, but as reciprocal modifications born out of different possible worlds rubbing up against each other – as we try to construct a subjectivity which can live in the world as an open multiplicity, one which has no origin and no goal and no centre. This is to understand the world as a continual opening without closure, as a perpetual disequilibrium, in which we must never explain too much, as Deleuze put it, or we lose the ability to multiply the world and to appreciate that multiplication. This is a genuine risk society.

Let's return to contemporary nature writing. In another variant of the craft, authors fix on various kinds of environmental apocalypse which snuff out cities. Running in an end-of-days bloodline which stretches from Richard Jeffries' (1885) *After London* through J.G. Ballard's (1966) *The Crystal World*, this strain of work has become ever more insistent of late. Of course, that's hardly a surprise. After all, we are in something approaching an environmental apocalypse right now[13]. But what is interesting is that many of these recent excursions are prone to read like a revenger's tragedy. In books like Liz Jensen's (2009) *The Rapture*, Barbara Kingsolver's (2012) *Flight Behavior*[14], Ali Shaw's (2016) *The Trees*, Jeff VanderMeer's (2014) *Area X* trilogy, Martin MacInnes's (2020) *Gathering Evidence*, Lydia Millet's (2020) *A Children's Bible* or even in Daisy Johnson's (2017) book of short stories, *Fen*, nature returns as an enveloping force which finds precious little room for the lives of human beings[15]. Nature either ejects the human outright or turns it into a mutation which resembles nothing so much as the extreme forms of life that we have been busy discovering of late (Toomey, 2014). Yet notwithstanding their gloomy, anxious prognosis, there are definite pleasures of schadenfreude associated with these books, the pleasures of deletion and of revenge and of life reasserted. Ha, nature got one back on you!

But if we are not to reach the kind of dark apotheoses depicted in books like these, in which the human is swept clear of the planet by some extrahuman force, we need to transform how we think about how the human thinks human. Guided by the work of writers like Eduardo Viveiros de Castro and Philippe Descola, I want to suggest another way of going on, one which would let us see the world anew and let us build ever more respectful cities, cities which no longer stand apart, cities which supposedly stand above the fray whilst actually initiating it, cities which have brought us progress as a sword to be wielded in favour of an attenuated version of humanity.

In other words, I want to propose an altogether more modest alternative to the city as a scythe. It is an alternative which would contain within it the seeds of something which might turn out to be kinder and less open to needless suffering and, just as importantly, might have genuine survival characteristics. It would see 'the human' not as some kind of a cultural or a biological given attuned to just one species but instead as a still unaccomplished task, both in the sense of adding lustre to the panoply of entities that have never been regarded as fully human and, equally, in the sense of chipping away at the notion of an absolute human uniqueness which is either 'not-animal' or 'animal – plus'. After all, it may be that human 'is less "human" on some registers than the devotees of anthropocentrism imagine. Accordingly, other aspects of human nature may be more human on an extended notion of humanity' (Connolly, 2017: 108). This alternative way of thinking emphasizes partial connections between unlike ways of life. Choosing an extended model of kinship and constant metamorphosis of forms, and respecting difference, it refuses to let the world go to pot. It is an obeisance to the practice of multiplying affinity, with the aim of producing a world in which more than human is more human because 'the common point of reference for all beings of nature is not humans as a species but rather humanity as a condition' (Descola, 1986: 120). Stengers sets out the choice we now have to make, one in which all of us

> [...] who were told stories since birth that there is something really special in being 'human' are at a bifurcation point: either we furiously keep to that narrative, or we accept that if there is a post-Anthropocene worth living in, those who live in it will need different stories with no entity at the center of the stage. (2013: 178)

But why bother with all of this fancy stuff about redefining what we mean by the human? Isn't this just a petty intellectual exercise with no real purchase on the world? I think not. It is increasingly apparent that how we think about the world not only needs to change but needs to be upended: we need to become other than what we are by being more than we are. But unless we can build more human cities where coexistence is not just a slogan, where diplomacy is not just another name for dominion, where we can experience 'the rude shock of the planet's otherness' (Chakrabarty, 2014: 23) as something other than just an additional weight to be borne, the planet is likely to falter. In other words, we need to alter our ways of being urban. If we carry on as we have up to now, building civilization on the back of barbarism, we will be left with cities that can only think dark thoughts, cities that can only twitch and groan as though they are caught up in a nightmare, but a nightmare that is being acted out awake.

A Resumé

After this brief introductory chapter, this book consists of another ten chapters, which multiply and build on these thoughts about how to construct a 'process of human development as neither liberation from Nature nor as a fall from it, but rather as a process of becoming ever more attached to, and intimate with, a panoply of nonhuman natures' (Latour, 2012: n.p).

In the second chapter, I attempt to summarize what cities are doing to the planet – and *all* of its inhabitants – as a prelude to engaging with the multiple set of beings we lump together under the sign of 'animals'. After the almost obligatory stop at the Anthropocene, I survey the effects of the handiwork of humans on what has become an urban planet – 'not in a good place' is the simplest way to put it – and begin the work of signposting where we need to go if we want to rewrite our networks of affinities so that cities can become safe harbours for all beings rather than a system of devastation.

In the third chapter, I consider the different ways in which animals have been considered in philosophy and social theory. Its main themes are the nature of thinking and the importance of symbiosis. They set the scene for what follows. The emphasis on thinking is an attempt to unsettle a word that we use all too casually as a sign of human exceptionalism while the emphasis on symbiosis reminds us that interactions among organisms don't always have to be antagonistic, dominated by competition, predation and parasitism. They can be cooperative too (Douglas, 2010), especially if we consider thinking as a verb rather than as a noun or an adjective (Ingold, 2015).

Then, in the fourth chapter of the book, using some of the voluminous scientific literature, I want to demonstrate that animals are not just 'scaled down versions of ourselves' (Godfrey-Smith, 2018: 10). They are not just the brutes of Dante's *Divine Comedy* – merely existing – whereas we superior beings are born to 'follow virtue and knowledge'[16]. They do not suffer, to use Heidegger's unfortunate phrase, from an 'abyss of essence' occasioned by how they relate to the world. Rather, they can be considered as different forms of thinking beings, as our companions in misfortune, unless, that is, we are bound to just one increasingly beleaguered image of the act of thinking which measures everything against the classical notion of the male human being sitting deep in thought, a notion which assumes that the quality of human cognition is singular and is the only way of lighting up the world. (In making this case, I will demonstrate a particular irony. Right at the time when we have come to understand that many nonhuman actors demonstrate at least some ability to cognize, and with it the realization that 'we' are more like 'them' than we had henceforth imagined, we seem to have reached an apotheosis in dealing out animal death, almost as though the boundary between human and nonhuman needs to be ever more strongly asserted as it becomes more and more threadbare.)

Armed with these insights about thinking and animals, in the fifth chapter of the book, I try to reinterpret how we think about cities. Can we get to a place where thinking is considered to be an attribute of all of the beings that inhabit cities, which, in turn, might lead us to consider their inhabitants as constituent parts of a common humanity which is no longer concerned with just one kind of thinking being? Or must we continue to regard the institutionalization and normalization of killing other beings by economy[17] and state as a norm, with all of its disastrous consequences? By addressing the case of the differential entanglement of city and animal agency through a series of four brief sketches – of sheep, horses, coyotes and chickens – I start to address this task and the fallout from it.

Chapters 6 and 7 are a chronicle of animal death in and because of cities. Animals have been killed in large numbers through history, as Lovegrove's (2008) history of the deliberate killing of wildlife in Britain shows only too well. But the growth of cities has both changed and accelerated animal death, as well as making it far more numerous. In Chapter 6 I outline the degree to which industrialized killing of various kinds of animal for food is both engrained into the very fabric of the city and sequestered from it. But this mass animal death exists as a shadow world of pain and suffering. This mincing machine is disconnected, out of sight and, more often than not, out of mind, even though it is a crucial element in the reproduction of the city. Though, by and large, companion animals are able to lead a life that casts the city in a more favourable light, for the majority of animals, the city is more like a continuous drive-by shooting. Indeed, 'if animals [Dolittle-like] [...] could talk, they wouldn't be pleasantly cooing and chatting us up.... They'd be screaming' (Dargis, 2020: n.p.).

Chapter 7 continues the chronicle of surplus animal death but it switches to the myriad other ways in which cities kill. Beginning with killing for sport, laboratory experiments, wildlife trafficking and pest control, I then switch to urban infrastructure. Mainly designed without animals in mind, the city's infrastructure acts as a snare and a scythe. To round things off, I turn to the issues of disease and climate change and show that, generally speaking, animals are in the same boat as humans but with fewer options.

The eighth chapter of the book shows that, though cities tend to be hostile environments for many animals, some animals are able to adapt and make parts or even the whole of the city into a more favourable and sometimes even welcoming space. Adaptation takes place in three ways, through behavioural change, through genetic mutations and through evolutionary shifts, where evolution is understood in a much broader way than usual as extended evolution.

In the ninth and tenth chapters of the book, I then move on to look at how cities could be changed so that they start to enact a different urban world. I want to take them away from their current emphasis on mass killing and reposition them as something larger and more human, as refuges for many kinds of being – including us. That requires a practical urban politics of mutual inclusion and mutual survival (Massumi, 2014), the barest outline of which I try to provide through five different but related steps – two in Chapter 9 and three in Chapter 10 – each of them aimed at unravelling and retying key practices. The solutions I offer may sometimes seem mundane, lacking in the kind of revolutionary brio that many people think has to be a companion to change. Other steps may appear, quite literally, outlandish. But there we are. They are just the minimum that is necessary if our cities are ever going to become more than a self-serving law unto themselves.

In the final chapter, I offer a series of extended conclusions about this book, framing it primarily as an exercise in 'alter-politics' (Hage, 2015), a politics of reimagination for a time of what we might call, following Sloterdijk, 'ontological emergency' in which spinning alternatives has become a necessity. In particular, the act of recognition of what we used to be so certain was something definitely human called 'cognition' can also be an opportunity for not just new forms of recognition of – and obligation towards – nonhuman interlocutors but also a way of glimpsing a world of diplomacy that we have not wanted to see, one in which 'conversations among ourselves have always had other participants' (Ghosh, 2016: 31). Cities could become summonings and proving grounds for all sorts of awarenesses and awherenesses – trails rather than territories.

So what is the task to hand that I am trying to address in this book? It is to begin to reinvent what we currently regard as human at exactly the same time as we try to rework the old saw that societies are known by how they treat their most vulnerable members, in order to span the abyss that has too often become our sense of connection with the world. That means getting away, in particular, from the notion that because another being is different it necessarily matters less. One logic that is often conjured up goes like this:

> It is the perpetual temptation, especially of the safe and privileged, to harbor the thought that those less fortunate than ourselves are also simpler beings to whom misfortune probably does not matter as much, or in the same vivid way, as it would if the same things are happening to us. (Korsgaard, 2018: 14)

This 'it's worse if it's happening to "us" than if it's happening to "them"' logic is applied equally to all manner of oppressed human groups and to many other beings as if they cannot possibly be as important as 'us'. But obligation doesn't have hard and fast boundaries beyond which sympathy is suddenly withdrawn. In a world of myriad partial connections, our obligations are multiple. They do not form a queue with, for example, the poor and downtrodden next and animals at the back. That queueing mindset is what has brought us to this pass.

How animals are treated is symptomatic of how we treat the poor and downtrodden and, indeed, the planet as a 'whole': 'practices of oppression, slavery and torture are historically inseparable from the question of the animal' and 'our concepts of man, humanity, and inhumanity are inherently bound up with the concepts of the animal, animality, and animals' (Oliver, 2009: 303). It isn't either us or them, then. It is both and.

Without a change of tack which allows all kinds of other beings to become people and therefore able to make a claim on us, as we make claims on them without even a scintilla of hesitation, we will not be able to provide the answers to our current quandaries or summon the political resources to carry them through. We will have set out on a journey which is going nowhere fast because we are tethered to our own sense of importance, which, in its current manifestation, works only by expending the lives of others. That change of tack means engineering a different mindset, a task which will involve intervening in a brew of feelings, reworking the categories that we commonly use in everyday life to signify difference, summoning new kinds of everyday virtue, and rebuilding the times and spaces in which we exist. We can then begin to change the ways in which the world can turn up to us and, in that process, save both ourselves and the other beings that compose the planet from being exiled. Simple! Nothing to it!

Of course, there are many and different political interventions that need to be made to get even halfway to such a point. Some of them clearly involve critique. After all, those oil, coal and concrete firms spewing out carbon dioxide and methane aren't simply going to go away without a fight. But, this book is also concerned with clearing the ground so as to enable new forms of *alter-politics* to come into being, politics that do not arise from an *anti-politics*, aimed at opposing what exists (important though such critique undoubtedly is) so much as from imagining alternative ways of being and fostering their potentialities by emphasizing partial connections between worlds that seem incommensurable (Hage, 2015). It is a politics which battles against the real primitives: those who want to partition the sensible into humans on one side and everything else on the other. It is an attempt to change what Wittgenstein called the 'propositional hinge' from which many cultures gain sustenance (Povinelli, 2016). It is 'alter' rather than 'anti' because it is not just a mere negative opposition (a conformation based on certain forms of oppositional thinking which have turned out to share rather more in common with their targets than was originally thought) but rather a positive reimagining and pursuit of radically other alternatives and possibilities. This stance, based on the premise that there is more than one critical mode to hand, is concerned with altering the premises on which politics is based and the beings with which alliances can be struck and to which obligations are owed.

In other words, the task is not just to provide ammunition for one side or another, but rather to provide another view which can come from outside of any expected political position and which might provide something like an enjambment, the political equivalent of a phrase from a poem that runs over into the second line and provides a sense of departure which is rooted in a current situation but changes the terms of what comes next (Hage, 2015)[18]. This does not mean ending up in the familiar roundelay of 'now you're saying it's acceptable to disregard capitalism', a stance which brings us back to the familiar score sheet of critique which allows so many people to feel that they have the world sorted – even if they clearly can't sort it (see Bessire and Bond, 2014). There are lots of questions and lots of answers and no stance can take them all into one account or one practice. In other words, I see both forms of politics, anti- and alter-, as necessary but neither as being sufficient by itself. However, bound together, they can provide the churn we need to make the reconciliations that have so far eluded us, using the city as our template, a city which is both the problem and – just maybe – a solution to the exclusions that have blinded us to what the earth could contain.

Notes

1 Figures do vary, according to how the data on the FAO website for 2014 at www.fao.org/faostat/en/#data/qc (accessed September 20, 2020) is interpreted. I have seen another figure of 77 billion and another of 113 billion being used. I have taken the lowest estinate here.

2   One meta-analysis suggests that 28 per cent of 'illegal' deaths of terrestrial vertebrates (mammals, birds, reptiles and amphibians) were directly caused by humans (Hill et al., 2019). Legal hunting was the main anthropogenic cause of death, except in the case of reptiles for whom the main cause of death was roadkill.
3   In which the stock view of the light emanating from cities at night as seen from above the planet is recast as the equivalent of the buboes caused by an actual plague.
4   Recent research (Riede et al., 2016) shows that tyrannosaurs could not roar but I claim poetic licence here.
5   We have more in common than we have wanted to admit; processes of corruptibility like ageing and death and affects like fear and joy.
6   Perhaps that explains the outbreak of recent books like Adam Roberts's *Bête* or André Alexis's *Fifteen Dogs* or Yoko Tawada's *Memoirs of a Polar Bear*, which imagine a world in which animals can talk. Or, indeed, the wonderful little commentary in Chiang (2019), 'The great silence'.
7   We could, of course, move the other way and expand the definition of animality to human beings, as Massumi (2014) does.
8   I am not sure that these rechristenings work. To my ear, at least, they sound as though they are trying too hard.
9   Equally, Latour and others make great play of a 'collapse of scales' but I would argue that cities have always been melting pots of scales and that, in any case, the notion of scale is a blind alley.
10 Just think of Aristotle for whom 'the slave is a living tool' (Nicomachean Ethics 8.11, 1161b, 6), an animal in all but name.
11 It is clear that our negative treatment of other life is bound up, in various ways, with some pretty toxic forms of masculinity as has been most graphically illustrated by the work of Carol Adams (see Adams, 1990; Glick, 2019).
12 Indeed, we might go further, as Hage (2015: 23) does, and argue that human beings are themselves made up of many realities, 'realities that are continuously present, even if they are overshadowed by more dominant ones', so that the possibility of making a switch in what we are is always there.
13 Another strain of work is represented by the growing body of Australian ecofiction, most especially when it tackles the subject of the fires eating up the continent, as in the work of writers like Alice Bishop, Eliza Henry-Jones, Mireille Juchau, Catherine McKinnon, Jennifer Mills, Alice Robinson and Alexis Wright.
14 Kingsolver (2019) has also written one of the great poems on environmental decline, 'Great Barrier'.
15 Another genre is typified by Cocozza's (2017) novel, which contrasts the 'uncivilized' life of animals with the apparently 'civilized' life of human beings, to the detriment of the latter. The point being that the line between the city and its apparent obverse, 'wilderness' or some such, is much thinner than we like to think.
16 Dante, *Divine Comedy*, Canto XXVI, lines 118–120.
17 Remembering that the etymology of the word capital is itself bound up with animals as the cognate words chattel and cattle. In later Middle English cattle meant 'movable property, livestock', including horses, sheep, asses, and so on. It began to be limited to 'cows and bulls' from the late sixteenth century. The term seems to have merged in with the Latin meaning of capital as property or stock at some point in its history.
18 I would want to follow Holbraad, Pedersen and Viveiros de Castro (2014) in insisting that alter-politics is about how things could be rather than should be. It always leaves an opening, a way out.

Part I

Cities

2
The Urban World

There is much talk nowadays of 'sentient' cities (Thrift, 2014). Usually associated with the loading up of cities with information and communications technology, and especially the plentiful use of big data combined with numerous little algorithms, each of them with their different filtering logics and probable associations, cities are apparently starting to become smarter. In one account, all that this means is that little algorithms are able to link people into ever larger networks of communication, thereby producing a permanently on 'ambient intimacy' (Ratti and Claudel, 2016) forged through all manner of prosthetic devices, new forms of citizenship and a general reorganization of the realm of movement so as to produce maximally efficient flows. In another account, cities are beginning to think big. All those little algorithms will gradually link up and cities will start to think for themselves. They may become 'conscious', that is, self-aware and with their own goals: information becomes revelation. In yet another account, which proves the immutable law that there is always someone willing to step up to the next level of exaggeration, cities will become a part of the singularity. They will morph into icy AIs whose thoughts and purposes will far outstretch our own ability to think thinking. If we're lucky they will keep us on as pets. If we're[1] not, we will become surplus to their requirements, thrown aside as a casualty of evolution.

But I want to argue that cities are already, or so I will claim here, deep reservoirs of nonhuman thinking. They are full to the brim with it. It's just that we don't see it that way. We don't acknowledge what is in front of us – a heaving mass of thinking space – because even now, after all of those endless criticisms of dualism, deep in the bones of Western culture still lies the notion that there are two kinds of object, human minds thinking away like crazy and all of the other less thoughtful or plain unthinking stuff. We find it hard to ascribe agency to anything other than us. Seen like this 'ontology first proceeds like an unobservant botanist who goes into the forest and discovers just two types of tree, and ends up as a tyrant who commands that only these two species must be recognized as legitimate objects' (Harman, 2016: 228–9).

And because we insist on the primacy of this certain kind of thinking being in advance, fuelled by what seems to us to be a patently obvious ontological difference which allows us to claim an exemption from the rules, we cannot produce cities that flourish, only cities that take – and take, and take, and take. Yet, like it or not, our cities are determinedly hybrid constellations of connections between a multitude of different kinds of being. It is just that too often they are the wrong kinds of connection, ones that wound and maim and kill.

I want to begin to outline these attachments in this chapter by sketching the current urban condition. We – humans and animals – live on what is becoming a predominantly urban planet, even when it isn't covered by concrete and glass. I want to outline some of the main ways in which this urban planet manifests itself as a surplus of death and suffering. I will start with what often seems like the inevitable prologue to such attempts – the Anthropocene. Whilst I am sceptical of its all-encompassing character as an explanatory motif – I doubt that anything encompasses everything – it is still a way into the current urban problematic. Then I move on to considering the ways in which the city is expanding its influence in all four dimensions. From there, I begin an assay of the damage done as this expansion has taken place. I then consider how the city might go through a kind of rebirth in which other kinds of humanity could flourish, a rebirth which would not only begin to reverse some of the worst damage but would also refigure what and why a city existed – on behalf of all of its inhabitants. This would be a plural and invitational city which allowed many different kinds of thinking being to exist alongside each other, not in harmony but in some kind of mutual accommodation, a city that would benefit not just animals but also ourselves.

The Anthropocene

It is often said that we have entered a new geological epoch called the Anthropocene, an epoch following on from the Holocene interglacial[2], a relatively benign period which already showed considerable human impacts, such as those arising from forest clearance for early agriculture. 'The Holocene was a freakish gift to humanity that we have exploited and taken for granted. We are now assisting at its funeral' (Forbes, 2018: 2). The Anthropocene's main characteristic is that it is made up from the detritus laid down by cities. In the Anthropocene, humans are the driving force. But that does not mean that humans are in the driving seat. Yes, they steer some things but other things are going notably awry because of their contempt for some basic rules of the road which means that they are destroying the safety structures that the whole planet depends on. Ignoring the rest of the planet and its myriad beings means repeating the human-centred mistakes of the past – but on a much larger and more destructive scale (Steffen et al., 2015). In other words, if you're just talking about humans you're not talking about the reality of the Anthropocene, you're talking about a fantasy made real in which the planet can be served up on a plate (unfortunately, as we shall see, that's how we have quite literally been proceeding). It is the difference between talking about cities *and* the Anthropocene – in which the epoch presents as a series of discrete problems that can be plugged in to policy and solved, or at least mitigated, by humans for humans – and cities *in* the Anthropocene, in which the epoch demands fundamental change in how cities proceed, which recognizes and listens to the demands of other beings as a fundamental part of any 'solution'.

A certain degree of wariness is in order when using this term, then, quite apart from the fact that its use has been devalued by a bout of intellectual inflation, by framing it as somehow a new phenomenon[3], and by the fact that it can be made to fit familiar, perhaps too familiar, cultural frames. As Sloterdijk (2018: 4) notes, 'The Anthropocene' conforms to two of the basic tenets of modern Western thinking that were stimulated by the notion of evolution and this should at least give us pause. So, it is concerned with the act of 'historicizing anything and everything, and of organizing all historical fields into eons, ages or epochs'[4]. Then, it is a historical narrative that promotes a stark moral choice, a choice which follows an apocalyptic logic that anticipates a system's death throes. It is history viewed from an end point.

Whatever the ins and outs of the definition of the Anthropocene (Ellis, 2018; Lewis and Maslin, 2018) and its cultural supports, it has become abundantly clear both that the rise and fall of city systems has had impacts on climate throughout history (e.g. Koch et al., 2019) and that whilst the latest manifestation of the urban realm may not lead to an absolute end point, it certainly implies some kind of terminus. We are reaching real tipping points. The atmosphere is warming rapidly. The oceans are warming rapidly too (Cheng et al., 2018). The finger of blame points firmly towards the energy demands of cities. Let's just take the atmosphere as an example. 'Heating and cooling the urban built environment alone is responsible for an estimated 35 to 45 per cent of current carbon emissions, while urban industries and transportation contribute another 35 to 40 per cent' (Davis, 2010: 41). It is not necessary to tell the rosary of the dismal effects of these demands in any detail – that has been done already and in profusion by a whole machinery of expertise (Warde et al., 2018). But, to give some sense of the trajectory that cities have both caused and against which cities will have to make their way in future, recent studies suggest that, even if the Paris Agreement emission reduction conditions are met, there is a substantial risk that the planet could be entering so-called 'Hothouse Earth' conditions in which, because of feedback processes, the climate will stabilize, in the long term, at a global average that might be some 4–5°C higher than pre-industrial temperatures, with sea levels 10–60 metres higher than today (Westerhold et al., 2020). In this case, many cities would become uninhabitable. Since the end of the pre-industrial period, temperatures have increased by 1.1°C, accelerating all the while (Steffen et al., 2018). There have been inevitable accompanying effects like sea level rise, which reached 0.25 millimetres per annum between 2014 and 2019, and an increase in ocean acidity of 26 per cent since the beginning of the industrial revolution (World Meteorological Organization, 2019). Absent any check on emissions, median warming of 3.2°C by 2100 is already a realistic expectation and there is only a 5 per cent chance that warming will be less than 2°C (Raftery et al., 2017). Even warming of 'only' 1.5°C will cause severe problems for some cities (Bulkeley, 2012; Fry, 2014; Klinenberg, 2016; Gottlieb and Ng, 2017), given not only that climate change is an uneven process, in which some regions of the world will heat much faster than others (Senivaratne et al., 2019; Wallace-Wells, 2019; Lynas, 2020)[5], but also that cities create much hotter conditions than the average in the first place. In short, we could arrive at climate conditions last experienced during the Cretaceous period 145 to 65.95 million years ago, when carbon dioxide levels reached over 1,000 parts per million, a simulation of which is provided by the 'levels of CO_2 in bedrooms at night and in poorly ventilated crowded places, […] under sustained conditions of such high carbon-dioxide concentration, people [will] suffer severe cognitive problems' (Forbes, 2018: 1).

Whatever the exact facts of the matter, and the still mainly unknowns like the role of clouds, the overriding question that arises is obvious enough: can we ever muster the agency[6] to do what now needs to be done to ward off the worst of these effects on cities which have themselves created the bulk of the problem? That question is complicated by the sheer scale of what is to hand and in more ways than are often acknowledged. There are already 7.7 billion people on the planet. By 2050, there might be nearly 10 billion (United Nations, 2019). It is a dubious proposition to argue that such a weight of humanity is amenable to the kind of one-for-all, all-for-one politics that is called for by those who dream about a world revolution. What is required is a different mindset which understands that bids for purity are anathema. In the Anthropocene, we have to talk about too much, and that is a major challenge unless a new kind of division of the labour of transformation can be constructed.

As Sloterdijk (2018) goes on to point out, an agential way of thinking begs another question. Who or what exactly is the culpable agency that has brought us to this current pass? If we are indeed reaching a point where late becomes too late, there would be no sense in putting an amorphous agency like 'humanity' on trial even though we might be able to argue that humanity, or at least the better-off part of humanity[7], bears a collective responsibility for the current state of affairs, if only through being guilty by virtue of Parfit's (1984: 67) famous dictum 'even if an act harms no one, this act may be wrong because it is one of a set of acts that together harm other people'. So which bit of humanity bears most guilt?

It might make more sense to allow the primary instigators of the Anthropocene – chiefly corporations and governments – to be brought before the courts on a charge of high crimes and misdemeanours. After all, as Heede (2014) shows, essentially 90 firms have been responsible for 63 per cent of all carbon and methane emissions from 1854 to the present, with more than half of those emissions having occurred since 1986. 83 of these firms are industrial producers of oil, natural gas and coal, and 7 are cement manufacturers. Of these 90 firms, 50 are investor-owned, 31 are primarily state-owned and are entirely government-run industries. With only four exceptions, all of these firms are still in existence and still going about their daily business. According to Taylor and Watts (2019), a more recent Heede study shows that since 1965 the top 20 oil, coal and gas companies have contributed 35 per cent of all energy-related carbon dioxide and methane emissions worldwide, while a study by Ekwurzel et al. (2017) found that from 1880 to 2010 carbon dioxide and methane emissions from the 90 biggest industrial producers were responsible for nearly half the rise in global temperature and nearly a third of sea level rise. Or, take the financiers who are providing the capital to allow all of this to happen. Between 2016 and 2018, JPMorgan Chase lent over $195 billion to gas and oil companies while Wells Fargo lent over $151 billion, Citibank lent over $129 billion and Bank of America lent over $106 billion. The top 33 banks have financed fossil fuels to the tune of $1.3 trillion since the Paris Agreement and the amount lent still increases year on year. And that's before we get to asset managers and insurance companies (Fossil Fuel Report, 2019; Yearwood and McKibben, 2020). On the grounds of their sheer recklessness, and not least their willingness to subscribe to notions and models of economic production as if they had no unintended side-effects or had side-effects that could be easily managed, or, worst of all, recognized the existence of side-effects but just didn't care about such piffling externalities, perhaps these corporations ought to be hauled before the courts on a charge of ecocide[8]. Indeed, many such lawsuits are now pending against them and their sponsor governments around the world, as part of a general rise in climate change litigation (Higgins, 2015; Laville, 2019). For example, in the United States, since 2017, 'eight United States cities, including New York and San Francisco, six counties, one state and the West Coast's largest association of fishermen have brought suit against a host of corporations […] for selling products that caused the world to warm while misleading the public about the damage they knew would result' (Jarvis, 2019: 28), while, not to leave the state out of things, Our Children's Trust filed suit against the US government attempting to secure a legal right to a stable climate and healthy atmosphere for future generations. (Though the suit was quashed by a Federal Court, this is unlikely to be the end of such actions in the United States. A similar suit is ongoing in Canada in a slightly different form.)

Alternatively, it might, I suppose, be appropriate to prosecute the well-off. For example, they are responsible for by far the largest part of energy use. The wealthiest 10 per cent of people consume about 20 times more energy overall than the bottom 10 per cent, wherever they live, and are responsible for half of all emissions. Indeed, so far as transport is concerned, the richest tenth of consumers use more than half the energy consumed by transport (Anderson et al., 2020; Oswald et al., 2020).

But it might also make sense to set up a preliminary hearing as to whether and how cities might be guilty of a dereliction of duty to their inhabitants. For example, carbon emissions are concentrated in only a small number of cities worldwide, which have carbon footprints that don't just generate emissions in their actual location but also in the many other locations where their imports are generated. Just 100 cities out of 13,000 drive 18 per cent of global urban emissions (Moran et al., 2018). In other words, some cities are clearly more culpable than others, providing a quality of life that doesn't even reach a minimal standard for some let alone all of their denizens and, at the same time, grabbing so much of the planet's resources that they are not just a threat to their own reproduction but an existential threat to the planet. But would all or some of them have to take the stand as guilty parties in a Noah's Ark class action brought by the impoverished and abused of every species – or at least those species that are left? Perhaps, if they are found guilty, a judge might mandate a form of community service that would involve recognition of some minimal form of responsibility for the damage that cities have done, such as declaring an ecological emergency over loss of wildlife, as cities like Bristol have done (Morris, 2020).

There is only one way to judge the outcome of such hearings and that is to gather the evidence and sift it for signs of not just past guilt but also future hope. One of the key messages of this book is that cities have access to a range of policies and practices that could turn things around and help us to stop mowing the planet of life by reworking what counts as together. The issue is – I won't say simply – one of political will. At the same time, it is also an issue of recasting our mindset so that 'in a world where everything is human, humanity [becomes] an entirely different thing' (Viveiros de Castro, 2013: 4).

The Urban Planet

We need to change things, we can change things. Indeed, not to put too fine a point on it, we must. The planet is becoming city, not just because more and more cities are growing larger and larger but because more and more life is coming under the sway of the urban. We live in an age of so-called 'planetary' urbanization (Brenner, 2014; 2018)[9] which has left no part of the Earth and its beings untouched by the products or the by-products of cities' industrial ecology[10]. Though exactly how and why all this is coming about may be open to dispute (Brenner, 2018), it is difficult to dispute the outcome: the idea of the city as a bounded spatial unit becomes ever harder to maintain and the extent of urban influence is much extended. Of course, this is not an argument that all cities have somehow become the same, existing as a singular condition. Rather, they have to be considered as an interconnected constellation, one in which the urban system and the earth system are merging.

The statistics[11] of this urban surge have been trotted out many times before but they still bear repeating: the urban population of the world has grown rapidly – from 750 million (29.6 per cent) in 1950 to 4.2 billion (55.3 per cent) in 2018 – and it is expected to surpass 6.4 billion by 2050

(United Nations 2018). In other words, we are heading towards a planet where 68.4 per cent of the human population will live in 'cities'[12] and where the other 31.6 per cent will be almost completely under those cities' thumb. What numbers like these reveal is not just a matter of degree. It is a shift in magnitude which started sometime in the seventeenth century when mercantile cities like London and Amsterdam began to extend their influence, drawing into their orbit all manner of entities – human and non-human, animals and materials – from farther and farther away. In the last 25 years, this shift has accelerated as world population has grown.

In the last 25 years, another step-change has also taken place. Cities have not just added population, rather like an athlete taking steroids, as the planet strains to accommodate an extra 75 million people each year. Many of them have also begun to sprawl over vast expanses of land (Angel, 2012). Though cities themselves still, generally speaking, take up relatively small percentages of land, they are growing fast. In the United States, for example, urban areas make up just 3.6 per cent of the total size of the 48 contiguous states, but an additional 1 million acres of urban area is being added each year, the equivalent of the footprint of Los Angeles, Houston and Phoenix combined (Merrill and Leatherby, 2018)[13]. In Britain in 2020, 8.3 per cent of the country's land mass of 90,500 square miles was counted as built up, tarmacked or paved over, compared with 7.7 per cent in 2010 (Hellen, 2020). (According to another study by the UK Centre for Ecology and Hydrology, 3,376 square kilometres of Great Britain was found to have been built up between 1990 and 2015, an increase from 5.8 to 7.3 per cent. This has meant a large loss of grassland in particular; phys.org, 2020.) But it has not been just the urbanization of the land surface that is involved. So, as we shall see, is the urbanization of the atmosphere – out into near space – and the urbanization of the depths too, down into the deepest underground. At the same time, all kinds of intensification have been taking place, too. For example, whereas cities have tended to be sites of more or less continuous 24-hour activity for many centuries, this round-the-clock activity is now unrelenting.

But cities are not restricted by their boundaries. Their influence reaches far and wide, hardly surprising given that they account for 90 per cent of global GDP. As already pointed out, they are the main source of global carbon emissions into the atmosphere. At least 70 per cent of these emissions come from the generation and use of energy for heating and lighting, transportation and manufacturing. Equally, cities dump 1.2 billion tonnes of solid waste each year, an amount that could easily treble by 2100 if current trends were allowed to continue (Schmitz, 2017). Then they remorselessly use up resources. For example,

> They use 60 per cent of available freshwater from across landscapes, and they utilize 70 per cent of wood available for housing and industrial activity. Seafood demand in the 740 largest cities appropriates 25 per cent of all the

marine production coming from marine shelf, coastal, and upwelling areas (Schmitz, 2017: 181).

Whatever the case, this urban stratum is – sometimes it seems remorselessly – increasing in scope and density[14]. Take just roads and railways as examples. The International Energy Agency has estimated that approximately 12 million kilometres of roads have been built since 2000. It is projected that more than 25 million kilometres of new paved roads will be built worldwide by 2050, a 60 per cent increase on 2010, roughly 90 per cent of them in tropical and subtropical regions with high biodiversity and environmental values (Laurance et al., 2015; Alamgir et al., 2017)[15]. Then take railways. Since 2007, China has carpeted its territory with nearly 20,000 kilometres of high-speed railways (as well as endless wireless networks). And there is no sign of any scaling back. At the last G20 summit, for example, world leaders pledged to invest some 60–70 trillion dollars into new infrastructure by 2030. In turn, the effects on the environment of this road and rail construction have often been drastic, from habitat conversion through poaching and illegal mining to wildfires and land speculation. Most seriously, roads and railways fragment habitats with clear effects on species loss. Major roads have split the Earth's terrestrial surface into approximately 600,000 patches of which more than half are less than a square kilometre in area and only 7 per cent are larger than 100 square kilometres (Ibisch et al., 2016). In one study, it was found that, on average, fragmented habitats lose half of their plant and animal species within 20 years, while some continue to lose species for another 30 years or more (Haddad et al., 2015; Nijhuis, 2015).

The urban stratum is also increasing in height (Graham, 2017; Thrift, 2017). It has more and more volume. The sky is getting closer. According to the work of the Council on Tall Buildings and Urban Habitat (www.ctbuh.org/), there are 126 buildings around the world that top out at over 300 metres, 1,317 over 200 metres and 4,238 over 150 metres. Tall buildings are what give the contemporary city its distinctive ability to draw a line in the sky, an ability which has existed only since the construction of the first metal-framed office skyscraper in 1885. This upward extension has been made possible by a series of technologies with their own histories and geographies, construction technologies like scaffolding[16] and the tower crane, and, most importantly of all, operational technologies like the elevator (Smil, 2019). The elevator first made an appearance in 1870 as a recognizably modern office building form (although it has been subject to many innovations since, from self-levelling to microprocessor-based controls)[17]. By 2017, the world had 14 million elevators. Around 1 billion journeys are taken by elevator each day. There are 66,000 passenger elevators in New York alone[18]. Again, 'skyways' and 'skybridges' which extend connectivity between buildings and other urban sites are becoming a standard installation in some cities[19], increasing the horizons of verticality.

Then, at ground level, there is a general reworking of geology, especially through landfill and reclamation. This has been a normal practice throughout history, of course, but the scale of activity has changed dramatically. Large areas of urban ground are now artificial: by one estimate, since 1985 5,237 square miles of artificial land have been added to the world's coasts – an area about the same size as the state of Connecticut or the island of Jamaica (Beiser, 2018). Landfill has become a norm[20], in particular as a result of the dumping of waste and general builders, aggregate[21]. Take just the example of the Crossrail tunnels in London. Three million tonnes of material from this project have been dumped in the Thames Estuary to create an island that will act as a nature reserve (Cronin, 2015).

Then there is more general reclamation, often using materials that are in shorter and shorter supply globally, as is the case with sand (Lamb et al., 2019). Sand is a basic ingredient of concrete and asphalt as well as being used more generally in reclamation. It is now being extracted with larger and larger machines, often doing considerable environmental damage in the process[22]. China is now the chief exponent: in 2015 alone it created the equivalent of two Manhattan's worth of new land (Beiser, 2018). In recent years, China has built up a large fleet of oceangoing dredgers, among the most technologically advanced in the world. The country's annual dredging capacity has more than tripled since 2000. Starting in late 2013, Beijing set these dredgers to work raising millions of tonnes of sand from the sea floor and using it to expand the pieces of territory it claims in the Spratly Islands. Within 18 months, these ships had built nearly 3,000 acres of new land. Another example is provided by the island of Singapore, which has a long history of land reclamation, beginning in 1822, and has grown in size by nearly a quarter (from 224 to 277 square miles) since independence in 1965 (Subramanian, 2017; Beiser, 2018). By 2030 the plan is for it to grow to 300 square miles. But the problem now is where to get material from to reclaim even more land, 'access to sand has become a matter of national security' (Comaroff, 2016: 2)[23]. Appropriate kinds of sand – 15 billion tons of which is reckoned to be used each year around the world (Beiser, 2018) – are in increasingly short supply, and there is a thriving illicit market.[24]

Then there is the ground underneath cities, through which pipes and cables crawl and interlace, and tunnels and boreholes and all kinds of shafts bore down into the earth. The humble pipe and cable still retain an influence on how cities are able to be present, wi-fi notwithstanding[25]. And the Earth has a very strong influence still on where and how these pipes and cables can be sited in cities. The distinctive skyline of Manhattan depends on the depth of the underlying bedrock but equally the closeness of the bedrock to the surface means that pipes and cables are often unable to be buried deep with all the complications that produces, assuming, of course, that builders and engineers know where they are in the first place.[26] So far as the tunnel is concerned, perhaps the biggest outbreak of large-scale tunneling in history has occurred quite recently as more and more cities have installed or extended subways. At the end of 2017, there were metro systems in 178 cities in 56 countries, most of which have substantial underground components (UITP, 2018). Most of the expansion since the 1990s has been accounted for by Chinese cities[27].

However, going underground at any scale is not an easy option for many existing megacities. These cities are often sited in low-lying areas which have high water tables and are also at risk of increasing maritime inundations. But on sites where the option is feasible, going underground has some obvious advantages, including leaving the possibility of a pristine surface[28], with all of the positive environmental consequences that flow from that, as well as some obvious disadvantages, of which cost is the main one[29]. That said, a number of cities do have extensive basement living. In cities like London, underground living is often an extension downwards by the well-off into the only dimension in which space is available[30], but usually, the basements of cities are occupied by the less well-off[31] – in Beijing, for example, an estimated 1 million people live underground in basements generally one to three floors deep which have been converted into cheap rooms. On a larger scale, cities like Chicago, Dallas, Houston, Oklahoma City, Montreal and Toronto all have extensive downtown systems of tunnels and larger spaces, which usually include retail spaces and the like, built to avoid the extremes of either summer heat or winter cold[32].

Finally, cities have also expanded outwards in time (Parkes and Thrift, 1980). The night has become a workspace for more and more people. For example, research in Britain (TUC, 2018) found that over 3 million people (11.5 per cent of the workforce) worked night shifts, the most common night-time industries being transport and logistics, protective services and care services. In the United States, the figures are, if anything, more pronounced with the main prevalence of shift work being among workers in service occupations, such as protective services – which includes police, firefighters and security guards – and food preparation and serving, and among those employed in production, transportation and material moving occupations. Unsurprisingly, shift work was least prevalent in professional and business services, followed by financial activities. Urban culture has often migrated into the night too, as a general lack of sleep, as different patterns of noise and light, as Dickens's night walks, as horror movies and as nightclubs. Byrne puts it nicely. For him the history of the city at night can be told via

> changes in [...] nightly celebrations and unwindings. [It is] accompanied by a bottle of Malbec, some fine Argentine steak, tango music, dancing, and gossip. It unfolds through and alongside illicit activities that take place in the multitude of discos, dance parlors, and clubs. Its direction [...] is determined on half-lit streets, in bars, and in smoky late-night restaurants [...] inscribed in songs, on menus, via half-remembered conversations, love affairs, drunken fights, and years of drug abuse. (2013: 126)

... 'what to make of a diminished thing'[33] The Urban Overdraft

This sprawl in all four dimensions has some pretty obvious consequences for the planet. Most particularly, it picks off yet more continuous areas of natural habitat and leaves a sometimes intercalated but more often discrete patchwork of environments, a state of affairs which generates enormous problems, from producing fire hazards (Davis, 2017) to pumping out carbon dioxide, nitrous oxide and particulates into each breath the city takes, from generating a mountain of waste to producing food in suspect and irresponsible ways, from traffic congestion clogging up the city's arteries[34] to social isolation[35], from brewing pandemics to producing an impoverished spatial grammar which often etch-a-sketches a much too tidy-minded visual homogeneity (which, ironically, then often dissolves into something that looks like a mess of pottage)[36].

And this sprawl in four dimensions doesn't stop at the boundaries of cities – insofar as cities have determinate boundaries nowadays. In these days of instant telecommunications, global supply chains and all kinds of externalities like emissions exported somewhere else, cities have impacts far beyond their supposed boundaries. Both rural areas and the ocean are now firmly under the spell of the urban. The urbanization of the countryside has gone on apace, forced by the techniques necessary to feed urban populations. It has been much remarked upon, not least because the demands of cities on the agricultural system have often produced sterile backlots in which sometimes nothing much lives at all except a few monocultural plants and animals.

Less remarked upon has been the way in which the ocean is becoming an even more important part of the make-up of the city[37], not just because the world's oceans are losing the power to stall climate change – which means that marine incursions are becoming ever more common (after all 75 per cent of all cities worldwide are now coastal[38]) but also because the world's oceans have their own distinctive planetary regulatory systems like the daily surge of phytoplankton and zooplankton, as well as a host of beings with likely important planetary impacts like algae and fungi. Of course, the ocean has always been a part of urban history – the first cities were located where they were as much because of proximity to the sea and its harvests as nearness to the land. But this relationship has now become crucial. Oceans and cities – even the cities far from any coast – are inextricably linked by the demands of their populations for food, as a means of maintaining crucial logistical networks, as places to dump trash like plastic – the first plastic bag recorded by a scientific survey of the ocean dates to 1965 (Gill, 2019) – and the human detritus of sewage, as recreational landscapes and, increasingly, as sites of undersea resources like minerals. Even in 1950, Rachel Carson remarked on the destruction wrought by cities on the oceans. That early on, she pointed out the deleterious effects of plastic, sewage, oil spills, various forms of pollution and the carnage of overfishing. In 50 years, time, she reckoned that the coastal ocean would be 'polluted beyond repair' and that the larger ocean would be succumbing to longer-term mixing. We may not be quite there yet but we are getting awfully close. Witness the depredations of so-called maritime industrialization, not just manic overfishing but seabed mining, shipping, fish farming, desalination plants, submarine cables, cruise tourism and the like.

What does all this up-down-out-round-and-back urbanization add up to? A lot is the answer. The sheer amount of planet-shaping that human beings now carry out, intentionally or unintentionally, is ranging beyond the extraordinary into the surreal. To give a point of comparison, take the generation of energy. The Earth receives 170,000 terawatts from the Sun. The primary production of the biosphere via photosynthesis is 130 terawatts. The flux of energy from the centre of the earth is about 40 terawatts. Our global civilization is now powered by around 13 terawatts of human-made energy (Morton, 2009). The point is that human beings already act as an energy source that begins to compare with plate tectonics in its magnitude and force. Or put the point in another way: every year, 'human activities move more soil, rock and sediment than is transported by all other natural processes combined' (Lewis and Maslin, 2018: 4).

For many people, the benefits of this latest round of urbanization have outweighed the disbenefits. Agglomeration was probably the only way to accommodate the weight of the ballooning world population and it has clearly paid dividends in terms of life span and general economic wellbeing. We also know all the arguments for why cities are good: they are founts of creativity from which invention of all kinds grows; they soak up and channel all kinds of human energies via various cognitive gadgets (Heyes, 2018)[39], oft-times to the good of their inhabitants; they concentrate resources into a whole set of public goods which provide a kind of commonwealth; they allow many different kinds of people to come into (mainly) peaceful contact; they promote their own kinds of everyday sociality which very often contain a kernel of modest but still significant virtue; they induce agglomeration economies which allow more to be generated from what otherwise would be less; they produce a landscape which can have its own distinctive beauties, so often documented on paper and screen that they have become another imaginary city [...] the list of credits is both a long one and it is an important one. It cannot be gainsaid.

But, and it is a big but, currently, cities also produce a whole set of debits in the planetary accounts, a global distemper that applies to *all* beings. The planet's carrying capacity is being challenged as never before (O'Neill et al., 2018)[40]. In particular, the latest round of urbanization has come at a cost in terms of the use of finite resources, a cost which the planet can no longer afford. Cities are already overdrawn at the bank of Planet Earth. The debt of carbon dioxide and methane[41] will soon be called in. In short order, many other debts are likely to be called in, too, as cities soak up future potential. So let's look at the make-up of the urban overdraft.

To begin with, the building of cities has created resource shortages. Take the example of a basic ingredient of cities, 'aggregate', of which there are many kinds, from the finest (the sand used for beach volleyball and for equestrian events) through gravel, crushed stone and all kinds of recycled materials. Natural aggregate is the world's second most heavily exploited resource, after water. Human beings are estimated to consume 50 billion tons of sand and gravel each year, almost twice as much as only a decade ago, nearly all of it driven by the explosion in the number and size of cities (Beiser, 2018). Mining of aggregate now exceeds natural renewal rates and it has been exploited exponentially, mainly because of economic growth in Asia. *Moving on…* Another basic ingredient of cities: concrete (Courland, 2011; Forty, 2012; Mattern, 2017). Concrete production has increased more than thirtyfold since 1950, and almost fourfold since 1990, nearly all of it for use in cities. Concrete is made from aggregate, water and cement. China used more cement just between 2011 and 2013 than the United States used in the entire twentieth century. It is an environmentally disastrous material, contributing about 8 per cent of carbon dioxide emissions. If the cement industry were a country, it would be the third largest carbon dioxide emitter in the world – behind only China and the United States. It contributes more carbon dioxide than aviation fuel (2.5 per cent) and is not far behind global agriculture (12 per cent) (Rodgers, 2018). *Moving on…* Waste. Mountains of waste have been created, including discarded mounds of aggregate like concrete, and a flood of plastic. Demand for plastic, a staple of city life, currently exceeds 300 million tonnes per annum accounting for 8 per cent of global oil usage and large amounts of water. Plastics are a major component of municipal waste and resulting litter, while microplastics and potential chemical leakage are global environmental concerns, not least because there is good evidence that they are entering the food chain. More than 8.3 billion tonnes of plastic have been produced globally since the 1950s, creating some 6 billion tonnes of plastic waste. Only 9 per cent of this waste has been recycled. We have already generated approximately 7000 million tonnes of plastic waste going into either landfill or the natural environment with a further 335 million tonnes of plastic produced every year. An estimated 15 million tonnes of plastic is being discharged into the oceans year on year with precious little understanding of the impact on marine life or the functional health of the ocean ecosystem (Geyer et al., 2017). *Moving on…* Water. Cities are suffering from major water shortages. Floods have become a constant in many cities, mudslides in some. Oceans touch more of the land. By 2040, 2 billion people will be affected by a global groundwater crisis whereby more water is being withdrawn than is refilling aquifers (Barbier, 2019)[42]. The weight of buildings bearing down on aquifers that are being so rapidly depleted means that some cities are sinking and, given the scale of sea level rise on some coasts, this creates a case of double jeopardy[43]. By 2040, water pressure will be a major challenge in some cities too. *Moving on…* Sea level rise. A recent estimate suggested that 340 million people are living on land likely to be flooded by 2050, the bulk of them in coastal cities (Kulp and Strauss, 2019). Many experts now believe that, as a result of greatly accelerating melt of the world's two biggest ice sheets, sea level rise could well exceed 1 metre by the end of the century which would engulf the homes of even more hundreds of millions of city dwellers (Horton et al., 2020). *Moving on…* Heat. The heat keeps on building. Deaths from thermal misery are increasing every year, especially in tropical and subtropical countries[44]. Some major cities, especially in South Asia and China, may soon become all-but-uninhabitable as wet bulb temperatures climb[45]. The combination of heat and humidity will be lethal for the narrow climatic envelope in which most human beings live. If global warming does exceed 3°C, about 1.2 billion of the world's population would be living in extreme heat (defined as an average temperature of 29°C), in 'mean annual temperatures warmer than nearly anywhere today' (Xu et al., 2020), affecting, in particular, the cities of India, Nigeria, Pakistan, Indonesia and Sudan. The number of potentially fatal heat and humidity events has doubled already between 1979 and 2017 and they are increasing in both frequency and intensity, especially hitting the cities of the Persian Gulf and the south eastern corner of the United States (Raymond et al., 2020). Things have been made generally worse by night-time temperatures which are staying stubbornly high because nights are warming faster than days (e.g. Im et al. 2017)[46]. *Moving on…* Natural disasters. Cities, as they have grown larger, are exposed to more and more risks. Natural disasters like earthquakes, cyclones and more general heavy precipitation events, as well as the consequences of heat and drought like wildfire, can do much more extensive damage than previously. For example, because of sprawl, fires are more likely to sweep into outer suburbs and small towns located in the so-called wildland–urban interface, with the bulk of them lit, carelessly or intentionally, by human beings. In the United States, for example, the wildland–urban interface expanded by a third between 1990 and 2010 and is expected to double again by 2030 while the number of residential homes in the interface grew by 32 million between 1990 and 2015 (Mietkiewicz et al., 2020). There is an inevitable economic toll to all of this. Take just the case of the United States again. NOAA data show that the frequency of billion dollar disasters has increased decade by decade. Though when adjusted for inflation the increase is less dramatic, it is still telling (Zagorsky, 2017). *Moving on…* Pollution. There is pollution pretty well everywhere. The air is often tainted[47], not just outdoors but indoors too (Twilley, 2019). Indeed, research shows that many air pollutants have higher concentrations in homes and offices than on the streets[48]. Pollution now kills three times as many people worldwide as AIDS, tuberculosis and malaria combined (Monbiot, 2019). The water contains all kinds of crud, as well as diseases. Mechanical noise is a constant urban accompaniment blurring apprehensions and disturbing the atmosphere. Traffic noise, mainly generated by roads, is audible by humans almost everywhere in the United States (Tennessen et al., 2018). And light blots out the night sky. Light at night – so-called ALAN (artificial light at night) – constitutes not just a massive assault on the ecology of the planet, it also has indirect impacts because, while about 20 per cent of electricity is used for lighting worldwide, at least 30 per cent of that light is wasted. Kyba et al. (2017) reported that even in the short period from 2012 to 2016 there was a dramatic increase in both the brightness of the metropolitan areas of the world and the geographic extent of light pollution[49]. One study in the UK found that only 22 per cent of the English population could experience 'truly dark skies', completely free of light pollution (CPRE, 2019). This, despite the fact that, since 2012, high-efficiency LED street lighting has been increasingly installed in much of the industrialized world so as to 'save energy'. But its overuse suggests that it is having major effects on light pollution. *Moving on…* Agriculture. The cockamamie agricultural system needed to supply cities with food is now so defective that it is a genuine threat to the commonweal. The resources needed to consume large mammals are consuming the planet, from the virtual water that needs to be expended to reproduce them to the plants that they need to eat to live. Approximately 85 per cent of the grain produced in Europe and the United States is fed to animals. In China, the proportion is already 65 per cent. Around 2 per cent of the world's best croplands will be lost by 2050 as cities come to take up three times as much land (Gu, 2019). Fish are being 'harvested' at unsustainable rates: the global biomass of predatory fish alone has declined by two thirds over the last century (Otto, 2018). *Moving on…* Soil. Scientists are concerned that the soil will stop acting as a carbon sink and start releasing carbon dioxide into the atmosphere[50]. Yields from the soil are steadily declining. The soil itself is disappearing as agro-industrial farming strips the ground bare: human land use has led to an estimated loss of $^{10}/_{14}$ kilograms of organic carbon from the Earth's topsoil, about 8 per cent of the top 2 metres of used land, and to topsoil being lost between 10 and 40 times faster than it is being replenished (Otto 2018; Laybourn-Langton et al., 2019). The planetary surface is wearing out: about one quarter of the terrestrial surface is now considered to be degraded, the result of erosion, pollution, compaction, nutrient degradation, salinization, and the loss of deep-burrowing and other kinds of earthworm (Otto, 2018; Stroud, 2019). Between a third and a half of the topsoil of the planet may have been lost in the last 150 years and topsoil can take a very long time to rejuvenate: according to an FAO representative, generating 3 centimetres of topsoil can take just under 1,000 years (though this is a global average and the process can be speeded up using appropriate farming practices; Arsenault, 2014). Decreasing productivity can be observed on 20 per cent of the world's cropland, 16 per cent of forest land, 19 per cent of grassland and 27 per cent of rangeland. A third of the planet's land is severely degraded and fertile soil is being lost at the rate of 24 billion tonnes a year (FAO, 2017a). About 30 per cent of the world's arable land has become unproductive owing to erosion (Laybourn-Langton et al., 2019). Unless new approaches are adopted, the global amount of arable and productive land per person in 2050 will be only a quarter of the level of 1960 because of growing population and soil degradation. Indeed, in some areas of the world crop yields are already declining. According to the FAO (2017a), if the current rate of degradation continues, with approximately 75 billion tonnes of fertile soil being lost to land degradation each year (IBPES, 2019), all of the world's cultivable topsoil could be gone within 60 years. *Moving on…* Trees. The intact forested landscape (i.e. forest untouched by significant anthropogenic activity) was reducing at a rate of 0.57 per cent a year between 2000 and 2013 (Potapov et al., 2017; Maxwell et al., 2019) and there is no reason to think that this rate has slowed down. Even in cities which desperately need more trees planted to combat pollution and heat, greening efforts are often moving backwards. *Moving on…* Planetary health (Haines, 2018) is inevitably affected. Emergent diseases, vector-borne diseases and water-borne diseases all travel more easily. The growing size of cities makes them into sinks for new kinds of zoonotic and other disease types. The obvious risk of a serious global pandemic suddenly appearing in one city and spreading via the airline system to all of the others has now come true (Keegan, 2018). There will be more. *Moving on…* Machines that produce dangerous levels of pollution also kill 1.25 million humans on the roads in traffic accidents every year and take up vast amounts of road and associated space, which the advent of autonomous vehicles could well make worse by boosting the number of trips (Calthorpe and Walters, 2017)[51]. *Moving on…* Living conditions. Cities hardly provide ideal living conditions for their inhabitants. The planet is beset by housing shortages and inadequate housing. On one estimate, the cities of the world contain 1.6 billion people living without adequate shelter. One in seven people on the planet currently lives in a slum and one in every four people will live in a slum by 2030. And that's before we get to the homeless. Then, as city buildings go higher, this brings its own problems, most notably more and more water pressure issues and the blocking out of natural light[52]. *Moving on…* Our urban habits have a downside for the human body itself. We bear the stains of our cities in the tissue of our lungs and guts. We accumulate damage to our heart muscle and circulatory systems. Our diets and lack of exercise are making many of us morbidly obese. We are becoming case studies in genetic and epigenetic damage. We are even putting limits on our cognitive powers through the influence of air and other kinds of pollution.

But It Isn't Just 'Us'

I could go on – and on. Obviously, this litany of unnatural hazards is hardly meant to be reassuring, although, as I will emphasize continually, the fact is that – even given the momentum now provided by climate change – many of them could still be fixed given the political will to spend money on the measures, large or small, that would solve each one for good, or at the very least ameliorate their worst impacts. It's not all doom, doom, doom. The solutions are there and they are available[53]. We could put the brakes on. We might not be able to come to a complete stop but we can certainly slow right down. The alternative is that we will become like those eighteenth-century prize fighters who had one of their legs pinioned to the floor so that the audience was guaranteed the entertainment of cuts and blows. We will limit our options just when we need to open them out.

But what can't be solved so easily is the damage already done – and that is continuing to be done – to the other inhabitants of the planet by these urban habits. They also suffer from the various watery inundations, from heat and fire, from pollution, from disease, from road traffic accidents and all the other urban externalities. But they suffer directly too – as entities that are purposely placed in the line of fire. For example, they are sacrificed on the modern-day version of the altar – the slaughterhouse killing floor – or through habitat removal or just through simple neglect but, for them, the sacrifice is continuous and indifferent and seemingly without end. Think of all these other beings on the planet for whom cities are often, at best, re-education camps, means of forced integration into the urban fabric, and, at worse, means of dealing out death, either purposefully or simply as a by-product of urban expansion. Meanwhile, extinctions are taking place at a rapid rate, very often linked to encroachment by cities. For example, one study found a 60 per cent decline in the population size of vertebrate wildlife between 1970 and 2014 (Otto, 2018) while another found that global populations of mammals, birds, fish, amphibians and reptiles not only declined by 68 per cent between 1970 and 2016 but also that, if anything, losses are speeding up (World Wildlife Fund/Institute of Zoology, 2020). One study suggests that a further 550 species of mammal will be extinguished by the end of this century, nearly all the result of human impact; for example, the correlation between past extinctions and population size is almost exact (Andermann et al., 2020). On the whole, for these other beings, cities aren't so much a commonwealth of life, more of a land grab, another version of settler colonialism. And the sacrifice isn't just all of those animals, it is also all of the lines of beauty that can never now be recovered and for which we have substituted only tawdry knock-offs.

In other words, we have become witchy. Like a modern version of Shakespeare's three weird sisters who were intent on whipping up the winds and raising storms, and on doing general harm to both people and animals, so through our actions we have learnt the joys of polluting and burning, of raising sea level, of increasing the frequency and windspeed of cyclones, and of conjuring up floods and mudslides, sometimes just for the hell of it – or so it can sometimes seem. But, in turn, we are summoning unintended spirits. We visit this rain of destruction on the planet and its inhabitants – all of its inhabitants – at our peril. The spells are going horribly wrong. They can't be confined. They are ricocheting around the planet. Peter Sloterdijk has written about urban 'atmospheres' which act as 'safety structures', immunizing their inhabitants from harm. But that is now an arguable proposition. Many modern cities' safety structures are, if anything, being made less safe by our actions. They do not provide immunity. Not only are their atmospheres being poisoned and laid waste but the risk of them being affected by extreme events has also increased. The off button no longer works. The toggles we once used are no longer connected or keep short-circuiting. The more affluent cities may have the resources to ward off a phenomenon like sea-level change through large-scale engineering projects[54] but in less well-off cities there is often very little in the way of protection or fallback, especially for the poor whose only recourse in many cities, even at the best of times, is an array of quotidian improvisations which, though they are often – quite rightly – hailed as a remarkable exercise in resilience and innovation (Simone and Pieterse, 2017), can only go so far. And at times of crisis, the state often just melts away and these urban inhabitants are thrown back on – very little. They are not just left to their own devices. They have been abandoned[55].

So the question now is whether these great cities will continue to act like the modern equivalent of Cobbett's 'Great Wen' – the 'monster' city that was forever hungry – or whether they can be transformed into something more friendly to life, something safer and more caring, an urban renaissance that really is a rebirth and not just another fudge. These cities would have as their goal a new kind of Aristotelian 'living well'. That would mean attempting to construct out of the coral of everyday interactions the urbanity that Aristotle so strongly valued but which cities so patently lack at present. What Aristotle in *Politics* called 'the constitution' of such cities – the 'ordering of the inhabitants', their immanent organizing principle supporting a good way of life – would stand in stark contrast to the brute-force urbanization that currently characterizes too much of what cities stand for – 'urbanization without urbanity' as Colebrook (2017) so aptly puts it. That would entail treating life very differently: life means *all* life.

Notes

1 Like Morton (2018), I am quite content to use the pronoun 'we' to characterize the human species. Though we may take in many identities, I cannot think of a way of functioning without it when discussing some of the issues I will be addressing. That said, it is clear that one of the purposes of this book is to problematize who is doing the talking when 'we' say 'we', and also to make clear that we will need to go beyond a 'we' that is centred on the human species alone.
2 I do not touch on the debate as to whether the Holocene ever really existed as a distinct epoch (see Lewis and Maslin, 2018) or on how far back in time anthropogenic climate change extends, as in debates on an early Anthropocene (Stephens et al., 2020).
3 As Davis (2016: 23) points out, historically speaking, it is hardly the case that climate change is a revelation: 'the deleterious consequence of economic growth, especially the influence of deforestation and plantation agriculture on atmospheric moisture levels, were widely noted, and often exaggerated, from the Enlightenment until the nineteenth century'. It surfaces again in Marx and Engels, attention to the scientific advances of their

day (Foster and Burkett, 2016), in Kropotkin's notion of progressive dessication (Davis, 2016), as well as in Ruskin's (1884) more visionary writings about the consequences of industrialization and a conflagration of 'plague winds'.
4   I have always been suspicious of this kind of cookie cutter thinking. It makes complex things too simple. Similarly, the concept of the Anthropocene is useful but once it falls into this narrative, it simply gets taken in by all of the other narratives that want to divide history into stages and epochs. Kidnapped by these interests, it becomes a stock explanation rather than a set of new questions.
5   See, for example, what is happening already to Arctic towns like Svalbard.
6   Some people would like to junk the word agency altogether and I understand their ambitions. But I cannot think of a better word.
7   By one set of UN estimates, developing countries are likely to bear an estimated 75 per cent of the costs of the climate crisis, despite the poorest half of the world's population causing just 10 per cent of carbon dioxide emissions.
8   In other words, this motley crew believed in prerogatives that they just didn't have, in the indulgence of their knowing ignorance, and in access to emergency exits that were never there. There are attempts to produce an international crime of ecocide and create a legal duty of care for life on earth (Monbiot, 2019).
9   Though this Lefebvrian term can be used in ways that are a little too absolutist, it is a valuable heuristic (Brenner and Schmid, 2013; 2015).
10 Quite literally, in the case of microplastics, which have been found on the highest mountains and in the deepest of deeps (e.g. Allen et al., 2019). In the oceans, the use of finer nets has revealed much higher concentrations of these particles than formerly thought (Lindeque et al., 2020).
11 Morton (2018) seems to think that assembling facts like these only creates an 'information dump' and does not live ecological knowledge. I disagree. Facts have their own forms of life. They are not 'inert', as Whitehead (1929) pointed out. Years of study by historians of science show this only too well. Making mute objects speak means asking them good questions and constructing devices that allow them to speak back, and one way they will speak will be through what we call facts. Just because a scientific machinery of expertise has been built up based on the apparatus of experiments, observations, equations, models and numbers does not mean that its output is somehow inauthentic (Edwards, 2010; Warde et al., 2018).
12 Of course, we need to be cautious about what we mean by a city. The widely naturalized assumption that cities are closely bounded and continuously built-up settlement units, and the concomitant understanding of urbanization as simply an expansion in the size and distribution of such units, is a suspect one. Equally, the statistics that derive from this everyday assumption are often questionable. What is happening instead is the imposition of something that is both porous and discontinuous and yet, at the same time, has a global reach (see Brenner, 2014).
13 This includes 2 million acres devoted to golf courses and another 3 million acres devoted to airports.
14 This tendency is well summed up in Hao Jinfang's by now famous science fiction story, 'Folding Beijing'.
15 The death of the Age of the Car has often been predicted but, at the moment at least, we are at peak car. There are an estimated 1.2 billion cars on the road worldwide and 75 million of them were sold in 2019 (www.statista.com/statistics/200002/international-car-sales-since-1990/). The attendant health and environmental consequences are legion. For example, in terms of planetary health, the annual toll of 1.35 million traffic fatalities recorded by the WHO (www.who.int/news-room/fact-sheets/detail/road-traffic-injuries) is one of the single largest causes of human death.
16 Specifically, the invention of tubes and ties and especially standardized systems at the beginning of the twentieth century. Bamboo scaffolding is widely used in Asia but there are issues over the ability to supply bamboo at the scale now demanded.

17 And by innovations, from pumps to overhead tanks, which allow water pressure to be maintained. Beijing currently has a rule that all buildings over five storeys have to have a pump installed but is thinking of changing it because of the energy demands. Water pressure is a constant unremarked-upon struggle in many cities, from Mumbai to Mexico City.
18 Beijing has the second largest number of elevators in the world. Its biggest problem now is retrofitting elevators to buildings that were built in a hurry and do not meet the standard of all buildings over six storeys having elevators. In China as a whole, the aim is to retrofit 3 million of these older buildings. Pay-per-ride elevators have been installed in some old apartment buildings with payment being made by swipe card. Although the solution forces residents to pay it also means that property companies cannot gouge them by charging for new elevators via inflated service charges. In richer cities like Beijing, Guangzhou and Shanghai, there is some prospect of targets being attained but in poorer cities neither municipal governments or residents necessarily have the wherewithal.
19 For example, as in Minneapolis, Hong Kong, Bangkok and in embryo in cities like Singapore, Seoul and Chongqing (Roxburgh, 2018).
20 By one estimate, 0.6 square miles of new ground requires 37.5 million cubic metres of landfill, about 1.4 million dump truck journeys (Comaroff, 2016).
21 In some cities, human interventions have led to a kind of reclamation by default. For example, much of central Seattle is built on and through a thick layer of sawdust dating from the city's peak logging days.
22 Sand is of many types, from fine river sand used for beaches and concrete to coarse sea sand used to create new ground. The upshot is that desert cities like Dubai have to import sand for building.
23 Other cities in the region have similar issues. About 6 per cent of Hong Kong's territory is reclaimed land. China's east coast is reckoned to have added 12,000 square kilometres in the last 40 years, much of it being in urban areas.
24 The global trade in sand is estimated to be worth $70 billion a year.
25 Think too of the undersea cables linking up the world's cities. About 97 per cent of global internet traffic and telephone calls are transmitted through just 200 undersea cables stretching for about 1.2 million kilometres. For example, 11 large cables, each roughly 25 millimetres in diameter, cross the Atlantic and come ashore in the UK, along with other cables arriving from the Middle East and Africa, via the Mediterranean. They surface at cable landing stations from where internet traffic and telephone calls are routed onwards (www2.telegeography.com/).
26 Often they don't. On one estimate £5.5 billion is spent in London each year on exploratory excavation just to work out what is where (Garrett, 2018). Most cities do not have comprehensive subsurface maps.
27 Beijing currently has the highest ridership in the world. Note that not all subway systems – including Beijing's – are continuously underground.
28 But remembering that burrowing underground is a key mode of survival for animals, and has been since earliest times (Martin, 2017), and that a subsurface lifeworld of great complexity has come into view over the last 20 years, thriving in an enormous freshwater reservoir of cracks and fissures. By some estimates, the deep biosphere could contain up to one third of Earth's entire biomass, including not just bacteria and archaea but also nematodes and non-animals like fungi and protozoa (Borgonie and Lau, 2017).
29 Although some cities are beginning to utilize caves for storage (e.g. the Hong Kong rock cavern strategy at www.cavern.gov.hk/home.htm) will utilize caves for warehousing and logistics, partly as a response to land shortage).
30 In the last 10 years, 4,600 basements have been granted planning permission to be excavated in London, nearly all of them in London's best-off boroughs (Garrett, 2018).
31 In many cultures, basements and cellars are seen as having touch of the illicit about them (e.g. in their role as nightclubs and various other 'dives').
32 There are also underground spaces like the Seattle Underground, which was constructed to facilitate the continued functioning of the city while large-scale terraforming was underway but has had an afterlife.

33 Robert Frost 'The oven bird'
34 But this effect varies substantially from city to city depending on its density and public transport infrastructure. For example, compare the built-up area of Atlanta and Barcelona, cities with an equivalent population (2.5 and 2.8 million). One occupies 4,280 square kilometres and generates 7.5 tonnes of carbon dioxide in transport carbon emissions per person. The other occupies 162 square kilometres and generates 0.7 tonnes of transport carbon emissions per person (Angel, 2012). Again, more than 90 per cent of trips in some North American cities are by private vehicles, compared to less than 15 per cent in Tokyo or Hong Kong.
35 In congested road systems, people tend to be isolated from other people. For example, compare the commute by Gravel (2016) in Paris on the metro and by foot, full of interactions, with his commute in a Georgia suburb, sitting isolated in traffic.
36 The obvious example is provided by China's building boom of the last 30 years. No wonder that President Xi is now calling for 'quality urbanization'.
37 For anyone who disbelieves this assertion, just look at a map of oil rigs off the Louisiana coast or consider the ship movements in areas like the English Channel as revealed by apps like Boat Beacon.
38 In the continental United States, although the coasts make up only about 20 per cent of the land, they account for more than half of the country's inhabitants (Berwald, 2018: 34).
39 Indeed, one could argue that cities are themselves cognitive gadgets.
40 One recent study (O'Neill et al., 2018) found that no country on the planet meets basic needs for its human inhabitants at a globally sustainable level of resource use. Whilst it is possible to argue about what the true carrying capacity of the planet may be (see Nordhaus, 2018), it is difficult to just wish the problems away!
41 The concentration of methane in the atmosphere has just reached an all-time high, with an accelerating rate of increase. Methane comes from natural sources, such as wetlands, and from human activities, including oil and gas extraction and livestock farming.
42 Indeed, 21 Indian cities are expected to run out of groundwater by 2020 if a run of low rainfall and droughts continues.
43 Probably the most severe case of double jeopardy is to be found in Jakarta. But Tehran runs a close second.
44 For example, in a typical year, longer and more frequent heat waves will kill more Americans than any other form of natural disaster, including floods, tornadoes and hurricanes. The most recent modelling of future heatwave deaths (Guo et al., 2018) suggests that in some countries, using the highest emissions increase scenario, deaths could rise by well over 1,000 per cent between 2031 and 2080. In some cities, the situation is already critical. For example, in August 2015, the Iranian city of Bandar Mahshahr suffered a heat index – combining temperature and relative humidity – of 73 degrees Centigrade (Linshi, 2015). But urban adaptation to extreme heat is possible – to an extent (Georgescu et al., 2014).
45 Twenty-four of the 100 most affected cities are in India (Urban Climate Change Network, 2015). China has equally severe problems. The North China Plain is one of the most densely populated regions of the world. It is likely to see major effects as a result of of climate change exacerbated by heavy use of irrigation which affects surface radiation, surface energy balance and boundary development such that surface humidity and temperature increase disproportionately (Kang and Eltahir, 2018).
46 In the United States, for example, 'summer nights have warmed at nearly twice the rate of days, with overnight low temperatures increasing 1.4 degrees Fahrenheit per century since 1895, when national temperature records began, compared to a daytime high increase of 0.7 degrees per century. (Nights have warmed faster than days during other seasons, too.)' (Pierre-Louis and Popovich, 2018).
47 Though much attention has been paid to China, according to the World Health Organization, India is home to the world's 14 most polluted cities, with Delhi being only the sixth worst. Toxic air caused 1.24 million deaths in India in 2017, or 12.5 per cent of the total, the second source of premature deaths after malnutrition (Balakrishnan, 2018).

48 One study found that the dominant source of higher volatile organic compounds in Los Angeles was consumer products like toiletries and cleaning fluids, not vehicle emissions (Twilley, 2019).
49 From 2012 to 2016, Earth's artificially lit outdoor area grew by 2.2 per cent per year, with a total radiance growth of 1.8 per cent per year. Continuously lit areas brightened at a rate of 2.2 per cent per year (Kyba et al., 2018).
50 The rate of increase in the amount of carbon dioxide released by the soil is outpacing that absorbed by plants. The soil contains more than double the amount of carbon dioxide found in the atmosphere, and it stays locked in the soil for hundreds or even thousands of years. But warmer temperatures and more carbon dioxide in the air are energizing the microbes that decompose organic matter in the soil, with the result that they release more carbon. This could induce a tipping point where the soil stops operating mainly as a carbon sink and starts acting as a net source of carbon dioxide (Bond-Lamberty et al., 2018).
51 On one estimate, 14 per cent of Los Angeles space is currently reserved for car parking (Chester et al., 2015). Of course, new autonomous vehicles may change all of this, allowing cars to be used more intensively as a result of treating them as shared platforms.
52 Living in shadow is becoming a problem in its own right, producing health problems like vitamin deficiency and myopia as well as greater energy usage – offices higher than 20 storeys are reckoned to use nearly two- and-a-half times more electricity per square metre than those with fewer than seven storeys. Some countries do have planning regulations concerning access to daylight but others have none (Zielinkska-Dabowska and Xavia, 2019).
53 Though some cities are in such challenging places that it is doubtful that any policy can rescue them. As a friend of mine said of Phoenix, 'You don't need a theory to explain this place. It's just a mistake.'
54 Stimulated by the Dutch experience and many other influences, many cities are now beginning to produce large-scale engineering projects to fend off water, such as the proposal for the 'Big-U' in New York.
55 Jakarta is perhaps the most extraordinary example of a city which seems to be in permanent crisis.

Part II

Life

3
Thinking Animals

All life. Cities are populated by all manner of 'nonhuman' things, far too various and variegated to be placed into just a few simple categories. Not that people don't try.

Take the serried ranks of 'animals', on which I concentrate in this book. The dictionary definition of animal covers a veritable host of beings: 'a living organism that feeds on organic matter, typically having specialized sense organs and nervous system and able to respond rapidly to stimuli' (www.dictionary.com). Animals share a number of characteristics in common: they are multicellular eukaryotes that, in general but with some exceptions, take in oxygen, are mobile, consume organic material and reproduce sexually. No one knows the exact number of animal species. Though a figure of 8.7 million is often cited (Mora et al., 2011), estimates vary widely as indeed this figure shows: it has a standard error of plus or minus 1.3 million.

Animals in Philosophy and Social Theory (and Biology)

But one thing we do know, they ain't us. Philosophers are a good guide to this proposition. They have been particularly good at contrasting humans with a broad-brush category of animal beings which, having been pulled into the human slipstream, can be regarded as subordinate. Kant has probably been the most influential. Simply put, he believed that animals are governed by laws given to them by their instincts whereas humans have 'autonomy', that is they are governed by laws that they give to themselves. Humans, in other words, are normatively self-governing, ruled by principles that they themselves take to be laws. 'Other animals, not being rational, cannot participate in the 'reciprocal' legislation from which moral laws emerge' (Korsgaard, 2018: 101). Put another way, humans are rational, that is they have the capacity to inquire into whether their reasons for their beliefs and actions are good ones, and to adjust those beliefs and actions accordingly[1]. They therefore have an intrinsic value.

For many continental philosophers, Heidegger is often the measure of, if not all, then many things. He is a good example of a philosopher who manages to elevate a common prejudice into a theoretical system of base and empyrean (Elden, 2006; Buchanan, 2008, 2012; Calarco, 2008; Glendinning, 2000, 2015; James, 2009; Oliver, 2009). Thus, Heidegger notoriously thought that only human beings had world. Material things like stones are simply worldless because they have no access to our kind of being. In contrast, animals (as Derrida and others have pointed out many a time, an all but meaningless category given the diversity of forms it covers) are 'poor in world'.

That does not mean that animals have no access to the meaning of being as such. For example, animals do have some kind of relationship with things. But though an animal can have a relation with a rock it does not understand 'rock' as such. The rock is given 'in some way' but not as a rock per se. According to Heidegger, animals both have and do not have world because they have no access to an ontological structure or a sense of self (though they are 'self-like'). They are 'immured as it were within a fixed sphere', never able to fashion their own sphere or be anything other than proper to themselves, never able to break through to the world as world. An animal cannot get out of itself – they are absorbed in what they are doing – they are confined to an environmental world (Umwelt), which is not the same thing as a world proper. They cannot jump away from that environment. They are trapped in their own being.

A whole series of deductions follow: animals are 'captivated', 'taken' or 'suspended'; they behave instinctually rather than comport; their being is already to be in a world so that they cannot transcend their circumstances; they do not exist, they 'merely' live. And, most significantly for this book, they cannot know death either. Rather they seem to simply come to an end and 'perish' (van Dooren, 2014). For Heidegger, only humans have openness to the world and consequently cannot be trapped in their own being, chiefly because of the capacity of language, 'the house of Being'. Only humans are world-forming.

> Heidegger is relentless on this point; indeed, like an avenging angel, swords crossed, he steps between the animal and the human being, in order to deny any ontological commonality between the two. He allows himself to be carried away by his anti-biological and anti-vitalist fervor to almost hysterical utterances, for instance when he explains that it appears that 'the essence of divinity is closer to us than what is so alien in other living beings'. (Sloterdijk, 2017b: 201)

We can take the point that Heidegger does not focus on animal life specifically: it is of interest only as it fits into the bigger picture of his ontological pastoral (Buchanan, 2008; Sloterdijk, 2012). That said, in Heidegger animals are clearly there with us in some way. They 'go along' with us. But a human kind of being-with is impossible for them. We can also take the point that Heidegger argues that animals have their own kind of 'wealth', they are not necessarily inferior for being poor in world. But we can still cavil with his depiction of animals. In our relations with them, for example, we may not forge a meeting of minds but we can still have a shared response to a common situation based not on a cognitive interchange but on an intertwining of bodily intentions, what Merleau-Ponty (1964: 145) calls a 'postural impregnation'. As James (2009: 39) points out, this 'unspoken dialogue of expression and gesture' is crucial to how we interact with animals.

But it is not just about us being with animals in this telegraphic way. For we have enough scientific evidence now to know that quite a few species of animals have something that looks suspiciously like world. Beasts are not just beasts. Animals are not just part of a 'covert throng of a surrounding into which they are linked'. In other words, we can now achieve the beginnings of an ontological analysis of other beings in ways which were not possible in Heidegger's time, though they are hinted at already in the work of far-seeing writers who are, like Merleau-Ponty, at least rough contemporaries; writers who took some notice of the contemporary scientific literature (Buchanan, 2008; Westling, 2014). And what the evidence shows is that at least some animals have something which looks very like world. They play. They deceive. They use tools. They have some sense of alternative behaviours and the futures that they might engender. They are not simply given over to tasks and unable to grasp them as such. They can achieve at least some distance from their environment. They can even disrupt it in various ways. In a few cases they have limited language-like capabilities[2]. It may be that some of them have been able to achieve self-consciousness (i.e. they can brand their thoughts as constituting an 'I'). In their own way, they are aspiring upwards too.

In other words, for some animals, and perhaps many animals, Heidegger was simply wrong. They can see into the, or rather, *an* open. We can deny this postulate only if we assume that there are just two options available to us – an animal is an instinctual mechanism or it is like us. But 'other stranger options could be available' (James, 2009: 45), different ways of knowing how to be in the world, different ways in which living beings can express themselves (Buchanan, 2008). In other words, as James goes on to conclude, we do not have to assume that there is one Big Problem – whether animals have minds or not – that has to be solved before we can make progress.

But Heidegger's philosophical worldview does still matter. While not dressed up in Heidegger's arcane prose, many human beings take much the same attitude to many (though not necessarily all) animals. Less that they are unimportant. More that they're just not as special as us. Of course, attitudes to animals clearly vary in and between human cultures. Some animals are pulled out for special treatment, either good (companion animals, religious taboos) or ill (farm animals, sacrifices) but whatever the species, animals are nearly always stepping stones, there to allow human beings to 'float on high'; as labour power wrought from animal proletariats, as affective props, as entertainment – or as food. Perennial accompaniments, vital elements of human animation, their flesh put to work or eaten for sustenance, they are a building block of many of the safety structures of modern life. In so many instances, we breathe only by relying on or taking away their breath.

But what if animals were counted as people, as a part of common breathed communities, each with their own melodies, to pick up on a word that Merleau-Ponty uses to such good effect? What then? After all, 'when it comes to relationships and mixtures of lifestyles, probably not a single life-form on the planet is limited to its own kind' (Thomas, 2017: xi). They are interrelated in myriad ways. Equally, what if we counted many animals as having valid subjective experiences which we might have at least some chance of accessing? We can certainly try to 'sneak up on them' (Prum, 2017: 8), not least because animals also shape their environment over time and in ways which can provide us with all manner of insights. Animals are not just passive bearers of evolutionary impulses. In other words, we must rid ourselves of the usual hoary clichés – humans have language while animals don't so animals have no relation to thinking and no sense of being beings as beings; animals 'perish' while humans 'die'[3]; animals are world poor, living in a 'dazed' or 'benumbed' state, simply existing, attached only to their own being, taken in by ttheir environment, while humans face the anguish of knowing[4]; animals 'stare', 'gape' or 'glower', only humans observe – the list goes on... Sometimes these distinctions are made simply to emphasize the unassailable authority (or 'infinite elevation', to use Kant's phrase) of the human species over all others. Sometimes they are used to denote the crystal clarity of human symbolic thought, as if human thinking is a kind of wellspring. Sometimes they buttress a simple correlationist position which relies on the irreducible dependency of subject and object, thinking and being. The net effect is clear, in any case. Large parts of the world are demoted to the category of 'the rest'. The parochialism of humans leads them,

> to divide up all that exists into our species on one side and everything else, from microbes to pulsars, on the other. (Imagine such a division from the standpoint of some other species – raccoons, say – and the oddity of a universe split up between raccoons and not-raccoons becomes absurdly apparent.) (Daston, 2019: 58)

As Harman (2016: 169) puts it more generally still:

> To modern philosophers it hardly seems to matter that grouping all of the trillions of non-human entities under a single lump term like 'the world' or 'extension' is a terrible oversimplification of a vast catalog of cosmic non-human entities, including such samples as dragonflies, positrons, spy satellites, melons, bridges and neutron stars. The obvious differences among these entities are treated as mere local permutations in a single 'nonhuman' category, while human thought is seen as so taxonomically special, so unprecedented in its ability to tear a hole in the fabric of the universe, that it deserves a segregated niche of its own.
>
> [*Source*: Harman, G. (2016) *Dante's Broken Hammer*. London: Watkins Media Limited © Graham Harman 2016. Reproduced with permission of the Licensor through PLSclear.]

As Derrida (cited in Derrida, 2017: 57) argues, in the case of animals a binary stance of this kind is 'compromised by a thesis on animality which presupposes [...] that there is one thing, one domain, one homogenous type of entity, which is called animality in general, for which any example would do the job'. But 'animals' is really just a 'median' catch-all for a myriad of species which vary so fundamentally in how they go on that grouping them together under a single noun is simply an absurdity.

This point has been made many times now in many different ways, most notably in the practice of artists and poets who deal in beings and environments which sum to something over and above their constituent pieces – just like cities. So Hopkins praises God for the variety of 'dappled things' in nature, like piebald cattle, or trout, or finches. He moves on to a landscape which has been 'plotted and pieced' into fields by agriculture. And on from that again to a general humility in the face of this profusion. One way of casting this book's approach is as a likeminded attempt to acknowledge all of these dappled things without reducing them to simply artefacts or appendages of human thought: '[…] animals are always the observed. The fact that they can observe us has lost all significance' (Berger, 2009 [1980]: 27; see also Burt, 2005). It is an attempt to bring to life a 'zoecentric' view of the planet's and equally cities' capacity to sustain life, a stance which can supplant the 'homocentric' view which has brought us into harm's way (Chakrabarty, 2015; Emmett and Lekan, 2016) for 'reality is too real to be translated without remainder into any sentence, perception, practical action, or anything else' (Harman, 2012). As Cartwright (1992: 1) puts it, we live in a 'dappled world' of 'ragged edges'; 'a world rich in different things, with different natures, behaving in different ways. The laws that describe this world are a patchwork, not a pyramid.'

However, none of the above is meant to imply that I think that all things have the same qualities. Quite clearly, humans have some very distinctive epistemic characteristics which animals do not have. They are not the same. After all, 'the idea that the human is not much more than a hollow fantasy coexists uneasily with the claim that humans as a species are a geological force' (Frost, 2016: 21). But animals have distinctive epistemic characteristics too (such as the types of affects through which they register the world). *'Not the same' is not the same as 'unequal'*.

> People are not more important than animals – not exactly because animals are just as important as people, but because the comparison does not make much sense. People and animals are the beings to whom things are important, and all importance must remain tethered to them. Everything that is important is important – to someone. To put it another way, everything that is good or bad must be good or bad for someone. We may, of course, be important to ourselves, and our own existence, among other things, may be a great good for us. But the other animals may also be important to themselves, in their way, and their own existence may also be a great good for them. (Korsgaard, 2018: 16)

Symbiosis: The Incorporation of Incorporation

One means of achieving at least some degree of closure on an attempt to describe cities as a colloquy of these different kinds of being, brought into occasional or more permanent alignment, is to portray them as 'relational', as occupying a world in which 'humans' and 'nonhumans' are analysed according to the relationships they possess with each other rather than the distinctions between them. This is an increasingly familiar approach in the social sciences and humanities, one which is still concerned with social relations but not with social relations taken as occupying a distinct ontological domain. Rather, *all* phenomena can potentially comprise or imply social relations and the kind of purposiveness that arises out of a constant searching for affinity (Connolly, 2017). But there is no solid doctrine of what those relations are. Taken by itself, however, these statements don't help all that much. The by now ritual invocation of relationalism says both too much and too little[5]. Multiplicity of relation is a banal observation. To mean something substantive, it needs flesh added to its bones so that it can articulate new meanings of 'we'[6], that little word with so many resonances – and so many pitfalls.

That flesh can be provided in at least *four* ways. One is by summoning the notion of what Deleuze called a 'disjunctive synthesis', a term that Deleuze borrows in part from Whitehead (Debaise, 2017a) to describe an open synthesis of relations based on continual divergence and incompletion as well as connection[7]. Both connection and disjunction, in other words. Never a binary. *Partial connection* (Strathern, 2020). This is a fundamental point since it means that explanation no longer has to revolve around making particularities converge on well-bounded, abstract but oft-times empty generalities (which themselves need to be explained) or parts on wholes (both of them being inadequate descriptions since they almost always 'presuppose existence as a totality or unity' (Debaise, 2017a: 50). Instead, everything is being constantly displaced in multiple divergent worlds through contingent 'cosmopolitical' articulations. Everything is asymmetrically implicated through these encounters. In turn, that means that rounded and well-mannered concepts will always struggle. Equally, there is never going to be a naked truth of being human that can be triumphantly uncovered[8], an exception that justifies rule.

The next way follows on: *entanglement*. All animals are societies, communities, collective existences, compounded from numbers of subsidiary individuals who often have little inkling of their place in any larger scheme of things but are invested in what, for them, constitutes their environment[9]. Even entities as small as cells are societies, each constituting their own ecosystems, constantly metamorphosing[10]. But there is more to entanglement than this. In order to survive, and contrary to the dominant evolutionary model of competition red in tooth and claw, living beings also routinely *cooperate* with other species in order to maximize their chances of survival. This is the phenomenon of symbiosis or, more accurately, symbiogenesis, in which 'unlike individuals [are brought together in order] to make up large, more complex entities' (Margulis, 1998: 9). Two or more[11] different species enter into a relation in which each needs the other and perhaps, beginning with that initial linkage, go on to form a composite organism based on reciprocal capture rather than complete absorption[12]. This line of thinking started in 1967 with Lynn Margulis's paper, heretical at the time, which argued that mitochondria and chloroplasts—two organelles within eukaryotic cells – were once independent organisms that, at some point in the distant past, merged with ancestral prokaryotic cells in a mutually enriching, symbiotic relationship. Following Margulis's prompts, Donna Haraway has probably done the most in the social sciences and humanities to emphasize the degree to which symbiosis is a prime mover of life. The conclusion that she and others draw from Margulis's work is easily summarized: 'partnerships of every kind are flourishing – trees and fungi, wolves and ravens, ants and aphids, ratels and honeyguides, badgers and coyotes, and many more. Even bacteria have mixed species relationships, probably more types than those of their domains' (Baynes-Rock, 2015: xii). Indeed, it now seems likely that the reason multi-celled organisms such as animals and plants exist at all is because of an ancient symbiosis in which a single-cell organism called an archaea trapped a bacterium. Rather than destroying it, the archaea merged with it, harnessing its abilities to produce energy and so producing mitochondria, the power generators of the cell (Imachi et al., 2020). In other words, co-evolution is evolution.

But symbiosis is about more than cooperative partnerships. It is about something closer to but not the same as actual mergers which are often both genetic and behavioural composites[13]. All animals turn out to be multispecies events. Rather than simply constituting an exchange of affects, symbiosis entails the 'transformation of one or both entities through the incorporation of one by the other' (Harman, 2018: 118). Above all, 'symbiosis generates novelty' (Margulis, 1998: 9) as each partner acquires complex novel traits which produce co-evolutionary diversification. Examples of symbiosis are routine in the natural world (Douglas, 2010), such as the squid that uses a specific bacterium to help with camouflage that matches the illumination from the moon in exchange for sugars that it generates (Poppick, 2019).

Bacteria and viruses are particularly important elements of symbiosis. Though bacteria and viruses, being prokaryotes and replicants respectively, are not classed as animals, they are immensely important biological actors. Just like many beings, bacteria and viruses are crucial inhabitants of cities. Microbial life like bacteria, archaea, fungi and protists (eukaryotes which are not fungi, animals or plants) like amoebas and diatoms are the most abundant living entities on the planet by far and are crucial to the make-up of materials like soil. There are an estimated 1.6 million distinct kinds of microbe on Earth (each of which is associated with at least one virus) and they make up perhaps half of the weight of life on the planet and about 93 gigatonnes of carbon in biomass (Montgomery and Bikle, 2016; Bar-On et al., 2018; Kuhn, 2019). They mark off the upper boundary of the biosphere, where bacteria are found at heights of 10,000 metres, and the lower, where they are found more than 3 kilometres below the surface of the land and sea (Wong et al., 2015; Smil, 2019). Many species of bacteria and archaea thrive in cities. For example, a study of houses in North Carolina, Florida and Alaska found 80,000 species of bacteria and archaea, concentrated not just on door trims, kitchen surfaces, toilet seats, pillow cases and the like, which might be expected, but also in showerheads, refrigerators, water heaters, dishwashers, even in stoves (Dunn, 2019).

Whereas there are tens of millions of bacteria in a square metre, hundreds of millions of viruses will occupy the same space. Trillions of virions fall from the sky each day, having been swept into the air and around the world by sea spray and dust storms. Often thought of as pathogens, viruses are much more than that. Viruses play a key role in the world. They are essential elements of everything from the human immune system to the human gut microbiome, from the ecosystems on land and in the sea (where just a spoonful of water is filled with millions of viruses (Gregory et al., 2019) to climate regulation. Viruses contain a vast and diverse array of unknown genes which they spread to other species, the result being that they modulate the function and evolution of all living things without being classified as alive. Yet we still know surprisingly little about the 4,958 virus species so far identified, yet alone all the ones that remain to be discovered. But what we do know is fascinating. For example, just as we have learnt that bacteria actively cooperate with each other, so we now know that viruses do the same. Viruses that infect bacteria, so-called bacteriophages, have surveillance mechanisms that garner intelligence on whether to stay dormant or attack, depending on the availability of new victims. It was long thought that these processes were passive but recent research in 'sociovirology' has found that phages actively 'discuss' choices via chemical signals (Dolgin, 2019).

There is no better illustration of the concept of coevolutionary symbiosis than the human body, which might be thought of as only part-human. Often thought of as entire unto itself, the human body is awash with other entities – bacteria, viruses, fungi[14] and archaea – which form a microbiome weighing in at around 3 lb made up of over 10,000 microbial species which is vitally important for corporeal welfare (all the way from newborn babies who receive essential microorganisms from their mothers through the work that microbiomes do every day in aiding the process of digestion to different microbiomes' likely involvement in fighting life-ending conditions such as diabetes, cancer and autoimmune diseases). Human cells are outnumbered by these other cells. By one estimate only 43 per cent of the human body's cells are human. By others, even less. Put another way, this microbiome is a second genome which combines its DNA with our own (Gallagher, 2018). Those trillions of constituent bugs are crucial elements of how we go on living and they are the outcome of a complex and mutable ecological relationship that numerous kinds of microbes, like the roughly 1,000 bacterial species that are present, have with each other – cooperative and otherwise – and with their hosts (Hinchliffe et al., 2016; Lorimer, 2016, 2017;

Lorimer et al., 2019; Proctor, 2019). But they are more than that, possibly much more than that[15]. We now know that this microbiome not only has the capacity to fight infection and cancer (Reticker-Flynn and Englemann, 2019) but also, through microbe-derived molecules, exhibits bidirectional links to the nervous system, influencing human behaviour and the brain (Zimmer, 2019a)[16]. For example, one recent study (Valles-Colomer et al., 2019) showed two particular groups of bacteria that are reduced in people with depression. Another suggests that bacteria may make as much as 95 per cent of the serotonin in the human bloodstream, meaning that a diverse symbiont community is producing mood.

Equally, this weight of microbes has major consequences for many inhabitants of cities if it is short-circuited. It has become apparent that as urban environments have become cleaner there are downsides as well as upsides (Richtel, 2019). In particular, declining family size, improvements in household amenities and higher standards of personal cleanliness resulting from all manner of hygiene products have reduced the opportunity for cross-infection in young families: many urban inhabitants have become too hygienic for their own good. They lack exposure to particular kinds of bacterial biodiversity, and especially to wild species. Lack of regular interaction with the 'friendly' bacteria and parasites that helped to teach and hone the immune system means that the immune system is more likely to over-react, developing antibodies and inflammation to many antigens that aren't actually dangerous. It becomes aggrieved by things like dust mites or pollen. It develops what are called allergies, chronic immune system attacks – inflammation – in a way that is counterproductive, irritating, even dangerous. There are related trends in asthma, inflammatory bowel disease, lupus, rheumatic conditions and coeliac disease (Dunn, 2019).

It follows from examples like these that organisms are never entire unto themselves[17]. The idea of a circumscribed, autonomous biological individual is a myth

> in any sense of classical biology: anatomical, developmental, physiological, immunological, genetic, or evolutionary. Our bodies must be understood as holobionts [integrated communities of species comprised of both host elements and persistent populations of symbionts] whose anatomical, physiological, immunological, and developmental functions evolved in shared relationships with different species. (Gilbert et al., 2012: 334)

Just like humans, then, animals are consortia. They are a living history of differential interaction which holds out the possibility of merger or even fusion. But that coming together is never usually a full assimilation. Rather, 'two become less than two but more than one […] to be a one takes much more than one' (Haraway, 2016: 262). Putting it another way, there is never full assimilation that produces a perfectly bounded whole: life is full of forces that are difficult to fit into a single template of a whole and nicely delineated constituent parts[18]. Rather, there is a continual process of cobbling parts of each other's lives together that is sufficient unto the task and that continues to unfold and evolve as a joint venture of becoming with, whether we are talking about the humble lichen or the human being, each of which have a freight of microorganisms. '[The] new paradigm for biology asks new questions and seeks new relationships among the different living entities on Earth. We are all lichens' (Gilbert et al., 2012: 336).

There is an important lesson to be taken from an emphasis on entanglement and symbiosis. That is not to place too great a dividend on simplicity. Whitehead (2015 [1920]: 143) famously wrote that,

> The aim of science is to seek the simplest explanation of complex facts. We are apt to fall into the error of thinking that the facts are simple because simplicity is the goal of our quest. The guiding motto in the life of every natural philosopher should be 'Seek simplicity and distrust it.'

In its fundamentals, life is complex. I am reminded of Dawkins arguing with Margulis in 2009 about the role of symbiosis. Dawkins, exasperated, asked her 'why on earth would you want to drag in symbiogenesis [to evolution] when it's so unparsimonious and uneconomical?' to which her answer was – I won't say simply – 'because it's there' (www.voicesfromoxford.org/margulis-dawkins-debate/ [accessed June 23, 2020]) This exchange is peculiarly relevant to cities, of course, which are chock full of redundancies and contingencies and feedback loops and unlooked-for interdependencies that can and do confound the expectations of even the most sophisticated theories, let alone the explanatory shortcuts we often deploy (Batty, 2018). Cities are the product of countless individual and collective actions that rarely conform to any grand plan. They are the product of ceaseless invention. They, quite literally, process.

Then, all living beings have feelings or *affects*, which means that, however primitive they may appear to be, they have at least a hint of a causal relation with the world. In other words, these different entities all think but they think in different ways according to what faculties they have been afforded by the process of evolution which award them with a multiplicity of centres of experience flowing from different parts of their body, which, in turn, have different capacities to feel and different capacities to locate those feelings (Debaise, 2017b). As Whitehead (1985, cited in Debaise, 2017b: 45–6) puts it,

> A flower turns towards the light with much greater certainty than does a human being [...] A dog anticipates the conformation of the immediate future to his present activity with the same certainty as a human being. When it comes to calculations and remote inferences, the dog fails[19]. But the dog never acts as though the immediate future were irrelevant to the present.

How living beings think depends not only on their different perceptual capabilities, then, but also on how these capabilities are linked together in a complex unity of experiences which produces their particular form of subjectivity. A plant is what Whitehead calls a 'democracy' which never comes together as one centre of experience 'with a higher complexity either of expressions received or of inborn data' (Whitehead, 1968, cited in Debaise, 2017b: 56) whereas an animal 'is dominated by one or more centers of experience', which together compose a complex and superimposed unity of experiences which have become consolidated (Whitehead, 1968, cited in Debaise, 2017b: 56). Human beings benefit from multiple centres of perception (touch, taste, vision, hearing, etc.) that are either lacking in other living things or work differently and which therefore give them different kinds of experience. As importantly, in human beings these centres of perception and the experiences that they engender are brought together in a centralized brain (though the human body has other sites of thinking too, like the gut).

Last, to add into the mix, in this account, the *'environment'* of living beings is a succession of questions. Their environment is never static and though it is inevitably shackled to the past, it is never entirely constrained by it since even the most ordered of orders has to be actualized and on multiple occasions, and according to the constant changes taking place in the environment.

> Everything happens in encounters. The capacity of a society is relative to its environment and vice versa. It is not possible to get beyond a form of empiricism where that which counts are the interactions in which living beings are engaged. (Debaise, 2017b: 75)

In other words, there is no mechanical repetition. The insistent particularity of each action cannot be transcended. The main point is that this does not involve having to posit 'the existence of memory, of a mind or of habit in order to establish the connection between […] heterogeneous acts. It is within the act itself, in its deepest reality, its very constitution, that this history is established' (Debaise, 2017b: 70).

To summarize, all ecologies are more than human. Human beings are only able to be understood as collaborations of unlike elements. Animals too. The same stricture applies to the atmospheres that they surround themselves with (Lorimer et al., 2017). Both human and animal terraforming is a grab bag of bits and pieces starting out as improvisations and then, for good or ill, becoming permanent connections with all manner of other beings (Descola, 2013).

Add these four relational propositions – partial connection, entanglement, affect and a dynamic environment – together and we start to get closer to thinking about animal thinking without reducing it to a model of the thinking of a particular group of human beings as the only way to understand understanding. They allow us to start thinking of the other in its own terms, on a level playing field, and without the narcissism that characterizes what that group characterizes as thought.

We must find another way for the world to make sense, in other words, one in which the light can always get in. We have never been human. But we could be. That is the task. But for that humanity to happen, we need to take in thinking across entities as a serious project, in that human and other kinds of being think very differently in ways which are not just a variation on a theme. All kinds of entities practise sense-making, though in different ways or, as Whitehead would have it 'the category of the subject is expanded to include everything that we know exists outside of the experience of the human subject' (Stengers, 2017: xiii). There is no need to haul on board the good ship explanation some kind of transcendent mystery, enclosed within itself (Viveiros de Castro, 2014). Rather, we just have to admit that we don't know what we can know and follow the trail of speculative thought where it might take us. Instead of an order, we are faced with an ongoing web of encounters united by the fact that the universe is present in each and every encounter as a constantly mutating sprawl; 'not an unconscious teleology, work of meaning, inclusive fitness, desire of the desire of the other, conflict or contract, but rather a becoming-other' (Viveiros de Castro, 2014: 218). This is a sprawl where, without denying that relations can have very different degrees of intensity, everything is, quite literally, related, is part of an enormous kin structure in which even the most distant of relatives is still a part of the family.

There is no hope of reconciliation, in other words, unless we radically change our perception of what 'we' are and how 'we' go on: 'the common point of reference for all beings of nature is not humans as a species but rather humanity as a condition' (Descola, 1986: 120). This is an alter-political project which involves the production of new existences which are not modes of knowledge that are adequate to a 'reality' but rather a series of imaginative leaps aiming towards an inter-related humanity that recognizes that 'we find ourselves in a buzzing world, amid a democracy of fellow creatures' (Whitehead, 1978, cited in Debaise, 2017a: 166), and that project must increasingly become focused on whether cities can be constructed in its likeness.

Notes

1 In fact, as Korsgaard (2018) points out, Kant's views on animals are nowhere near as stark as often made out. So for Kant, if we kill animals it has to be done swiftly and without pain. It must never be done for sport. Generally speaking, he does not think we should inflict painful experiments on animals either. Making animals work is allowed but only within their capacities, working animals should never be killed just because they have ceased to be useful. 'Any action whereby we may torment animals, or let them suffer distress, or otherwise treat them without love, is demeaning to ourselves' (Kant, 1997, 27: 710). But, as Korsgaard underlines, these are obligations to ourselves as expressions of good moral conduct. Animals are a kind of moral conduit.
2 The latest research shows that even one species of mouse indulges in conversational episodes (see Zimmer, 2019b).
3 A distinction which is engrained in many theologies. Think only of the Christian notion of an end of times after which the dead will rise up. They will enter the city and be transformed. Other beings are not included. They cannot make the climb to the high places.

Their flesh remains corruptible. No sheep will 'rise from the earth, whole and round and white, like silly clouds' (Mcfarlane, 2017: 27).
4   I take these terms from Heidegger partly because he at least tries to argue the distinction whereas in many works it is all but taken for granted.
5   So, for example, like Harman (2018), I do not hold that every being is defined purely by its relations. Beings have a certain integrity. But unlike Harman, I do not insist that they can only come into contact with each other via a 'mediator'.
6   I have wrestled with the notion of both 'we' and 'human'. To begin with, there are liberal definitions of 'we' and 'human' which have, over many centuries, been used to exclude. Equally, the act of inclusion in these categories can be thought of as a means of assimilation to dominant values and practices. And that's before we get to the usual charges of smuggling in racism, heteronormativity, and so on. So I will have to rely on the reader's good sense.
7   Morton (2017: 1) calls this an 'implosive whole' in which 'entities are defined in a non-total, ragged way' but, so far as I can see, it's much the same thing.
8   In a sense, this is akin to Tarde's conception: all things are persons. In turn, thinking becomes about thinking the other's thought. But alien thought is neither a belief nor a set of propositions. It is *a practice of sense-making*. Thought exists inside its expression. And it does this by recruiting new intermediaries that, quite literally, make sense to it and of it (Candea, 2012).
9   The notion that society is a general term is found in Tarde, of course, but in a number of other authors too, for example, Ruyer's (2016) metaphysics.
10 Some authors like Margulis argue that the cell is the basic template for life. Other entities like viruses do not have the social characteristics that mark them out as alive. They are neither prokaryotes nor eukaryotes.
11 There are examples of three-way symbiosis, for example, such as the case of the proto-carnivorous Roridula, which is inhabited by two species of bugs which live their entire lives on the plant and are found nowhere else. The bugs eat the prey trapped by the plant and the plant benefits from the nutrients in the bugs' faeces. But the plant does not want too many bugs since they suck its sap and so the arrangement is policed by a spider which feeds on both the trapped prey and the bugs, so stabilizing this symbiotic triangle (Thompson, 2018). Equally, much attention is now being focussed on groups of species that form complex ecosystems symbiotically linked (Douglas, 2010). In other words, many symbioses are 'nested' (Favini, 2020).
12 Creatures of all kinds come together to make what in psychotherapy is called a 'third being'. These third beings are more than the sum of their parts and they have their own existence as a knot of relations that boost what it is to be alive.
13 Indeed, symbiosis can even function more or less effectively according to personality. Thus, one study found that, in the case of elk being picked clean of ticks by magpies, shy elk and bold magpies were the ideal personality fit, giving each personality type the best outcome (Found, 2017). Another study found that aggressive spiders in so-called mutualistic relationships were at a disadvantage compared to docile spiders. But what is meant to be mutualism can be upended by personality too. One study observed how bolder cleaner fish tended to cheat on mutualism by consuming the protective mucus around their client fish and then swimming off, not bothering to eat parasites in return (Klein, 2017).
14 Fungi are getting ever more attention as elements of a human mycobiome. It seems likely that the interaction between bacteria, fungi and viruses will prove pivotal for all kinds of health.
15 No wonder that directed evolution of microbes has become such a large area of scientific and engineering research. It is even attempting to synthesize insect mating pheromones cleanly, cheaply and on an industrial scale, with the goal of fending off agricultural pests through confusion rather than just extermination.
16 Though the exact mechanisms through which this influence takes place remain elusive. Most work shows correlations, not causes. It is not that surprising though. A number of parasites are known to exercise a kind of mind control on their hosts.

17 Indeed, organisms themselves are constantly changing format. The tadpole and the frog or the pupa and the butterfly are examples of a common natural strategy which probably evolved to access different food sources. The baby and the mother could be seen as another example.
18 The idea of a whole and parts is deeply suspect. Animal communities usually muddle along by using rules which produce inexact but serviceable outcomes (see Esponda and Gordon, 2015, on ants).
19 We now know through numerous scientific studies that dogs do calculate and infer in their fashion, but the point can still stand.

4
Animals Thinking

If there has been a radical reworking of philosophical and social theoretic traditions concerned with humans and nonhumans, the same reworking has occurred in science too. A growing tradition of scientific research suggests not only that thinking is a multifaceted characteristic shared by many different forms of being but also that there are many different evolutionary roads to intelligence. Intelligence has emerged multiple times independently and in different forms. For example, what conscious subjective experience does for us has become open to debate. Often seen as the key to being human, as what sets us apart from animals, it is not at all clear that some other beings do not have this quality to a greater or lesser degree (Godfrey-Smith, 2018)[1]. Meanwhile, what has been regarded as an animalistic quality – instinct – is no longer regarded as just a reflex action. It always contains a potential excess of behaviour arising out of a certain plasticity of orientation and content which can produce spontaneity and unpredictability, inventiveness and expressiveness, in many beings (Massumi, 2014).

It is a measure of how far we assume that human ways of thinking must be the measure of thinking that we assume that vision is the primary means of recognizing one another and knowing things. For example, the test of whether an animal has a sense of self is often assumed to be mirror self-recognition[2]: does an animal see itself in a mirror's reflection? But, as Gee (2013: 166) points out, such a test is biased towards human capabilities and expectations: 'the ability to recognize oneself in a mirror is […] a somewhat contrived special case of a much more general ability to distinguish between oneself and other creatures, based on senses that aren't necessarily visual'. In other words, 'some animals', mental skills may be more impressive than we imagined, while the mirror test may say less than we thought. Moving forward in our understanding of animal minds might mean shattering old ideas about the mirror test and designing new experiments that take into account each species' unique perspective on the world' (Preston, 2018: 2). It is a human tendency to judge other beings by the same yardsticks we adopt[3]. But in large parts of the animal kingdom, it is the orphan senses of smell or sound that reign supreme[4]. What is it like to exist in an olfactory world like a dog which mixes up play, sex and eating or to sense with sound like Nagel's bat? All manner of animals have greater olfactory capacities. Quite a few animals can identify kin and non-kin by smell from their urine. Many animals can distinguish other similar animals and, indeed, different humans by smell. Smell is now seen as an important moment in spatial orientation too. Or take the case of the medium of sound. All manner of animals are much more acutely aware of sound than we are and use it as their primary sensory register. Knowing through sound may not be knowing in the same way as knowing through looking is sometimes represented, as abstract and formal (though there is a tradition of thought that sees looking as a kind of grasping). Rather, it suggests a different form of resonance with the world (Helmreich, 2016). Sense of self may well adhere just as strongly in these other sensory registers, in other words. We cannot assume that animals have fainter versions of our own kind of experience when very often their experience is just different. It could even be, for example, that most animals just aren't interested in looking in a mirror!

Animals in Science

Our relationships with animals in cities can take many forms: selfless love, vile cruelty, anthropomorphic projection, profit, indifference – the list goes on. Until recently, though, it was rare to find the animal being included in the loop as anything other than a correlate of human wishes and desires (Despret, 2016). It is debatable that animals were ever thought of as just Cartesian clockwork – with what Descartes described as 'no thoughts' – but what is clear is that they are now regarded as a much more complex proposition than formerly[5]. They have danced along our margins but now they are beginning to be seen by many as entities with their own motives and thought worlds. So the question now being asked is no longer 'do animals think?' but 'what do animals think?' In other words, as already pointed out, our appreciation of animal thinking does not have to be premised on qualities that they apparently lack and that we apparently possess: they are not the full stops at the end of thought.

Why? Because whereas once practitioners of research into animal cognition and behaviour were sometimes seen as the poor relations of biological science, they have now become mainstream (see reviews in Andrews, 2015; 2020)[6]. It may be that animals were once thought of as somehow lacking in thought, as just a bunch of 'instincts', but as more and more researchers have begun to ask questions about animal thinking and behaviour so a correspondingly enlarged landscape of inquiry has opened up. Now we can think of animals as displaying a plurality of forms of thinking and awareness. We might argue about what significance that thinking and awareness has, but more and more rarely do we argue about its presence. New findings about animal cognition occur on a regular basis.

> We hear that rats may regret their own decisions, that crows manufacture tools, that octopuses recognize human faces, and that special neurons allow monkeys to learn from each other's mistakes. We speak openly about culture in animals and about their empathy and friendships. Nothing is off limits anymore, not even the rationality that was once considered humanity's trademark. (De Waal, 2016: 4)[7]

We now know that animals – not all animals but certainly some – teach, innovate, calculate and exhibit social learning in ways which allow us to think of them as occupying distinct cultural niches. In turn, it also seems likely that these cultural qualities have triggered bouts of gene–culture co-evolution in at least some species – genetic differentiation has followed cultural diversification in both sperm and killer whales and it seems that sponge-carrying dolphins and tool-using New Caledonian crows are likely going the same way (Whitehead and Rendell, 2015; Laland, 2017).

All this said, it hardly needs pointing out that much of what has been discovered about animal thinking has been achieved through an implicit comparison with human cognition and/or with tool-using[8]. But, as already pointed out, whether these are the right gauges is an open question. After all, many animals have sensory capacities that human beings don't have, capacities which allow them to think different things differently. For example, animals can have apprehensions of space we can only speculate about, such as two different and independent visual fields or binocular vision or an ability to see pretty much everywhere at once or see colours we cannot even imagine[9]. What is that like? Again, how do various night hunters apprehend a world with an extra retinal layer? And what is it like to have an eye and brain that can be heated up to produce extra processing power to track changes in the environment, as happens with at least one fish (Young, 2005)? Animals dwell in umwelten which give them very different cues as to what the world is and how to go on, very different aesthetic sensibilities (like crafting nests), which we may well under-appreciate, and very different pleasures (like song, aerial acrobatics or the joy of running) (Herzfeld, 2016; Horowitz, 2016; Safina, 2016). To ask 'what do animals want?' is a question that can now be asked anew as we have realized that they have capacities we had never thought of as capacities. Increasingly, their realities speak to ours, even though we may be able to hear only a part of the conversation.

Quite rightly, much attention has been focused on the conventional range of land and sea mammals (and especially large mammals like elephants, various primates[10] and cetaceans[11]) and the multiple findings about their high levels of sentience have now become commonplace, even humdrum. So instead of producing a long list of all these current findings, which, in any case, many authors have summarized in depth (e.g. Andrews, 2015), I want to concentrate on thinking in four sets of living beings that until now have been relatively neglected, namely birds, fish, cephalopods and insects.

Birds

So let's move first to airspace. Trillions of flying organisms occupy the troposphere. It is a vital piece of habitat (Diehl, 2013). Take the 200 to 400 billion **birds** on the planet, probably making up as many as 18,000 species in all (Barrowclough et al., 2016). We now know that this 'staggering array of species' varies in multiple ways including 'plumage, form, song, flight, and behavior' (Ackerman, 2020: 1). They range from the vesper flights of swifts, birds which never land on the ground and which in the late evening and just before dawn rise up with the flock right up into the air to heights of about 8,000 feet from whence they can survey the land and orient themselves (Macdonald, 2020), to the Australian white-winged chough, which is always found in tight-knit bands. They build nests in common and bring up their young together. But they also indulge in fights with other groups and even enslave these groups' young (Ackerman, 2020).

Most importantly, many birds can accomplish considerable mental feats with brains that in a number of species are the equivalent of primates and have the wherewithal to display consciousness (Herculano-Houzel, 2020; Stacho et al., 2020), using a whole range of senses and consequent forms of affect. For example,

> There's a kind of bird that creates colorful designs out of berries, bits of glass, and blossoms to attract females, and another kind that hides up to thirty three thousand seeds scattered over dozens of square miles and remembers where it put them months later. There's a species that solves a classic puzzle at nearly the same pace as a five year old child, and one that's an expert at picking locks. There are birds that can count and do simple math, make their own tools, move to the beat of music, comprehend basic principles of physics, remember the past, and plan for the future. (Ackerman, 2016: 1–2)

Equally many birds, especially corvids and psittaciformes, can innovate and improvise (Emery, 2016). They show both a large range of behaviours and, most importantly, considerable plasticity of behaviour. We can see this in the multiple examples of new behaviours spreading and becoming locked into bird species. We can see this in the clear examples of deceptions that demonstrate an ability to construct a model of what other birds are thinking and think one step ahead of them by, for example, hiding and protecting caches of food. We can see this in planning for the future. We can see this in sophisticated forms of navigation that demonstrate an ability to gather and integrate a whole range of information from geomagnetism to odour and use selective forms of memory. Take just the fulmar. As Nicolson points out, in order to make journeys quartering the Atlantic in search of food, they have to know what they are doing. They are not just following blind instinct. On one journey, for example, bird 1568 flew nearly 3,900 miles in just over 14 days. He travelled to the Charlie-Gibbs Fracture Zone because of an accumulation of knowledge about where to find food, which is clearly a feat of memory.

> He knew there was a predictable food source there, because he had spent the first few years of his life wandering the oceans exploring and expanding his knowledge […] So many birds go to the Mid-Atlantic Ridge to fish that he probably followed others there. The Mid-Atlantic Ridge was ingrained in his mind as a source of well-being. (Nicolson, 2017: 34)

Fish

Now let's take a dive into the water and into the aqueous realm of fish, into the lakes and rivers certainly, but mainly into the oceans, which are nearly 4 kilometres deep on average and probably occupy some 90 per cent of the biosphere's available living space by volume (Scales, 2018). They produce more than 50 per cent of planetary oxygen and absorb 25–35 per cent of human-created carbon dioxide emissions. The planetary surface is more water than land (in a ratio of 70 per cent to 30 per cent) and 'the oceans are alive. They are literally brimming with life' (Flusser, 1992 [1987]: 66). Though it would be going too far to argue, in terms of biomass, that sea creatures are the quotient and land creatures are the remainder, still fish (and other marine denizens like arthropods[12] and molluscs) are a significant part of the planet's biological load (Bar-On et al., 2018). There are roughly 30,000 species of fish at large, which, like birds, display an extraordinary range of behaviours, including cooperation with each other and with other species, tool use, acute spatial coding, at least a rudimentary first-person perspective, perhaps even facial recognition (Scales, 2018; Woodruff, 2020).

Fish have often been dismissed as marine versions of ciphers staring glazedly ahead, thinking placed firmly to automatic. But we now know that many of them may have inner lives based on their acute senses – fish have sharp senses of (colour) vision, acute hearing and a versatile acoustic range, which means that they are constantly chattering; as well as good senses of smell and taste and touch, and feelings like anxiety and depression. Like birds, they have extremely accurate navigational systems and many have complex social lives and ways of signalling including many different means of using sound: some participate in an underwater dawn chorus (Scales, 2018). Fish even have distinctive parenting styles. They are now known to be able to innovate (e.g. by hunting new kinds of prey) and to learn from each other (Balcombe, 2016; Scales, 2018). Indeed, some fish seem to outperform primates on certain specified mental tasks.

Just like the fulmar, some fish which travel long distances clearly have a strong locational memory learnt in part from others. For example, cod are highly vocal and have very elaborate calls compared with many other fish. They have traditional feeding and breeding grounds which have been established over many hundreds or even thousands of years. Many young fish will follow the older fish to these grounds. 'In experiments, introduced outsiders who learned such preferred locales by following elders continued to use these traditional routes after all the original fish from whom they learned were gone' (Safina, 2020: 161).

Fish are hardly the only aqueous denizens. So far as the oceans are concerned, all manner of other animals inhabit the deep from crabs that can solve mazes (Greenwood, 2019) to cephalopods whose form of intelligence we have only just begun to understand. Of these other species, a particularly widespread group are jellyfish (Berwald, 2018; Williams, 2020), an important element of the ocean's plankton. They are found in most of the waters of the Earth. But, in certain senses, jellyfish are a mystery. It is not easy to count them. It is unclear whether their numbers are increasing, as was once widely believed, or we are simply seeing evidence of brief population explosions. We cannot be sure how many species there might be (at best guess (Berwald, 2018), probably 600 species of true jellyfish, 100 species of box jellyfish and another 100 siphonophores, and at least 4,000 species of hydrozoans). What we do know is that they are having more and more impacts on cities where they block up power station inlets, sting unwitting swimmers and often seem able to survive in heavily polluted environments. They can also have major environmental effects, taking over seas where overfishing has been rampant, as in the waters around Namibia where jellyfish now outnumber fish by 2.4 to 1 (Berwald, 2018).

Cephalopods

Carrying on in a marine vein, there are the molluscs known as cephalopods, of which there are reckoned to be at least 800 living species. There are two main types: Coleoidea, which includes octopuses, squid and cuttlefish[13]; and Nautiloidea, represented by *Nautilus* and *Allonautilus*[14]. They are ecological keystones in that they provide abundant food for oceanic predators of many kind[15]. Recent research shows that these animals, unlike molluscs in general (typified by animals like clams and snails), have developed complex nervous systems and, as a result, have what can only be described as a degree of intelligence[16]. Furthermore, it is intelligence of a very special form which has existed over a very long time scale as a result of a different evolutionary route (Staaf, 2017; Amodio et al., 2018):

> cephalopods are an independent experiment in the evolution of large brains and complex behavior. If we can make contact with cephalopods as sentient beings, it is not because of a shared history, not because of kinship, but because evolution built minds twice over. This is probably the closest we will come to meeting an intelligent alien. (Godfrey-Smith, 2018: 9)[17]

Probably, out of all the cephalopods ('head-foots'), most work has been done on the octopus, of which there are about 100 different members in the genus (Mather et al., 2010; Montgomery, 2015; Godfrey-Smith, 2018)[18]. Hampered by a solitary lifestyle (which may, however, promote a very high degree of individual variability)[19] and by a short life span (usually around 2 years with the smallest species only living 6 months to a year and the largest managing 3–4 years), octopuses still seem to demonstrate a remarkably complex form of cognition but they manifest it in ways that depend upon their own array of senses, which dictates how they can be smart (Amodio et al., 2018). Thus, octopuses taste/touch with their entire bodies (Lesté-Lasserre, 2020), have blue copper-based blood, can squeeze through the tiniest of cracks, are jet-propelled, have three hearts and can change colour (in about 30 milliseconds)[20], texture and shape so as to deceive numerous predators[21], to communicate visually with conspecifics[22], and maybe as a pure aesthetic act in some cases. What is clear is that they learn and they are extremely flexible and curious learners with quite distinctive individual characters. They originate all kinds of behaviours, including play with objects that take their interest for no reason except that they take their interest, and the use of various elements of the environment to make tailored spaces. Their intelligence is distributed around their bodies in a way that no vertebrate can emulate[23], probably at the cost of less integrated perception but with the advantage of having a much less clear dividing line between self and environment. Thus,

> the relevant contrast in the octopus is not 'body rather than brain'. In an octopus, the nervous system as a whole is a more relevant object than the brain: it's not clear where the brain itself begins and ends, and the nervous system runs all through the body. The octopus is suffused with nervousness. (Godfrey-Smith, 2018: 75)

This very diffuseness makes it more difficult to recognize the octopus's intelligence just as its solitary nature (which begins with the fact that after they hatch they are on their own) means that many tests based on the norms of human intelligence (e.g. self-recognition[24]) simply do not apply in the same way. At the risk of repetition, animals like octopuses manifest an intelligence. They can reveal different personalities. They understand sequence and planning – though the 'reasons' for their actions may sometimes be opaque. They communicate with each other. They play. They observe. They watch closely. They learn. It is a brave person who says that there is nothing going on there but simple conditioning (Schweid, 2014). But how do we describe this awareness?

A Cephalopod Digression

Writers like Taussig (2019) have produced wonderful ethnographies which attempt to give voice to animals as part of an assemblage of concerns. But somehow that voice still remains faint except insofar as it relates to human concerns. It is as if 'all the ways you imagine us […] are always amputations' (Powers, 2018: 3)[25]. There is, however, one interesting attempt at an answer to this conundrum. It is provided by Vilém Flusser (2011 [1987]) in what is, by any account, a remarkable book. Flusser attempts to conjure up the world of a particular cephalopod, the less than a foot-long vampire squid (*Vampyroteuthis infernalis*), which lives in the low-oxygen, high-pressure abyss of the ocean depths and is broadly distributed around the world, moving through near-total darkness. He makes much in general of octopuses' non-vertebrate evolutionary path, one in which animals are not 'hung by an internal coat-hanger' (Flusser, 2011 [1987]: 31). In other words, Flusser wants to talk about a group of animals whose fundamental bodily tendency is to twist over themselves but who, for all that, are vertical beings formed in the shape of an open palm with the cranium on the bottom (the opposite of humans), who Flusser described – mainly incorrectly as it turned out – as fast and ferocious carnivorous predators with teeth in the mouth, on the tongue, in the oesophagus and even around the suction organs along the eight tentacles, who could walk, project and swim via fins, had glands that expelled ink and venom, had red skin and blue eyes[26], and seemed to have an extraordinarily complex sexual life. Can we conjure up how an animal like this thinks and feels? After all, some have argued that the current situation arises from an incapacity in human reason which means that thinking the other has limits which cannot be broached, a scepticism that goes back a long way:

> if cattle and horses or lions had hands and do the work that men can do, horses would draw the form of the gods like horses, and cattle like cattle, and they would make their bodies such as they each had themselves. (Xenophanes of Colophon [c. 570? – c. 475 BCE] cited in Daston, 2019: 47)

Flusser attempts to build up a picture of a creature which, because of its deep-sea haunts, is different from other octopuses in a number of ways, most notably in that it has lost its ink sac and the most active chromatophores, has grown two retractile filaments which are likely tactile sense organs, has developed photophores and the ability to produce a bioluminescent cloud and has evolved a gelatinous tissue consistency. But Flusser's account shows the rub of these kinds of speculative exercises in that science has moved on (Dickey, 2012). For example, Vampyroteuthis is not, as Flusser would have it, a fearsome predator. Its 'teeth' are cirri not spines and the vampire squid subsists on 'marine snow' – faeces, mucus, bits of dead plants and animals, and anything else that falls down from the surface of the ocean (Staaf, 2017). But, even as Flusser wildly over-reaches in scientific terms, he also manages to imagine a different kind of world, a volume rather than a plane or a surface in which things are taken in rather than just touched.

> He lives in three-dimensionality: he licks it with a tongue covered with teeth. This is why he did not pass from the second to the third dimension when he erected himself, as did men. But as he erected himself, he twisted the third dimension into a spiral in order to penetrate a kind of fourth dimension, the coil […] His posture does deny the second dimension, as ours does, but perforates the third dimension like a screw. We navigate the world perpendicularly, and he spirally. […] For us, the shortest distance between two points is a straight line. For him, the shortest distance is a coil, which makes the two points coincide when retracted. (Flusser, /2011 [1987]: 76–7)

Flusser also tries to draw a fanciful picture, a 'fable' as he himself describes it, of a heavily sexualized vampire squid culture in which 'his language's syntax, the play of colors over his skin, is the logic of sex' (Flusser, 2011 [1987]: 83). The vampire squid thinks but its practices of reflection are not based on objects but rather on information directly stored in the nervous system, which makes up a complex system of fluidic memory expressed as lights, colours and sounds, as gestures and caresses, as new skin paintings, as periodic violence and as cloud messages soaking through pores.

> Vampyroteuthis collects information by means of his tentacles and bioluminescent organs. He paralyses this information […] in order to transform it into workable 'bits'. His nervous system will codify this information: it will symbolize it. […] Once codified into colors, lights, or gelatin clouds, the information will be emitted. And this emission is received by other Vampyrotheuses by means of their tentacles and bioluminescent organs. Through this process, acquired information is stored in the memory of the species. This is vampyroteuthian history. And the collection of emissions supported by the secretions is vampyroteuthian culture. (Flusser, 2011 [1987]: 90)

Insects

Back into the air. As many as 10 quintillion **insects** (as well as arthropods, arachnids, and other members of the phylum Euarthropoda) are estimated to live on the planet, about 200 million insects for every human being (McAlister, 2017; Sverdrup-Thygeson, 2019), many of whom also occupy airspace. Formerly thought of as akin to automata, with no light switched on inside, we can now be pretty sure that encomiums to insects' swarm intelligence, first made in the nineteenth century by Darwinist writers on animal consciousness like George Romanes (2016 [1892]), are indeed accurate, though to what degree remains a matter of controversy. Individually, most insects' brains are tiny, having just a million or so neurons, compared with a human being's 86 billion neurons. For all of the talk of insects having midbrain structures that can compensate, this deficit is hard to just gloss over, although recent research suggests that number of neurons should not be the measure but rather their complexity – on this measure bees, for example, do rather well. Certainly, many eusocial insects like bees and ants, and arthropods like the velvet worm[27], exhibit plastic and flexible behaviour. They can master some forms of conceptual learning and are adept at certain kinds of non-linear problem solving. It may be that 'some social insects can categorize, extract and organize their knowledge' (Kirksey, 2016: 23). For example, even with so few neurons, ants can encode complex memories, know about time and place, and communicate with each other by releasing pheromones, through the medium of tactile stimulation, and through sounds generated by making chirping noises. And ant colonies have corporate memories that individual ants don't have which are retained through a variety of means. The older colonies tend to make more stable, 'wiser' judgements (Gordon, 2018). Bees make an even more compelling case for being thought of as thinking beings of a kind. It is not just that 'whatever it feels like to be a bee, it feels like something' (Keim, 2016: B8). Though some caution is in order, it seems that they are capable of 'offline thinking' about the spatial locations that they visit (Chittka and Wilson, 2018; 2019), manifest the ability to predict what will happen in the future as a result of self-generated movements, display a degree of foresight in constructing their homes, can determine the quality of pollen they collect through gustatory, olfactory, mechanosensory and visual cues (Nicholls and de Ibarra, 2017), use simple tools which they learn about by observing skilled demonstrator bees (but then can improve upon), are capable of 'numerosity'[28], can perhaps recognize faces, likely hold an internal representation of shape, which can be accessed by a range of different senses, demonstrate metacognition (knowing their own knowledge), seem to fall into both optimistic and pessimistic emotional states, and, though this is certainly contested, it may even be that they dream. In other words, 'perhaps the problem is not that insects lack an inner life, but that they don't have a way to communicate it in terms we can understand' (Chittka and Wilson, 2018: 1).

There are a few insects that may show even greater acuity than bees. For example, paper wasps, like rats, geese and cichlid fish, exhibit transitive inference (the ability to compare indirectly) (Tibbets et al., 2019) while the case has been made that praying mantises, of which there are about 2,500 species, are 'aspiring vertebrates' (Angier, 2017). They have stereo vision (the only invertebrate so far for which there is definitive evidence) as well as a fovea, enabling the mantis to track prey, which consists not only of other insects but, in the case of the larger species, small birds. It seems that this relative of the cockroach has made a step upwards in terms of insect cognition, perhaps the result of being a climax predator and having an immense appetite which means that it needs to feed regularly. Certainly, they show signs of being able to calculate strategically and not just react.

The importance of insects to the environment is paramount. Take the case of flies. Flies are ubiquitous – it has been estimated that one in ten of every species ever described (about 160,000 in all) is a fly (McAlister, 2017)[29]. They are vital to the wellbeing of the planet. They pollinate many flowers, including those of fruit trees. They control pests, for example some species[30] eat aphids that would otherwise destroy many plants. They are a key food source for all kinds of animals, especially birds. They decompose waste. The list goes on and on. Flies also exhibit complex behaviours (e.g. intricate dance moves to attract mates). They don't just react instinctively. Studies show that their brains make decisions based on several different inputs – smell, memory, hunger and fear, for instance.

To illustrate the impact of the fly on the environment, take just one example: the humble marmalade hoverfly which – like many insects[31] – makes mammoth migrations. Wotton et al. (2019) estimate that up to 4 billion hoverflies migrate in and out of southern England each year[32]. Each fly can travel as much as 50 to 100 miles in a day, and over the course of a year's migrations hoverflies can cycle through several generations. The voracious larvae produced by migrating hoverflies every year in southern England devour on average some 6.3 trillion aphids – about 400 for each larva – which have a combined weight of around 6,350 tonnes. The flies, one of the most frequent flower visitors, visit billions of flowers each year and then, as the insects make their way along their migration route, they carry the pollen grains from the flowers over long distances. Wotton et al. estimate that hoverflies import somewhere between 3 billion and 8 billion pollen grains into southern England in the spring, and then export 3 billion to 19 billion pollen grains with them as they fly south again in the autumn. But the insects are not just important for the prey they eat and the pollen they carry. They are also nutrients. Many are eaten by predators; others fertilize the soil after they die. They comprise about 73 tonnes of biomass, amounting to some 35 million calories.

Decline and Extinction

Like birds, fish and cephalopods, insects can do some remarkable things, down to cases like that of the humble whitefly, which not only deceives individual plants that it attacks by eliciting a response that is anti-disease rather than anti-insect, but also by spoofing their alarm system so that they spread an erroneous message to neighbouring plants (Zhang et al., 2019). But this hasn't stopped them from being vulnerable to human depredations. Whereas the dramatic decline in many bird and fish populations has been frequently documented, it is only recently that insect population decline has moved into the limelight. I will end this chapter by summarizing what we now know as a harbinger of what is happening to many wild animals as cities expand their reach.

There are some worrying signs that insects are environmentally stressed, mainly because of the use of non-specific insecticides and intensive industrialized agriculture more generally, as well as the spread of new pathogens, general global warming and, in cities especially, artificial light (Owens et al., 2019). Though studies tend to be rare, it may be that we are seeing a long-term decline in the fly population, and in the insect population more generally (Vogel, 2017; Goulson, 2020). One recent review and analysis of 73 studies (Sanchez-Bayo and Wyckhuys, 2019) suggested that the total mass of insects worldwide may be falling by as much as 2.5 per cent a year. More than 40 per cent of insect species were declining and their rate of extinction was eight times faster than that of mammals, birds and reptiles. Another study (van Klink et al., 2020) from 166 long-term surveys in 41 countries on five continents found land-based insects declining at nearly 1 per cent a year or almost 9 per cent a decade, though freshwater insects were holding their own. If even the lower of these estimates proved to be accurate, it would be an exceptionally serious issue, threatening food systems and planetary ecology more generally. More specific studies also give cause for concern. One report suggested that the biomass of flying insects in Germany has dropped by 76 per cent – regardless of habitat type – since 1989[33] (Hallmann et al., 2017). Another found an 80 per cent decline in the abundance of flying insects hitting car windscreens in rural Denmark between 1997 and 2017 (Møller, 2019). Another report again found a 30 per cent decline in grasshoppers in Kansas prairie over the past 20 years, partly perhaps because of nutrient dilution as a result of climate change (Welti et al., 2020). One other report (Lister and Garcia, 2018) found a worrying marked decline in the phylum of arthropods more generally in a Puerto Rican rainforest between 1976 and 2012, and parallel decreases in lizards, frogs and birds who feed on them, mainly because of climate warming. Since arthropods comprise as much as two thirds of terrestrial species, this is an important finding with likely flow-ons for the biodiversity of tropical urban areas.

In other words, insects, like many other animals, are under the cosh and there they will remain until cities stop encroaching on their habitat, tackle climate change far more forcefully and halt the surplus of killing. Which brings us on to the question of death.

Notes

1. Even meanings can be processed unconsciously. Sequences of words flashed up so quickly that a person has no idea that they were shown them at all can still register in the brain.
2. Research shows that chimpanzees and orangutans definitely have this capacity. So, probably, do elephants and dolphins. After that, things get more problematic although one recent study suggested that the tiny cleaner wrasse may have it too (Baraniuk, 2018; Preston, 2018).
3. Even vision is problematic. What about animals that have more than one visual representation of the world, like frogs and a number of birds (Godfrey-Smith, 2018)? Or animals that see and/or can be seen in ultraviolet?
4. 'To what organic sense do we owe the least and which seems to be the most dispensable? The sense of smell. It does not pay us to cultivate it or to refine it in order to gain enjoyment; this sense can pick up more objects of aversion than of pleasure (especially in crowded places) and, besides, the pleasure coming from the sense of smell cannot be other than fleeting and transitory' (Kant, 2006: 46).
5. There is even some controversy about what might be included as 'animal'. Ctenophores (comb jellies), the 8,500 species of sponges and myriad placozoans are often neglected, not least because they do not belong to the clade with bilateral symmetry, but their genomes are not so very different from those of bilaterian animals (Neff, 2018).
6. A search of Google Scholar currently yields over 200,000 citations.
7. As I was writing this book, it was found that both horses and pigeons can recognize and respond to different written words (which is not necessarily the same as 'reading' them) and that corvids seem to have mental models and can plan several moves ahead as a result (e.g. Gruber et al., 2019).
8. The latest animal found to be using tools is a type of pig (Bernstein et al., 2019)!
9. Humans are trichromatic. They see colours as a combination of red, blue and green, thanks to three types of light-sensitive proteins called opsins. By contrast animals like dragonflies have no fewer than 11 opsins.
10. Recent remarkable work by Eckert et al. (2018) shows that chimpanzees have a model of the world that not only includes their knowledge of the world but also includes inferring what others themselves know about the world. In particular, they seem to demonstrate the same means of statistical inference as humans.

11 Latest findings on whales, for example, include: that some species go through 'cultural revolutions', completely changing/simplifying their song repertoire every few years, songs can be adopted by other populations and some populations have their own dialects (Weintraub, 2019).
12 Thus, the Euarthropoda krill contributes a quantity of 400 million tonnes to global biomass, similar to the biomass of humans and cows (Bar-On et al., 2018). Krill feed whales, seals, seabirds – and us. Whales have been discovered to have a vital role as ecosystem engineers, in that they transfer nutrients from the depths where they feed to surface waters where they defecate, thus spreading fertilizing iron that sustains phytoplankton and so krill (Nicol, 2018).
13 Recent research (Reiter et al., 2018) shows that cuttlefish make their thoughts visible on their surface – the inner workings of the cuttlefish's brain are reflected on its skin. Now all that is needed is to be able to interpret what those thoughts are!
14 In the Coleoidea, the molluscan shell has been internalized or is absent, whereas in the Nautiloidea, the external shell remains.
15 A single sperm whale can eat between 700 and 800 squid every day. 'Back in the 1980s, scientists calculated that the mass of cephalopods eaten by whales, eels, and seabirds outweighed the total marine catch (fish, cephalopods, and everything) of all fishing fleets around the world' (Staaf, 2017: 3). Of course, many cephalopods are adept at eating each other too. There are almost no catch limits on cephalopods around the world and there is also a substantial problem of bycatch in the case of some species. Generally, however, cephalopod populations seem to be holding up reasonably well.
16 For up-to-date news, see *The Octopus News Magazine Online* (TONMO) at www.tonmo.com/ (accessed June 24, 2020).
17 Indeed, they have even been held up recently as examples of the Hoyle–Wickramasinghe hypothesis as having arisen from virus-driven extraterrestrial genetic enrichment or even squid and octopus eggs preserved in icy bolides traveling across space (Steele et al., 2018).
18 The genome of the octopus shows a staggering level of complexity with 33,000 protein-coding genes – more than in *Homo sapiens* (Albertin et al., 2015).
19 Although there have been recent reports of 'octopus cities' in Australian waters, which may or may not suggest a higher degree of sociability (Godfrey-Smith, 2018).
20 Though it seems that octopuses are colour blind and therefore cannot see colour in conventional ways, it is likely that they can 'feel' colour through their skin.
21 Indeed, it may be that losing a shell, which made octopuses more vulnerable to predation, also forced their intelligence (Amodio et al., 2018).
22 Octopuses have been portrayed as solitary animals but recent work (Scheel et al., 2017) shows quite frequent interaction in some species and even clumped dens.
23 For example, their arms have around two thirds of their neurons and these seem to have recurrent connections that may give each arm short-term memory (Godfrey-Smith, 2018).
24 But they can and do recognize and like and dislike individual humans.
25 Powers is referring to trees but the same stricture can be applied to animals.
26 Colour-changing abilities are useless in the dark environment of the deep and red is as good a colour as black in the deep sea since red light is the most readily absorbed by water.
27 Velvet worms, cousins of arthropods, are extraordinarily social. They sleep together in piles, share food and give birth to live young, which remain with their parents for a period (Sullivan, 2020).
28 One recent paper goes so far as to argue that bees know how to count (Howard et al., 2019). The insects were apparently able to add or subtract on demand, learning to perform arithmetic by following instructions given to them. However, there is some scepticism about this result.
29 To give some sense of comparison, there are approximately 5,400 species of mammal on the whole planet (McAlister, 2017).
30 Remembering that in many flies the eating is done by both the larva and the adult.

31 One US ladybird migration was large enough and dense enough to show up on radar as a weather system (Kennedy and Matias, 2019).
32 The true number is probably higher, because the radar system used to track these insects can only spot insects flying above 450 feet.
33 The fall was even higher (82 per cent) in summer, when insect numbers reach their peak. This research captured all flying insects, including wasps and flies which are rarely studied, making it a much stronger indicator of the depth of decline.

Part III

Death

5
The Animal City

Introduction

In cities all kinds of different thinking things are placed together in Gary Snyder's 'one big empty house'[1]. Cities are common ground, even in those cases where animals are regarded as pests. The degree of commonality may vary but it is there all the same, for all of the misconstruals (Diski, 2010: 56). Equally cities are grounds for common thought. That thought may be multiple, distributed, spasmodic and more often than not undocumented, but that does not mean that it doesn't exist. Cities are a project of composition, interconnected, always dynamic, constituted from a whole mass of modes of existence which includes but is certainly not restricted to various human habits and practices. This process has been most fully documented for various kinds of ecology. But in many ways the true salon of 'ecology without nature' (Latour, 2004) is now the city. Cities contain all manner of beings brought together by the heightened levels of intensity that result from cohabitation, commensality and commerce. As that convergence happens, so cities exhibit emergent tendencies through a process of reciprocal capture in which beings fold into each other in new combinations through various kinds of co-invention like symbiosis and parasitism. Of course, some care needs to be taken here. Words like composition and interconnection and emergence can cover a multitude of sins, acting like a magic wand 'to account for whatever it is that we do not know how to explain' (Shaviro, 2015: 32). Anything and everything can be included.

That caution made, cities are more than just an 'ontographic' (Bogost, 2012) gallimaufry of different things placed together; though, that said, the very fact of contiguity is often important. To return to the content of a previous chapter, they are symbiont organizations. As has already been pointed out, symbioses are not wholes, of course. They are 'diversities of co-evolving associates' (Margulis, 1998: xx). That means that they are always partialities that induct a set of actors into living in reciprocal relationships with one another. The unity, such as it is, is like that of the body: it 'is that of a co-functioning: it is a symbiosis, a "sympathy". It is never filiations which are important, but alliances, alloys' (Deleuze and Parnet, 2007: 69). But what if these alliances get out of joint? That, I would argue, is what has happened in contemporary cities, leading to surplus animal death. Note the use of the adjective surplus. Like humans, animals are dying all the time – from predation by other animals, from disease, from all manner of adverse environmental events, from random accidents, and so on. That is a part of life. But what we have now is something very different. Animals are being killed in a kind of urban-induced frenzy, as the following chapters demonstrate. That is a bald statement and there are all kinds of nuances that need to be injected into it. For example, some of the animals that dwell in cities live longer than they would in the wild and are able to reproduce on a larger scale. But, generally speaking, what we see is an imbalance which needs to be righted and for all kinds of reasons, including massively adverse environmental effects, mortal threats to human beings like pandemics, and a simple sense of what is just and what isn't.

Whereas, until recently, many changes in urban ecologies were identified as purely negative, there is a strain of ecological writing which is becoming more common, one that in its more extreme forms can be seen as near to Panglossian in its outlook. New, more mixed ecologies are identified as coming into existence, many of which are urban, which are clearly 'better' in the sense that they are more biodiverse or will become more biodiverse as evolution takes its course (Thomas, 2017). These examples are used as a means of arguing that, at least in the long run, all can be for the good[2]. Fuelled by perpetual transformation, more biodiverse ecologies will spring from the wreckage of environmental disaster and produce new possibilities out of the human occupation of the planet. Nature is given a turbo-boost, not a punch in the guts.

But a word of warning is in order. Such judgements need to be tempered. Nuance is all. Yes, new ecologies may emerge but often only over the very long term (Wilson, 2015). Meanwhile, we have a forced march in which the killing and predation is all on one side. Take just the case of animals. Certain animals – like dogs or cats – have commensal relationships with human beings in which their species gets some advantage from the relationship. But others are in a relationship where the advantage is, to put it but kindly, unclear, and seems closer to continuous abuse, unless one subscribes to the idea that genes are the basic units of evolution and a certain kind of biological replication is all the explanation needed.

Body Count: How Cities Relate to Animals – and How Animals Relate to Cities

Cities have always included animals in some shape or form. There is no time in which animals, however humble, have not been present. They are woven into the city's history. Whatever role they take – oppressed, defiant, companions – they are always there. Just a brief glance around the environs of any contemporary city will reveal birds, from generalist scavengers like pigeons and crows, as well as predators like hawks and other raptors, to water birds like herons and Canada geese[3], to garden birds like starlings, finches, sparrows and, latterly, ring-necked parakeets[4] as well as their traces – like bird droppings – for us all to curse. In North America, such a glance could well provide a glimpse of a a rat or a squirrel or a chipmunk or a fox or a coyote or a brief flashing image of a bobcat or even a prairie dog. The sidewalk may be heaving with so-called pavement ants, subsisting on a diet of junk food. It will undoubtedly, of course, take in numerous dogs and cats, some of them very possibly feral. In the suburbs, depending on location and the presence of green corridors, it is likely to include deer of various kinds[5], elk, bears, javelinas, boar[6], bobcats, mountain lions, coyotes, foxes, raccoons[7], opossums, wild turkeys, feral chickens, iguanas, lizards, giant land snails, or, in some cities, snakes like rattlesnakes or even boa-constrictors and pythons[8] (Donovan, 2015). In the ponds and watercourses, diverse forms of aquatic life live, though only a few thrive. Feinstein (2011) lists 135 common North American urban mammals, birds and insects. In other words, animals have come to town.

Now walk inside. In the world's densest cities, the indoor biome is often bigger than the outdoor space, at least in terms of residential floor area[9], and it is the most intensely inhabited part of the city, given that urban dwellers in cities of the North spend as much as 80 to 90 per cent of their time indoors. (Indeed, surveys show that for both the US and the UK the figure seems to be about 90 per cent, though one UK survey put the figure as high as 95 per cent; Roberts, 2016; Twilley, 2019). Yet scientists know almost nothing about the beings that inhabit this space alongside us, often living in environments much more extreme than they would have encountered previously. But what is remarkable is the sheer diversity of life found there. Dunn (2019) and associated researchers have catalogued over 200,000 species living in Western homes. The bulk of the 200,000 species were prokaryotes like bacteria and archaea discovered in dust, bodies, water, food and intestines. There were 40,000 species of fungi. The rest were insects, animals and plants. Some houses were found to have as many as 200 arthropod species, including centipedes and millipedes (Twilley, 2019). Indeed, there are 'hundreds of species [of arthropods and insects] that have lived in homes long enough to evolve specific adaptations for indoor dwelling' (Dunn, 2019: 137). Many of these different animals are regarded as pests to be annihalated, like certain species of cockroach which thrive in houses (not least because they are becoming increasingly resistant to every chemical thrown at them) but are comparative weaklings in the wild – indeed there are no wild populations of the German cockroach. Bedbugs and the larvae of the two types of clothes moth are also on the list of unwelcome animals that thrive indoors, their populations expanding because of factors like hotter winters, natural fibres and warm homes. Others, like the ten species of spiders found in each North American home are, on the whole, beneficial. They feed on what we regard as the less pleasant indoor insects such as roaches, earwigs, flies and clothes moths, and they rarely bite. But, on the whole, we know remarkably little about these different kinds of insect, to the extent that new species of camel crickets have been able to spread through North American homes without anyone knowing, until very recently, that they had even done so (Dunn, 2019).

Of course, different kinds of animal have different kinds of connection with human beings and with the city. For some, cities are almost cosy sinecures, for rather more they are landscapes of fear. O'Connor (2013) provides perhaps the best classification. To begin with, there are 'domesticated animals'. These can be divided into two kinds, namely companion animals, which are owned, captive-bred and act as a social resource, and livestock, which are owned, captive-bred and act as a material resource. Then there are 'wild animals'. Some of these (synanthropes) willingly live in urban environments. They can be divided into many kinds: for example, commensal animals live alongside humans in cities and reap the benefits – like food. Some are 'adapters' who have passively entered a synanthropic role because their range has been encroached upon by the human built environment – like many garden birds. Others are 'adopters', actively moving into the urban environment – like foxes. Some commensal animals – like geckos or rats – live most of their lives on urban buildings, some in domestic structures, others not. Then, finally, there are 'wild animals'. The vast majority of these atanthropes do their utmost to avoid humans – and cities. But some show a certain propensity to interact under very specific circumstances – like Baynes-Rock's (2015) Ethiopian hyenas, which show more behavioural flexibility in urban situations[10]. I will use this classification at various points in the next three chapters.

Animal Agency

We must be careful not to automatically cast animals as just passive beings in the urban brew, whether that passivity comes from genes or human intervention – or, indeed, a mixture of the two brought about by domestication (Despret, 2016). Indeed, the presence of domesticated animals has brought about substantial changes in human societies. For example, there is fairly good evidence that, tethered to the invention of the plough, domestication produced greater inequality because, around 4000 BCE, certain peoples came to own draught animals (especially oxen) and ploughs, and with them the capacity to decouple wealth from labour, extending production and surplus by making land more valuable and human labour less so (Smith, 2011; Bogaard et al., 2019; Fochesato et al., 2019; Bowles and Choi, 2020)[11].

But animals are more than just convenient adjuncts, living property allowing certain people to store wealth and others not. Agency is relational and animals can also have considerable agency in how they inscribe relations of exchange and proximity. They do not just conform automatically to human wishes, as anyone with a dog or a cat can attest. Animals can mould us too. 'Beings learn either to ask that what matters to them be taken into account or to respond to such a demand. And [...] they learn to do so with another species' (Despret, 2016: 20). But, until comparatively recently, many studies of human–animal interaction took animals to be ciphers although there is all kinds of evidence that their interactions with humans are complex and can result in many different kinds of outcome – from the most brutal genocide to at least temporary truces (Baynes-Rock, 2015), from mutual ignorance of what is important to each party to deep and lasting knowledge which extends the worlds of both parties, from mere exploitation to complicated emergent intersubjectivities arising out of mixed animal and human cultures. These interactions produce 'an association of associated worlds' (Despret, 2016: 166) which challenges the proposition that 'humans are the actors of history, animals are not' (Brown, 2015: 8). Human and animal worlds are blended together in all kinds of combinations. Take the cow. 'Not only are cows no longer wild but there is now attached to them a world of stables, hay, hands that milk, Sundays, human odors, touches, words and cries, fences, paths, and ruts. Attached to them is a world that has modified the list of what affects and constitutes them' (Despret, 2016: 165). Nothing about this is meant to imply that these associations of worlds are necessarily either 'good' or 'bad', rather that they are there and need to be taken into account.

Clearly, the association of human and cow is weighted in favour of the human being. But associations can run the other way, as non-domesticated animals show all too well. Some invasive species really are invasive, species like the fire ant, the Asian termite, giant Asian hornet, the gypsy moth, the emerald ash borer, the Asian carp, the snakehead, a couple of species of python, the olive ebola bacterium, and the West Nile virus, to name but a few. As a cautionary tale underlining what this can mean for cities, take just the example of the humble quagga mussel and zebra mussel. These small freshwater mussels are natives of the lakes of Southern Russia and the Ukraine. But they have escaped these confines because of human activity, especially ballast discharge from ships, and are now invasive species of some power in North America, the UK, Ireland, Spain, Italy, the Czech Republic and Sweden. Notoriously, they were carried to the Great Lakes in the late 1980s by ships. There, the mussels' population numbers exploded. By 2012 their population in Lake Michigan had reached a density of 10,000 per square metre. By 2015 it had reached 15,000. By one estimate, there were 950 trillion mussels in the lake with quagga mussels reaching a density of 7,790 mussels per square metre (Hoddle, 2019). The lake became markedly clearer because the mussels filter fed the plankton that typically grew there, as well as killing other native mussels and clams (on the other hand, some fish populations expanded). This was a serious inconvenience for human activity, to put it mildly, and an industry has grown up attached to the mussels which tries to mitigate the damage they do, damage which is usually reckoned to be in the billions of dollars worldwide. One estimate of the annual cost of mitigation in just the Great Lakes puts it as high as $500 million per annum (Mukherjee, 2017)[12].

Death

What all this means is that we can never predict with absolute certainty what will come out of an interaction between humans and animals. That involves a quality best described as 'interagency' (Shaw, 2013: 11). The history of the colonization of North America not just by settlers but also by domestic animals shows this well enough (Collingham, 2017). Many of the newly landed settlers chased the English dream of the yeoman farmer, constructed on ideas about land ownership, the proper way of farming and the right way to eat food that they found difficult to translate on to a terrain where it was difficult 'to harness their animals' movements to serve the cause of permanence' (Anderson, 2004: 83). Equally, indigenous peoples had no category for living chattels: 'they granted individual propery rights only to animals they had killed' (Anderson, 2004: 38). Indeed, initially, they assumed that the new animals were wild and possessed spiritually powerful connections. The settlers constantly tried to keep their animals within the boundaries of possession, boundaries that both their and native animals constantly escaped, invaded, migrated across or just plain ignored. Thus, migrant animals like cattle that the settlers brought with them soon strayed, often trampling indigenous peoples' gardens as they ranged widely, and became feral or semi-feral. Meanwhile, native animals changed their habits in reaction to the newcomers. For example, predators attacked migrant species like sheep. The wolf is a case in point, a problem that had not been encountered by English husbandmen for many centuries. Eradicating wolves proved to be an exceptionally difficult task. Wolves weren't interested in emblems of ownership and the colonial order butted up against the wolves' ways of life. So, 'by the turn of the nineteenth century wolves' actions had fundamentally altered English colonizing, shifting frontier settlers' actions away from enclosure and improvement and toward the free-range animal husbandry and hunting that became characteristic of an American version of colonization' (Smalley, 2017: 8). But, they were also subject to persistent campaigns of eradication by cattle ranchers intent on forming a 'red meat republic' (Specht, 2019) through a re-orientation of the Plains ecosystem from grass–bison–nomad to grass–cattle–rancher.

Equally, the difficulty of restraining migrant animals led to innovations which then reverberated on the human world. Take the case of barbed wire. Initially introduced as a way of restraining domesticated animals in the uncapped spaces of the American West, its simple technological barbarism helped to fuel new modes of warfare and incarceration which had never originally been envisaged. From barbed wire came not only a means of keeping animals in defined territories but also trench warfare and concentration camps (Netz, 2009).

Clearly the issue of agency is a complicated one, therefore, arising out of round after round of interagency. But, just one word of warning. For all of the studies that have appeared stressing the multispecies nature of animality, the complexity of hybrid human–animal networks, and the unexpected consequences of entanglement, what often seems to shrink into the background is the issue of killing. I am not arguing for an easy denunciation of killing and indeed some of these studies have highly nuanced takes on it (e.g. Probyn, 2016; Crowley et al., 2018). Similarly, it is the case that cities seem to provide favourable environments for some animal species, in part because of not just human–animal entanglements but also specific human interventions on their behalf. Yet somehow the very complexity of these studies, and their tendency to 'flatten' animal cognition (Langlitz, 2019), seem to take away from the force of the act of killing, whether it is the consequence of a gun, a Larsen trap, containerized gassing (see, for example, www.livetecsystems.co.uk/containerised-gassing-units/), a drift net or the slaughterhouse line. Conjugating the relations between humans and animals in these networks, as Probyn puts it, and writing about the minutiae of ethical judgements that are needed in order to pay attention to their situations sometimes not only seems to filter out the 'dark phenomenology' (Roden, 2014; Sparrow, 2014) of fear and suffering (Berger, 2008) but also seems to re-install the animals as mere ciphers in a human world, not least because of a certain kind of inherent reasonableness that only just skirts the boundaries of justification. I'm not sure what the answer is or might be to this situation and I'm certainly not trying to rain on the parade but neither do I think that this is a minor issue.

Different Agencies

I need to be more specific. What is clear is that different kinds of animal have different kinds of agency. In this section of the chapter, I will offer four very brief sketches of the differential agency of animals whose interactions with cities have been particularly notable, each in their different ways, as part of a multispecies history and geography – and a multispecies city (Brown, 2016). What these histories tell us, is that, like it or not, the city is permeable. *Sheep*, historically one of the classical livestock animals, are regarded as a humdrum rural animal located at a distance from the city yet they are still one of the main urban food and apparel sources. They are the guts of the city. *Horses* were for a long period of time a mainstay of urban life and one of the main means through which cities could become ambulant entities. They were living infrastructure. They have been both domesticates and to a much lesser degree, livestock. Now they are chiefly a middle-class recreational accoutrement, mainly restricted to the city's outskirts, except for ceremonial occasions, police enforcement, and the like, more equestrian performer than equestrian breadwinner (Walker, 2008). *Coyotes* were 'wild' animals but now they are well on their way to becoming one of the most successful urban immigrants (DeStefano, 2011). They are becoming city as they move from being adapters to being adopters. Finally, I want to consider just one more domesticated animal, the *chicken*, as a segue into the next chapter. In one account it has triumphed as a species by becoming all but ubiquitous. In another, it has become simply a fleeting moment in a worldwide flesh trade, a living commodity that is sacrificed daily in order to keep the city's human inhabitants moving.

Domesticates: Sheep

The story of animal agency is well personified by the example of an animal which has been domesticated for 11,000 years and is one of the most familiar of all familiar animals. Sheep are very often thought of, in the West at least[13], as amongst the most stupid and pliable of beasts – and therefore as utterly malleable. Indeed, their supposed qualities have entered the base vocabulary of many languages – as sheepish, bleating and fleecing, as well as in all kinds of sayings – as standing for a mindless lack of individuality (Armstrong, 2016). Sheep are like blank, little clouds dotting the landscape and making it familiar. Surely, they are just ciphers, put there to provide meat and wool for humans? And yet research shows that even these supposedly dozy and disrespected animals have 'extensive spatial memories, ample capacity to learn from experience and a highly developed ability (beyond that of dogs, and comparable to humans' own) to identify individuals by their faces, even after long periods of separation' (Armstrong, 2016: 20): sheep even have particular friends in their flock. If they lack social intelligence, it is almost certainly because of ways of farming that make socialization difficult (Franklin, 2007).

Whatever the case, sheep have been the means by which all kinds of landscapes have come into being. They provided the raw material – wool – for the first English agribusiness, promoting large-scale international commerce, and changing England's countryside forever in the process. The wealth gained from these sheep still survives in the form of the churches, abbeys and cathedrals, castles, guildhalls, barns and granaries that dot the landscape. In effect, large amounts of the English landscape became both a giant pasture and a repository of wealth that would be carried forward, as Marx noted, into manufacturing, slavery, industry and colonialism. By Tudor times, sheep outnumbered people three to one. Winder (2017) has even argued that sheep-rearing imbued the national character with certain characteristics drawn from their husbandry.

Then, there was Spain. Spain came to rival England as a competitor in wool production. Its merino wool, produced via transhumance, came to dominate the Spanish economy. In turn, for both England and Spain, sheep were the imperial animal par excellence spreading out into the colonies of Mexico, Australia and New Zealand[14]. There sheep changed the landscape, becoming the foundation of a particular variant of ecological imperialism which changed the landscapes of these countries. These Old World animals produced enormous changes in the New World. In Mexico, to begin with, Spanish pastoralists treated the country's Central Highlands as an open commons, as it had been in Spain, allowing sheep the luxury of uncontrolled grazing, which meant, in turn, the despoliation of the crops and gardens of the indigenous peoples, a major change in overall vegetative cover and the importation of pathogens which native animals were defenceless against (Melville, 1997). In Australia and New Zealand, following on from the example of the enclosure of the Scottish Highlands, similar consequences followed, including the displacement or just deletion of the indigenous population and the transformation of the native ecosystem (Collingham, 2017). In Australia, for example, sheep 'swiftly killed off ground cover and compacted the soils, resulting in less rain and a reduced ability to absorb moisture, along with increased instability and liability to erosion on slopes' (Armstrong, 2016: 97). In New Zealand, in some ways more suited to raising sheep, by 1860 there were over a million sheep in the country, by 1880, 13 million, and, by the end of the century, 20 million (Armstrong, 2016). A land of forests and wetlands had become a land of pastures, shaped by sheep, resonating to their bleating and baaing. That fate was sealed by following the Australian example with the inauguration of refrigerated shipping from New Zealand to the United Kingdom in 1882. This was the beginning of a thriving trade in frozen sheep carcasses which undercut the price of British lamb and mutton and, in time, helped to change British working class diets (Collingham, 2017). One hundred years later, the country's sheep population peaked at some 70 million sheep (Armstrong, 2016). As is clear, sheep were one of the mainstays of the Age of Empire and of its attendant ecological imperialism (Collingham, 2017). In 1929, there were 700 million sheep in the world. Of these, one third were located in the British Empire. (By then, the UK had only 30 million sheep.) Food and empire, empire and food. Or, more accurately, imperial city and food, food and imperial city.

Sheep meet an industrialized death. Increasingly, they are meat animals, their life premised upon the fact of their demise. They are the original dead labour. Leaving aside all kinds of suspect farming practices, from mulesing to tail docking to pizzle dropping to castration, many sheep suffer concentrated confinement during transport to slaughter or live export overseas sometimes in terrible conditions. There is then the process of slaughter itself, sometimes in a different country after a long journey. For example, in the case of Australia, over 2 million sheep a year are exported to countries like Indonesia, Malaysia, Israel, Mexico, Japan, China and Saudi Arabia. To give some sense of the conditions, even the Australian government recorded half a million deaths occuring during these voyages between 2000 and 2012 (Armstrong, 2016).

The question of how to ascribe agency to these animals like these is a live one. After all, sheep have been domesticated over many millennia now. Their very bodies are, in part, an outcome of human impulses. Equally, they are tied into human patterns of activity and regulation from cradle to grave. Their characteristics as animals are part of human-inspired networks, for all the talk of flat networks in which all kinds of entities act and can act back. But this does not mean that they are mere ciphers. Humans have also had to adjust their practices to the sheep's characteristics and not just the other way around. And that is to ignore the fact that one-way accounts that attribute agency only to human influence neglect the fact that for sheep it is the presence of each other that still counts most, not the presence of humans.

Domesticates: Horse

Then animals have been tools providing the kinetic energy for human movement and expansion. Take the example of horses, an example of such importance that it has been argued by Reinhard Koselleck that history should be split into just three phases – pre-horse, the period of the horse (the 'equine age') and post-horse. For the more than 6,000 years when horses were the most important animal for humans, their dominant characteristics were 'rapid acceleration and high velocity' (Raulff, 2017: 9). For all intents and purposes, being fast meant being mounted or being transported in horse-drawn chariots and carriages. Though the horse might have been used as a pack animal, it was its speed which set it apart (Walker, 2008).

Though no one knows exactly when horses were first domesticated, it happened later than cattle domestication. Perhaps before but certainly by the fourth millennium BCE, horses were being tamed and ridden with the result that humans could become more mobile (Roberts, 2017). Why horses in particular? Horses seem to have the characteristics that make them good human allies. They are predisposed to co-operate. They can read human emotions and they are also able to influence human behaviour: 'horses not only wish to communicate, they recognize humans as capable of receiving communications' (Roberts, 2017: 260–1). They were one of the spearheads of the age of animal traction[15] and, as domesticates, a more complicated story than that of sheep.

Horses have been used as tools in three main arenas. First, in agriculture, as adjunct labour, since time immemorial. The acme of their use in agriculture in the West was probably in the nineteenth century. There, the demands of a rising urban population coupled with the need for more rather than fewer horses to pull the first mechanized agricultural instruments like combine harvesters (which only saved human labour by increasing animal labour) meant that many farms were given over to growing feed (especially hay and oats), mainly for urban horses. 'The 3 million horses that inhabited the cities of the United States in 1900 consumed 8 million tonnes of hay and almost 9 million tonnes of oats a year. Twelve million acres of land were needed to produce that quantity of fodder – about four acres per horse' (Raulff, 2017: 31)[16].

Second, in war. Though the horse is a prey animal whose natural inclination is to flee, horses were exceptionally effective instruments of killing.

They were also the means of general transportation which allowed armies to campaign and empires to be built, a means of rapid medical evacuation from the battlefield, a potent form of communication and, of course, haulers of heavy loads of all kinds, from provisions to munitions to artillery. It is no exaggeration to say that the horse revolutionized warfare and that technical inventions like the stirrup and various refinements of the saddle made the horse an ever more effective instrument of war, a prey animal made into a predator that allowed territory to be dominated and then subdued and appropriated. 'To see history from the horse's perspective means to conceive of it as a mover, as a vector' (Raulff, 2017: 341). But obviously the horse's role in animating war came at a considerable cost. Take just the First World War where animal casualties – not just horses but also mules, donkeys, dogs, cats, pigeons, canaries, even camels – were on an epic scale. Of a million horses recruited by the British Army to serve in the War, nearly half died as a result of injury or enemy fire. In 1916, on just one of the days of the Battle of Verdun, 7,000 horses were killed. By the Second World War, the toll had climbed again: the German Army, which had utilized around 1.8 million horses in the First World War, used a further 2.7 million in the Second World War, mainly on the Eastern Front where the terrain dictated a different kind of war from the mechanized Western Front. Of these horses, 1.8 million perished (Raulff, 2017)[17].

Third, in the city. Indeed, by the late nineteenth century, the city was probably the main consumer of horses. Horses were ubiquitous, often urbanizing more rapidly than people. They were commodities for sale, even in death[18]. Their manure was a commodity. They delivered the bulk of commodities too. They were sometime products of breeding programmes that suited them to urban conditions. They were objects of numerous urban regulations. They required regular maintenance, from farriers to, latterly, veterinarians. In the cities of the United States, for example, there was, on average, 1 horse for every 20 people though some cities had higher ratios – New York's ratio was 26.4 – and others, especially in the West, lower. By 1900, 130,000 horses were working in Manhattan alone (McShane and Tarr, 2007).

Meanwhile, London had some 300,000 horses living within its boundaries (Raulff, 2017)[19] and these indispensable 'living machines' (McShane and Tarr, 2007; Tarr and McShane, 2008) all required prodigious amounts of feed and water (Thrift, 1990), the bulk of which came to the literally named Haymarket (until it was moved to a new location in 1830 because of the pressure of traffic in the vicinity), 'as well as in Whitechapel, Smithfield, the Borough, and from 1800, in Paddington' (Velten, 2013: 45). Between 1827 and 1828, more than 26,000 loads of hay and straw were registered with the toll collectors. Horses were ubiquitous as draught animals, drawing loads as diverse as rubbish, timber and stone, as haulers of omnibuses and trams[20] and fire engines, as drawers of an abundance of different types of coaches and cabs and carriages and carts, and as objects of conspicuous consumption, and the urban fabric was physically configured to take the horse population into account – mews and stables, coach houses, livery, horse fairs, street design, horse troughs, pavements and kerbstones, mounting blocks, slaughterhouses[21] – all the paraphernalia of an equine city, a city with its own distinctive smells and soundscape made up of the crack of whips, the din of wagon wheels and horseshoes on cobbles, the shouts and screams from ubiquitous traffic accidents, and the periodic racket of horse-drawn vehicles marking out the course of each day and reaching a crescendo in the morning and evening rush hours. The city was physically configured to allow horse labour to labour and relied on an enormously complex division of labour from fodder merchants to farrier, from whip-makers to makers of straw sun hats for horses, from ostlers to grooms (Forrest, 2016) as well as a mass of distinctive knowledge and guilds and accompanying spaces like horse markets: in other words, the whole character of London's streets was often dictated by the needs of working horses. Even in medieval times, London's first mayor had decreed that the 'overhanging projections on jetties on the upper floors of houses had to be at least high enough for a man on horseback to pass under' (Velten, 2013: 45). By the nineteenth century, London was an equine city of vanners, sweepers and bussers whose daily round was dictated by the availability of all kinds of horses, heavy or light, (see Forrest, 2016: 157–63), and was configured in ways which relied on the horse as a means of transportation. (At least to begin with, the coming of the railway only increased the demand for horses, needed to service the stations and depots.)

And it was in the city that many horses – used and then used up – met their deaths[22]:

> For the horses living in and consumed by the nineteenth century city […] it was no healthy environment. Their muscles, tendons, hooves and joints could only endure the harsh work of providing draught power […] for a few years before they were sold on for commercial use to pull lighter loads, or allowed to return for their final years to the countryside. City horses went into retirement at the age of five and had an average lifespan of ten years. This was true of omnibus horses, while tram horses tended to be exhausted after four years. For many the end came even sooner by way of permanent lameness, a sad fate concluded with the veterinarian's bullet. Between 1887 and 1897, the employees of the New York ASPCA[23] […] put down between 1,800 and 7,000 horses annually. Contrary to the popular notion, the dead animal was not left to rot in the gutter: the disposal of carcasses was a mechanized process […] In the cities of European countries where horse meat was eaten, you would often see groups of horses, many limping on three legs, making their weary way to the slaughterhouse. In France, owners had their horses shaved before slaughter to make use of the horsehair. (Raulff, 2017: 30–1)

Of course, since the mid-twentieth century, horses have been cleared out of most cities[24]: it is now a matter of some amazement that the city of Dakar in Senegal used horses as a preferred means of transportation until quite recently (Hartocollis, 2019). The horse has been relegated to featuring in sporting fixtures or to acting as a middle-class plaything, a status that it already had in parts of the nineteenth-century city – bred, cared for and admired as repositories of skill, as sentimental bonds and, straightforwardly, as reflections of their owners' social and cultural capital. The days of Koselleck's era of the horse and of an equine city have drawn to a close. That said, it is hard to deny that, so great has been their influence, 'without the horse, humans would be different' (Walker, 2008: 193). And so would the city.

As importantly, as horses have ceased being beasts of burden in many parts of the world, they are generally being shown more respect. There are, of course, numerous historical instances of extraordinarily strong relationships between rider and horse. But they were probably a rarity overall. Now horses can often be cosseted: in many cases, they have crossed the line that separates animals from companion animals. Though it would be difficult to say that this relationship went as far as that found in Siena's annual Palio race where the winner is always the horse, not the rider, and where the horse can still win without its rider, relationships between riders and horses nowadays are often close and their general welfare has no doubt improved as a result[25].

Synanthropes: Coyote

What about wild animals? Something rather different happens with just a few of them. They actively change their behaviour in response to human inundation. And they can do this quickly if needs be.

Take just the case of the genuinely wily coyote. Coyotes have lived near or in urban conglomerations for many hundreds of years. For example, they were undoubtedly present in the Aztec cities of Mesoamerica, as well as in the indigenous American settlements of Chaco Canyon in what is now New Mexico. But their real expansion into cities en masse dates from the early twentieth century when they first attracted attention in the cities of Southern California and Arizona (Flores, 2016). Part of the reason for this initial ingress was undoubtedly the curbing of enormous stray dog populations in American cities through dogcatchers, dog pounds and leash laws in the late nineteenth century, which gave them a new niche. A further spur to urban colonization was provided by rural eradication policies. Idiotically shot and poisoned to the tune of around 500,000 animals each year by the US government and hunters, the coyote has changed both its breeding strategy and the kinds of spaces it inhabits, moving into and colonizing cities. In an adaptation that biologists call fission-fusion, when coyotes come under pressure from hunters their packs split up into lone animals and pairs, they start producing much larger litters of pups and they migrate into new areas[26]. 'By the late 1970s [they had colonized] all of North America – they even swam cold Atlantic waters to Cape Cod. Unless they stowaway to Hawai'i, they colonized their final US state, Delaware, in 2010' (Flores, 2016: 8). Moving south, they have now reached the Florida Keys (Klein, 2018). In 2010, they crossed over the Panama Canal. The only thing that seems to have stopped them from entering Colombia and the cities of South America seems to be the rainforest called the Darien Gap[27]. The cities of North America have fallen one by one. By the 1970s coyotes were already an urban presence in Los Angeles and Denver and they were spotted in Chicago by the 1990s[28]. By about 2000, pretty well every major city in the United States had a coyote population, including New York where they first appeared in the Bronx in the 1990s and where, by 2015, they had formed a relatively robust population, one even being spotted in Central Park (Flores, 2016).

Coyotes have been extensively studied as they have moved urbanwards as a paradigmatic example of an urban carnivore/omnivore which lies somewhere between a synanthrope and a misanthrope, in that most urban coyotes avoid areas of high human use (Gehrt et al., 2010). Their behaviour in cities is adjusting: urban coyotes tend to be more nocturnal than their non-urban conspecifics, occupy smaller home ranges, have higher population densities, have different predator avoidance behaviours and will even build dens in quiet alleyways or parking garages (O'Connor, 2013, see the papers collected at the Urban Wildlife Information Network at https://urbanwildlifeinfo.org/). They are able to take advantage of a wide variety of foodstuffs – coyotes are omnivores who will eat anything from rodents to berries, not to mention the discarded remains of fast-food orders and every now and then a household pet – helped by a relatively small body size, and an opportunistic attitude (DeStefano, 2011). But they do not subsist exclusively on anthropogenic foods in cities, a common stereotype (Gehrt et al., 2010). They have become so successful that they can become a nuisance, leading some cities like Denver and Montreal to introduce 'hazing' policies which aim to make coyotes more wary of humans by inducing humans to change their behaviour (Caron, 2018). They seem to have relatively high survival rates in cities, with rates for pups up to five times higher than in the wild. Indeed, vehicle collisions seem to be one of the most common causes of death. That said, some coyotes have learnt where it is safest to cross roads and how to avoid traffic based on its speed and volume.

The net result of urban colonization is that the coyote population has recovered from human depredation (Flores, 2016), at least in part; aided by genetic hybridization (Heppenheimer et al., 2018) and, most ironically of all, by the extirpation of grey wolves, cougars and jaguars from large parts of North America, which gave the coyotes the freedom to travel more freely. So successful has the coyote become that people can now hunt them legally within the boundaries of some US cities, with the inevitable result being tragic accidents (Romero, 2017). But urban coyotes can actually benefit human urban dwellers by eating rodents like rats, which can spread disease, by culling feral cats, which prey on songbirds, and by killing the ubiquitous Canada geese.

Three different kinds of animal agency, then. Some animals, like coyotes, have displayed considerable agency. But then there are those animals which have become subject to industrialization and commodification and have very little agency at all. Their lives have become nothing but a faster and faster way of being consumed in the service of the bellies of urban inhabitants (Despret, 2016). The sheep is one example. But the logical endpoint of this process is another animal – the chicken.

Domesticates: Chicken

Animals are involved in all kinds of relationship with humans that involve dealing out death. That has been the case for many millennia. Though the evidence is disputed, human beings, in conjunction with long-term environmental change (Faith et al., 2018), may have hastened the end of numerous species of megafauna herbivore (Milks et al., 2019). Indeed, by one estimate, 'the few million people alive at the end of the Pleistocene killed a staggering one billion very large animals' (Lewis and Maslin, 2018: 107). (Certainly, the extinguishing of megafauna herbivores by whatever means may even have accounted for some part of the Younger Dryas cooling of climate because of a decline in atmospheric methane.)

But amongst those animals that are domesticated for food, the relationship often seems to be much more extreme: a case of survival but only by being consigned to the third circle of hell as generalized, industrialized and commoditized 'meat', a reduction of life to the lowest common denominator – shredded and pulverized body parts. Industrialized violence at its most extreme, in other words, in which animals are turned into a 'gigantic chunk of private property' (Morton, 2017: 26). Property rights written into the flesh. Not bare life, barely life at all.

Of course, the search for food and sustenance has always shaped cities but this search has now gone into overdrive. Sometimes it seems more like a death drive. Engelen (cited in Kuper, 2017) has argued that 'we will need more food in the next 40 years than all harvests in history combined'. Yet, by one estimate (Steel, 2009), contemporary cities already rely on a global hinterland at least 100 times larger than their inhabited extent, a hinterland in which servitude and death, because of agricultural monocultures, dietary change, habitat extinction and the general machinery of industrial killing are facts of animal life. Of course, cities have nearly always been built on the cries of bewildered and terrified animals and their screams as they are put to death in order to reproduce the city, whether in the form of food or the many animal by-products that make our lives comfortable[29]. But for some animals those cries and screams have now become just another normalized brick in a commodified wall, described by J.M. Coetzee (1999: 21) as 'an enterprise of degradation, cruelty and killing which rivals anything the Third Reich was capable of'.

Likewise, Derrida (2008: 26) argued that the situation can be likened to one in which:

> instead of throwing a people into ovens and gas chambers (let's say Nazi) doctors and geneticists had decided to organize the overproduction and over-generation of Jews, gypsies and homosexuals by means of artificial insemination, so that, being continually more numerous and better fed, they could be destined in always increasing numbers for the same hell[30].

It is worth dwelling for a moment on the facts of the matter, before returning to them in more detail in the next chapter, because they show just how far we would have to backtrack to produce a city that was not abusive of other species.

As a segue into the next chapter, take just the case of the humble chicken (*Gallus gallus domesticus*), the ultimate industrial animal, of which the 'vast majority inhabit a shadowy archipelago of enormous poultry warehouses and slaughterhouses surrounded by fences and sealed off from the public' (Lawler, 2015: 5)[31]. If there were an animal which has replaced the horse as the urban animal par excellence, the chicken would be a prime candidate – the animal as an entirely fungible commodity with a turnover (life)time second to none. We live, now, in the city of the chicken, not the city of the horse. There are an estimated 22.7 billion chickens living on Earth at any given time (Bennett et al., 2018), at least ten times more than any other bird, 40 times even the number of sparrows. Chickens constitute the ideal global urban meat – versatile, affordable, subject to no particular religious taboos, and able to be quickly converted from live flesh into multiple kinds of processed cuts, chunks, patties and nuggets: the average American consumed around 64 lb of chicken in 2017, up from 10 lb in the 1930s and 33 lb in 1980, largely as a result of the proliferation of branded chicken products (Striffler, 2005; Moch, 2020). Chicken surpassed beef in terms of overall consumption in 2010 (Mock, 2020).

No wonder that 69 billion chickens were slaughtered in 2018 (Ritchie and Roser, 2019), including 20 million each week just in the UK[32]. This is a form of living property which is, in effect, dead on arrival. Subject to thousands of years of genetic sorting since their domestication in southern Asia around 8,000 to 10,000 years ago (Potts, 2012)[33], by one account the modern-day broiler chicken, which now grows three times faster than its distant ancestor, wearing out its own body as it does so, is no longer an animal but a genetically engineered monocultural technology with model numbers to boot, the result of most broiler chicks being produced by only three companies (Weis, 2013), with each product model being carefully evolved to suit a particular consumer market.

The chicken is the ideal commodity form – it produces itself rapidly and out of sight in a never-ending just-in-time chain that reaches from broiler breeding units to farms to slaughterhouses to processing plants. Little wonder that chickens outnumber humans by three to one, far more than other human-induced animals like cats, dogs, pigs, cows and even rats (Lawler, 2015). But most of them will live only 5–7 weeks, as opposed to their natural lifespan of 10 or even 20 years, the result of a steady increase in growth rates since the 1960s which has condemned them to earlier and earlier obsolescence. Many would be unlikely to survive if left to live to maturity: a chicken 'can't be allowed to live any longer because its genetics are so screwed up. Stop and think about that: a bird that you simply can't let live out of its adolescence' (farmer cited in Foer, 2009: 113)[34]. During this attenuated lifetime, most of them will live in densely packed conditions, squeezed into the equivalent of the space of an A4 piece of paper, existing as a malformed cog in a complex mechanized system of 'computer software, electricity, transportation vehicles, refrigeration, feed-processing factories, and more' (Bennett et al., 2018: 7).

This process of industrial incapacitation (Blanchette, 2020) means that they will never be able to manifest the oft-times impressive cognitive abilities that recent research suggests that they may well have, abilities that grow out of the acute senses of hearing and sight that the original ground-living red junglefowls needed to survive. So, chickens have been shown to have impressive recall, being able to memorize over 100 other chicken faces and 'recognize familiar birds after several months of separation. Chickens also remember humans and have been shown to turn away from the countenances of people they dislike' (Potts, 2012: 39). They are able to grasp abstract concepts. As well as being able to locate hidden items, 'three day old chicks are [also] capable of identifying a whole object when part of it is obscured – a feat not accomplished by human babies until four to five months of age' (Potts, 2012: 39). They can also anticipate the future and practise self-restraint, qualities that for a long time were thought to be unique to humans and primates. They have acute social intelligence, based not only on dominance hierarchies but also on a complex 'chicken talk' involving the use of all the bodily senses to convey intentions and send messages. They often form close relationships and they can often show strong individual character when they are allowed to manifest it.

The development of the chicken into a mass commodity which is the most traded animal protein in the world, with a market share in 2017 of approximately 35 per cent of the 335.9 million tonne meat trade (Ritchie and Roser, 2019), is an extraordinarily recent historical phenomenon. Before the First World War, chickens were usually to be found on small farms and in suburban backyards, often kept mainly for their eggs, usually cared for by women and children and providing a supplement to household income[35]. It is only really since 1923 – when the first chickens were mass farmed purely for the East Coast urban market in the United States – that chickens have been living and dying in a commoditized way (Foer, 2009). Indeed, chicken was still something of an afterthought on most American farms until the Second World War when urban markets, production, consumption and price all began to align, boosted by the fact that, unlike beef, chicken was not rationed. No wonder that American broiler[36] production almost tripled during the war (Striffler, 2005). By the 1960s true factory farming had arrived, based on both vertical and horizontal integration, on 'advances' in breeding, on the adoption of antibiotics and hormones, on high meat yields and on new processed products. The American chicken farm is made up of a set of as many as 18 broiler houses which can house more than 10,000 birds at a time and produce up to 135,000 birds each year, 'marketing about two million birds from a single operation' (Smil, 2019: 148)[37]. In England, factory farming is growing too (Hinchliffe et al., 2016). In 2020 there were 1,092 permitted intensive livestock facilities housing over 40,000 chickens, either as broilers or layers (Colley and Wasley, 2020). Seven out of ten of the largest intensive farms in the UK were in the poultry sector, each marketing over 1 million birds in a year.

It's not a lot of fun being a broiler chicken. Kept in extraordinarily cramped spaces, it is no surprise that in the UK 'the mortality rate prior to slaughter is around 5 per cent' (Potts, 2012: 154). By the time that they reach the slaughter weight of 2–2.5 kilograms and their 5–7 weeks of life are up, in effect they are still only babies (Foer, 2017). About a third of these chickens will develop heart and lung problems and more than half will have severe walking problems. Most spend 90 per cent of their time lying down. But for the producers what counts is what counts: in the US in 1925, the age to market of a broiler was 112 days and live weight was just 1.1 kg. By 2017, the age to market was 48 days and live weight was 2.3 kg. What counted was less food for more weight with a faster turnover time (Smil, 2019).

As for battery hens (intensively farmed egg layers[38], usually killed at around a year or 18 months) they will spend their lives in often execrable conditions, deprived of any means of displaying the behaviours that make them chickens before being slaughtered as 'spent', sometimes debeaked. Meanwhile 'male chicks, extraneous to the egg industry […] are destroyed within twenty-four hours of hatching. Each year in the US alone more than 272 million male chicks are disposed of by gassing, microwaving, smothering, or maceration […], their collective remains used as pet food' (Potts, 2012: 159). Globally, an estimated 4–6 billion male chicks are slaughtered in this way every year (Le Blond, 2018). Why this scale of killing? Because male chicks lay no eggs and don't grow fast enough to justify the cost of feeding them up for meat[39].

When it comes to slaughter of broilers or battery hens, there is also the ordeal of transportation, especially when it involves long journeys. Then, in the slaughterhouse, further cruelties can await. Humane slaughter is still a distant goal. To give some sense of this, in the United States, where the wellbeing of chickens is not covered by animal welfare acts, around 2.8 million broiler chicks were boiled alive in de-feathering tanks in 2002, having missed the stunning baths and the blades at throat-cutting stations. In the UK, where chickens are covered by animal welfare acts, around 50 birds an hour are reckoned to be conscious when their throats are cut, and up to 9 in every 1,000 birds are boiled alive (Potts, 2012)[40].

The net result of the rise (if that is what it can be called) of the chicken? Chickens now have a combined mass exceeding that of all other birds on the planet. Their discarded and fossilized bones, preserved within landfills and mass burial sites, are likely to be so numerous that a case has been made for the chicken as the primary biostratigraphic marker species for the Anthropocene, even given their low skeletal density, a 'near synchronous global signal of change to the biosphere' (Bennett et al., 2018: 9). Their bones will signal 'human' just like concrete and plastic.

Food

What the example of the chicken also points to is the intense importance of food to the existence and life of cities through history (Steel, 2009; 2020). Arguably, animals' role as meat is now *the* prime relationship between animals and cities. Cities are best represented as gigantic mouths, gaping maws which consume more and more flesh. An obvious enough point you might think but what is surprising is how little attention was paid to either animals or food in many parts of the urban literature until comparatively recently[41]. That is surprising since both animals and food have loomed large in a number of disciplines. Take just history. So far as animals are concerned, they have been firmly on the radar in subdisciplines as diverse as environmental history, intellectual history, the history of consumption, histories of science and technology, and global or world history (Fudge, 2002a). So far as food is concerned, studies have been made in economic, social and cultural history since at least the Annales School (though only relatively recently has food and its ecological impacts figured large in topics of immense historical importance like empire and war; but see Collingham, 2012; 2017; Ross, 2017). However, an urban interspecies past has now been well and truly discovered (see Atkins, 2012; Nance, 2015; Brown, 2016; Bull et al., 2017; Domanska, 2017; Kalof, 2017; Kean and Howell, 2018; Wischermann et al., 2018).

The comparative lack of involvement with the business of animals and food has occurred even amongst those who are expected to plan and manage the contemporary city. Only just over 10 years ago, Morgan (2009) castigated urban planners and architects for this omission. But, since then, the situation has changed, with much more attention given to innovations like 'continuous productive urban landscapes' (Morgan and Sonnino, 2010; Morgan, 2014). More than 140 cities have already signed the Milan Urban Food Policy Pact. But when Lang (2020: 67) asks if it is too much to ask each city to conduct food audits and plan how their city can improve land use and food systems, in the case of many cities the answer is still 'yes'. Cabannes and Marocchino (2018) call this the missing link in urban planning. Though most urban planners, for example, would be aware of issues like food deserts in cities and the need to strengthen food systems, and have passed local food ordinances, food action plans and the like, few would probably think of cities as a crucial part of what the EAT-Lancet Commission calls the 'great food transformation', not surprisingly given their limited food powers. But in the cities of the Global South, especially, this kind of urban planning will soon become a matter of survival (Cabannes and Marocchino, 2018).

The divorce between urban affairs and their sustenance, which echoes the division between mind and body, might be considered bizarre but there are good reasons for its continuance. In particular, food is often considered to be 'rural' and therefore (quite literally) out of bounds. Those sheep and cows grazing in apparently verdant fields – if they're lucky – are an accompaniment to the main urban event, a kind of spatial footnote, even as they pass through urban dwellers' guts. But they aren't footnotes. Without a radical change in how we govern 'rural' areas, cities are going to run into increasing problems. The countryside needs to become a much more important item on *urban* policy agendas, rather than simply a 'dumping ground for urban externalities' (Steel, 2020: 209). For cities, some of the biggest threats to their inhabitants now come from their rural hinterland.

Take a particularly dramatic example: dosing animals, fish and (unbelievably) plants with antibiotics, so building microbial resistance. More than half of all of the antibiotics used worldwide are administered to livestock, often to whole flocks or herds regardless of the number actually infected, and in some countries they are still given out routinely to promote growth. It is likely that farm animals are a leading cause of growing antibiotic resistance.

China is the world's largest consumer of agricultural antibiotics, out dosing even the United States 2013 study by the Chinese Academy of Sciences (Chinese Academy of Sciences, 2015) found that 147,000 tonnes of antibiotics are consumed in China each year, more than half the global total, with 52 per cent being used in animal husbandry. In the US, 70 per cent of antibiotics amounting to 9,700 tonnes are consumed by livestock each year. It is thought that lack of antibiotics that can combat antibiotic resistant bugs will mean more people die from these infections than cancer in 20 years' time. It will mean STIs becoming impossible to treat. We could return to a situation like the one before antibiotics when 40 per cent of the population died prematurely from infections that cannot be treated. So rural agricultural practices directly threaten the health of urban dwellers[42].

Or one other example. Food security. Take China again. Chinese cities rely on just a few crops and animals for sustenance. But, as recent events have shown, their food supply can be rapidly threatened. African swine fever was only first reported in August 2018 but by the end of August 2019 the entire pig population of China had dropped by about 40 per cent because of this virulent disease. China accounted for more than half of the global pig population in 2018, and just the epidemic there (ignoring its spread into Southeast Asia) has killed nearly one quarter of all the world's pigs either directly through the disease or through culling to try to halt its spread.

Again, fall armyworms – the larvae of the moth *Spodoptera frugiperda* – have descended on 11 provinces in China, consuming vital crops like rice, corn and soybeans.

Notes

1. Gary Snyder (1993) 'Ripples on the surface'.
2. Even Kirksey (2016) comes close to this stance at times.
3. Canada geese have spread out from North America to parts of Europe and New Zealand. For example, they were first introduced into Britain in the late seventeenth century as an addition to King James II's collection of waterfowl in St James's Park in London.
4. Ring-necked parakeets, originally from India, have proved very successful synanthropes, establishing themselves in 35 countries on five continents. Introduced into the UK some time around the 1930s onwards through a series of small-scale escapes, breeding populations had become established by the 1960s. There were reckoned to be about 8,600 breeding pairs in 2013, outnumbering barn owls, nightingales and kingfishers (see Heald et al., 2019). There are estimated to be tens of thousands living in London (Hunt, 2019).
5. Muntjac deer have proved particularly successful at adapting to suburban life.
6. Which have been found in or close to the centres of Rome and Barcelona, not just in their suburbs.
7. Which also go to prove the fact that introductions can take place in all kinds of directions. The raccoon was introduced into the wild in Germany in 1934. There are now around a million raccoons living in Europe, including 600 raccoon 'families' living in Berlin (Donovan, 2015).
8. Indeed, the number of snakes living in Bangkok has increased rapidly because of the growth of the city and an increase in flooding.
9. By one estimate (NESCent Working Group et al., 2015), indoor Manhattan's estimated residential living space area now exceeds Manhattan's outdoor land area by a factor of nearly three to one.
10. And which, by the way, challenges the assumption that the route to intelligence is necessarily through the formation of complex social hierarchies. In hyenas, a case can also be made for the so-called cognitive buffer hypothesis; that is, that their intelligence (which is high) has emerged as an adaptation to dealing with novelty and change in the environment (Johnson-Ulrich et al., 2018; Benson-Amran et al., 2016; Barrett et al., 2018).
11. Equally, certain animals like horses make it possible to extend communication and with it the capacity to carry out activities like gathering taxes which are crucial to the foundation of states.
12. That said, there has also been some natural pushback. Some species of duck have learnt to eat the mussels in Lake Erie (Marris, 2011).
13. Though not in other cultures. For example, in China sheep are thought of as gentle and placid but also as 'stubborn, strong-willed, passionate and capable of militancy' (Armstrong, 2016: 20). In Japan, where sheep were late introductions, are relatively rare and therefore stimulate only a few cultural cues, it is possible for people with no preconceptions to perceive sheep as mindful, even uncanny (Armstrong, 2016).
14. Of course, sheep were also found outside the main imperial locations in places like the American Southwest.
15. Other traction animals have existed, of course, especially camels. Camels had been domesticated by the middle of the third millennium in Central Asia and what is now Iran and their use spread from there.
16. Horses were also food too and a horsemeat industry still thrives in many parts of the world.

17 The toll of war reached out in other more indirect ways too. For example, in the Second World War, as many as 750,000 British pets were killed in just 1 week of 1939 as a result of a public information campaign on air raids which recommended their destruction if they could not be sent to the countryside forthwith (Campbell, 2013; Kean, 2017).
18 Most especially, in Chicago, the largest horse market in the world, where 18,000 horses were sold every year (McShane and Tarr, 2007).
19 There was also a substantial population of donkeys. By 1893, there were about 13,000 of them (Velten, 2013).
20 The London omnibus company owned 10,000 horses by 1890 (Velten, 2013).
21 One London slaughterhouse killed 26,000 horses every year in the 1890s (Velten, 2013).
22 Not all handlers and dealers were cruel, by any means, though some undoubtedly were. As Forrest (2016) points out, horses were often regarded as fellow labourers and treated accordingly.
23 American Society for the Prevention of Cruelty to Animals.
24 By the Second World War, there were about 40,000 horses left in London but thereafter they declined rapidly in number (Velten, 2013).
25 Maybe the horses will come again (see Edwin Muir's famous poem, *The Horses*).
26 Something similar may now be happening with golden jackals in Europe. Golden jackals, who once inhabited only the continent's periphery, now greatly outnumber Europe's wolves, totalling around 117,000 by the latest official estimate (by contrast, the highest estimate of European wolf numbers is around 17,000) (Gorman, 2019).
27 Camera traps have caught them heading that way.
28 It is estimated that 3,000 to 4,000 coyotes now live in Chicago.
29 Such as the leather that is used for shoes, coats and bags, and in chairs and in cars and the fur still used in some clothes and other fashion accoutrements.
30 A new round of this imposition is currently arising out of gene editing.
31 www.factoryfarmmap.org
32 The global figure may be an underestimate. The British poultry sector is one of the largest in Europe, contributing more than £3 billion to the economy annually. It is also becoming more intensive. The chicken industry saw a 27 per cent rise in the number of poultry farms holding 40,000 or more birds between 2011 and 2017 (Farming UK, 2018).
33 Although ongoing DNA and dating research may bring this date forward. Domesticated chicken bones have been found in the Indus valley from as early as 2500 to 2100 BCE. Their spread is coincident with the establishment of new trade routes. So they were introduced to the Iberian Peninsula by Phoenician traders in the first century BCE and to the New World by Spanish colonists in 1500 CE (Bennett et al., 2018).
34 A eugenicist would no doubt be proud.
35 Though some quarters of cities like London specialized in rearing poultry, often in truly awful conditions. Hence Poultry and Scalding Alley. By 1850, Leadenhall was the largest poultry market in the city (Velten, 2013).
36 Straightforwardly, chickens raised solely for meat.
37 Some large operations run as many as 18 broiler houses (Smil, 2019).
38 According to the British Egg Industry Council, in 2019, over 13.1 billion eggs were sold in the UK making the country 87 per cent self-sufficient. Since 2006, egg consumption has grown by 3 billion eggs, www.egginfo.co.uk/egg-facts-and-figures/industry-information/data (accessed August 10, 2020).
39 There is a potential solution on the horizon. This is to determine a chick's gender in the egg before it hatches through a simple chemical marker. The first eggs guaranteed not to involve mass slaughter of males have gone on sale in Germany. Meanwhile France is banning culling of unwanted male chicks by the end of 2021 and a German court has ruled that the practice can continue only on a temporary basis.
40 Though new means of slaughter involving suffocation using carbon dioxide may spare more of them this experience.

41 In the urban historical literature, for example, subjects like the Paris Commune have been covered almost ad nauseam. They fall in with a received view of what ought to be regarded as important. But what anyone was eating in cities and how the food got there has, until recently, been by and large restricted to a more specialist (though burgeoning) urban food history literature (e.g. Baic, 2016; Assael, 2018), even when commentators point out that, if there was one obsession that united the inhabitants of the Paris Commune, as the siege dragged on, it was where the next meal was coming from.

42 Efforts to reduce the use of antibiotics on farms, which have been strongly urged by the WHO and others, have been slow to take effect, and the problem appears to be growing (Richtel and Jacobs, 2019). Some urban areas, for example in eastern China, are particularly badly affected by overuse.

6
The City of Surplus Death

Cities have always been concentrations of violence and sometimes even outright battlegrounds. That is not at issue. Riot, affray, fracas, melee, scuffle, skirmish, assault, fight, mayhem, brawl ... all these are a part of a common urban linguistic currency. Shots and sirens and shouts of warning or aggression still constitute a familiar element of the urban soundscape of many cities, producing landscapes of fear that attach not just to humans but to animals too (Gaynor et al., 2019).

But cities kill humans in many ways, some of them more, some of them less dramatic. Of course, there are the outright spasms of destruction that result from warfare, which have been documented so many times by geographers and sociologists since earlier work by Hewitt (1983) and Forbes and Thrift (1986) (see especially Graham, 2010). This destruction kills animals too, as the field of warfare, ecology (Hanson et al., 2009; Machlis et al., 2011; Hanson, 2019) has shown only too well. Many animals die, not just in the heat of battle, caught in the crossfire or co-opted into martial service, but from all manner of institutional and socioeconomic factors associated with mobilization and logistics (Gaynor et al., 2016). Many, many animals, of all kinds die (Yong, 2018). For example, as wars have spread back and forth across parts of Africa over the last few decades, they have been an important factor in the decline of large wild mammals, not least because a large amount of the conflicts have taken place in biodiversity hotspots (Hanson et al., 2019). In parts of Africa there is a direct correlation between frequency of conflict and the population decline of large wild herbivores in supposedly protected areas, though few actual extinctions. In the Gorongosa National Park in Mozambique, about 90 per cent of the large mammals were shot or died of starvation in the wars that ravaged the area (Daskin and Pringle, 2018)[1]. When people declare war they also declare war on the natural world. But the death toll of animals in urban areas affected by war is usually very hard to access. There are often few or no records but rather scattered stories of ravaged zoos – only 96 of Berlin Zoo's 16,000 animals survived the Second World War – or of cats and dogs euthanized or destined for the pot.

These landscapes of fear extend to the day-to-day violence that continues to plague every city to a greater or lesser degree – both purposeful (murder, assault, rape, domestic violence, mugging, and so on) – and 'accidental' (road accidents, domestic accidents, and the like). And there is also all of the silent violence that infests cities, most of it to do with the differential life chances that affect various sections of the population brought on by being exposed to killers like poverty or pollution. Animals are caught up in many of these events, usually as innocent bystanders. Indeed, we might say that one of the things we share in common with animals is the mass death occasioned by cities. Yet we make very little of this connection.

Then there is the exercise of cruelty, a common human trait (Taylor, 2009). Sometimes cruelty to humans and cruelty to animals intermix in cities. For example, Ritvo (1987) documents the connection made between cruelty to animals and bad behaviour by the lower classes by Victorian humane campaigners. To them, it was self-evident that not only were animals objects of their compassion (which they undoubtedly were) but also didactic instruments through which it was possible to instill a greater degree of benevolence into the lower classes, who lacked vital moral feeling. Meanwhile the members of upper-class culture were naturally kind to animals (except those they shot in what were often extraordinary numbers; Lovegrove 2012). Indeed, sometimes explicit comparisons were drawn between noble animals and the nobility.

It may be – the idea is contested – that violence between humans has been decreasing over time (Pinker, 2012) but correspondingly violence against other beings still hangs like a pall over the proceedings. Indeed, it may be that there is an inverse relationship – *we are doing more violence to other species as we do less to our own*. On one view, as wars have declined, the liberal warfare state has transferred its attentions to other beings. For, after all, there is something warlike as well as industry-like about the way we now treat many animals. It is as if they were inhuman opponents whose sufferings can therefore be the more easily justified.

No doubt it would be possible to argue at length about the sources of human violence and whether they are a part of our animal heritage or a perversion of it and still come to no conclusion (Thrift, 2005). But what is very clear is that humans have always done their worst to others who are regarded as lacking some essential element of humanity; usually arranged in a strict hierarchy according to how sapient – and therefore how capable of true humanity (and therefore individuality) – each individual could be considered to be. Until recently, white upper- and middle-class males were taken to be the high point of humanity and accordingly they were usually the freest from violence (and the freest to deal out violence, though usually indirectly through the various apparatuses of the state). As a result, violence towards enslaved people, violence towards women, violence towards various ethnic groups, violence towards disabled people, violence towards pretty well anyone considered to lack one or more elements of humanity … these have all been staples of city life[2]. The list goes on with all manner of reciprocal complications of class and status and gender and sexuality and ethnicity, allowing some humans to lord it over the other humans who are considered to have 'dehumanizing' characteristics, which are often conceived in animal terms. Today, patterns of human-on-human violence in cities still tend to adhere to these hierarchies as a powerful shadowland of battery and assault, misogyny, general mistreatment or simple indifference. 'Humankind' can quickly run out of road. It still has some way to go if it is to become a broad church when it cannot even control violence among its own members.

Yet, at the same time, treating human beings like vermin can also stem from a recognition that vermin is precisely what they are not: 'people may know full well that those they treat in brutally degrading and inhuman ways are fellow human beings, underneath a more or less thin veneer of false consciousness' (Manne, 2017: 2). Violence to others may then just as easily reflect a desperate attempt to assert social norms, a distorted sense of moral entitlement which paints those affected as deserving of their fate, or even a bizarre feeling of unfairness eating away at restraint. In other words, adverse judgements are often accompanied by doubt, ambivalence and a kind of fear that giving recognition to others' humanity allows those others to judge you too. According to this kind of logic, perverted forms of enforcement then become necessary.

Violence to animals can often suffer from the same kinds of doubt and ambivalence and a comparable discomfort that they might in some way be judging us. But though animals may be denied sentience by human absolutists, though it might feel good to have power over animals if you are a sadist[3], though it might be thought best to walk on by, not knowing too much about animal suffering lest it disturbs the equilibrium of our daily lives, still, at the very least, much of contemporary humankind seems to have a sense that a relationship with animals requires more nuance, if not as yet complete rethinking. We cannot just be beastly to beasts – though we still are.

Whatever the exact case, it has only been relatively recently in the historical record that violence towards animals in cities has come under serious question as their separation and sequestration has raised questions in the wider culture about the problematic role of animals, questions that were rarely asked before. First, there is the question of *what an animal consists of*, both as a thinking and a feeling entity, an extension of the thoughts in previous chapters. After all, formerly, it was often argued that animals were just bundles of instincts and so they could be acted upon with impunity. Second, *the question of differential separation* because animals were themselves becoming subject to rules that mandated some of their number as companions and others as food animals, thereby legitimating violence towards certain kinds of animals and not others. And, third, *the question of sequestration* because the lives and deaths of food animals were increasingly displaced to rural hinterlands where they were out of sight and out of mind, only being present and presented in urban areas as sanitized parts of corpses, as 'meat', as dead stuff without a specific origin, even though that origin weighs on us in all kinds of ways: 'in the methane emissions of cows, in cardiovascular diseases for meat eaters, in trees that are cut down as part of the deforestation that is required to grow […] tons of grain […]' (Despret, 2016: 82). In other words, we see contradictory strands of practice, some that favour animals, some that most decidedly don't, threading their way through recent history.

These three questions are clearly worth examining in more detail since they happened in lockstep with the development of cities. That examination made, I will then pass on to considering how the answers have produced an industry which supplies the food needs of cities through mass killing.

What Is an 'Animal'?

To begin with, the idea that animals were only bundles of instinctual reflexes was gradually displaced both by Darwinism[4] in its more sophisticated versions (which also, of course, brought into question as never before the question of the animal origins of the human) and by a growing strand of behavioural research which also began in the nineteenth century and which has been given greater and greater scientific credence, especially in the last 30 years or so. As outlined in Chapter 4, we can now think of animals as thinking, conscious entities that feel something more than simply instinct[5].

Our perceptions of Western thinking on the environment, nature and animals have been shown to be a stereotype. Histories of natural history (e.g. Jardine, 1996; Curry et al., 2018), sustainability (Warde et al., 2018) and of everyday attitudes to animals have all undergone substantive revision as it has become clearer than ever that thinking about the environment and nature was diverse and could cut across established discourses. Yes, on one side there has been a tradition of slaughtering animals without repair, exemplified in England by the Preservation of Grain Act, passed in 1532 by Henry VIII and then strengthened in 1566 by Elizabeth I. These acts, often called the Vermin Acts, put a bounty on the head of a multitude of native species which were thought to be in competition for food – kites, ravens, choughs, woodpeckers, shags, kingfishers, badgers, foxes, wild cats, pine martens, stoats, weasels, polecats, even hedgehogs (which were thought to suck milk from the teats of cows at night – as a result, half a million were killed in the latter half of the seventeenth and first half of the eighteenth century). The Act wasn't repealed until the mid-eighteenth century by which time it had permanently changed English ecology (Lovegrove, 2008). But there has also been a consistent alternative strand of thought throughout Western history which has always questioned any depiction of animals as just put there for us to use as we see fit, a strand which has become increasingly mainstream in fits and starts, gradually changing the population's ethical compass. It has been a curious hybrid of particular interpretations of Christian teachings, revolutionary fervour, concerns about diet and health, and the gradual rise of practices of appreciation that extend a right of existence and care to animals that were formerly regarded as resources. Take just one example of such an extension embodied in a single person, Florence Merriam-Bailey (Kofalk, 2000). In the latter decades of the nineteenth century, milliners used the feathers, heads and even sometimes whole carcasses of a range of different birds to decorate increasingly elaborate hats. This fashion led to the deaths of about 5 million birds a year worldwide.

Merriam-Bailey was a part of a successful grassroots movement that put a stop to the trade in the United States. Soon hundreds of other women protested against the millinery industry's use of birds, an effort that led to the passage in 1900 of the Lacey Act, which prohibited trade in illegally acquired wildlife, and the Federal Migratory Bird Treaty Act of 1918, which protected migratory birds. But she didn't stop there. Convinced that being exposed to birds in the wild would lead to a growth in sympathy for birds, she urged that they be observed quietly in their natural habitat. At the age of 26 she published the first field guide to native birds, one of ten books she wrote in her lifetime[6]. Merriam-Bailey was also in effect, one of those who established a new practice of relating to animals in the United States, namely birdwatching. The upshot is clear. There are now reckoned to be some 45 million people who watch birds 'around their homes and away from home' in the United States (United States Fish and Wildlife Service, 2016)[7]. One of the needlessly tragic consequences of the Trump government's roll-back of environmental protection has been that it has attacked some of the legislative achievements of the legions of bird admirers.

This care for animals like birds has transmuted into an efflorescence of institutions, many of which have very large memberships. In the UK, for example, there are animal protection societies like the Royal Society for the Protection of Birds (founded in 1889 and, like its American counterparts, started as a result of action by a group of women to stop the trade in feathers), which now has a membership of over a million people, through to animal protection institutions like the Royal Society for the Protection of Animals (founded in 1824) and the People's Dispensary for Sick Animals (founded in 1917) – as well as innumerable other animal charities.

In other words, animals have been the object of twists and turns which have given some of them more cultural latitude. But the process has been differential with certain animals locked out of consideration as somehow less worthy, a calculation based on two simple equations: 'Dead animals are translated into pounds of meat, deceased humans into persons' (Despret, 2016: 82). Worthy animals are cossetted. Animals deemed unworthy are killable. The translation of animals into meat depends upon the dismal path to the slaughterhouse already followed by the chicken in the previous chapter and the way in which everyday life depends on that path for succor. That is where we now must tread.

The Differential Animal

As the examples of birds and hats shows, in many countries at many times, cruelty to animals was regarded by many as, if not a sine qua non of daily life, then as something to be passed by as inevitable[8]. This attitude and its critics are famously encapsulated in Hogarth's set of cartoons of 1751, *The*

Four Stages of Cruelty, which are a rich mine of meanings as both a form of moral instruction and as a catalogue of the cruelty on display in the street in English cities at the time. In them, not only are animals seen as being subjected to all kinds of tortures but these tortures are also seen as being a precursor to acts of violence to humans, and especially women. Produced inexpensively so that they might circulate among 'men of the lowest rank', it seems likely that the cartoons had some effect on public opinion as part of the campaigns leading up to the first bans on animal cruelty in England, the *Cruel Treatment of Cattle Act* and the *Cruelty to Animals Act*, which passed into law in 1822 and 1835, respectively[9].

Domesticates/Companion Animals

Part of the pressure for these laws clearly arose from a general change in moral sentiment towards animals that has been great enough in many parts of the world that a recent Gallup poll (Rifkin, 2015) was able to suggest that 32 per cent of Americans believe that animals should be 'given the same rights as people [to be free from from harm and exploitation]', and that only 3 per cent believed that animals require little protection from harm and exploitation 'since they are just animals'. It is, in many ways, a remarkable change. After all, 'humankind and its hominid ancestors have been on this planet for about 4 million years. For something like 3,999,850 of those years hardly any human devoted [themselves] to the prosperity of another species' (Cocker, 2018: 6). A good part of that cultural shift has likely arisen from the closer emotional relationship many people have formed with certain kinds of animals, in part because of the elimination of 'childhood familiarity with using and killing animals [which allowed] more adults to question utilitarian relations with animals altogether' (Brown, 2016: 245). The separation into different types of animals deserving of more or less affection was more complex than is often allowed (Tague, 2015). But what is certain is that, as Keith Thomas (1983) so famously documented, the growth of a new emotional palette allowed for certain animals to take on an existence in the home and apart from the herd. They were allowed to become individuals, pets – or what are now called companion animals – which were judged (or indeed bred) to have lovable characteristics. Indeed, a failure to love these animals is now often regarded as a sign of cold-heartedness.

This cultural shift was an extended process which seems to have gone hand in glove with urbanization (Bradshaw, 2017)[10]. In England, for example, by some point between the late eighteenth and early nineteenth century, attitudes to companion animals had already changed so much that many people had come to regard love of pets as a moral virtue. 'Pets, being neither fully human nor fully part of the animal world […] offered a unique opportunity for eighteenth century Britons to articulate their view of what it means to be human and what their society ought to look like' (Tague, 2015: 2). Pets could be simultaneously human and nonhuman.

But it had not always been like this. During the eighteenth century, when pet-keeping was becoming a much wider phenomenon, many people still regarded the keeping of a pet as an open question or even a mark of extravagance: 'material and emotional resources that should have been devoted to humans, in this view, were devoted to the care of creatures that God had intended to serve humans as labour or food. Pet keeping was, at best, a useless luxury; at worst, it was actually sinful' (Tague, 2015: 2). Though it is clear that the keeping of pets is synonymous with urbanization and industrialization, the story is clearly more complex than that and more nuanced, involving gender (pets were often regarded as a female preserve), and growing consumerism (including larger homes, manuals on how to care for pets, changing consumer tastes, new pets like guinea pigs, health remedies, sales of pet food like dog's meat and pet accessories like collars and spaces that declared a love for animals like pet cemeteries). It also varies according to the kind of animal (Danahy and Morse, 2017). For example, whereas, in the UK, dogs were widely accepted as pets by the end of the nineteenth century (Chez, 2017), cats did not gain this kind of acceptance until the early twentieth century (Bradshaw, 2017).

Whatever the case, pets are now a staple of life in cities around the world, a focus of intense emotional investment[11]. As a result, they are one of the mainstays of the urban economy. They are a common sight on urban streets. Large areas of the city are reserved for them one way or another, for example, the pet cemeteries that show their owners' post-mortem devotion[12]. And pets are increasingly fitted to urban needs. Living in cities has prompted people to opt for smaller dogs which are better suited to smaller spaces: the average weight of a British puppy has shrunk by about 12 per cent and the average size of a dog has consequently fallen (Economist, 2016)[13].

Contemporary reported figures on pet ownership are inexact, but in many countries they are high and getting higher. For example, until recently the United States has had the largest population of pet dogs and cats globally, with an estimated 78 million dogs and 85.8 million cats in 2015 (Okin, 2017; ASPCA, 2019) Somewhere around 43 per cent of US households and 46 per cent of UK households now have a companion animal of some kind (with many having more than one). Urban figures are hard to come by but, on one analysis, it was estimated that in 2012 there were approximately 1.1 million pets in New York City (600,000 dogs and 500,000 cats), or an ownership rate of about one pet for every three households[14]. No wonder that the US pet products industry was worth some $95.7 billion in 2019 (www.americanpetproducts.org/press_industrytrends.asp).

Furthermore, pet ownership is spreading rapidly around the world. For example, there has been a 51 per cent increase in the number of dogs kept as pets in the developing world, up to 243 million, since 2003. Cat ownership has increased at a similar rate, to 126 million (Tahir, 2017)[15]. In countries like China, as one instance, the days when Chairman Mao denounced pet ownership as a bourgeois distraction are gone. A large increase in pet ownership has occurred at the same time as a wider animal protection movement has gained some traction (Li, 2018). In the larger cities like Beijing and Shanghai, pet dogs have become so popular that the law restricts owners to one dog a household and bans large breeds in cities (Bradshaw, 2017). Even so, in 2018 China overtook the US to become home to the world's largest population of cats and dogs – 188 million – a number projected to grow to 248 million by 2024.

We rarely think about how the city manifests itself to all of these pets. Take the example of dogs. Dogs' main sensory conduit into the world is smell and though it may be a myth that dogs have a sense of smell that teeters close to the supernatural, it is quite clearly smell that acts as a key to many of their social and other interactions. To them, the city is a complex smellscape (Horowitz, 2016; Berns, 2018; Howes, 2018). How does a city reveal itself in olfactory terms? Virginia's Woolf's (1988 [1933]: 21) evocation of Elizabeth Barrett's dog, Flush, on his first visit to the city can help:

> For the first time he heard his nails click upon the hard paving-stones of London. For the first time the whole battery of a London street on a hot summer's day assaulted his nostrils. He smelt the swooning smells that lie in the gutters, the bitter smells that corrode iron railings, the fuming, heady smells that rise from basements – smells more complex, corrupt, violently contrasted and compounded than any he had smelt in the fields near Reading, smells that lay far beyond the range of the human nose; so that while the chair went on, he stopped, amazed, defining, savoring, until a jerk at his collar dragged him on.

Not that all pets are treated as well (or sometimes as badly) as Flush. They bear a cost to their companionship. But things have got better in many countries. By one estimate, in the 1960s, about one quarter of the dog population in the United States was still roaming the streets (whether owned or not) and 10- to 20-fold more dogs were euthanized compared to the present. However, since the 1970s the number of cats and dogs euthanized in animal shelters has declined sharply from somewhere between 13.5 million and 20 million then to probably 1.5 to 2 million now (Rowan and Kartal, 2018; Horowitz, 2019; ASPCA, 2019), the result of a change in attitude from worrying about how animals were killed to objecting to them being killed at all (Fudge, 2008; Brown 2016)[16].

Domesticate or Synanthrope? Dwellers on the Urban Margins

But there are also domesticated animals who stray, and animals which are feral or at most partially domesticated. So-called 'village' dogs are a good example of a series of animals that dwell on the edges of human being. Not feral but not domesticated either. Often described as superbly adapted free-roaming scavengers, the 850 million village dogs in the world occupy a particular niche which allows 'dogs [to be] in the absence of a human owner' (Srinavasan, 2013: 110). They are found in many countries, although India's significantly named 'street dogs' are often pulled out as the exemplar of an environmental niche in which dogs have existed for centuries[17]. But 'if humans were to disappear, the village dog niche would disappear and village dogs would become extinct. Dogs would not take up residence in the wild because that niche is already taken – by wolves, coyotes, and jackals' (Coppinger and Coppinger, 2016: 43).

Though generally ignored, these kinds of dogs can be the subject of campaigns of eradication. For example, Egypt is reckoned to have some 10 to 15 million street dogs, which are often feared as possible rabies carriers (Samaan and Spencer, 2020). They have been subject to systematic poisoning, but so long as the rubbish and detritus of cities continues to mount, especially since pigs no longer occupy a niche in Egyptian cities as scavengers since an outbreak of swine flu led to their mass culling in 2009, their numbers are unlikely to be drastically affected. Again, a middle class more and more used to domestic pets is increasingly prone to defend them.

In Western cities, the equivalent of these dogs is the legion of 'stray' dogs – stray being a contentious term, of course (Greed, 2017). These dogs have been a constant of urban life but the very fact that they are now called strays indicates that they have become the subject of the forces of regulation of public space, something that only happened in most cities in the nineteenth century as dogs became a common part of bourgeois households and now standard practices like 'walking the dog'[18] became general. All kinds of institutions arose as a result of a shift to understanding all dogs as adjuncts of human beings. The market got in on the act – specialized pet shops became a normal way of acquiring pets. But so did the state and the developing institutions of civil society, institutions like the first dogs home at Battersea in London, the 'Temporary Home for Lost and Starving Dogs', opened in 1860 by Mary Tealby. Strays became the unloved companions to 'pets', a threat to property, order and sanitary resolve rather than an animal friend (Howell, 2015a; 2015b). The Battersea Home illustrates this move all too well: dogs that could not be restored to owners or rehomed were put down. The Home only

> seems to have become truly viable when it started working with the police[19], receiving the dogs that they had been charged with rounding up since the passing of legislation in 1867 and 1871. [...]
>
> By the late 19th century, particularly during the rabies scares, the Home was barely able to keep up with the many thousands of dogs that it needed to put down each year, even with the aid of the humane gas chambers invented by the eminent surgeon and sanitarian Benjamin Ward Richardson. (Howell, 2015b: n.p.)

The situation is now much changed. One estimate made in 2017 by The Dogs Trust put the number of strays in the London region in 2016/17 at 7,767; a substantial decrease since the turn of the century (Dogs Trust, 2017)[20]. In other cities, the numbers of strays can be larger. For example,

Detroit, with a much smaller population than London, has been reckoned to have a stray dog population of between 20,000 and 50,000 dogs (though the latter figure is almost certainly inflated) (Stafford, 2019).

Dogs stray in cities for all kinds of reasons, from their owners moving and abandoning them to their having escaped or been stolen. Usually, though not always, they then become parts of small scavenging packs until they die or are captured and sent on to animal shelters where, in cities like London, they are usually rehomed (Beck, 1973). Often numbers of strays vary with the state of the economy. For example, in 2015 it was estimated that there were as many as 1 million stray dogs in Greece as a result of the deep recession there.

But it isn't only dogs who stray, of course. Cats are an issue too[21]. Many cities have a major cat issue. Rome, for example, is famous for its population of feral cats, estimated to number at least 300,000 at last count. In Beijing it is estimated that there are between 200,000 and a million stray cats (the wildly differing estimates show how difficult it is to count these animals). This is despite the notorious fact that thousands of the creatures – both feral and abandoned – were rounded up in preparation for the 2008 Summer Olympics[22].

Domesticates/Livestock

In contrast to pets and strays, there are what might be thought of as the living dead. Farm animals were always excluded from the privileges of conviviality, even though research shows that farmers often have complex emotional relationships with their animals (Despret, 2016; Young, 2017 [2003]; Gillespie, 2018; Walling, 2018). At about the same time as pets first came to be regarded as a separate animal category, meat-eating started to move from a mark of distinction which was the preserve of a small and wealthy section of the population to a more general condition of life. This shift probably took place first in England. By the eighteenth century, boosted by new animal feeding practices, new breeds and land enclosures, England had more domestic beasts per acre, and especially cattle, than any country in Europe, with the exception of the Netherlands (Fiddes, 1991; Vialles, 1994). It had a reputation as a flesh-eating country (Velten, 2013), one in which meat from farm animals was replacing meat from game. One result was that London increasingly became the focus of a continuous flow of animals, often travelling large distances. Tired beasts approached the city from all directions (Velten, 2013). In addition, attitudes to meat-eating had changed more in England than elsewhere in Europe as a particular sense of a world – and the animals in it – was boosted by industrialization and colonization. The latter decades of the nineteenth century then saw a further emphasis on meat-eating brought about by a general rise in incomes and more and more meat imports from Australia and New Zealand, hastened by the advent of dis-assembly lines and refrigeration, which produced wholesale industrialization of the industry.

But there was more to the process of industrialized 'meatification' than the increased demand resulting from the restructuring of production and consumption. Part and parcel of that increased demand was what Remy (2016) has called the 'de-animalization of the animal'. Gradually, the most recognizable features of an animal were hidden from public view as 'consumers reconciled themselves to industrial meat production by distancing themselves from industrial meat production' (Specht, 2019: 260). This process happened in a number of ways (Despret, 2016). To begin with, the animal was disassembled and reassembled as types and forms of meat – as pork and ham and beef and veal and as prime cut, fillet, cutlet, chop, burger, and so on. Then, anything that might remind the consumer of its animal origin or its killing was effaced. In the slaughterhouse, evidence of anything that looks like a real animal – ears, heads, tails, hooves – is removed so that it cannot disturb the consumer's equanimity when eating. Finally, the industry depicted itself as a means of making goods and not as a mass killing machine. It traded in an industrial vernacular of graphs, charts and statistics expressed in pounds and tonnes which allowed contemplation of killing animals by glossing over the killing and brutality. These animals' lives counted – but not as lives. Instead they had become part of an anonymous execution machine which is dedicated to the Latin word for executioner – *carnifex* or 'meat-maker'[23]. The net result of this work of forgetting is obvious enough, in any case:

> All that reminds us of the living animal [...] has [...] disappeared. The most recognizable features of what animals once were are now hidden. [...] there has been a gradual withdrawal of enthroned calf heads occupying merchants' stalls and of the bodies, still whole and sometimes unplucked, of chickens and game birds. The culmination of this concealment can be found today in the hamburger, which constitutes nearly half of the consumption of beef in the United States. (Despret, 2016: 83)

The Great Separation

So far as the city is concerned, the industrialized manufacture and mass consumption of corpses went alongside a general separation of food animals from cities by means of the growth of the modern slaughter and meat-packing industry with its practices of dissociation of the animal which walks into the slaughterhouse from the meat-bearing carcass that is trucked out. This is the business of surplus death: 'species, ecosystems, habitats, relationships, and connections that sustain the web of life on Earth become collateral casualties in the rush for consumption. [...] monstrous cruelty and massive wastage are hidden within organized invisibility' (Rose, 2011: 28).

We turn away from these actions, as though they are one of those regrettable parts of life we can do nothing about, and so we allow them to continue to foster our inhumanity. This is one definition of disgrace, of course: a turning away (Rose, 2011). It is deeply engrained in how we currently live. It is about passing over the bodily suffering of supposed other beings or reserving that suffering to ourselves as the only beings who can truly think (Diski, 2010).

In past cities, domesticated animals had often lived cheek-by-jowl with humans. For example, until the end of the nineteenth century, so-called backyard cows were common in American cities like Seattle. Indeed, in some cities milk cows (but not steers, horses or hogs) were allowed to run loose and graze, even in downtowns, though ordinances were gradually brought in exerting greater control over 'unruly behavior' and where they could graze (Brown, 2016). In any case, living so close to animals meant that ignorance of consequences could not exist. There was no turning away. Killing was a part of daily life in which cattle could be driven

> along city streets to be slaughtered, chickens' necks were broken on the spot in markets, and the blood and guts of eviscerated beasts were often on display for all to see. The cries of frightened and thirsty beasts mixed with the strong and penetrating smells of blood and manure […]. the activities of slaughterhouses were often open to public view. (Velten, 2013: 35)[24]

Gradually, many city-living animals like horses and cows and pigs became more tightly controlled and then were exiled from cities, in the case of cows and pigs as meat production systems became less and less local and middle classes became more and more vocal. Equally where animals died became a matter of spatial conflict and control. In London, there had been a continual battle to push slaughterhouses out of the city which had begun as early as the thirteenth century. But even sanitary legislation had little effect. Slaughterhouses continued to operate. In 1873, there were still 1,500 metropolitan slaughterhouses. Even in 1905, there were still 350 (Velten, 2013). In the end, the decline of slaughterhouses in London occurred simply because of a lack of livestock to be slaughtered:

> most of the live cattle imported into London were foreign and because of disease restrictions went via the abattoirs at Deptford: imports of […] beef from Australia, New Zealand and South America grew […] and an increasing proportion of domestic beef was country-killed and shipped directly to London […] Private slaughterhouses […] persist[ed] […] until 1927 when they were finally abolished. (Velten, 2013: 37)

In New York until well into the nineteenth century,

> thousands of head of cattle – whipped by country drovers, nipped by city dogs – were driven to the East River slaughterhouses every Sunday afternoon for the Monday market. […] [and you couldn't miss] an 'overpowering stench' [which] announced the propinquity of 'pig town', a district extending to the Hudson with piggeries in backyards and 'bone boilers' on every block […] these [were] smoking metal tubes, moated by heaps of bones, 'collected from the retail butchers whenever it best suited their convenience', no matter how long they had been rotting in the alleys behind their shops […] the char yielded by burning animal bones was used by the city's sugar industry: the

black bone dust whitened the yellow stain left on the crystals by the refining process. (Santlofer, 2016: xvii)

A total of 375,000 cattle, sheep and pigs were butchered in the city in 1853 at 206 slaughterhouses but their presence had become more and more oppressive. So, for example, in 1850 a city ordinance barred mass daytime herding below 42nd Street, the first sign of sequestration. A forest of regulations gradually grew up which made it more and more difficult to slaughter close to the customer. So it was that killing at a distance – and consequently away from the public gaze – began to become, statistically, the main form of relationship between humans and animals via the industrial production of corpses to feed city populations, a process first rolled out in the slaughterhouses of Chicago and then become general (Fitzgerald, 2015)[25].

By the 1870s, new kinds of slaughterhouses gradually developed in cities which replaced the neighbourhood slaughterhouses of old. They utilized industrial technologies of extermination based on detailed divisions of labour, carefully arranged spaces and all manner of specialized instruments in order to make it possible to produce meat and move it long distances. At the same time, these slaughterhouses displaced labour that was increasingly regarded as physically and morally repellent from public view so that it could be hidden in plain sight, so to speak (Pachirat, 2011). Smelling, seeing, hearing and touching slaughter was relegated to a company of lost souls who, quite literally, did all of the dirty work that turns individual thinking animals into the generality of 'meat'.

The new generation of slaughterhouses tended to occupy specific districts on the outskirts of cities. Thus, the modern slaughterhouse was, for all intents and purposes, invented in the square mile of 'the yards' of Chicago.

> In the square mile at its prime stood numerous packinghouses, ringed by railroad lines adjacent to the tens of thousands of animal pens of the Union Stock Yard. Train tracks encircled the stockyard and delivered a constant flow of livestock to the Chicago market and then the world. Railroad docks stood ready to unload the massive quantities of animals, to be sold to packers daily in the huge fairground. During World War One – the height of its history – some fifty thousand people found employment in the stockyards and adjacent Packingtown. Tens of thousands of cattle, calves, hogs, and sheep changed hands every day in the market. Afterward, about one third reboarded trains and headed to slaughterhouses further east. The rest met their fate in Packingtown.
>
> Unloaded on the docks that could handle hundreds of livestock railcars at a time, the creatures were counted and accounted for, then driven to the sale pens. Once sold, employees weighed and then drove them to the abattoirs that sent them off as meat products […] Thanks to the by-products industry, various animal parts became combs, buttons, lard, fertilizer or even pharmaceuticals as the packers used everything, as the cliché said, but the squeal of the vanquished hog. (Pacyga, 2015: xi)

Slaughterhouses were subject to continuous organizational and technological improvements, not just an immense investment in capital equipment (necessitated by the need to get meat to cities as rapidly as possible), or the growth of effective bureaucratic structures, but also the advent of mechanical refrigeration in the 1890s and the subsequent use of railroad refrigerator cars. Again, whereas carcasses had been moved by hand on overhead rails in the slaughterhouses, the meatpacking companies now installed an endless chain to move the bodies around the killing floor by power, thereby producing a continuous process which it is often claimed was the inspiration for Henry Ford's automobile assembly line and which places systematic killing and the subsequent processing of the resultant carcasses into meat right at the heart of industrial civilization (Edgerton, 2006).

From the 1950s on, slaughterhouses gradually made their way to the margins of cities. Now, they are all but invisible, which is, of course, the point. The modern industrialized slaughterhouse is large. There are about 800 federally inspected slaughterhouses in the United States but only a few of them account for most of the killing. For example, only about 50 plants are responsible for 98 per cent of cattle deaths and the subsequent processing of the carcasses (Corkery and Yaffe-Bellany, 2020a). But the modern industrialized slaughterhouse is also anonymous. It 'blends seamlessly into the landscape of generic business parks' (Pachirat, 2011: 23). The blood flows, but only a few workers have to see it. Within the slaughterhouse itself, the actual act of killing is a cloistered-off affair which only a relatively few workers are closely involved in (Blanchette, 2020). Much of the slaughterhouse is taken up with processing the carcasses into meat, carried out by workers like ear cutters in aptly named spaces like the gut room, the head line and the viscera table. It is in the anonymous confines of the 800 federally inspected and 1,900 non-federally inspected[26] slaughterhouses that, in the United States in 2019, according to US Department of Agriculture figures (USDA, 2019) 9,339,249,000 chickens, 227,660,000 turkeys, 129,913,000 pigs, 33,555,000 cattle and 587,000 calves, 59,000 bison, 675,000 goats, 27,544,000 ducks, and 2,321,000 sheep and lambs met their end.

> The slaughterhouse I worked in continues to operate today. It employs close to eight hundred nonunionized workers, the vast majority immigrants and refugees from Central and South America, Southeast Asia, and East Africa. It generates over $820 million annually in sales to distributors within and outside the United States and ranks among the top handful of US cattle-slaughtering and beef-processing facilities in volume of production. The line speed on the kill floor is approximately three hundred cattle per hour. In a typical workday, between twenty-two and twenty-five hundred cattle are killed there, adding up to well over ten thousand cattle killed per five-day week, or more than half a million cattle slaughtered each year. (Pachirat, 2011: 17–18)

Many of the lines on which these animals are killed are under constant pressure to speed up. One answer has been to breed animals so that they are more easily killable amd disassemblable by 'relatively regularizing and standardizing their bodies in terms of weight, tendons, posture, and fat-to-muscle ratios' (Blanchette, 2020: 231).

And now a new form of sequestration is taking place on the production side too. 'Concentrated animal feeding operations' (CAFOs) in the United States have allowed more animals like cows, pigs and chickens to be produced whilst reducing land, feed, and labour costs (Fitzgerald, 2015). The result is that 'more than half the country's beef now passes through some five hundred feedlots that each fatten fifty thousand cattle or more a year' (Brown, 2016: 224), allowing steers to be sent to market within 16 months (as opposed to 4 or 5 years in the early 1900s). Taking their cue from this model, perhaps 70 per cent of UK farm animals are now thought to live in intensive indoor units (Colley and Wasley, 2020). Chickens, pigs and cows are being taken off the land and housed in huge 'intensive' animal confinement facilities, so-called super- or mega-farms which house a minimum of 1,000 beef cattle, 2,000 pigs or 40,000 poultry. In 2017, there were already at least 217 of these intensive cattle farms in the UK which have restricted or zero access to pasture. The largest farms fatten up to 6,000 cattle a year on 'feedlots'.

This is the latest manifestation of a certain kind of high-throughput low-cost industrialization: cow, pig and poultry populations are increasingly concentrated at every point in their life course in order to gain economies of scope and scale, including moulding the animals' own compromised bodies, in order to fit the demands of homogeneous production, and never mind the risks that concentration produces like disease incubation (Hinchliffe et al., 2016). At the same time, their experiences become ever more distant from those who eat them: they are invisible. Yet cultural changes mean that this industrial model and its associated stunning and killing technologies (Edgerton, 2016) increasingly finds its legitimacy challenged and the erosion of the cultural value of meat production, even in national cultures like the United States whose identity is bound up with meat like beef, is clearly causing problems for the industry, whether in the form of vegetarianism or proposed taxes on meat.

And there is no getting away from these deathly facts by veering into what might look, at first sight, like kinder practices. For example, meat production may be bad. However, surely milk and cheese are OK? In fact, milk and cheese production – cheese, in particular, is a fast-growing industry producing some 22 million tonnes a year worldwide – doesn't win any medals either, not least because the dairy industry is intimately connected with the meat industry (Layton, 2019). To begin with, the natural lifespan of a cow is about 20 years but most dairy cows are slaughtered at somewhere between 3 and 7 years of age, worn out by the pressure in the industry to increase productivity (in the United States, for example, milk production per cow increased by 13 per cent just between 2007 and 2016 (Gillespie, 2019; Layton 2019))[28]. In the United States, which has 9.3 million dairy cows

(3 million of which are slaughtered every year), dairy cows are separated from their mothers at birth, raised until they are about 18 months old, and then artificially inseminated. Nine months later they give birth. They are then inseminated once a year so that they keep on producing milk (Gillespie, 2018). And, of course, as with the chicken, males are surplus to requirements, killed right away or reared for meat and slaughtered within 6 months. Many dairy cows are kept indoors most of their lives – already at least 10 per cent of UK dairy cows are housed indoors all year round (Meager, 2016). Some of these cows are tethered in 'tie stalls'[29]. In the United States, approximately 40 per cent of dairy farm cows are kept in tie stall barns that restrict movement for all or part of the day (Robbins et al., 2019).

Postdomestic Food Systems

In any case, what we see is that the emotional redefinition of what constitutes an animal has combined with the sequestration of the business of killing away from the public gaze which, in turn, has allowed an epistemic blind spot to be produced that allows all kinds of repugnant practices to be passed over in thought, even when the evidence is on the plate in front of you. The net result is that cities now are full of a 'postdomestic' ignorance in which,

> people live far away, both physically and psychologically, from the animals that produce the food, fiber, and hides they depend on, and they never witness the births, sexual congress and slaughter of these animals. Yet they maintain very close relationships with companion animals – pets – often relating to them as if they were human. (Bulliet, 2005: xx)

The removal of meat consumption from its production is easily illustrated. Take the example of New York's foodshed, first investigated in the 1920s. It comprises, at a minimum, approximately 20,000 restaurants, 13,000 food retailers, 1,600 public schools, numerous hospitals and other non profit service providers, 90 farmers' markets, an enormous distribution centre at Hunt's Point (which includes produce and fish markets) as well as several other store-owned and specialty distribution centres, 53 United States Department of Agriculture inspected slaughterhouses, and more than 80 live animal markets that slaughter on demand (Barron et al., 2016)[30]. In 2002, the last date for which there are detailed figures, about 2 million tons of meat entered the city, of which only 22,000 tons came from overseas. Almost 75 per cent of the domestically sourced food had an origin from within the northeast (though that does not mean that it was all produced there). About 1,057,000 tons of live animals and fish[31] entered the city, of which 247,000 tons was international. Remarkably, there seems to be no reliable data that describe precisely how much food is consumed by New Yorkers, a fact that sadly is mirrored in many other cities around the world. Equally remarkably, there is rarely data that allow urban food supplies to be exactly traced back to their origins, though a burgeoning literature on foodsheds and local food systems is gradually putting this to rights. Usually, the trace can only be followed back to whoever is the previous immediate distributor, although some North American cities like San Francisco, Philadelphia and Vancouver have tried to study their pattern of food origins in more detail, a pursuit being taken up in a burgeoning literature on North American and European foodsheds (e.g. Horst and Gaolach, 2015).

Whatever the case, most residents of most cities have no idea of the enormous complexity of the food system or of the origins of their food. The rough estimate of 30 million meals served up in London each day in 39,338 food service outlets (of which about 15,500 are restaurants) is simply an accepted part of the weave of everyday life. This fact holds true even for the majority of these restaurants and food outlets since they usually rely on distributors and middlemen to procure their food and therefore have only a vague idea, if any, of its origin. Again, the fact that so many people's jobs rely on the food system is simply taken to be a fact of life. (In the UK, for example, the food labour force numbers 3.95 million but only 11 per cent of them work on farms, fishing boats and greenhouses (Lang, 2020). The rest are involved in food manufacturing, services and consumption, mainly in or near cities.)

In other words, it is an anonymous fact of urban life that food turns up on the plate. That the flesh of animals is often being offered up to satisfy urban dwellers' demand for food is passed by with a proverbial shrug. Not that visibility would necessarily produce a wholesale switch in behaviour – after all, in earlier cities, seeing animals killed (or, indeed, killing them oneself) did not necessarily produce a mass outbreak of sympathy, a fact that still holds true even now in many live food markets around the world. And the press of everyday life often acts as a tranquilizer dart: you might well wake up with a jolt in the middle of the night and realize, guilt-stricken, that you need to address what your food habits are doing to the planet and its inhabitants. But then you wake up the next day and there is a long and pressing list of things to do. As long as this conveyor belt of distractions continues to roll, the situation never has to be confronted.

The Results

Whatever the rights and wrongs of the case, it is an immutable fact that the business of killing has now reached epic proportions. Humanity is going on a killing spree. Take only the case of 'meat' (i.e. dead animal) production. Global meat production has risen from less than 50 million tonnes in 1950 to more than 300 million tonnes in 2015 (Smil, 2019). Included in this figure are 1.5 billion pigs, half a billion sheep and 50 billion chickens (Thornton, 2019). By one reckoning, on current trends, just the next 10 years will see a 14 per cent increase in pig and beef consumption – in killing pigs and cows[32], not to put too fine a point on it – worldwide and a 20 per cent rise in chicken consumption. And that's before we get to other poultry and to animals periodically defined as sources of meat like goats and horses and ostriches and even dogs[33].

But producing meat is causing an environmental disaster of epic proportions. Feeding people through means of the current resource-intensive system is degrading the ability to feed them. The facts are well-known but they still bear repeating. As Harwatt et al. (2019) point out, if the livestock sector carries on in its current guise, by 2030 it will make up 49 per cent of the emissions budget for 1.5°C. Given that the production of meat, milk and eggs has already increased from 758 million tonnes in 1990 to 1,247 million tonnes in 2017, and is likely to increase still further, there is an increased probability of exceeding emissions that could limit warming to between 1.5°C and 2°C. It also means that 'the removal of CO_2 from the atmosphere through restoring native vegetation will be limited, and threatens remaining natural carbon sinks where land could be converted to livestock production' (Harwatt et al., 2019: 1; see also Harwatt, 2019).

Equally, according to Poore and Nemecek's (2018) meta-analysis, meat and dairy farming are extremely inefficient ways of eating food. They provide just 18 per cent of calories and 37 per cent of protein. But they use 83 per cent of farmland as well as producing 56 to 58 per cent of agriculture's greenhouse gas emissions. Though roughly twice as much land is used for grazing worldwide as for crop production, that land produces a very small amount of the protein that we eat. Even the very lowest impact meat and dairy products cause more environmental harm than the least sustainable cereal and vegetable growing. (That said, there is substantial variability between different ways of producing the same food. In the worst case, raising beef cattle on deforested land results in 12 times more greenhouse gases and uses 50 times more land than beef cattle grazing on natural pasture.) In other words, moving to meat-free diets will have a transformative potential, not least because the land required for carbon emissions reduction could be used as a carbon sink as natural vegetation re-establishes itself and the carbon in the soil builds up again.

Not all is gloom, though. The Food and Agriculture Organization of the United Nations (FAO) (2020) argues that global meat production *may* have begun to stall or even fall. Certainly, beef consumption is declining now in a number of countries. But, pig[34] and chicken consumption still seem to be trending upwards, though recent outbreaks of disease have badly affected pig production in Asia. Equally, the planet *may* have reached 'peak pasture' given that since 2000 the amount of land used for grazing has declined by 1.2 per cent of total global land area (although land used for feed has continued to increase) (Bullard, 2020).

Industrialized Hunting

But it is not just farmed meat from the land that is at stake. Commercial or commercialized hunting, mainly for food, still remains a major activity. Take the case of bushmeat – meat from wild animals used for food. By one estimate, bushmeat hunting threatens 301 terrestrial mammal species including 126 primates, 26 bats, and 65 ungulates such as deer and wild pigs with extinction (Ripple et al., 2016). One important offshoot of hunting is the bushmeat trade. A large number of species are killed for bushmeat. For example, in 5 months in 2006 one estimate had nearly 1.5 million animals being killed for bushmeat in Cameroon and Senegal, some of them for local consumption but far more now being killed by commercial hunters (Fa et al., 2006). One of the primary markets for bushmeat is large cities of the Global South (e.g. the cities of Vietnam where eating bushmeat is a status symbol) but cities of the Global North are not immune. While some bushmeat is brought in legitimately, customs confiscations have shown that bushmeat is for sale illegally in Paris, New York and London.

But it is in the sea that the volume of wild animal killing explodes. There mass hunting is still the chief mode of dispatch. The death toll arising from the demands of cities strikes animals in the sea as well. Fish are on the front line of this urban slaughter, as one of the primary determinants of an estimated death toll of somewhere between 1 and 2.7 trillion fishes that are killed by humans each year, usually by asphyxiation (Balcombe, 2016). They are the subject of what is best described as industrialized hunting, fed by the invention of the trawl, fishing's version of the plough (which first appeared in embryonic form in the seventeenth century), purse seines (which first appeared in the 1850s), long lines and large combined netting operations (which first appeared in the nineteenth century) and, finally, steam and then internal combustion engines powering larger and larger boats able to reach deeper and deeper waters (Fagan, 2017). Now, fishing by some 4.6 million vessels (2.8 million of which are motorized) has become unsustainable. According to Fagan (2017) peak 'capture' (of marine) fish occurred in 1996 when 86 million tons of fish were caught. Since then that number has apparently plateaued (but see Pauly and Zeller [2016] for more disturbing figures). However, while industrial catches have been declining in general, artisanal, small-scale catches and recreational landings have increased, though on a much more limited scale (Fagan, 2017)[35].

Fishing is as important as farming in the history of the feeding of many cities[36] but it receives much less attention, even though fish are now the most traded commodity in the world (Fagan, 2017) and 'between 1961 and 2016, the average annual increase in global food fish consumption outpaced population growth and exceeded that of meat from all terrestrial animals combined' (FAO, 2018: 2). Fish suffer greatly for their prominence, not least because for marine and freshwater fish pretty well nowhere is safe from the hunt to serve urban appetites (Probyn, 2020). By one estimate (Fagan, 2017), only three fifths of 1 per cent of the ocean is truly protected from the 4.6 million fishing vessels currently extant on the planet[37] though it is true that, just as on the land, a few species of fish serve as the main urban food animals: they are the 'beef of the sea' (Fagan, 2017). In the United States, for example, four species predominate – salmon, sea bass, cod and tuna – each of them caught in a roundelay in which, in 2005 for example, the United States imported more than 5 billion lb of seafood, practically double what was imported 20 years before, and during the same period, saw a quadrupling of seafood exports (Greenberg, 2010; 2014; Kurlansky, 2020). But it is the Chinese distant water fishing fleet which now drives overfishing (FAO, 2018). China is currently the biggest seafood exporter. Its population also accounts for more than a third of world fish consumption caught globally too, a figure growing by 6 per cent a year. The Chinese distant water fleet, supported by government subsidies[38], has been estimated to number at least 2,600 vessels with 400 new vessels coming on line just between 2014 and 2016. But a more recent study (Gutierrez et al., 2020) suggests that the size of the fleet could be three times larger than this and includes large illegal 'dark fleets' that do not advertise their position. Many of the vessels are large trawlers which have moved into new fishing grounds like West Africa as they exhaust old ones, notwithstanding the institution of a Chinese government catch reduction policy. No wonder that the FAO (2018) now reckons that 90 per cent of the world's fishing grounds are fully exploited or facing collapse. Generally speaking, there is a decline in catches as the large industrial fishing fleets ply their rapacious trade.

> The FAO recently calculated that 29 per cent of fish stocks were being fished at biologically unsustainable levels, down from a peak of 32.5 per cent in 2008. In 2011, 71 per cent were being fished at a sustainable level, a sharp decline from 90 per cent in 1974. (Fagan, 2017: 298)

The shortages caused by the largely indiscriminate slaughter often seem to drive only more slaughter. For example, the latest extension of the killing is into the mesopelagic, the layer of the ocean below a few hundred metres into which little light penetrates but which contains an estimated 10 billion tonnes of fish. Mesopelagic fish species connect primary consumers and predators in oceanic food webs, and their slow growth and reproductive rates make them highly vulnerable[39]. Having pillaged shallower waters, permits are now being issued to net fish this layer[40].

Ironically, much of the by-catch from fishing – mainly fish and other marine species caught unintentionally, either while targeting other species or because the fish caught are undersize – will be reserved for producing fish oil and fish meal, made mainly from the leftover bones and offal of fish caught by commercial fleets, in order to sate the demands of farms, especially factory farms, for animal feed or for the use of fish farms in order to feed domesticated fish[41].

The rise of fish farming means that fishing is no longer only about hunting. Fish-farming has become a major industry in response to the decline of wild stocks, especially in China. In 2016 farmed food fish comprised 46.8 per cent of the world's total fish production, up from 25.7 per cent in 2000 and 13.4 per cent a decade earlier (Fagan, 2017; FAO, 2018). Though the amount of wild fish caught since the late 1980s has barely changed, over half the fish eaten in the world – by one lower-end estimate, as many as 37 billion fish a year – now comes from aquaculture (FAO, 2018) and fish farms are still continuing to expand, though more slowly[42]. But fish-farming comes with a list of negatives, like pollution and algae bloom, attracting parasites, and spreading diseases, apart from the fact that it requires the death of many other wild fish like sardines and anchovies as feed in order to sustain the salmon and other farmed fish. That said, 'within a few generations [it is likely] that almost all the fish eaten on earth will be farmed' (Fagan, 2017: 303).

Our attitude to killing fish is utterly contradictory. Just one example will suffice. We demonize the shark as a fearsome predator, ready to bite bits off a human being at the drop of a hat, as though it was snatching candy. But sharks kill only 10 to 20 people each year[43]. Meanwhile we are killing up to 73 million, yes 73 million, sharks a year (Clarke et al., 2006)[44]. There are more than 500 species of shark, ray and skate, many of which, not surprisingly, are endangered, but sharks that live in the open ocean are in particular danger because they are being forced to share large parts of their habitat with fisheries. For example, longline fishing operations[45] encroach on almost one-quarter of the area that pelagic sharks cover each month. In some regions, the overlap is even higher (Warren, 2019).

Insects?

And then, to conclude, there are the insects. Not so long ago, insects were regarded as off edible limits in many food cultures though they were used in other ways[46]. But it may be that insects will become the last food frontier, farmed in the same way as many other animals as a new kind of meat. In some countries, insect larvae are already coming to be regarded as normal fare while, in the UK, South Africa and other locations, insect farms are being set up which will farm the larvae of flies so as to make feed for farmed fish, poultry and pets, acting as a substitute for the two main sources of animal protein – soybean and fishmeal – both of which have exceptionally adverse environmental impacts.

Notes

1 Though it is important to note that, in this case at least, intensive intervention after the war restored much of the wildlife.
2 This violence is nowhere better typified than by the nineteenth- and twentieth-century eugenics movement, which attempted to apply the breeding principles used to select animals to human beings. This kind of reproductive control still surfaces periodically in various issue of reproductive justice and the unequal control of populations. It also transfers over to animals: how much right do we have to change them? Is it ethical to grow human organs on or in animals?

The City of Surplus Death

3 Some limited research suggests that extreme violence towards animals can be a precursor to serial killing.
4 Indeed, Darwin showed very considerable sympathy – I think that is the right word – to both animals and plants, most notably in *The Expression of the Emotions in Man and Animals* and even his book on the humble earthworm, *The Formation of Vegetable Mould Through the Action of Earthworms*, and in his remarkable series of books and monographs on plants (see Thompson, 2018). In his later life, he was a noted campaigner against animal cruelty.
5 Though as Massumi (2015) points out, it is entirely possible to reframe instincts as far more plastic and malleable than they are often characterized.
6 As if to show the links to the rise of other important institutions of care for the environment, her older brother, Clinton Hart Merriam, later became the Director of the United States Biological Survey (now the United States Fish and Wildlife Service) and one of the founders of the National Geographic Society.
7 In the UK, the Royal Society for the Protection of Birds reckons that about 3 million adults go actively birdwatching.
8 Not that the presence of animal cruelty laws always provides an index of a positive civilizational atmosphere. For example, as the Chancellor of Germany, Hitler passed comprehensive laws banning animal cruelty, though how far they were enforced is an open question. The laws forbade all unnecessary harm to animals, including the inhumane treatment of animals in film production, and the use of dogs in hunting. Livestock were supposed to be killed humanely. In 1936, a special law was passed regarding the humane dispatch of lobsters and crabs. Pets who were terminally ill were supposed to be euthanized. Nazi Germany was the first country in the world to place the wolf under official protection. It was also the first country to host an international conference on animal welfare (in 1934). In 1938, animal protection was gazetted as a subject to be taught in public schools and universities. When the Nazis invaded France, animal protection laws were put into place there too (see Sax, 2000).
9 There do not seem to have been any animal cruelty laws anywhere in the world until 1635 when the Irish made a law forbidding tying horses directly to the plough by their tails and pulling the wool off sheep instead of using clippers (Korsgaard, 2018).
10 Even in the seventeenth century, members of elites often had 'pets'. For example, John Evelyn kept a tortoise whilst Samuel Pepys kept a monkey and a tame lion. But this was also the beginning of another way of treating animals. Men of science gathered in private to administer opium to dogs – and then dissected them (Willes, 2017).
11 Perhaps the best index of this is divorce. UK figures show that one of the main points of contestation in many divorces is ownership of pets. Equally, pre-nuptial agreements that specify who in a partnership owns a pet are becoming more common too. There are many other indexes too such as the rise of veterinary practices – there are now over 20,000 practising veterinarians in the UK, for example. Equally, there is the rise of pet health insurance, a staple in the UK which is now spreading rapidly in the US.
12 Such as New York's Hartsdale pet cemetery, opened in 1896 (and officially incorporated in 1914), which now contains some 80,000 former pets (Tague, 2015).
13 Though urban dogs exhibit another characteristic typical of those living in cities. They are becoming more and more obese. For example, in the United States obesity amongst dogs (and cats) has risen (along with insurance claims for ailments related to being overweight).
14 Dog-walking is, of course, a major form of urban social interaction for both dogs and humans.
15 The corresponding figures for the Global South were 137 million dogs and 126 million cats.
16 It isn't just about euthanasia, of course. There is also the vexed issue of spaying and neutering and the treatment of the pet. One survey of British dog owners found that more than a quarter believe that it is acceptable to leave a dog alone at home for up to 10 hours a day, even though they are sociable pack animals (Newkey-Burden, 2019).

17   Mumbai is often regarded as a sanctuary city for these dogs.
18   And, indeed, the massive industry that has sprung up around the care of dogs as they have become standard urban accoutrements, like the rise of dogwalking services, dog carers, and so on.
19   Though the famous article by Charles Dickens had already helped to bring the Home into the public eye (see Dickens, 1862).
20   The situation was more robust in New York. In the late nineteenth century, dogcatchers rounded up the city's stray dogs and transported them to a crowded dog pound, where they were loaded into large crates and drowned in the East River. In one incident documented in 1887, more than 700 dogs were disposed of in this manner in a single morning. In 1894, a New York State law abolished the dog pound and the American Society for the Prevention of Cruelty to Animals (ASPCA, founded in 1866) took over the care of homeless dogs and cats in the city.
21   Cats were first taken into Battersea in 1883.
22   It's still not clear whether those cats were euthanized or simply died from disease in shelters.
23   The carnifex was the public executioner of Rome, who put enslaved people and foreigners to death, but not citizens. The office was considered so disgraceful that the carnifex was not allowed to reside within the city. The similarities to the current situation are almost too great!
24   Also of note were all of the trades that depended on slaughterhouses, many of which involved noxious production processes: tanning, glue, catgut, tallow, colours like Prussian Blue, and the range of pies and offal.
25   Though South Omaha has an equal claim to this dubious crown (see Pachirat, 2011).
26   These cover 95 per cent of all deaths. They exclude slaughter on farms. Geese, guinea fowl, ostriches, emus, rheas and pigeons are not included.
27   Milk is, of course, produced by many animals, far more than first thought, even including 'insect milk'.
28   In the United States, milk production per cow increased by 13 per cent between 2007 and 2016 (Gillespie, 2018).
29   For a long time, there were numerous dairy cows in London. By 1850 there were 20,000 dairy cows in London, mainly living in cowsheds, some of which housed as many as 500 cows. Even after the railways started to bring milk into London, dairy cows remained a feature of London life – in 1906 there were still 15,000 cows in London and the last herd survived until the 1960s (Velten, 2013).
30   A number of smaller slaughterhouses, mainly halal, are not inspected (*New York Times*, 2016).
31   About 60 per cent of fish was East Coast wild caught.
32   Nearly half of the beef consumed in the United States is found in the form of the hamburger, a deracinated slab of 'de-animalization'.
33   This is to ignore the trade in animal products which are not food-related. Most recently, donkeys are being slaughtered in many parts of the world in order to satisfy the Chinese desire for medicinal products.
34   For example, according to the *Rabobank Global Meat and Poultry Outlook* (2018) (https://meatindustry.ru/upload/iblock/c78/c78a2abcec71d6d2c6e7574f01e21a5e.pdf) the total world trade of pork was estimated at approximately $20.5 billion in 2018. Four exporters dominate the market: the European Union, the United States, Canada and Brazil. China is the number one global net importer. China is the only country whose government keeps a strategic pork reserve.
35   Recreational landings are modest in comparison, not least because catch-and-release has become more common. A recent study (Freire et al., 2020) found that recreational catches have increased from 280,000 tonnes in the mid-1950s to about 900,000 tonnes in 2014. The hunting of sharks and rays for 'fun' accounts for as much as 6 per cent of the catch, and this is having real impacts on the prospects for these species.

36 Fishing, often large-scale, was integral to the lives of most early cities, which tended to be located near to estuaries, lakes or rivers and often included complex fish-processing facilities. It can be argued that fishing came before farming and was sometimes more important in allowing cities to be established.
37 A recent study (K.R. Jones et al., 2018) found that just 13.2 per cent of the world's oceans could be classified as 'wilderness' (i.e. areas less affected by human activity) – mostly located in international waters near the Arctic, Antarctic and around Pacific Island nations, or in the open ocean.
38 Though China, like many other governments, is trying to cut back on these subsidies.
39 Furthermore, these species play a critical role in transporting organic carbon to the deep sea; the effects of harvesting this biomass on marine carbon cycles are completely unknown.
40 Other deep sea activities like seabed mining are likely to extinguish all kinds of rare maritime dwellers like, for example, the scaly-foot snail whose shell is armoured with multi-layered iron sulphide so that it can with withstand the pressures at depth.
41 According to one report, deep sea trawlers are catching 42 per cent more fish than they report. In the past 65 years, they have caught 11 million more tonnes of fish than they have reported. The situation is particularly serious so far as deep-sea fish are concerned (Webster, 2018).
42 In the United States. fish-farming began in the 1960s on the northeast coast and by the late 1980s and early 1990s had begun to make its way up the coasts of Canada.
43 Some 1,657 shark incidents have been recorded in North American waters since 1900, of which 144 were fatal. In Australia the corresponding figures are 904 and 259, in South Africa 395 and 96. Only 17 shark attacks have occurred in British waters since 1785, and only one proved fatal. Each year, on average, cows kill seven people in the UK.
44 One estimate goes as high as 100 million. The result is clear anyway. The great white, hammerhead, oceanic whitetip and thresher have all fallen in number by 90 per cent in the past 60 years.
45 The method uses lines that can reach 100 kilometres in length and include hundreds of hooks. It is the fishing practice that catches the most pelagic sharks.
46 The obvious example is cochineal, a red dye extracted from the tiny cochineal insect that parasitizes the prickly pear cactus. It became closely associated with the projection of Spanish imperial power. So rich was the cochineal trade that it was ranked second only to silver as the most valuable export from Spain's American colonies, more profitable even than gold. Its use only died out as synthetic dyes became available.

7
Not Meat But Still Dead

Not every animal that is killed purposefully in the service of the city's inhabitants is there to produce meat. It is worth considering just how toxic cities can be for other animals around the world as well as meat animals[1]. Consider just four examples of direct killings.

First, there are the animals that are killed for sport (though some may then become meat). Consider the commercial shooting of pheasants, partridges, grouse and wildfowl in the UK. This industry has grown by 5 per cent each year by volume of birds killed over the last decade. Take just the case of pheasants. Out of the approximately 43 million non-native pheasants released into the British countryside each year (as opposed to the 3–4 million released in 1970), about 13 million pheasants are shot (Avery, 2019; Pringle et al., 2019)[2]. Many of these pheasants are intensively reared. The country's ten biggest game shoots released 1.4 million birds for shooting last year – more than the smallest 3,000 shoots combined. On many estates, up to 600 birds can be killed for 6 days a week for the length of the season in a kind of gigantic shoot-em-up game but with real deaths. Millions of pheasants and partridges are being dispatched in this way, resulting in a glut. Many of these birds are not eaten but dumped in landfill or left to rot. Only 6 per cent of pheasants make it into the food chain through licensed game-processing plants. Since many of the clientele for the large-scale shoots live in cities this death toll is an urban issue.

Then there are the animals that are killed to service science and medicine. Mice, rats, guinea pigs, birds and fish constitute a massive worldwide market. For example, the global market for gene-altered mice is predicted to expand by 7.5 per cent a year to over $1.59 billion by 2022, with mice selling for as much as $17,000 a pair. One company, Jackson Laboratory, has 11,000 strains of mice in its catalogue and is adding around another 600 each year, boosted by gene-editing technologies like CRISPR–Cas9 (Einhorn, 2019).

Statistics on animals used up in medical testing, for example, by being given cancer or transplanted organs, are imperfect. For example, the United States counts only warm-blooded animals in research, teaching, and testing except for rats, mice, fish and birds that were bred for research. The EU counts all vertebrates as well as cephalopods like octopuses and squid. Currently, no country counts all invertebrates (e.g. fruit flies and nematode worms). One 2005 estimate (Taylor et al., 2008) found that 115,300,000 animals were killed each year. Another later estimate (Lush, 2014) put the

2012 figure at 118,390,040. However, these figures are likely to be underestimates since they do not include figures for countries like Brazil, India and especially China. China is becoming a major centre for animal testing. In recognition of this fact, Charles River Laboratories, the world's largest provider of animals for medical testing, now has 650 employees in in Beijing and Shanghai (Einhorn, 2019).

Then there are animals that are trafficked. These animals are likely to have shortened lives in collectors' hands, even if they do not die while in transit, or they are transported only as deracinated body parts, as in the case of black bears in Myanmar (e.g. Auliya et al., 2016; Nijman et al., 2017). Or they may simply become part of the wildlife farming industry: notoriously, in China, nearly 20,000 wildlife farms have raised species including peacocks, civet cats, monkeys, porcupines, foxes, racoons, bamboo rats, squirrels, snakes, toads, ostriches, wild geese and boar as part of an officially sanctioned policy of 'wildlife domestication'[3] (Standaert, 2020). One study (Scheffers et al., 2019) found that one in five vertebrates that live on land is traded in wildlife markets, often to satisfy urban consumers' whims and fancies as either entertainment or meat. A total of 5,579 of the 31,745 vertebrate species analysed – about 18 per cent – were being bought and sold around the world. This number includes more than 2,000 birds and nearly 1,500 mammals, many of which are captured illegally from the wild, although the figures also include legal farmed trade. The study looked only at land-based vertebrates. If invertebrates and water-dwelling animals had been included, the number of traded species would have been much, much higher.

Finally, there is the eradication of 'pests'. The pest eradication industry has a long history in cities (Biehler, 2013; Velten 2013), as has the history of its different modes of killing, from traps to dichlorodiphenyltrichloroethane (DDT). Pest controllers' vans are a standard sight in many cities, 'controlling' many different kinds of animals, not just rats and mice[4] – still the bulk of the market – but also a vast panoply of insects, from moths and beetles and wasps, through cockroaches and termites[5] and bed bugs to the threat of vector-borne diseases that are carried by mosquitoes, sandflies, triatomine bugs, blackflies, ticks, tsetse flies, mites and lice.

There are no reliable figures on how many animals classed as 'vermin' (a loaded word that in many places has given way to less stark descriptions) are killed this way. But we do know that there are 40,000 pest control companies worldwide, generating sales of around $18 billion per annum, mainly targeted at urban commercial and residential space. The global market, driven in part by urbanization and its effects like piles, of compost and rubbish, litter, birdfeeding and poorly maintained sewer pipes, as well as by warmer weather, increasing resistance to rodenticides and a particular boom in cockroaches (that rats in particular love to eat), is growing by around 5 per cent per annum (Rentokil, 2018). Pest controllers also figure, along with many other actors, in the agricultural areas that feed cities. It is commonplace to trap beavers and possums, poison rats, mice and cats, shoot and poison badgers and wolves and squirrels, gas rabbits and generally do away with millions of animals that might threaten agricultural production. Then there are the secondary effects. For example, rodents can take many days to die from poisoning, during which time they are often predated. Recent UK government figures show that 90 per cent of barn owl carcasses contained rodenticide (Harrison, 2020)[6]. In other words, to get in the way of the agrilogistic machine is many times a death sentence.

Some pests, like the fly, have dwindled in their impact on cities of the Global North (mainly because of the decline of the horse as an urban dweller) but others persist. But pest control is rarely a rout. Take the case of that ultimate urban survivor – the rat. We know that the black rat was present in Roman London, though it has now been joined by the brown rat, which first entered the city sometime in the first half of the eighteenth century (Velten, 2013). Rats have been urban survivors for so long because they are clearly intelligent animals. For example:

> rats are capable of reliving memories of past experiences and mentally planning ahead… They reciprocally trade different kinds of goods with each other, understand not only when they owe a favour to another rat, but also that the favour can be paid back in a different currency. When they make a wrong choice, they display something that appears very close to regret…. Rats can be taught cognitively demanding skills such as driving a vehicle to reach a desired goal, playing hide-and-seek with a human, and using the appropriate tool to access out-of-reach food. (Andrews and Monsó, 2020: 2)

Rats also seem to demonstrate empathy. A number of experiments show that rats react to other rats' suffering in ways which demonstrate something that seems suspiciously like care. Partly because of these qualities of cognitive agility, it is widely recognized that rats cannot be exterminated en masse. Their populations can only be 'managed' and a good part of the reason is the nature of urban environments.

New York, which comes third after Chicago and Los Angeles in one ranking of America's 'rattiest' cities, is a case in point. An urban construction boom meant more digging up of burrows, forcing rats out into the open. Milder winters – the result of climate change – make it easier for rats to survive and reproduce. And the city's growing population and thriving tourism has generated more rubbish for rats to feed on. In 2017, the Mayor of New York called for 'more rat corpses'. He unveiled a $32 million assault on rats, which included not just increased litter basket pickups but also the deployment of solar-powered, rubbish compacting bins and rat-resistant steel cans as well as more culling: for example, the city uses dry ice to smother rats where they live. But in 2018, city health inspections still found 30,874 instances of 'active rat signs' (such as sightings and droppings) at buildings and properties, nearly double the number of instances found in 2014 (Hu, 2019)[7].

Mean Streets

The killing doesn't stop there, though. For many animals, a city's layout and design resembles a gigantic snare, suddenly snapping down and catching them in its embrace. Urban infrastructure kills animals, lots of animals. It really does. Most of the time, though not always, this is because of lack of thought or simple indifference, not any kind of conscious plot. It's rather like the way that women are designed out of urban space and time by the assumption that men are the default (Criado Perez, 2019) – urban spaces become indifferent, exclusionary or downright lethal for animals because no thought has ever been given to their presence except in the guise of pests, food or pets. A few simple examples will suffice to make the case.[8]

Let's begin with buildings or, more precisely, windows. Bird strike into windows has been claimed to be the second largest source of avian mortality (Klem, 2009)[9]. In the United States, a benchmark study by Klem et al. (1990) estimated that each building in the United States kills between one and ten birds every year. Using 1986 US Census data, they then estimated that a yearly range of some 97.6 to 975.6 million birds were being killed. (This number must have risen considerably since given the continuing increase in new construction across North America[10].) A more recent estimate (Loss et al., 2018) gives a slightly higher range of between 365 and 988 million birds. In Canada, one estimate suggests that about 25 million birds die each year in that country from window collisions (Machtans et al., 2013). There are 4,000 species of migratory birds in the world and they are especially affected by cities because they are so susceptible to artificial light at night (ALAN)[11]. Their deaths are concentrated in particular brightly lit cities which lie on spring and autumn migratory routes. In the United States, for example, that means especially Chicago[12], Dallas and Houston followed by cities like New York, Los Angeles, St Louis and Atlanta (Horton et al., 2019). There are some estimates for individual cities. For example, it is thought that between 90,000 and 200,000 birds are killed in building collisions in New York each year.

Next, take the case of power lines. They might look harmless but they are mass killers. All kinds of animals, particularly birds, collide with or are electrocuted by power lines each year. How many? No one really knows for sure. Around the world, power line bird collision may cause more than 1 billion deaths. In the United States, one estimate (Loss et al., 2014) is that between 12 and 64 million birds are killed each year at US power lines, with between 8 and 57 million birds killed by collision and between 0.9 and 11.6 million birds killed by electrocution (Nuwer, 2019). Between 10 and 41 million birds are killed annually by power line collisions in Canada (Bernardino et al., 2018). These kinds of death rates rank power lines above deaths from wind turbines[13], which are more often picked out. In both cases, certain species seem more susceptible than others. It's not just birds, of course. Other animals are susceptible too, as the periodic brown-outs and blackouts that occur in cities from animals eating through cables show only too well.

Then take the phenomenon of roadkill (Forman and Alexander, 1998; van der Ree et al., 2015). As Knutson wrote in his aptly named field guide, *Flattened Fauna* (cited in Kroll, 2018: 2): 'Fast cars and hard-surfaced roads have produced the entire flattened fauna described here in less than an eye-blink of evolutionary time'. Indeed, so great is the toll that it may even be having evolutionary consequences (Brady and Richardson, 2017). Attempts to document roadkill first took place as early as 1935 but the statistics are still uncertain, not least because other animals hoover up roadkill at some pace. However, it seems likely that roads are the largest cause of anthropogenic mortality, after legal forms of killing, for many vertebrates. The number of animals killed on the roads each day in the United States is estimated at over a million per day, with 340 million birds alone killed annually. In Canada the annual toll of birds is 13.8 million. In Sweden 8.5 million. And so on. Other countries have comparable levels of avian mortality (Schwartz et al., 2020). In the United States, another estimate is that 365 million vertebrates are killed on the roads each year, 1–2 million of which are deer. 'This annual number of [killed] animals also includes 1.2 million dogs, 5.4 million cats, and between 4,000 and 5,000 humans' (Kroll, 2018: 3). Roadkill is estimated to be responsible for 50 per cent of the deaths of endangered Florida panthers[14]. And so on.

In all, between 350,000 and 27 million birds are estimated to be killed on European roads each year. In the UK, numbers of animals killed are probably in the millions, with one estimate totalling 2.5 million (Schwartz et al., 2020), a toll headed by badgers and pheasants and the estimated 100,000 hedgehogs killed each year[15]. Another recent study (Baxter-Gilbert et al., 2015) showed that insects, too, are prone to a very high risk of roadkill incidence[16]. Some animals are clearly more susceptible than others. Take the case of barn owls in the UK, a species that is currently doing quite well, in part because of the human provision of more nesting boxes (80 per cent of barn owls now use them). Even so, about a third of the barn owls that fledge each year are killed on motorways and dual carriageways (Harrison, 2020). Barn owls fly low and slow as they hunt along verges and field margins, looking down at the ground. That makes them vulnerable to fast-moving traffic, particularly if a road has no trees along its margins that will force them to gain height. (Of course, it is worth remembering that roadkill is also a substantial source of food for scavengers like crows, vultures, foxes, bears, and many insects. Indeed, ominously perhaps, some of the most successful birds in recent times have been those that feed on the dead. They are also likely to become victims themselves as they fail to dodge the traffic.)[17]

Animals are also a substantial risk to human life where roads are concerned. Kangaroos are involved in over 80 per cent of the 20,000-plus vehicle-animal collisions reported each year in Australia (Berlin, 2019). In the UK, between 2005 and 2017, 100 people were killed in accidents where an animal was involved, with a further 14,173 injured.

It is not just roads acting to kill and cut off habitats. There are also the railways. Around the world they kill many wild and domestic animals – from reindeer through elephants and bears to cows (Borda-de-Água et al., 2017). In the UK, deaths, which are less extensive, nearly all involved damaged fencing which allowed animals to stray on to the line. Most of the deaths were outside urban boundaries but within the main urban fabric. Overall deaths increased by 13 per cent between 2003 and 2014 (Rail Safety and Standards Board, 2014).

And it doesn't stop there. There is also bird strike. Aircraft in the United States strike more than 13,000 birds per year[18] (Kroll, 2018). But far more birds are actually killed by programmes to eradicate birds that might be involved in strikes around airports. For example, nearly 70,000 gulls, starlings, geese and other birds were slaughtered in the New York City area, mostly by shooting and trapping, after the 2009 accident in which a jetliner was forced to land in the Hudson river after birds were sucked into its engine (Associated Press, 2017). Again, aircraft are so sacred that the curlew, an endangered species in southern England, was the subject of licences granted by Natural England permitting the destruction of up to 854 of the birds and their eggs or nests near to airports between 2014 and 2019 (Rochard and Horton, 1980; Carrington et al., 2019).

And there is ship strike too. Though exact figures do not exist, many animals must be killed. For example, 'it seems reasonable to say that every year at least ten whale deaths are caused by colliding with ships moving through North American waters and between 80 and 100 manatees meet their end by Floridian propellers' (Kroll, 2018: 4).

These are all direct deaths but urban infrastructure also shortens lifespans. For example, noise from transportation networks is a global source of habitat degradation. It impairs species' abilities to: attract mates, rear offspring, forage and feed efficiently, communicate, defend against disease and avoid predators. It also alters the sounds that animals produce, as well as how these vocalizations travel. Though there is evidence that the populations of many species of animals may be adapting to traffic and other urban noise, producing different sounds in cities (Tennessen et al., 2018; Sueur et al., 2019), the adaptation can hardly be called optimal. And the noise is not just from transportation networks on land either. In the oceans, noise is an increasing problem adding another stressor which both causes deaths (e.g. as a result of panic dives by cetaceans) and cuts lives short. Evidence is growing concerning the problems arising from the noise created by military sonar, seismic surveys, oil drilling, dredging and ship engines. Short, loud blasts of sound can cause physical damage; persistent background noise, especially from shipping, can alter a host of systems and behaviours, from communication to feeding. Different marine animals have different hearing ranges, which means that the picture can be very complicated. Even so, no one denies that human beings have addled the ocean soundscape. Obviously, data are sparse but we know that global ship traffic doubled between

1950 and 2000, boosting the overall sound level by about 3 decibels a decade. Because sound travels through water differently from the air,

> the blast of a seismic air gun used to map the sea floor for oil and gas can be as loud as a rocket launch or an underwater dynamite explosion; ship engines and oil drilling can reach the roar of a rock concert [...] Some of these sounds are audible for hundreds of kilometers. (Jones, 2019: 159)

Finally, to add to the continuous cull that cities cause, there is extirpation – the local extinction of a species, though it still might exist elsewhere, as a result of the continuing growth of cities whose infrastructure cuts up, cuts off and mangles habitats. Some commentators argue that this is a much more serious problem than is often recognized since it reduces a species' population, genetic diversity and geographic range, and brings it closer to extinction through the death by a thousand cuts. Certainly, the fracturing of habitats by cities is becoming of ever greater concern. For example, local freshwater ecosystems are being threatened by the greater calls cities make on water supplies (Fitzhugh and Richter, 2004), though many of the problems could be solved by more efficient use of water and the implementation of less damaging strategies for storing and diverting water. Again, various butterfly populations have been extirpated in many cities, though sensible use of parkland could ameliorate the process (Bonebrake and Cooper, 2014). The list goes on.

Sometimes the Shoe Is on the Other Foot

But it's not all one way. Cities provide new spaces for animals and they also make these spaces into a melting pot for evolving diseases. Three quarters of the new or emerging diseases that infect humans originate in animals and urban activity multiplies the risks of contagion substantially. Most animals carry a range of pathogens – bacteria and viruses that can cause zoonotic disease as they spill over into humans. A pathogen's evolutionary survival depends on infecting new hosts – and jumping to other species is one way to do this. Cities make this feat much easier to achieve (Bloomfield et al., 2020), as the food poisoning from salmonella and campylobacter, bacterial pathogens commonly found in farm animals, shows only too well. Lyme disease is another well-known bacterial disease, a pathogen transmitted by ticks which have become infected after feeding on deer, birds or mice with the disease. It is linked especially to patchwork woodlands caused by the suburban expansion of cities. However, it is viral diseases which now take up a large amount of our attention because a number of animals are reservoir hosts. It seems likely that the number of viral zoonotic diseases is increasing as domesticated animals like cattle, sheep, pigs, dogs and goats increase in number and as wild animals that have adapted well to living in cities – like rodents, bats and primates – bulk up their populations and live close to one another in ways that would never happen in the wild, leading to the emergence and propagation of zoonosis (Quammen, 2012; Frutos et al., 2020; Johnson et al., 2020). The 1918 'Spanish flu' pandemic probably originated in a pig farm in the Midwest of the United States. The HIV/AIDS epidemic of the 1980s and on originated from great apes. The 2004/07 H7N7 avian flu pandemic came from poultry. Pigs were the source of the swine flu epidemic in 2009. More recently, it has been discovered that severe acute respiratory syndrome (Sars) came from bats, via civets, while bats also gave us the Ebola infection and the Nipah virus. Again, Middle East Respiratory Virus (Mers) seems to have originated in bats (though dromedaries are implicated as intermediaries). The coronavirus called SARS-COV-2, which causes the acute respiratory disease COVID-19, may have originated in a live animal market in a Chinese city which sold wild meat, probably from bats, possibly intermediated by the much-persecuted pangolin (Campbell and Park, 2020 is the best general summary)[19] (though the bulk of 'wild' meat in China is actually farmed, often to compensate smallholders for losing market share to large livestock firms). In other words, humans may well find that the interaction between cities, their food systems and wildlife provides a running tally of pandemics because we destroy the natural environment of animals like bats, leading some of them to adapt to an anthropomorphized environment where, for example, they can feed on the number of insects drawn to lamplight. The result is that different species cross in ways that would not have occurred in the wild.

Those approximately 2 million human deaths arising from zoonotic diseases every year might be counted as the animals' only means of revenge, I suppose. It's a funny kind of revenge, though. Animals get viral diseases too and, in the case of farm animals, are often culled in very large numbers if a viral disease strikes them. (In the UK, for example, foot and mouth disease claimed the lives of 442,000 farm animals in 1967 and over 6 million more in 2001, many of them slaughtered as a preventative measure rather than infected with the disease.) And, then, as if to add to the consequences of COVID-19 viral transmission, because of low demand from the catering industry, dislocated supply chains and virus-induced low worker attendance at slaughterhouses leading to some closures, farm animals were on the front line. Chickens were 'depopulated', to use the industry parlance, in their millions: in the UK, at least 400,000 chickens were killed (Kevany, 2020b). In the US meanwhile, one company euthanized nearly 2 million chickens in just a month, as well as 61,000 laying hens (Hauser, 2020). Pigs were killed too. Pork-processing capacity in the US fell by nearly 40 per cent. The result? In Iowa, 600,000 pigs were killed. In Minnesota another 90,000 (Corkery and Yaffe-Bellany, 2020b). As many as 10 million pigs may have been killed in all via anaesthetic overdose, gassing, shooting, electrocution, blunt force trauma or even ventilation shutdown (Kevany, 2020a)[20]. In Denmark, millions of mink farmed for their fur, were put down because of a mutated coronavirus infection that was apparently spreading from them to humans. To add to this global death toll, many laboratory animals were euthanized as well. Still, all that said, some wild animals did enjoy the benefits of a so-called 'anthropause' like reduced noise and traffic, leading to animals wandering through locked-down cities, animals never seen before in cities exploring urban environs, normally nocturnal animals appearing in the daytime, animals like birds calling with much improved quality at lower amplitudes, and so on (Stokstad, 2020; Derryberry et al., 2020). On the other hand, a number of urban natives like rats suddenly found their diets severely reduced (Rutz et al., 2020; Zhang, 2020).

And Don't Forget Climate Change

What often also goes unremarked on is that all manner of interactions between the growth of cities and human-induced climate change – like greater incidence of wildfires – affect many other beings as well as humans[21], a point that that doyen of American conservation, Aldo Leopold, who famously wrote of the need to extend obligation and responsibility beyond the human by way of a land ethic, would no doubt have made – if he hadn't died fighting a wildfire in 1948 (Warde et al., 2018).

Climate change challenges animals just as much as humans. For example, one thing that is still unclear is the effects of the new more frequent and intense fire regime on the animals that live in and around the forests which now interdigitate with cities to a much greater degree. The same stricture applies equally to flooding, pollution, heat, sea level rise and many other stressors. But, in truth, there are no really accurate estimates of the numbers of animals killed in forest fires, heatwaves or floods, or who die from the various kinds of pollution, in or around cities. But we know that these effects are unlikely to be positive, to put it but mildly. Farmed animals can die in their hundreds of thousands. For example, in 2018 Hurricane Florence swept through North Carolina. The resulting floods killed at least 3.4 million farm animals. Where wild animals are concerned, numbers of deaths are far more difficult to count.

Take just fires again (Pyne, 2015; Kodas; 2017; Struzik, 2017; Scott, 2018). One RSPCA estimate from Australia reckoned that in the 2009 'Black Saturday' fires in the state of Victoria, up to 1 million animals died (Verghis, 2019). In the more recent 2019/20 fires, 800 million wild animals were estimated to have died in the state of New South Wales alone (Dickman, 2020). But the 2019/20 Australian bushfires show the rub[22]. All kinds of figures were bandied about with the most authoritative estimate being that nearly 3 billion Australian wild animals were in the path of the fires (which does not mean that 3 billion wild animals died) (Dickman et al., 2020). But they were necessarily estimates. This figure, like others, relied on estimates of the average densities per hectare of mammals, birds and reptiles and then multiplied these figures by the amount of land hit by the fires. But, fish, insects and invertebrates were excluded. Obviously, large animals, like kangaroos or emus, as well as many birds, can move away from a fire as it approaches but less mobile species and smaller animals that depend on the forest itself are more likely to die. Indeed, some animals can become extinct, simply because of their limited range[23]. Even many of those animals that survive an actual fire, either by fleeing or going underground, will die later, because of smoke inhalation or because of lack of food in the area (so-called 'starvation events') or because of lack of shelter or because they fall victim to introduced predators such as feral cats and red foxes. Even those birds and animals able to flee to unaffected areas are rarely able to successfully compete with animals already living there and succumb within a short time (Nimmo et al., 2018; Zielinski and Zachos, 2018).

Climate change can interact with animals and cities in other ways too. Take the movement of animals. Just like humans, many animals are now involved in great migrations to new areas of the planet. But the movements can be far more specific than that. Live export of farm animals is a $21 billion global trade which is reckoned to involve nearly 2 billion animals each year (Osborne and van der Zee, 2020). In particular, live farm animal exports to the cities of the Middle East have risen steadily, the result of rapid urban population growth coupled with increasing demand for meat and dairy products (especially in cultures whose norms mean that meat may be understood as a marker of a family's ability to provide, and serving meat to a guest is a gesture of hospitality). The conditions for rearing these animals from birth in situ are often inappropriate since they require large amounts of water and they are being made ever more problematic by the water stress induced by climate change. For example, dairy cows, mainly imported from America and Germany, can drink 30 to 50 gallons of water a day. Cattle reared for meat may consume slightly less water, but the amount is still sufficient to encourage water-scarce and increasingly urbanized countries to look for ways to attenuate the amount of time they have the animals in their care (usually 6 months at a maximum) (Michaelson and van der Zee, 2020).

Or take the issue of urban food security more generally. Much attention has been given to the difficulties that animal food supply from the land will face as a result of climate change. But the oceans are just as important, and just as badly affected. For example, recent studies have shown that oysters are shrinking in size, and their shells are becoming weaker. Sardines are also declining in size, the result of a lack of food which can mainly be attributed to ocean warming (Bremner, 2020). Over the last 10 years, sardines have lost two thirds of their average mass in the Mediterranean while those in the Atlantic off France have lost half of their weight. Shortage of food is also cutting short the lifespan of sardines in the Mediterranean. The average lifespan has fallen to 1 year from 3 years a decade ago. Even more worryingly, climate change, combined with nutrient pollution from farming and industry, is driving oxygen from the oceans, threatening many species of fish – especially larger fish – in the process. Around 700 ocean sites now suffer from low oxygen levels, compared with 45 in the 1960s (Laffoley and Baxter, 2019).

Stop the Killing

Whatever happens next, one goal must be to create a city which calls a halt to unnecessary killing and puts a damper on the associated suffering. We need to inject a measure of clarity here, however. Killing and suffering are both parts of life. You might even argue, as Lestel (2016) does, that meat-eating is an acknowledgement of an evolutionary impulse that entails killing in order to live and that carnivory is just as or more ethical than vegetarianism (though even Lestel considers factory farming to be a 'crime against the living' (p. 91). Whatever the case, there is no simple answer to be had. The choice between 'animal rights' and the 'greater human good', like the choice for or against anthropocentrism, is a false one. 'Both of these proceed as if calculation solved the dilemma and all […] we have to do is choose' (Haraway, 2008: 87). For example, predation is one of the primary engines of evolution. But that doesn't mean that human beings have been given a licence to kill without restraint: the killing of animals is never 'comfortable or clear-cut, never straightforward. Our existence on the planet is a problem, but it isn't a problem to be solved' (Diski, 2010: 297). It is a dilemma which isn't going to go away.

Relatively few people nowadays argue that animals were put on the planet just to serve our needs by, quite literally, 'sucking up living labor' (Marx, 1867: 179). But still, there is an inclination, insofar as people want to think about the issue at all, to think that the billions of animal deaths caused by humans every year are, if not unimportant then not as important as our own, and, to a greater or lesser extent, unavoidable. Animals' deaths are the price we have to pay, regrettable as that may be. They are the collateral damage of modern life, the blood sacrifice that has to be made to keep cities fed and profits flowing. We may not like it but it's a regrettable fact of life. Not so. This is a choice that has been made and choices can be altered.

At the same time, we also need to be careful not to let the fact of these deaths distract us from farmed animals' often restricted lives. As one farmer puts it (cited in Foer, 2009: 115) 'people focus on the last second of death. I want them to focus on the entire life of the animal.' Many animals live as well as die in appalling conditions: think back to the chicken and the cow and the pig (Velten, 2007). Being a commodity is not much fun, in other words. It is true that most people are ignorant of the precise facts about these conditions, but that is in part because they avoid seeking them out. This tendency to elide thinking about cruelty might be thought of as being a bit like sympathetic magic: if you think about it, you become involved in it. Indeed, you might then have to extend sympathy to the unfortunates (Hume, 2010). So, best not to think about it.

Whatever the case, what we have now is something different from the casual cruelties of yore, bad enough as those might have been. Now we have something that does not acknowledge or honour animal life or death or suffering but instead hides it away as part of an industrial machine that wants to standardize and cauterize in order to make beings killable (Haraway, 2008).

The killing often lacks any thoughtfulness, both in the sense of thinking about how animals are being killed, and in giving thought to them as beings that we might respond to and honour in some way. No rituals here, then, to salve our conscience. No thought that this killing might be counted by some as murder – that's a word reserved for humans (Derrida, 2008; Haraway, 2008). Instead a machine, one that generates an atmosphere of disregard, not even disrespect. To say that this behaviour is suspect is neither to underestimate its complexity, nor the urgency of a change of heart. It is about coming to understand that we are an accidental species not so very different from those that we lord it over and that 'sentience, that seemingly quintessential human characteristic, is an artifact maintained by human exceptionalism – and has given up with hardly a whimper' (Gee, 2013: 167), falling to the ground just like many of the other pillars of human exceptionalism.

But It's Not Quite That Simple

But the toll of surplus death generated by cities comes with its own quandaries. There isn't an easy 'just stop killing things' fix. As Haraway (2008) points out, issues that involve this kind of responsibility are never a matter of simple calculation. Two examples will suffice. One is that the rise of the companion animal has spawned a burgeoning pet food industry which largely relies on animal products. In 2017, the global pet food industry was worth $94 billion and it is expected to grow much further (Fleming, 2018)[24]. For example, in China, where pet ownership has historically been rare, the market grew by 100 per cent in 2017 and in 2019 pet food overtook baby formula as the highest-selling imported product on China's biggest shopping day of the year, Singles Day (Tang, 2019). If China follows the same trends as other countries there will soon be millions more pets – and a correspondingly larger demand for pet food. On one estimate, as much as a quarter of the impact of world meat production can now be attributed to the pet food industry (Fleming, 2018). If that estimate is even close to correct, the industry is having a very large environmental impact, paid for in animal deaths and environmental damage (such as carbon dioxide production and faeces (Okin, 2017), showing that not all the consequences of symbiotic relationships are necessarily good ones.

The other is that, in many parts of the world, on the list of anthropogenic causes of death, the biggest urban killer of birds (and, indeed, many other animals) is probably the humble domestic cat gone feral (Marra and Santella, 2016). By one estimate, cats kill 1.3–4.0 billion birds and 6.3–22.3 billion mammals annually in the United States (Loss et al., 2013a; 2015). Unowned cats[25], as opposed to owned pets, cause the majority of this mortality, which suggests that, sometimes at least, cities or at least parts of cities – may be safer places for birds and certain other animals. In Australia, the situation is even worse proportionately. There some 2–6 million feral cats roam freely. In addition to mammals, many of which are near to extinction, these cats kill an estimated 377 million birds and 649 million reptiles every year (Woinarski et al., 2015; 2019; Aguirre, 2019). In New Zealand similarly, one estimate (Van Heezik et al., 2010) is that the country's 1.4 million cats alone kill at least 18.76 million animals a year, including 1.12 million native birds.

In other words, in a topsy-turvy anthropogenic world, it is not possible to avoid uncomfortable judgements which may well, for example, involve reparative killing of some 'awkward' animals – not just cats but also feral pigs, goats, rats and squirrels, as well as ocean dwellers like the crown of thorns starfish, which is busily hoovering up Great Barrier Reef coral – in order to save others. However uncomfortable it may be, killing sometimes has to be placed alongside care. Equally, the justifications for making animals killable in these situations – for example, balancing ecosystems or controlling 'invasive' species – are not all the same or equally reprehensible (Ginn, 2014; Ginn et al., 2014; Crowley et al., 2018). To insist on a hard-line animal rights discourse can sometimes be a way of avoiding choices about coexistence that have to be made to preserve other animals and general biodiversity. In Australia, New Zealand and in many other locations these are not choices that can be shied away from. We can abhor animals being carelessly killed. That's one thing. But we cannot shuck off all responsibility for surplus animal death unless we also reckon with the surplus animal deaths caused by some other animals. After all, we caused many of these problems in the first place.

Notes

1. Of course, animals in cities are also responsible for human deaths, though nowhere near as many. For example, as cities have expanded they have often encroached on prime snake territory. About 11,000 people a month are thought to die from snakebite, and a further 450,000 suffer life-changing injuries (Casewell and Ainsworth, 2019). Most of these deaths and injuries occur in remote areas of sub-Saharan Africa, South Asia and Latin America, not in urban agglomerations.
2. The rest are expected to make their own way, resulting in a bonanza for crows, ravens and other avian predators, and for foxes and badgers, as well as very large amounts of roadkill which benefit buzzards and kites (Pringle et al., 2019). The pheasants also present a real problem for certain kinds of British wildlife, especially reptiles which they will kill (such as the adder which is now endangered, in part because of the surplus of pheasants). Other European countries release far fewer birds. Three million captive-reared birds are released in Spain and 15 million in France.
3. One study by the Chinese Academy of Engineering put the value of the wildlife industry at $18 billion with 6.3 million practitioners (Wang et al., 2020).
4. Pigeons are also a target in some cities, though birds are a small percentage of the market.
5. Which, in many places that use wood construction, can be more destructive than fire or flood.
6. Some US states like California have passed laws outlawing rodenticides, even though that means more mice and rats.
7. Many other US cities have large rat populations, including Chicago, Philadelphia and Los Angeles.

8   The fact that most figures are broad estimates reflects the fact that, until relatively recently, figuring out these numbers was a very low priority, an index of the lack of attention given to these issues.
9   These figures are contested, though. The British Trust for Ornithology has estimated that up to 100 million birds strike windows each year in the UK, and that a third of them subsequently die – a calculation based on the number of ringed birds found dead near windows. By contrast, the UK's largest bird charity, the Royal Society for the Protection of Birds, does not see windows as being a major threat in the UK (McDonald, 2013). See the nascent Global Bird Collision Mapper at https://birdmapper.org/app/ (accessed June 30, 2020).
10 Though Klem et al. (2009) make another estimate of approximately 34 million annual glass victims across urban areas of North America north of Mexico during the main migratory periods in autumn and spring.
11 Songbirds are especially badly affected. They tend to emit faint chirps called 'flight calls' during migration and are more likely to chirp when they see the bright lights of a city, luring other birds in (Erickson, 2019).
12 On one estimate 5 million birds from as many as 250 different species fly through Chicago's downtown every autumn and spring.
13 For the purposes of comparison, in the United States between 140,000 and 328,000 birds are killed by monopole turbines every year, with mortality being greater the taller the turbine (Loss et al., 2013b). Much of the death toll can likely be halted by painting one blade black, which seems like it might reduce bird fatalities by as much as 70 per cent (May et al., 2020).
14 https://projectsplatter.co.uk/ (accessed June 30, 2020).
15 Remedial action was taken here. A highway was engineered to be more permeable, using underpasses, which has at least mitigated the killing (Kroll, 2018).
16 As are snakes, drawn to the warmth of the roads as a place to bask.
17 Of course, there is a strong spatial pattern to roadkill. For example, Kreling et al. (2019) found that urban areas close to wildland where a road forms a geographical boundary were particularly susceptible.
18 Though this is likely an underestimate since the Federal Aviation Administration does not mandate reporting and small birds would probably be killed unnoticed in many cases. There is also some evidence that quieter engines in modern jets are making it more difficult for birds to evade them.
19 Wildlife farms and markets in China have now been closed down but, sadly, a trade in 'medicinal' products will continue.
20 Generally, the pigs had grown too big to be slaughtered commercially. Pigs are raised to grow to about 300 lb over about 6 months. Pigs that grow overly much above that weight are unsafe for slaughterhouse workers to hoist up along the slaughter line. So farmers were forced to kill them and dispose of their carcasses (Blanchette, 2020).
21 Though it is also worth noting the numbers of humans killed who met their deaths because they had refused to leave or had gone back for their animals.
22 One solution to fire is often made out to be backburning. Australia's dry bush has co-evolved with fire, so regular planned burning can be a good thing, especially if it takes up the native 'little but a lot' practices that are now becoming popular. But that is only true up to a point. A number of rare species depend on 'old growth' bush up to 100 years old, and over-frequent burning can put them under long-term threat (Nimmo et al., 2014).
23 For example, in the 2019/20 Australian fires it is possible that a host of different insects with limited ranges have become extinct, such as velvet worms, trapdoor spiders and alpine grasshoppers. On the other hand, fire beetles head towards the fires to mate (Sullivan, 2020).
24 In 2014, UK pet owners spent about £6 billion on pets. In the same year, US owners spent about $60 billion (Bradshaw, 2017).
25 Unowned cats include farm cats, strays and cats that are completely feral.

8
But Some Animals Do Adapt to the City

Cities clearly promote intense mixing under conditions which are often very challenging to life (heat, noise, aridity, pollution, etc.) and act to force physiological and behavioural change. Some animals cannot survive in urban conditions but others thrive, sometimes for obvious reasons, other times less so. Very often the survivors tend to be generalists like the three main commensal rodents (the house mouse, the black rat and the brown rat) or birds like pigeons (*Columba livia* or rock doves)[1], originally coastal and mountain dwelling birds. Domesticated some 5,000 to 10,000 years ago as a food source, they escaped and can now seemingly live anywhere[2]. There are also the parasites like bed bugs and head lice. In the chapter that follows, I want to consider some of the evidence for positive adaptations like these. I will begin with changes in actual behaviour. Then, I will consider animal adaptation through two other lenses, genetics and evolution, in order to show just how quickly some animals can adjust to an urban milieu, far more quickly than was originally believed.

In making this survey, it is important to note that cities do not consist of one environment to which animals adapt. They are composed of myriad habitats, some, like central business districts often all but concreted over but offering rich sources of food for certain opportunists, others like the great indoors making space for certain specific species, and yet others, like parks or river courses or areas with large gardens or even golf courses acting as major green spaces. Animals tend to adapt to these and other specific spaces, and a few generalist animals can be found in many of them. The centre of a city like London, which has a network of centrally located parks, is more friendly to wildlife than the centre of a city like New York, where green space is, Central Park notwithstanding, much more limited[3]. But in the central city, as well as in other scattered urban locations, brownfield sites can rapidly transform into what Mabey (2010 [1973]) famously called the 'unofficial countryside', odds and ends of spontaneous green space which can often harbour a rich ecology. Farther out, cities turn into a complex mosaic of different kinds of edge habitat which can make an easy home for some kinds of wildlife, especially because of deliberate feeding practices which may well encourage animals to set up shop. For example, there is a multi-billion-dollar global industry dedicated to feeding wild birds in residential gardens, which has increased the resource base open to many bird species. In Britain, it is estimated that up to half of British homeowners feed the birds in their gardens (using mixes and types of feeder that have become more and more complex and species-specific), providing enough supplementary food to help to support approximately 196 million birds (Orros and Fellowes, 2015). This feeding has had lasting effects on the size and mix of bird species (with some species becoming more abundant and others fading) and is at a sufficient scale that it is having evolutionary impacts (Plummer et al., 2019). Farther out again, in some countries like the United States, we arrive at what might be called the 'wilderburbs' (Bramwell, 2016), developments so far out in the countryside that they share the inherent risks that are found there, including wild animals which can be distinctly unfriendly, but from which residents often still expect to be protected in the same way as they do from natural hazards like wildfires.

Finally, all of these patches of habitat are connected up in different ways which can help or hinder animal lives, given that many animals move around between them. Many of the species that now live in cities do not have shuttered territorial geographies. True, some species, like pigeons, tend to stick to tight territories close to where they were born, But others are more mobile (Hodgetts and Lorimer, 2018). Indeed, to add to the complexity of animal movement in the city, some species also have considerable intra-species variation. English foxes, for example, can take on at least four guises – breeders, subordinates, juveniles and transients – which imply quite different urban geographies.

> On a map ... draw a circle and label it 'Fox Family 1'. In this group, perhaps, there is a mated pair and cubs... Draw another circle which slightly overlaps the first. This is 'Fox Family 2'. Again, there is a mated pair and their cubs, but there is also a yearling vixen who has not reproduced. She is a subordinate, helping to raise her younger brothers and sisters. Finally, write transient wherever you like […] many young foxes […] have neither territory nor family. (Brand, 2019: 61–2)

In some cities, conscious efforts have been made to produce wildlife corridors that aid animal mobility. In others, little has been done to annul the effects of both the scale of habitation and the different infrastructural networks that connect up and service human populations – roads, railways, canals, dams, pipelines, and so on – all of which are likely to cause isolation of habitats.

Behavioural Adaptation

Cities, understood as this mosaic of different environments, act as forcing grounds, providing all manner of opportunities for new behaviours to arise, many of which I have already documented, in species like the hyper adaptable coyote or the hardy red kite. Animals must improvise to survive in what, at least to begin with, is a foreign and volatile habitat, bringing together species which might have never interacted before and isolating others, a habitat in which they 'must locate and exploit new food resources, deal with new predators and competitors, develop different navigation strategies …. and overcome elevated levels of noise and light pollution' (Barrett et al., 2018: 1). That improvisation produces new behaviours, aided by the fact that cities can make animals more cognitively flexible. Some of those involved in the rapidly expanding subfield of animal cognition, cognitive ecology, argue that cities may even be making urban-dwelling animals more intelligent in the sense that they seem to outperform their wild counterparts on tests that measure behavioural plasticity, likelihood of changing behaviour, less neophobic attitudes, and general levels of innovation in both individuals and social systems (e.g. Greenberg and Holekamp, 2017; Johnson-Ulrich et al., 2018; Barrett et al., 2018; Bisceglio, 2018). They learn faster, in other words. Instances of novel urban behaviours that demonstrate such expanding 'intelligence'[4] (a contentious term given how hard it is to work out what is being measured and how to measure it) and, as importantly, novel behaviours that vary between different groups of the same species, are legion. In some of the urban locales of Japan, crows have learnt to crack open nuts by dropping them beneath the wheels of cars (Sax, 2003; Schilthuizen, 2018; Ara et al., 2018). Some go further and have learnt to wait at intersections for the lights to change to red so that they can walk out and collect their prizes. In Uganda, chimpanzees have learnt to look left and right before and whilst crossing busy roads. In the Netherlands, sparrows nest in cycle racks, and in Mexico City sparrows and finches line their nests with cigarette butts (because the nicotine acts as an insecticide). Noisy miner birds have learnt to open sugar packets while great-tailed grackles pick dead insects off car number plates. Grey squirrels are continually upgrading their abilities to get into bird feeders (Barrett et al., 2018). In a number of places, sparrows and pigeons have learnt to use motion sensors to get inside enclosed shopping malls so that they can forage for food. In Toronto, bees have even started to use plastic films and foams to line their nests (Gibbens, 2019).

The most successful animals can be regarded as 'nuisances', by virtue of their prevalence in cities and their often bolder temperaments, which lead them into increased contact with humans and very likely riskier behaviours (though in these same animals cognition is also used to avoid dangerous human activity and dangerous sites) (van Dooren, 2020). But, to go into more detail, it is worth taking up just two examples. The first is the rhesus-macaque monkey, which is now widely distributed through Indian cities[5] and growing in numbers all the time (Barua and Sinha, 2017). On one estimate there are some 500,000 of these monkeys living in northern and northeastern India, around 55 per cent of which live in or near to human habitation. They often do quite well living in cities, not least because through religious and other practices they have become a part of how humans define themselves (Fuentes, 2007). They have developed novel and bold foraging behaviours like bipedal 'begging' for food from tourists and pilgrims, an activity mainly undertaken by high-ranking individuals, as well as a certain form of what looks like bartering with humans. Equally, they have developed new banks of knowledge which include all the possible opportunities to forage for food (Donovan, 2015). They are likely to choose territories that are rich in opportunities, raid gardens and crops, break into houses and cars, open rubbish bins and other objects, and even process foods differently[6]. And, finally, they have cascaded these novel behaviours and knowledges down through social groups – groups which themselves often vary in their behaviours, from parents to offspring, from group individuals to other group individuals (Barua and Sinha, 2017). As importantly, these social learning behaviours are heterogeneous – not all rhesus-macaques do them or they do them differently. The second example is the crow (which I take to be a catch-all for the genus *Corvus*, which takes in ravens, rooks and jackdaws as well). Crows are extremely successful urban colonizers, possessing mental acuity which is probably on a par with monkeys and apes, 'the result of flexible and complex social lifestyles, long life spans, and large brains' (Marzluff and Angell, 2012: 3) in which part of the forebrain, the pallium, does the heavy cognitive lifting instead of the cerebral cortex in mammals (Nieder et al., 2020). Most recently, they have been found to have 'sensory consciousness': they knew what they had seen. Cities provide these exceptionally intelligent animals with myriad new food and other opportunities and, as a result, they interact with humans in numerous ways which Marzluff (2014) argues may even be co-evolutionary. In particular cities, there is evidence that their behaviour varies as a result of different kinds of experimentation ranging from the use of new forms of materials for nest-building to sheltering in the lee of certain types of buildings for protection in storms rather than trees (van Dooren, 2019). In other words, the dispossessed can take back at least some limited possession of the city and in some cases, especially for generalists, the city is actually a more favourable habitat. Urban macaques and crows illustrate once again the fact that 'just as much as animals have a history of their relations with animals, so also animals have a history of their relations with humans' (Ingold, 2011: 61).

But there is more to it than this. What we are seeing in a number of instances are animal cultures coming into existence which attest to the fact of what has famously been called 'multiculturalism beyond the human'. Rather than animal ethnography, we need animal ethology, in other words. Indeed, some have argued that the study of animal cultures is simply rerunning the history of cultural anthropology, becoming increasingly reflexive as more and more 'there' is discovered. Of course, certain aspects of the shift to the study of animal cultures are still hotly disputed. For example, it is still a moot point whether these animal cultures grow more and more complex over time, though, as in the case of macaques, clear examples have been found of very different behaviours existing between groups and of new behaviours spreading through groups, some of them sometimes imported by newcomers. In other words, animal cultures can and do have cultural diversity. Even in advanced primates like chimpanzees, all kinds of arguments still rage but what is clear is that these mammals are not just 'mired in a primitive state of nature', forever condemned to repeating past behaviours (Langlitz, 2018: 2). A widely accepted theory like dual inheritance, which understands animals as able to pass on behaviours through both genetic and cultural transmission, or the call to preserve biocultural diversity rather than biological and cultural diversity, both make the point in different ways.

Now there is a further twist which amply illustrates Hacking's well-known looping effect in which new norms can create all manner of different kinds of human and animal hybrid cultures which produce their own new norms. Of course, a number of these cultures have been in existence for millennia but what is interesting is how many of them have come into existence comparatively recently as cities have spread as well as the degree to which they can vary from city to city. As the examples of macaques and crows also both show, not just animals but also humans have had to make accommodations. But it is more than just accommodation that we are seeing now. New practices are being invented on both sides of the supposed fence and are passing into the urban everyday as hybrid ways of life. There are all kinds of tensions, to be sure, but there is also a degree of hope that some of these practices may end up being of mutual benefit, as Haraway (2003) has argued for a considerable period of time.

Genetic Adaptation

Given the point that cities include numerous kinds of habitat, evidence is mounting that certain of the animals living in cities are not only undergoing behavioural but also genetic and epigenetic change (change in which existing genes are switched on or off by novel environmental conditions). The examples of these changes are growing day by day into a compelling case for the city as an evolutionary forcing agent promoting actual selection for different coping mechanisms (Shochat et al., 2005; Alberti, 2015; Albert et al., 2017; Schilthuizen, 2018) via direct urban stressors like pollution, drought, heat and changed biotic interactions as well as different incidences of 'natural' stressors like habitat modification, food quantity, predation and overcrowding (see table 1 in Alberti et al., 2017). It is clear that genetic change can take place much faster than originally thought, in other words, not least because so many organisms are hybrids (Thomas, 2017). Genetic change can also be boosted by the actions of viruses, which act as genetic forcing agents under some circumstances: viruses can insert themselves into an animal's DNA and sometimes thereby change the course of evolution, both because the genome's immune system is stimulated and because ancient viral DNA is re-activated (Zimmer, 2017). Then there is the presence of all manner of epigenetic factors, the changes brought about by genetic expression, or silencing, rather than by the genetic code itself. It follows that something like a city, which is a conglomeration of new barriers and flows and, by extension, a means of transport and new amalgamations of of all kinds of genetic material, can act as a brewhouse for evolutionary change which is clearly genetic but can also be, at the same time, behavioural and morphological.

Take the insect realm to begin with. The textbook case is the London peppered moth, which turned from pale to black when the soot from the Industrial Revolution turned the bark of the city's trees black[7]. Then it turned pale again when clean air laws were enacted. Or there is the humble water flea (*Daphnia magna*) found in many urban garden ponds. It is changing its proportions of body fat, proteins and sugars through faster growth and development and has begun to differ genetically from its rural cousins, especially as a result of higher rearing temperatures (Brans and Meester, 2018). Or there is the mosquito dwelling in the London underground and feeding off the blood of its commuters. It turns out not only to be genetically different from its above-ground cousins – which feed mainly on bird blood – but also varies genetically from line to line. This differential in the mosquito's genetic make-up seems to be occurring globally whenever humanity has gone underground (Schilthuizen, 2018).

Above ground, similar changes are occurring amongst mammals and reptiles. Some are particularly spectacular, especially those that represent birds adapting to a more urbanized life. For example, in the United States, cliff swallows' wing shapes have been growing slowly shorter, making it easier for them to turn and take off rapidly. Roadkill casualties among these swallows have declined as a result. Something similar seems to have happened to US starlings since their introduction in the last quarter of the nineteenth century. Shifts in beak size and bite forces have been observed in urban house finches as a response to the growth of bird feeders which dispense larger and harder seeds than would be found in their natural food (Marzluff, 2014). Urban blackbirds have gained shorter, stubbier bills, sing at a higher pitch earlier in the day (like most city birds), have lost their urge to migrate, start breeding and nesting several weeks earlier, and are more even-tempered and less shy (Otto, 2018). Meanwhile, the wings of urban pigeons are growing darker as they dispose of heavy metal toxins through their feathers (Chatelain et al., 2014). Lizards in some cities are evolving longer limbs and more toe lamellae, which increase locomotory performance on artificial surfaces (Johnson and Munshi-South, 2018). The list goes on.

Already genetic differences are occurring *between* urban populations of animals in the large: gene flow may actually be increasing among urban areas as a result of inter-urban connectivity. For example, the pigeons of New York, Baltimore, Washington, Providence, Philadelphia and Boston all have similar genetic signatures. However, the pigeons of Providence and Philadelphia have a different signature, presumably because the straight line distance of 305 kilometres that separates New York and Boston is a band of green space which acts as a barrier to mixing (Carlen and Munshi-South, 2020). It seems as though large-scale urban 'sub continents' are being set up where pigeons may evolve differently in the future. In the west of the United States, black widow spiders seem to show a similar pattern of gene flow as a result of urban connectivity, perhaps because the spiders like to build their webs in parked cars that then move them around (Miles et al., 2018).

But, generally speaking, what can be seen in cities is the growth of small, isolated populations *within* cities as a result of loss of habitat, producing, in turn, an associated loss of genetic diversity within populations (as in the case of bobcats in Los Angeles, which have experienced habitat fragmentation and severe population bottlenecks associated with the pesticides consumed by their rodent prey) and increased differentiation between populations (as in the case of Manhattan where there is evidence of reduced dispersal of rats across the island's less residential Midtown region and the formation of two distinct evolutionary clusters in uptown and downtown Manhattan (Coombs et al., 2018). There is more intensive selection, in other words. Genetic mutation rates are also raised by air and other forms of pollution, as well as the existence of all kinds of pesticides (Johnson and Munshi-South, 2018).

Evolutionary Change

Evolutionary change has often been interpreted as simply a matter of genetic change. But the picture of evolution has altered, moving away from the neo-Darwinian synthesis between Darwin's theory of evolution and genetics towards something much more variegated. It now incorporates many more kinds of influence. To begin with, understanding of the gene and genetics has expanded substantially. Evolution is now understood as an active cellular process, one that is regulated epigenetically and that can produce rapid and often quite large changes via mechanisms like horizontal DNA transfer, inter-species hybridization, symbiogenesis, whole genome doubling and what can even prove to be a massive restructuring of the genome (Shapiro, 2011). Then, it is also understood as drawing on more kinds of adaptation which are extra-cellular. As a result of genetic and behavioral adaptations, which are repeated in many urban-living species, new species are likely to come into existence (though we live in a time where what exactly a species might be is a matter of some debate). That said, we are not there yet: the gene pools of different cities have not joined up to produce conformity to just one norm (Thomas, 2017). But new hybridizations are definitely occurring in particular cities as a result of adaptive radiation to new urban niches – the issue then becomes whether they are going to become general enough to count as new urban species. What seems likely is that the strong selection induced by cities will shorten the time to speciation (Otto, 2018).

What lessons are we able to draw from this rapid urban genetic and, of course, epigenetic change? One story that you hear quite often is that the system that an animal like a sheep or a cow or a pig or a chicken is caught up in is to the animals' ultimate evolutionary advantage: these meat animals are lucky critters. They have us. It's part of an evolutionary deal which maximizes genetic survival: existence at pretty well any cost for the sake of more replication (Morton, 2018). Thomas' explanation is typical:

> For [...] chosen animals [...], we have entered an era of mutual benefit. This might seem odd because we [...] kill our cattle and sheep to eat their meat. This is hardly to their individual advantage. Yet this is little different from the way oak and pine trees benefit from the presence of squirrels and birds. [...] The oaks and pines sacrifice most of their offspring to the rodents and birds that will harvest them. But, in the long run, the trees benefit because the squirrels and nutcrackers also plant their seeds in places where new trees will eventually sprout. [Similarly] most individual [...] domestic animals will die to feed us, but humans ensure that some live, and these in turn spawn subsequent generations. (2017: 44–5)

The result is an evolutionary bonanza as domesticated mammal flesh multiplies to feed us and those mammals turn up evolutionary trumps: 'Where wild beasts once roamed, livestock now graze. Around 30 per cent of the world's productive land is covered by pasture, supporting enormous numbers of large mammals' (Thomas, 2017: 45).

But I am wary of this 'gee, really it's all for the best'/selfish gene argument and for a number of reasons[8]. I want to make three points, each of which are part of an argument that evolution is a much more plastic and multipolar process than formerly thought. The *first* is about individuation and innovation. Just as in the case of humans, animals can have very different characters and these characters are not just incidental (Gillespie, 2018; Rees, 2018; Walling, 2018): each encounter is shaped by them, however minutely and however trivial any variation may seem. The role of individual animal characterization has only just begun to be studied in depth (see Laland, 2017), probably because of a residual fear of Lamarckism, but it seems to me to be crucial for it suggests that every animal, just like humans, can – at least potentially – be a valuable part of a what looks like an unproblematic species whole.

Long ago, ecologists and ethologists like Lack and Tinbergen started down the line of careful and systematic observation of animal societies and, as importantly, of the individual animals that comprised them. They criticized 'both field scientists who indulged in lazy anthropomorphism, and those who insisted on setting up "artificial standards of simplicity". In particular, they objected to the dismissal of any apparently sophisticated animal action as "instinctive"' (Rees, 2018: 3), in effect arguing that humans have been setting the questions and then marking the answers. This tradition of careful and systematic observation has been continued by successive animal behaviourists and ecologists. Indeed, individual identification has become a central moment in the recording and analysis of individual and group animal interaction. Attempts have even been made to try to write stories of these interactions from the animals' points of view (e.g. Swart, 2010)[9].

The question of animal innovation follows on. As Laland (2017) points out, the question before the question, so to speak, is whether animals can be considered as 'innovative' at all. Perhaps changes in their environments prompt changes in behaviour in an all but mechanical way? Three questions arise from challenges like this. If innovation does indeed exist, who is doing the innovating? Are there particular individuals or personality types that are more prone to innovation? Again, when innovations are observed spreading through animal populations, is this because of social transmission or has each new adopter simply learnt it independently? The answer to each of these three questions – observed in primates, birds and fish – is as follows.

Animals innovate. Observations of primates, birds and fish all bear out this statement. They innovate within the bounds of specific animal cultures which themselves can be more or less innovative, but innovate they undoubtedly do. Some individuals are more likely to innovate than others. The young are more likely to explore a new task. More mature animals are more likely to solve it[10]. Species that are more dependent on manipulative and extractive foraging tend to be more innovative (and are probably more likely to survive). Species that have larger and more complex brains (like primates, corvids and cetaceans) are more likely to have high-fidelity transmission mechanisms, tend to learn more rapidly, are more innovative and show signs of 'general intelligence', that is of general mental abilities like reasoning. A recent study by Ducatez et al. (2020) of thousands of reports over the past 60 years found 3,800 instances of birds engaging in innovative behaviour to find food, many of them stimulated by human encroachment. For example, herons have been repeatedly observed using bread or insects as bait to lure fish into snatching distance, a behaviour learnt from watching humans. Peregrine falcons use the gust of wind from trains to help them catch birds flushed out of trees. Similarly, cormorants in New Zealand use the strong currents left by ships' wakes to go fishing. Great blue herons hunt squirrels on golf courses. And so on. (Importantly, the study also found that the more innovations were described per species, the more likely it was to have stable or increasing populations.)

Animals pass on these cadenzas in a variety of ways. Animals (even down to fruit flies and bumblebees) copy (and the ability to imitate means that animals must have at least a scintilla of comprehension of the goals and activities of the animal they are copying, as well as the incentive to build up stores of knowledge of activities like foraging or migratory routes or the best places to find food as well as what to fear, what calls and gestures to make, and what social conventions need to be kept to). Animals are more likely to learn from close associates, parents and elders, of course, but also the group to which they belong and friends. There is clear evidence, for example, that animals as varied as cows, sheep, llamas, baboons, parrots, flamingos, horses, hyenas and grizzly bears all have friendship networks and likely learn from them. There are sex differences in some cases but it seems that many animals make and learn from friends and nearly all of them learn from parents and elders. What all this means is that not only is there variation within species upon which evolution can act but also that there do seem to be processes that seem awfully like cultural transmission which enshrine local cultural knowledge and allow it to persist[11]. This cultural knowledge can be extraordinarily distinctive. At the same time, such distinctive cultures, which are usually locationally specific, can be extinguished if a group is caught in the crossfire between urban development and greed. In other words, just like human cultures, animal cultures can be eroded and then snuffed out, sadly too often only at the point when we have come to recognize their existence in the first place. Cities have a major role in this excision. As human development shrinks habitats into patches, the resulting isolation produces cultural impoverishment (e.g. in the complexity of birdsong), and animal cultures significantly decline in variety with the result that 'traditions that helped animals survive and adapt to a place begin to vanish' (Safina, 2020: 135).

In other words, we should take individuation seriously as an evolutionary process but one in which the distinguishable entity is framed as an effect of individuation: the individual is replaced by a never-ending process of various operations of individuation which, in turn, make the unfolding of future individuations possible, leading to progressive modification (Scott, 2014). This approach means that the individual is never just an epiphenomenon but neither is it separate either: the individual neither comes into existence alone nor exists alone. The individual is always understood as 'relative to the milieu associated with its existence' (Simondon, 2012: 7) and it can never be defined in isolation. It is 'always more than one' (Manning, 2013). Equally, individuation does not exist without individuals: the whole grows by altering itself, including what can count as an individual at all. Of course, individuals cannot have agency that is independent of the corona of the collective that defines them or the different roles they have been assigned, some of which are more mobile than others. But their particular style of taking part in the collective means that they are able to influence specific events (whilst disappearing into the mass when it comes to other events). So DNA, for example, is not just a static code, it is a set of potentials, which are able to unfold in various directions, and which do not attain their form except in the actual process of unfolding[12].

Taking individual animal characterization seriously requires us to agree that there is, at a minimum, subjective experiencing of some kind[13], an ability which both feeds into and arises out of goal-directed associative learning (Ginsburg and Jablonka, 2019). In contradistinction to those who believe that only linguistically endowed humans have this ability, I would argue that many, perhaps even most, animals possess it, though to very different degrees. After all, to make obeisance to Deleuze, working through the medium of authors like Simondon, thought isn't necessarily representational – it doesn't function by making pictures of the world, which can be judged as true or false depending on their degree of accuracy. Rather, thought is creative, and always connected to that which it thinks about.

Equally, thought is always and everywhere collective. We might think of the issue at hand as how to think a multiplicity but a multiplicity that still has little flashes of individuality constantly firing off as the load of interaction passes between its different elements, generating novel behaviours. Mostly, all that results is attunement to the status quo but, every now and then, these little flashes can drive an innovation which might be important in the larger scheme of things, driving more general change in social systems[14]. Urban environments are particularly likely to force innovations that work at this level. For example, in urban areas one kind of humble ant has been observed switching mating systems and forming supercolonies rather than single colonies (Buczkowski, 2010). If there is one criticism of the human use of farm animals that might be made, apart from the endemic violence, it might be that the conditions under which they are kept, combined with other factors like breeding, might prevent these kinds of innovations from taking place by trapping species in a human-induced amber. Such animals have no means of potentializing and therefore evolving. Whatever the case, in many animals, individuality can surely be counted as an important moment in evolution, one that is both singular and collective.

Which brings me on to my *second* point. Evolution has never just been a matter of survival of the fittest genes in any case (Shapiro, 2011). To begin with, we live in a period when even some of the basics of genetics are being challenged. For example, recent work has complicated what we think of as processes of genetic drift (through the now common piece of wisdom that as much as 80 per cent of what was once thought of as 'junk' or non-coding DNA actually has some sort of function and by the discovery that there are 'de novo' genes that do not evolve from existing ones) and may even challenge what we think of as constituting a gene (Levy, 2019).

But, in any case, recent work has challenged a narrowly gene-based account of heredity. In this model, evolution is driven by other imperatives too, imperatives that are now being recognized in models of so-called 'extended evolution' which emphasize not only competition but also cooperation. There are epigenetic factors, of course, arising especially from environmental factors – like cities –– which add all kinds of plasticity, not least because many kinds of animals, just like humans, change their environment. These factors are now counted as much more important than formerly. There are behavioural factors which arise from imitation and social learning and which depend on behaviual repertoires that form 'animal traditions' (Avital and Jablonka, 2000; Jablonka and Lamb, 2014) which may well drive gene-culture co-evolution, as in the case of the innovative foraging skills adopted by some dolpins and corvids and not others (Laland, 2017).

Talking of animal traditions, there may well be symbolic factors too. Some writers now believe that there is a symbolic dimension to evolution

(Fuentes, 2009), for example. It is worth remembering Darwin's original work of 1871, *The Descent of Man, and Selection in Relation to Sex*, in which the aesthetic dimension of mate choice also takes on a role, driven by the demands of sexuality. Take the case of birds. Mate attraction is a

> more open-ended, unconstrained, and dynamic challenge than [tasks like] opening a seed. Each species evolves its own solution to the challenge of intersexual communication and attraction – what Darwin called independent 'standards of beauty'. […] it is no surprise that each of the world's ten thousand plus bird species has evolved its own, unique aesthetic repertoire of ornaments and preferences. (Prum, 2017: 10)

But this is not just about mate-signalling, a classical utilitarian argument which sees these standards of beauty as just another aspect of natural selection. They are more than that – they imply genuine aesthetic choice based on subjective evaluations, choice made for its own sake. (Perhaps, because since most of the choosing is being done by females, it therefore somehow matters less? Certainly, Darwin struggled with matters like imputing agency to women and aesthetic discrimination to non-Europeans; Richards, 2017). But the result is clear, in any case. Evolution can have a 'decadent' quality in that sexual ornamentation may not only fail to signal all that much about objective mate quality, but may actually lower the chances of survival and fecundity of not just the signaller but also the chooser (Prum, 2017; Richards, 2017).

And so to the *final* evolutionary point, which is closely related. We cannot let species thinking overwhelm us, as though species were separate monads whose only point is to reproduce adaptation by natural selection like a whirring machine. To begin with, the distinctive cultural knowledge of certain groups means that 'a species isn't just one big jar of jellybeans of the same colour' (Safina, 2020: 150). Then, it is just as important to preserve the connections between species as within (and in many cases, those connections are indeed what keep many species going). We return to symbiosis again. It is not parts or wholes that keep things whirring along. Rather it's partial wholes dynamized by encounters that can sometimes redefine the nature of the connections. For example, certain whales like rorquals have been found to breed between species that seem to be phenotypically distinct, an intermingling which was once thought to be out of bounds to them as distinct species (Weintraub, 2019). A case like this defies any simple Darwinian theories. Darwin argued that many species evolved when they became isolated from others of their kind, accumulating differences as they adapted to a new environment. But whales like rorquals roam over the entire ocean, and there are no geographic barriers that isolate them. Instead, at least some whale speciation seems to have been driven by culture or even personal taste, a process that also seems to have occurred between other mobile species – like modern, Neanderthal and Denisovan humans.

Humans

To conclude, none of this is to say that animal and human evolution are identical. Humans have a much-expanded capacity for cultural evolution and gene cultural co-evolution (Laland, 2017; Chater, 2018; Heyes, 2018). At birth, the minds of human babies are only subtly different from the minds of newborn chimpanzees: they have a friendlier temperament, their attention is drawn to different attentional cues like faces, voices and bodily motions like gesture, and they have a better capacity to learn and remember. But these relatively small differences in their start-up resources are then exposed to febrile human environments like cities, which can and do change very rapidly, giving the babies a rocket-like cognitive boost which stems from the way in which these differences are able to be slotted in to so many different situations; 'distinctively human cognitive mechanisms are tracking targets that are too fast for genetic evolution' (Heyes, 2018: 208). Non-specific, generic skills are the prime focus of genetic evolution. But how they are actualized will vary markedly precisely because they are generic. This is the phenomenon of cultural evolution. Though many animals undoubtedly have cultures which vary they tend to do so more slowly with the result that they are more easily locked into particular sets of behaviours. Not so for humans, which need nimble and easily exchangeable cognitive mechanisms which must change faster than genetic evolution could ever foster in order to keep up with the constant changes in their environment.

> For example, *social learning* strategies track 'who knows' in a particular social group […]. *Imitation* tracks communicative gestures, ritual movements, and manual skills that change as groups find […] new group markers, bonding rituals, and technologies. And *mindreading* […] must not only track externally driven change in the phenomena it seeks to describe […] but also self-generated change. (Heyes, 2018: 208, my italics)

Human evolution is a particularly acute case of 'gene-culture co-evolution' (Laland, 2017), with human cultural activity both speeding up the pace of genetic evolution and treading its own path. Cities are an important part of this process of enhancing plasticity, one in which cultural evolution now dominates as populations have scaled up, producing environments in which innovations have a far better chance of both being adopted and becoming more general, the result of widespread teaching and a corresponding ability to concoct much greater levels of high-fidelity transmission, as well as greater flexibility of response: 'larger or denser populations not only generate more innovations, and more complex innovations, but are capable of preserving them for longer, leading to bigger cultural repertoires' (Laland, 2017: 258).

But human evolution is continually dependent on other, nonhuman, actors to produce its own evolution – and increasingly theirs, too – as cities also show. The problem is that this fact often goes unacknowledged, even though perhaps the main driver of human evolution – social bonding – is, in fact, quite often extended to making investments in other species. The lack of acknowledgement of this fact leads to what are called, to put it kindly, abuses hatched out of cultural evolution. But this very fact also means that they are reversible. So let's engage reverse gear.

Notes

1. These urban inhabitants are also better able to tolerate lead, have better defences against parasites and suffer lower predation from falcons in the case of darker morphs.
2. In fact, pigeons often only have relatively small populations living in cities but because they tend to be concentrated in city centres they are a prominent feature of urban life in many parts of the world (Fuller et al., 2009).
3. Though Central Park has its own ecology, including an estimated population of over 3,000 squirrels which act as an isolated colony which has evolved its own unique behaviours such as timed avoidance of dogs. Between 6am and 9am every day, the time when dogs are allowed off the leash, the squirrels retreat to the trees, before one makes a call to sound the all-clear.
4. One irony is that this greater flexibility may make these animals more of a 'nuisance' to humans and therefore more rather than less threatened.
5. Macaques are found making their way into many other Asian countries, for example in Malaysia (see Fullerton, 2019). There are inevitable stresses as they make greater human contact.
6. These new behaviours have, of course, provided numerous opportunities for conflict with humans, as found with other species like baboons in Africa as well.
7. We now know that the DNA-jumping responsible for the moth's shift to black occurred in the north of England about the year 1819.
8. As I hope I am making clear, the study of evolution has changed quite markedly over the last few decades (Losos, 2017). The idea of adaptive convergent evolution, that species which evolve independently are likely to end up with similar features, these being the limited range of solutions that arise from the challenges that predominate in particular environments, has become a commonplace. At the same time, the role of contingency has also been underlined (which is not the same as arguing that evolution is random or haphazard). In any case, the range of endpoints is still large!
9. None of this is to suggest moving towards a folksy, anthropomorphized interpretation of individual animals but those who work with them will often attest to the presence of real and often very different individual animal personalities and the absolute necessity of being able to recognize this variation in order to produce a satisfactory working relationship.
10. Some species actively teach their young, though the evidence for this behaviour currently spans a curiously diverse group of animals, from meerkats to ants (Laland, 2017).
11. In other words, in the case of mammals at least, the brain has driven its own evolution. The bigger the brain grows, the greater the power of a species to evolve biologically.
12. The classic exposition of DNA as the monarch of evolution is provided by Dawkins' account of the selfish gene. But, as Jablonka and Lamb (2014) point out, Dawkins makes three errors. First, he assumes that the gene has to be copied with a high level of fidelity to be a unit of evolutionary change. Second, he assumes that the relationship between the replicator (gene) and the vehicle (body) is unidirectional. Third, he assumes that the gene is the only biological hereditary unit.
13. This is not the same as arguing that life and consciousness are identical.
14. The work of Tarde is an inspiration to many on this point.

Part IV

A New Settlement

9
Dreaming More Human Cities 1

In 2015, President Xi Jinping gave a speech in the United States. Part of it was a reminiscence about his time living in a small, remote and impoverished village. One of the things he picked out from his time there was the lack of meat in the villagers' diet. 'One thing I wished most at the time was to make it possible for the villagers to eat meat to their heart's content […]' By the time he returned to the village in the same year, everything had changed.

> I saw black top roads. Now living in houses with bricks and tiles, the villagers had internet access. Elderly folks had basic old-age care, and all villagers had medical care coverage. Children were in school. Of course, meat was readily available. (Xi Jinping, 2015)

President Xi had got his teenage wish. In China, meat-eating is now general. Since 1980, meat consumption has quadrupled (Brighter Green, 2011). People ate about 74 million tonnes of pork, beef and poultry in 2017, around twice as much in absolute terms as the United States[1], according to US agriculture department estimates, though still only half the per capita meat consumption of the US[2]. More than half of that figure was pork. Since China began opening up to the world in the late 1970s, pork demand expanded by an average of 5.7 per cent every year, until 2014. Like other meat producers, Chinese pig farmers went on a building spree, constructing huge intensive farms[3] to capture a bigger share of the world's biggest pork market, while leading producers overseas have been changing the way they raise their pigs to meet Chinese standards for imports[4]. (That said, pork demand has now hit a ceiling, well ahead of most official forecasts. Sales of pork have fallen for the past 3 years as concerns about threats to health, the rapid spread of diseases like pig 'blue ear' and most especially African swine fever[5], and adverse environmental impacts have come to the fore.) But, as we have seen in the previous chapter, this slackening in demand does not necessarily help matters. A change of urban direction in China is needed – as elsewhere – towards cities which both share with and value thinking life more fully[6]. The issue is how we get there.

There is, of course, the question of *whether we should be living in cities at all*. The story of the long march of civilization didn't have to include cities as an inevitable waystation. Humans and cities aren't necessarily joined at the hip[7]. After all, settled urbanism, as opposed to temporary settlement, has a complex stop–start history, a tangled history which includes systematic inequality, the patriarchal control of women and enslaved people, and the history of domestication. For much the largest part of human history, most humans probably lived in small, mobile, dispersed and relatively egalitarian bands[8]. Of course, we cannot simply revert to such an unsettled condition, not least because modern cities are already premised on movement (Amin and Thrift, 2002) with many inhabitants (though by no means all) leading mobile lives.

Given where we are now, the idea that we could suddenly fold up the whole of the urban enterprise and start again is not remotely realistic. But it is realistic to think about what kinds of cities we want to live in – notice the use of the plural of kind here: there is no one solution. We are going to have to radically redesign cities, constituting a community of communities whose roots are diverse and act to promote symbiosis, all the while understanding that what counts as a city can vary enormously. That is going to require a radical alteration of the global urban landscape but, given the scale of the transformation that has taken place over the last 50 years which has already produced one such transformation, it is certainly not beyond our wit or will. Then, in the longer term, perhaps other forms of lower impact inhabitation might become apparent as our cognitive and affective baseline changes. That said, the task will be made more difficult by the fact that it will have to take place against the background of an increase in ecological domino effects in which one tipping point fires off another one (Rocha et al., 2018), the result of which is that not only that we are moving into the era of the so-called standardized disaster in which disasters become commonplace in some cities – but that they will likely manifest as not one but a string of multiple disasters following one after the other from which it will be correspondingly more difficult to recover. These strings of disasters will test cities to the limit and, at the same time, they are as likely to distract as concentrate attention on the changes that are necessary to overcome them[9]. But I am still hopeful. Cities may have created a large part of the devastation that we now face but they are also the resource from which and with which we can grow a forest of solutions.

So What Needs to Be Done?

There is a moment in many books where there has to be a change of gear towards concrete policies and practices that affect outcomes. This is it. Inevitably, with such a move comes the risk that the emperor turns out to have no clothes. It is all very well talking about recasting cities as arenas of constant interspecies connection, as knots of obligation, as means of redefining the composition of humanity, as places where hospitality can take on new forms. But that stuff's all a bit up in the air, isn't it? What are the actual practical changes that are necessary? However, the extraordinary thing about the current conjuncture is that there is no need to indulge in magical thinking (which is not to say that some magical thinking wouldn't come amiss). Quite a few of the leaps of imagination have already been made. There is a whole suite of policies and practices which – if they were acted upon swiftly enough and at sufficient scale – would change things rapidly, perhaps even sufficiently rapidly to head off some of the more disastrous urban outcomes that lower on the horizon (though I suspect that, given the forward momentum we have now introduced into the planetary system, some disasters are now inevitable). In other words, the die is not cast, though it is unlikely that we can throw a six. In the rest of this chapter and the next I will consider five knots of practices – some familiar, some less so – that need to be unravelled and retied in order to found a new more inclusive urban order which, as a result, has genuine survival characteristics. (Of course, it is impossible to produce a detailed compendium of every single knot. In any case, that has already been attempted by many other authors [e.g. Hawken, 2017]).

In the final analysis, it will be the political problems that are the most daunting barrier to instigating these policies and practices. In particular, there is the problem of how to get things done with some considerable sense of urgency in polities that do not seem equal to the urgency of the case, as well as the problem of what democratic governance can deliver more generally. For example, do we want a representative public (Brennan, 2017)? In which case, what would that public be representative of (Amin and Thrift, 2014)? Could we get to Latour's 'parliament of things' or similar? How many powers would we have to remove from entrenched interests and how would we call a halt to the inevitable counter-reaction? How would the internet figure in all of this? These are just some among a range of questions to which many forests have been sacrificed without any definitive resolution.

Then there is the problem that, though policies may abound, they are often cut off from one another with the result that momentum is lost. What we sorely need is some way of *aggregating* them. Take climate change and cities. A number of important books on a green new deal have tried to offer solutions at a national or international scale. But the best opportunity may arise out of cities which are practised in both innovation and implementation at operable scales, often through founding urban living labs and other experimental institutions (Sengers et al., 2020). The transfer of policy knowledge between different cities around the world has undoubtedly started to increase. For example, the number of formal inter-urban organizations which are attempting city-to-city learning has multiplied: Barber (2017) lists just those concerned with environmental and climate change matters – the Global Cool Cities Alliance, the C40 Cities Climate Leadership Group, the Climate Alliance, the Covenant of Mayors, Energy Cities, the International Council for Local Environmental Initiatives, MedCities, Alliance in the Alps – but there are many polycentric organizations that have also taken up these matters as part of a broader portfolio such as the United States Conference of Mayors, EuroCities, United Cities and Local Governments, and Metropolis.

Another problem is that persuasive powers are in short supply. Though it is clear that many, many people want something different, they have little conception of how different that different will have to be, and of either the benefits of setting out or the sacrifices that are going to be needed to get there. We undoubtedly need more political structures that are able to work over the very long term. But at the same time, we need to come to terms with what has been called the small bowel of communication, the flyby of undigested opinions and pure prejudices that currently pass for a lot of public discussion. This means dealing more effectively with affect but such a project is still in its infancy and unfortunately the problems we face are not.

This affective work is part of the issue of a more general change of mindset which would allow us to feel the planet differently – as a 'system of engendering' (based on the principle of dependency) rather than a 'system of production' (based on the principle of freedom) (Latour, 2018). The idea that we might suddenly switch to new ways of thinking cities as knots of obligation might seem outlandish were it not for the fact that there are so many populations that have made similar affective and cognitive journeys. Dominant cultures are more fragile than we often think. They can be displaced. Consider the many examples of epidemiological interventions like innoculation which were initially treated with suspicion and even hostility but have become accepted practice, except by a small fanatical rump. Think of the way in which civil rights have become an increasing matter of concern in the United States. Think of the way in which patriarchal cultures have changed in many Western countries. Think of the way in which gay and lesbian people have become a generally accepted part of the social landscape. Think of the way in which secularism has taken hold in many formerly religious countries. Think of the way in which a notion of 'environment' was forged and became dominant in just a few decades, taking on its own experts and institutions in the process (Warde et al., 2018). But also remember the salutary example of the way in which communist leaders in Eastern Europe attempted to forge a dominant culture of socialist morality over two generations of indoctrination only to see the whole thing fall apart, as old traditions surged back (Gintis et al., 2015). The point is that these transitions – forward or backward – were not lengthy. On the whole, they took two to three generations or even less. So, there is hope that something similar can be achieved so far as making cities a functioning part of the planet. But it is not at all clear that we have the vocabulary we need to describe what we need to do. We are still struggling to redescribe the urban world in terms that start to lay down a different discursive medium which is both a base and an aspiration. Yet redescribing what we have in terms that simultaneously make it apparent what the stakes are will be a necessary step.

We might also begin to *feel* differently about cities as this work of imaginary reconstruction takes place. There might be more empathy for – and inclusion of – other beings. I will leave the more general issue of cities that can take in many lives until the last chapter, whilst noting that, in the final analysis, without a change in mindset, it seems unlikely that it will ever be possible to get to cities that will give something back to every inhabitant, all of them a part of the same web of relationships.

So, given this very brief excursion into politics (for an expansion, see Amin and Thrift, 2014; 2016), what can be done to produce a commensal city? Over this chapter and the next, as I have already indicated, I want to point to a set of five knots of practices (two in this chapter and three in the next), some of them familiar, some less so, that, were they to be instigated would produce a more thoughtful city, a city in which the contributions different kinds of being make to the planet are valued for more than just having a utility which is measured out in their blood and bones. That means thinking about cities in a non-doctrinaire way, as exuberant, even exorbitant, forces, driven by aesthetic as well as instrumental motives, just as Darwin proposed a theory of aesthetically driven sexual selection, to go alongside the theory of natural selection. Such would be *an anthropogenic rather than a anthropomorphic city*, a city which is perpetually in an unfinished state, constantly in-between, and able to take in the combined work of many partially connected lives lived with many partially connected others, whilst still being able to achieve a state of something like mutuality. Ingold (2015) calls this *a 'humanifying' city*, one which is there to work out what being human might actually be by reinhabiting what counts as ordinary life, through the process of reworking its allegiances. Cities need to be better at producing these speculative coalitions which promote more cooperation between human and nonhuman (accepting that the boundary between the two categories is porous anyway, to put it but mildly) rather than just dominion. Generating collaborative 'what might be possibles' becomes a part of what the city is about. The go-beyond becomes an institutionalized fact of life.

Re-representation

First, re-representation. There is a long and honourable tradition of reimagining cities. But that tradition is hampered by its own epistemic bent towards visibility and a corresponding emphasis on nouns rather than verbs. It tends to see finished product, in other words, not the vitality of process. It tends to fix on the architectural bubblewrap of world-making rather than on gardening with the grain of the practices of urban inhabitants – of whatever stripe. But there are grounds for hope. Humanity has always imagined other lands, whether we are talking about a secret commonwealth of witches and demons, the supposed delights of a promised land or, even, so-called intangible products and assets, products that we can neither see nor touch that have gradually been brought into the frame of everyday existence. We need to turn this fictive impulse into a worthwhile reality, unsullied by the constant background noise of so many pointless deaths and so much mistreatment.

There is, in other words, a pressing need for a politics of imagination which can re-represent cities as kaleidoscopic entities taking in many beings at once. What could cities be? We start from the premise that there is a gulf between what we have and what we need. But we must also factor in the issue that we cannot know precisely what we do need. A coalition of all manner of peoples needs to work on imagining the city anew and that means going beyond stock phrases like the sustainable city, the ecological city or the circular economy, which are so easily subverted or subsumed. There are so many avenues to explore. Cities need radical redesign on practically every dimension (Escobar, 2017). They need to look and feel different. They need to be different. They need to stand for difference. This kind of ontological politics, based on acting out cooperation between many unlike and partially connected sources, is often prefigurative. Its proponents behave according to the rules of the society they hope to create by inventing new embodied disciplines, calling for inspiration taken from all manner of sources of inspiration like information technology, writing, art, drama, even dance, in order to generate multiple imaginaries (Anderson, 2015; Davis and Turpin, 2015: Fry, 2017; Latour, 2016a). They walk the talk. Take just the case of art. Artists have striven to produce ethico-aesthetic representations of the multiple spatial dimensions of the landscape of cities, representations which are at one and the same time different means of thinking and owning to responsibility (e.g. Abrahams et al., 2016). They work with the mechanics of space in order to challenge the familiar by drawing on inspirations as diverse as early maps, neuroscience, weaving and nanotechnology. In their hands, space becomes a kind of dreaming but about new possibilities, a dreamtime in which streams of diagrams and illustrations joined by tracks and trails (a theme I will return to) produce a profusion of detail which can generate new spatial scores. Artists like Jessica Rankin, Julie Mehretu and Josh Dorman are all struggling to produce these kinds of picturing, which challenge the bounds of what is regarded as legibility and illegibility in order to recast the moment of first contact and so decolonize cosmology (Demos, 2016).

And now we have all of the supposed benefits that have flowed from the explosion of mapping associated with reams of geodata. The conventional map has been unseated by the profusion and complexity of available locational information and the ability to navigate via GPS, developments which have enabled landscape imaginaries to come into being which are able to involve different kinds of speculation, critique and invention. The result is that the 'liquid, hidden' (Calvino, 2010) richness of being in cities has begun to be unveiled and, as it has been unveiled, so it has become increasingly appreciated. Whether we are enabling a new process of locution that allows us to speak the infrastructures that transport the livelihoods of cities (Amin and Thrift, 2016), or appreciating the complexity of life down to bacteria, fungi and even the viruses that hover on the edge of urban life

(Cheshire and Uberti, 2016), or etching the processes involved in urban physical formations like heat or humidity or condensation in novel ways, maps have increasingly been able to be used as means of not just illustrating but exploring cohabitation with all manner of beings in numerous inventive ways (see Brook and Dunn, 2013; Kurgan, 2013; O'Rourke, 2013; Milner, 2016) so as to plot new destinations. Though too often these exercises have fallen back on reproducing their own terms of reference instead of enacting a diplomatic enterprise spanning many worlds, this is becoming a new age of writing on the landscape, in which all kinds of beings can come into close communion, guided by the contours of the land, and knitted together by a commons that has been refigured to include many more beings. Sinclair (2010) notes how, in the 1970s, J.G. Ballard's *Crash* and Richard Mabey's *The Unofficial Countryside* between them stood for such an act of urban reimagination, producing out of apparently contrary visions what were the defining texts of the moment. On a larger scale, something similar is required again now, one which addresses the world differently, not just through a change of vocabulary but a change of syntax too. The lineaments of it are there already, a tantalizingly vast bank of different practices, skills and re-representations. But they have very rarely been put together as a kind of practical science fiction traversing many different worlds and possible outcomes.

Why this emphasis on re-representation? For many reasons, some of them practical, some of them not. But what seems clear is that to escape the current situation will require a rebooting of the affective infrastructure of the city and that rebooting means being able to see, hear, smell, taste, touch and generally sense things differently. This is a different kind of construction project from the physical vicissitudes of the urban fabric but it is just as important. For example, there has been much talk of a 'collapse of scales' of late. But what this might mean in practice (if anything) and how a new more productive resolution can be arrived at out of current instabilities and fragilities – and, yes, mysteries – in the fabric of everyday life now awaits a new Picasso who can unwind and rewind existing spaces and times and conjure up new apprehensions of cardinals like inside and outside (Clark, 2017; Fuller and Goriunova, 2020).

Build Cities Differently

Second, there is the actual *physical construction* of cities. There is no reason to think that we could not find mutual accommodations that allow all beings to have an influence on what we build. For example, instead of thinking of cities as somehow set apart, we might rechristen them as multispecies landscapes to which we could give care and from which we could derive comfort. As the scripted metrics of landscape urbanism are replaced by ecological urbanism (Mostafavi and Doherty, 2015; Waldheim, 2016), so the ambition of city builders has gradually changed from building buildings and infrastructures to building ecologies which deny the occlusion between the 'urban understood as external to ecology' and the 'ecological understood as external to the city'.

Let me point to one of the most successful multispecies landscape features as a prompt: the approximately 1 million miles of British hedgerow. Very much a construction meant to serve the ends of human beings by enclosing property, since its inception in the thirteenth century the hedge has become an extraordinarily diverse linear reservoir of all kinds of life. Animal life, of course, and of all kinds, mammals, amphibians, insects. But also plant life: trees, shrubs, climbers, herbaceous plants and grasses (Wright, 2016). The hedgerow suggests a particular form of city, one which makes room for others, one which no longer regards everything as an untapped resource, one which thinks generously, one which is not sealed off, even though it still creates boundaries. This is a city where humanity is no longer a distinctive category because it includes everyone in a quiet and functional wildness. This is a different form of the human community because 'being-in-common – that is community – can no longer be thought of or felt as a community of humans alone; it must become multi-species community that includes all of those with whom our livelihoods are interdependent and interrelated' (Gibson et al., 2015: 36). Human sociality is just one manifestation of this interrelatedness among many and cities need to acknowledge this fact rather than fall back on the architectonic hierarchy that is so often produced. As Latour (2014: 8) puts it, we 'need to reopen negotiations with the other collectives on the composition of a common world' and we will have to do part of that work of diplomacy through the lens of the city's built form.

Of course, as I have already pointed out, by default cities do make room for all kinds of beings who adapt to the human presence which is itself adapting to what it has wrought. Cities are already multispecies coalitions. Pass by all of the companion animals that were addressed in Chapter 6 and, as I have already pointed out, there is still a multitude of animals making their way through urban landscapes. There are 'wild' animals like foxes, flying foxes, langurs and coyotes, or pigeons and penguins and seagulls and rosy parakeets and red kites, animals that have adapted to fit in with human schedules and routines, though they may also have achieved part of their ascendancy through competitive release, that is the lack of competition from species who have not been able to adapt (van Dooren and Rose, 2012). British seagulls (mainly herring and lesser black-backed gulls) are one example. Their populations are growing rapidly in cities. There were estimated to be 473 urban gull colonies in 2015, up from 239 in 2000. One study found that they spend two thirds of their time in urban and suburban areas and a third in rural green areas. They congregate at places and times where food is likely to be on offer and use the city as a general resource relying on a large range of different kinds of food (Spelt et al.,

2019). (Gulls' nests in one British city included not only the bones from 40 kinds of food but also plastic forks, spoons, cable ties, rubber bands and human hair.) British pigeons have become urban denizens in large numbers too. One estimate is that a million pigeons now live in London. They have a life expectancy of around 4 years and then die, usually unseen[10]. Again, red kites, once a common sight over English medieval towns, where they helped to keep the streets free of the bodies of dead animals[11], have now returned. Reintroduced into the UK in 1989, hundreds now 'commute' in every day into the city of Reading where they are purposely fed by humans in well over 4,000 gardens (Orros and Fellowes, 2014). As I have already pointed out, crows have also proved extraordinarily adept urban colonizers. So adept, indeed, that they may even be suffering from high cholesterol as a result of their changed diet, which tends to include fast food scavenged from rubbish bins and dumpsters (Buehler, 2019). Crow populations do fluctuate in cities. After an attack of West Nile virus, they are now re-establishing themselves in New York. So, too, are a few ravens, part of a dramatic increase being observed in areas where they are willing to live (Taft, 2016). Other animals than birds have also proven to be extraordinarily successful urban colonizers too. In Europe, it is the red fox that struts and postures in cities too numerous to name. In the UK, they have been found in towns and cities since at least the 1930s. Whereas the rural population of foxes in the UK has declined, in cities foxes, like coyotes, have continued to increase in number, certainly to well over 50,000 animals, boosted by easy food sources including feeding by humans. Some cities have very high densities. For example, one study of the Brighton suburbs found around 12 foxes per square kilometre (Brand, 2019). In North America, as we have seen, it is the coyote whose presence is most felt, even though foxes are present in large numbers in many North American cities, too (Day, 2007). The density of these different animals can cause problems. Research shows a correlation between how many animals of a particular species are present in a city and public perception of them as a nuisance. So, for example, the presence of some birds – like seagulls and pigeons and parakeets[12] – can cause real tensions and even culling. Revealingly, they are often described as 'anti-social'. That phrase immediately questions what we mean by public space in cities: are these birds part of a public or off to the side (Trotter, 2019a, b)? Instead of introducing a raft of preventive and disruptive measures[13], why can't we live alongside them?

After all, as Marzluff (2014) points out in the case of mass bird feeding, what we are seeing is a kind of co-evolution. Our culture changes as new practices like feeding unfold, and as the cultures of birds react to them. But birds have also changed our culture. This back and forth could be a model for future more resilient cities, cities in which we pay back for the disruption we have caused. But care is needed. Grand statements need to be tempered by actual dilemmas. For example, as Marzluff also points out, dense populations of a few species that are particularly able to adapt to urban life as it currently exists can threaten biodiversity. But they can also hold out the possibility of a new beginning if the relationships with these common urban animals can be leveraged to construct new ecological webs.

Where all of these different animals live and die varies immensely within the city. That said, some areas of the city are clearly more convivial to them than others. One good proxy is tree cover. For example, in Los Angeles, a map of the city's tree canopy shows that the wealthy areas of West Los Angeles and Los Feliz have a canopy of more than 35 per cent. In less well-off South Los Angeles, by contrast, coverage is between 10 and 12 per cent. But this measure shows something else too: environmental injustice: Often it is the more well-off areas of cities that are also the richest in animal life[14]. Even animal ecology can have a class dimension, in other words (Grove et al., 2015). Biological wealth is unevenly distributed (Turner et al., 2004). For example, in American cities, 'a vast majority of all urban residents live in neighborhoods that harbor fewer bird species than are found on average throughout the city' (Marzluff, 2014: 215), though some cities, like Denver, have put in place schemes that attempt to right the imbalance. In other words, in cities biological wealth and economic wealth are correlated (Turner et al., 2004). (Marzluff, 2014).

Whatever the case, much more can be done to produce a city whose physical form is facilitative of inter-species survival, a city which acts like the hedge. There are all manner of actions that can be and are being instituted. Many of these policies are aimed primarily at boosting human welfare but they benefit animal welfare too.

For example, there are policies that diminish the light and noise pollution which has had such negative effects on all kinds of beings. Consider just the overabundance of light. Only 20 per cent of mammalian species are diurnal like human beings. Nearly 70 per cent of mammals are nocturnal. The rest are crepuscular (active at dawn and dusk) or cathemeral (active during both day and night). Many animals are becoming increasingly nocturnal in cities[15] as they try to avoid human disturbance, and especially artificial light (Bennie et al., 2014; Gaynor et al., 2018), with all manner of consequences from altered diets to general effects on the food chain. But many animals are still stressed by the rhythms of artificial lighting. They look for oases of darkness. More of these can be provided by cutting down on artificial light at night, building in different ways and reconsidering everyday objects. It has been estimated that something as mundane as vehicle headlights results in 100 billion insect deaths each summer in Germany alone (Carrington, 2019). Again, lights can be turned off when buildings or parts of buildings are not in use. Specific buildings can also be tweaked. For example, the Federal Aviation Administration has said that it will change the lighting on airport communication towers across the US after its research found that birds are attracted to the steady red lights that highlight obstructions to pilots at night and then die by colliding with them or their surrounding wires (Millman, 2016). Flashing lights will be used instead. (Research has found that the static red lights commonly found on all kinds of communication towers attract birds – often in large migratory flocks – which then circle the light repeatedly, often collapsing of exhaustion and dying on the ground. Longcore at al. (2012) estimated that 6.8 million birds a year die in the US and Canada due to collisions with communication towers.

All manner of other simple changes to infrastructure are possible that benefit all urban inhabitants and not just humans. Power lines can be buried underground, rerouted or marked in various ways so that they are more visible to birds. Conductors on pole tops can be insulated, and poles designed so that birds cannot make contact with live components. The growth of 'transit ecology' means that it is possible to redesign roads so that they are more friendly to animals that want to cross them as well as providing roadside habitats that animals can use. Buildings can be reworked too, sometimes quite simply. For example, there are policies that transform rooftops. They can be a boon if carried out at scale. One recent audit of London central business districts identified, out of London's 100 square kilometres of roofspace, nearly a square kilometre of space that could be converted into rain gardens, green roofs, agriculture and green walls to the benefit of both humans and nonhumans. Paris is trying to increase the amount of rooftop urban gardening, aiming to transform the roofs of office buildings and other spaces into 100 acres of garden over the next 2 years. A survey of New York found that there were 300 acres of roof suitable to be laid down to agriculture, apart from already existing projects like the nearly 1-acre rooftop farm at Brooklyn Grange (Cohen and Reynolds, 2016). Montreal has just opened the largest commercial rooftop greenhouse in the world. The list goes on. Again, painting city roofs white (or now superwhite) so that they reflect heat is a simple action which ultimately benefits all. New York has already painted more than 5 million square feet of its roofs with a reflective coating. Los Angeles is replacing some of its dark asphalt roads with brighter materials that reflect heat, as is Tokyo. Another policy is to make ventilation corridors out of wide tree-flanked arterial roads allowing cool air to flow down into the city, an idea taken up by cities like Stuttgart which benefits all beings.

Finally, there are the policies that promote more wildlife-friendly corridors in cities through the retention and enhancement of gardens, trees and allotments, and the construction of more parks, small and mini-forests and lakes, as well as more general policies that boost so-called green infrastructures which both sustain and are sustainable (Dover, 2015; Blum, 2016). Additionally, a whole set of new forms of expertise has grown up which govern what has become a very significant land use, a patchwork of edge habitats in which many animals now live, which are increasingly being linked up so as to avoid extirpation (Marris, 2011).

It is vital not to think of cities as simply ecological deserts, then. As already noted, certain animals and plants don't just struggle in cities. They thrive. For example, in one 30-year study of a garden in Leicester, 474 plants, 1,997 insects, 54 birds and 7 mammals were recorded.

In New York, 227 bee species have been recorded. Cities are often, in some senses, more biodiverse than many other ecosystem types, especially intensively farmed agricultural areas. As one instance, in Los Angeles, there are 145 species of trees, compared with 50 to 60 native trees in Southern California (Marris, 2011). Many other cities would show similar arboreal species counts (Wood, 2019).

Retaining, planting and maintaining trees[16] is a policy no-brainer for many reasons[17]. Trees soak up carbon dioxide: it is a fact that restoring natural forest is currently still the best way to remove atmospheric carbon (Lewis et al., 2019). Apart from shade and shelter, they provide air filtration – their leaves absorb and filter air pollution. They provide a source of cooling – the water evaporating from their leaves can cool a neighbourhood by a few degrees during the hottest periods. They provide improved water quality and stormwater percolation. And they provide personal health benefits like better physical and mental health (Schmitz, 2017)[18]. (More generally, on one estimate, around the planet there are some 2 billion hectares that are suitable for reforestation, an area larger than South America.) No wonder that the history of urban trees has become of such interest[19]. After all, tree planting has been an integral part of the history of cities, from the tree-lined promenades of the seventeenth century through the construction of boulevards in the nineteenth century, from the various park movements that intersperse urban history through garden cities and new towns through to the too often bland plantings that characterize so many urban developments today (Johnston, 2015; 2017)[20]. But now urban tree planting may well become a survival characteristic (Goodwin, 2017; Pearlmutter et al., 2017).

However, at the same time, trees in cities are under constant threat from development, climate change, insects, diseases and fire. A study by Nowak and Greenfield (2018) which analysed tree cover in US cities and their surrounding areas reported that tree cover in these areas was declining at a rate of some 175,000 acres, or 36 million trees, every year. At the same time, impervious cover (roads, buildings, etc.) was increasing significantly with the result that 40 per cent of these impervious surfaces were found in areas where trees used to grow. The total loss of tree cover from 2009 to 2014 was estimated to be 1 per cent across cities and their surrounding areas. In the UK[21], which is about 13 per cent forested[22], similar rates of reduction have been found in some cities. It has been estimated that 150,000 trees have been removed from urban highways since 2010 and only 113,000 have been replaced. In Australia, one study (Amati et al., 2017) estimated that between 2008 and 2015, metropolitan regions suffered a 2.8 per cent vegetation loss, equivalent to 1,586 square kilometres, a larger area then the City of Brisbane. (But there were large variations between the regions with some cities suffering a large amount of tree loss made up for, to some extent, by growth in shrubland area and even turf). This tree loss is a tragedy in its own right for many species but it also means less rainfall run-off mitigation, less pollution reduction and greater energy use (especially because use of air-conditioning will be greater).

Another powerful policy is the better use of gardens. Gardening is more than just a recreation with no larger lessons to hand[23]. After all, at last count, just in the UK alone, there were an estimated 10 million acres of garden taking up approximately one quarter of urban land cover (Loram et al., 2007), most of it consisting of a patchwork of small gardens (although it should be added that according to Bonham [2019] only 62 per cent of this space in Great Britain is estimated to be taken up by actual vegetation). Further, in part because of the increase in built-up land, the area devoted to gardens is expanding (except in cities like London where planning regulations allow housing development in gardens because they are classified as built-up land) (Hellen, 2020). Even in a smaller country like Finland, there are at least a million properties with some kind of lot. So, this is an artform with a real capacity to exert change[24]. Indeed, as Marris (2011) points out, gardeners working together can actually have a very considerable impact on the way cities function for wildlife. I have already noted the example of feeding birds. There are many other examples from the insect world. Garden ponds of many different types have become an important resource for amphibians (Hassall, 2014) and aquatic insects (some of which are suffering particularly severe declines[25]), as well as for birds who feed on the insect plumes above them. Then there is a thriving movement to construct more urban beehives, so successful that in London (where the number of registered hives has increased from 2,287 in 2011 to 4,844 in 2019) the new hives have been accused of squeezing out wild bees (Webster, 2020). But more can still be done. For example, take the case of conserving insects in New York:

> If New Yorkers planted more fertile plants and loosened up their gardening standards, bees zooming across the five boroughs could tie isolated specimens together into a metapopulation. If they were willing to plant species with less pest resistance, and accept the tattered leaves and petals that come with it, there would be more food available to the insect fauna. (Marris, 2011: 146–7)

Gardens would have to become less structured, in other words, with more native species, less hybrids, less fertilizer, less lawn, much – much – less pesticide[26] and more connection to the art of connection. If they did, and their owners were willing to accept the change to the less cultivated (but not slapdash) aesthetic that came with it, they could well become a catalytic force (European Environment Agency, 2013; Goulson, 2019).

Then, take the case of the oceans. Apart from policies that simply call a halt to overfishing – and enforce it properly – as well as producing more and more marine reserves, especially ones that aren't just ignored[27], there are simple measures that can be taken in the water in or near to cities. For example, in South Florida zones in which boats that cause wakes are prohibited have allowed to

> give some respite to the manatee [while] the International Maritime Organization has shifted shipping lanes away from right-whale habitat and [...] created seasonal speed limits for large ships when they have no choice but to share their sea lanes with whales in what is now sometimes [...] called the 'urban' or 'industrialized' ocean. (Kroll, 2018: 4)

Whales are a particular problem. They suffer from ship strikes and entanglement with fishing gear and other debris, especially in waters like those off New York where they are becoming more common, as well as some level of disturbance from whale-watching. Apart from imposing speed limits, which, if a 20 per cent cut in speed were generally applied, would lessen ocean noise pollution by two thirds and reduce the chances of a ship colliding with a whale by 78 per cent (Seas At Risk, 2019), other solutions include dividing shipping lanes and producing quieter ocean transport (Jones, 2019)[28].

What these brief examples show, as well as the example of migratory birds set out below, is that the designers of cities are becoming increasingly aware of the need to construct places of coexistence for all so that all may flourish. But this is never going to be a simple task. Given what we now know about how cities affect biodiversity, produce new predators and competitors, influence water tables and biogeochemical processes, induce different forms of nutrient cycling and promote micro-evolutionary change as a result of genetic differentiation, it ought to be possible to produce more resilient regimens that can be beneficial for all urban actors. But this will never be an entirely joined-up process – cities are dynamic entities in which change is the norm. Take just the example of birds. For birds to do well in cities, a whole series of additive actions have to be put in place like providing more vegetative cover, encouraging human feeding of birds, which, as already pointed out, is often a surprisingly important supplementary food resource, and providing appropriate habitats like reworked gardens, as well as the ameliorative actions like reworking city buildings, reducing light pollution and redesigning transport routes. But the outcome of these actions will never be entirely predictable, even if we wanted it to be. And it needs to be kept in proportion. Part of, if not the main reason, for animal deaths from anthropogenic causes is simply loss of habitat to cities. The problem is that, while we know that this loss of habitat is occurring (especially if indirect losses resulting from the demands of cities, like deforestation for construction materials or palm oil, as well as farming, are included), it is very difficult to quantify how many and what animals are adversely affected. We have case studies but the overall figures are often estimates at best.

Loss of habitat leads us directly to the issue of how we share and spare land, by giving added weight to land in which animals can thrive or by leaving it outside of the formal urban corona. Land sharing involves finding ways in which wildlife can thrive within the human-dominated environments of cities as well as in agricultural areas (where low-yield agriculture is often cited as a solution). That involves working out means which enable high density urban populations and wildlife to coexist. Such land sharing solutions are in their infancy, both in terms of what they consist of, and perhaps more significantly, how to implement them, given especially that many animals do not confine themselves to one place. But that does not mean that no progress has been made. Migrant birds are a good example of what is required and it is worth dwelling on this instance. For example, birds that winter in Africa represent one third of all European breeding bird species, including species that have disappeared from many areas of Europe within a lifetime, such as nightingales, turtle doves and spotted flycatchers. Migrant population densities are key general indicators of the capacity of the environment to retain biodiversity generally. Migrant birds also bridge the conservation continuum between local solutions, which generate questions like 'how many green spaces and trees are needed to make a city welcoming?', and global solutions, which generate questions like 'how do we establish a network of habitats and legislation in each stop on the flyway so that no link in the chain is missed?' Solutions that work for migrant birds will often work for much of the biodiversity that needs to be retained to maintain functioning ecosystems on a global scale. But, at present, the populations of migrant birds are under severe strain come what may – from shooting, from mechanical agricultural practices like mowing, tilling, seeding and harvesting which kill fledglings (Tews et al., 2013) – and from cities.

Take the issue of bird strike into windows, which is inevitably tied to this migratory agenda. It is no surprise that Toronto, San Francisco and a number of other North American cities have changed their building code to protect migratory and other birds, whilst others like New York and Chicago have also introduced legislation to adopt similar measures (Poon, 2019). Take the case of Toronto and the Toronto Green Standard, established in 2010 and revised in 2014[29]. A disproportionately high number of bird fatalities tend to occur in Toronto because of its location adjacent to Lake Ontario – at the confluence of the Atlantic and Mississippi Migratory Flyways – and because of the fact that it contains one third of all of the tall buildings in Canada. Bird mortality is disproportionately higher around mid-rise and high-rise buildings, which are concentrated in urban areas like Toronto. So, buildings in that city are expected to use less clear and reflective sheet glass, which birds often strike, so killing themselves, incorporate translucent, opaque and low reflectance glass, include awnings and overhangs, avoid design traps and cut night-time lighting so as to minimize 'fatal light attraction'[30].

Land sparing is often depicted as though it is the opposite of land sharing, in that it argues that separated and very high-yield agriculture and concentrated tightly bounded cities may indeed be less friendly to animals but that the intensification of the use of space they both represent can be used to conserve more untouched habitat in which animals can thrive. However, as many observers have pointed out, this is a false dichotomy (Ansell et al., 2016), not least because the one does not necessarily imply the other and because the distinction is more difficult to make in practice than it is on the page[31]. Cities need tight allocation of land and land that is more friendly to animals but the two don't have to be mutually exclusive, especially since both in certain forms can actually be used to justify more encroachment. In the main, Chinese cities are renowned for the fact that they have grown fast, gobbling up agricultural and wild land and, at the same time, hardly featuring as havens for wildlife. But the Chinese government is increasingly aware of the need to protect non-urban and especially agricultural land. It is designating red lines for land use (as well as energy and water consumption) beyond which urban growth will not be allowed to go so as to guarantee food supply and cease damaging China's increasingly fragile ecology.

Of course, the ultimate land-sparing and land-sharing solution is the one offered up by Wilson (2015: 3) – so called half-Earth, the set aside of 'half the planet, or more', for nonhuman life in order to halt species decline and general damage to ecosystems. The idea is not to divide the planet into two halves but rather to set aside large areas of contiguous land which can function as genuine ecological cradles and start to make reparations for all of the killing on a planet where one third of land is under intense pressure (Jones et al., 2018). This may seem like an optimistic goal but then again perhaps not. On Wilson's figures, reserves already cover 15.1 per cent of the Earth's land area (but only a paltry percentage of the planet's ocean area). Another 35.3 per cent of unprotected lands would therefore need to be devoted to conservation, either through being set aside or restored (Dinerstein et al., 2020). Of course, any such move would require moving away from the archaic agricultural systems that currently feed humans and farm animals, and from growing plants that provide agricultural products at extraordinary ecological cost like palm oil, systems that have swallowed up enormous amounts of land for what are often limited returns. After all, there is really no reason why humans have to be in the picture – quite literally, in the age of the camera phone – everywhere on Earth. That said, the idea of half-Earth is controversial for a number of reasons. To begin with, there is the question of which half of the earth needs to be fenced off. This is a complex issue: the wrong half would be a disaster. For example, does the land need to coincide with the land where most species are? On this index, chosen carefully, only 17 per cent of the world's land surface could be arranged to protect 67 per cent of the world's plant species, for example (Pimm and Joppa, 2015). Or, so far as the rarest plant species are concerned, much less again. Meanwhile, many protected areas are probably safe come what may – steep slopes in mountainous areas, deserts, and so on (Joppa et al., 2008). Then, and following on from these examples, there is serious debate about exactly how much land is really needed to assure good protection of wild animals. Not surprisingly the answer is contested. How many biomes are needed, for example? A half-Earth, properly partitioned, would preserve 85 per cent of life's diversity according to some commentators and also go some way towards stabilizing climate change (Dinerstein et al., 2019; 2020, Strassburg et al., 2020)). But an answer like this has to be hedged with all kinds of caveats. It would have to include certain biologically well-endowed areas to make sense. It would need to include a variety of similar kinds of area to spread risk. And so on.

Of course, land sharing and land sparing doesn't take place just in space. It also takes place in time. The occupancy of the city varies through each 24-hour cycle and different beings are more prominent at some times than others. So animals often play a larger part on the urban stage when humans are sleeping – or at least they did when cities were less frenetic. Sleep is something that all mammals and most other animals do but often at different points in the 24-hour cycle and for widely varying periods of time. It is a form of nourishment which has waned in human history in concert with the rise of the city with its loud noises (whether they were the jangle of medieval church bells or the contemporary roar of traffic), lighting technologies which have evolved from the deeply shadowed assonance of gaslight to the glare of white LED bulbs and powerful smells which have created miniature spatial and temporal ecologies (Handley, 2016). There is no reason why some of the rhythms of the city could not be adjusted to allow different species uninterrupted breathing space, as well as promoting all manner of inter-species interaction[32]. They could be given back their night walks.

But all this 're-naturing' of cities is just a start. We also need a basic change in urban style which recognizes that cities cannot continue growing in the way they have been. Regimented and inflexible cities that balloon outwards cannot survive if we want other beings to survive, yet alone ourselves. The best cities are compact in contrast to the many new cities around the world that sprawl endlessly (Guangzhou is a good example: between 1990 and 2015, its population increased by 925 per cent from 2,485,072 to 24,657,221 but its footprint increased by 3,284 per cent. Houston is another. The overall metro area population of Harris County has grown from 2,818,199 in 1990 to 4,538,000 in 2015. At more than 600 square miles, its footprint now occupies the same space as Chicago, Cleveland, Detroit and Philadelphia combined.) But the best cities also leave room for unexpected combinations. They co-evolve through a constant metamorphosis of forms, taking care not to assume that any one form is definite or definitive. This stricture means taking much more notice of infrastructure as a vital element of cities, of course (Amin and Thrift, 2016). But it also means understanding building as a process in time and not as a one-off finished product. Buildings are constantly supplemented and extended, opening up new possibilities for coexistence (Cairns and Jacobs, 2014). They decay. They may be saved by repair and maintenance – or not. Equally, they can resonate with many different senses at once (sound, smell, touch, taste, parts of the visual spectrum that resonate outside the perception of human beings but can be translated into new palettes, and so on).

We can begin to picture a city in which change and decay are not just regarded as a part of what a city is, but as a valuable resource for certain of its inhabitants which doesn't have to be corrected and brought into line at all costs. This will be a city that to our eyes will look messier, disconnected, even fragmented. The key words are adaptability, adjustment, variegation, redundancy, emergence (Moore, 2016). The city won't be created from whole cloth but will spot opportunity (Gravel, 2016). It is very close to what Moore calls, describing London, a 'slow burn city', a continually emergent city of incremental transformations in which urban ecologies are renewed through change, not devastated by it: 'it renews through consuming itself, through changing its physical and cultural fabric, its buildings, neighborhoods and traditions, from one thing into another, but without devastating what is already there' (2016: xix). As a result, it is full of unruly places where one side of the street is not only very different from the other but can sometimes be counted as a whole other world (Bonnett, 2014; Foer et al., 2016). Cities that follow this model are like the hedge. They are complex, highly adaptive ecosystems whose resilience has emerged over time and is premised on flexibility and diversity. They are therefore suited to change, unlike merely complicated systems, which can fail when just one element fails (Marohn, 2020). One thing is certain: if this vision of a city comes about, cities will look markedly different. They will be messier – less anaemic, darker at night, less tidy, sometimes even ramshackle – for a start. Complicated, but in a good way. Instead of manicured gardens and backlots, the predominant aesthetic is likely to be much more informal, both more devoted to growing food and more wildlife-friendly. The cities will be filled with trees and shrubs. Cities like this will welcome other forms of life as an addition to the city's commonwealth in a 'partially connected commons' (de la Cadena, 2015: 285).

Whatever happens, much of this urban renaissance will have to take place on the back of existing urban stock – on what's already there. Fry (2017) calls this metrofitting, unsettling the settled so that it can dance to a different drum (Amin and Thrift, 2016). We cannot just start anew. We will have carry out mass retrofitting. This is an extraordinary challenge – to re-purpose and re-inhabit what is already there and this time to do it right, and to do it against a background of recurring crises.

Notes

1. China has surpassed the United States as the world's top producer of pigs and chickens. It also raises two thirds of the world's domestic ducks and 90 per cent of geese used for meat. Beef output from cows and buffaloes is still relatively low but growing fast. Dairy is an expanding industry too. Since 2000, consumption of milk products has tripled.
2. China is hardly the only large producer of pigs. For example, there are 50 million pigs in Spain, more than the human population. This figure is an increase of about 9 million animals since 2013. In Spain, a particular problem is water use. Each pig consumes 15 litres of water a day, more than is used by the cities of Zaragoza, Seville and Alicante combined. Spaniards consume about 21 kilograms of pork each year (Burgen, 2018). I neglect pigs in this book but for a superb rendition of the 'life' of pigs in the United States as an exercise in managing a probabilistic totality see Blanchette (2020).
3. Most of these are near the major cities.
4. As in the EU, the use of growth hormones is banned in China.

5   A disease which has led to the culling of over a million pigs and a corresponding cut in China's stock of live pigs by a fifth. It is estimated that that China will produce 150 million to 200 million fewer pigs in 2019 because of deaths from infection or culling. Given that 700 million pigs are slaughtered each year, this is a massive hit (Zhong and Tang, 2019).

6   A draft animal welfare law has circulated in China but has never been passed. There are no nationwide animal welfare laws in China though there is some specific legislation concerning treatment of animals in research and zoos.

7   This thought has been a constant over many decades. For example, Marx and Engels, from The Communist Manifesto on, 'argued that population should be dispersed and the enormous urban concentration characteristic of capitalism should be broken down' (cited in Foster and Burkett, 2016: 25). It's a similar kind of story in the work of writers like William Morris (cited in Mackall, 1922: 305), who famously wrote of a sustainable and decentralized society 'For this is what I want done in this matter of town and country: I want neither the towns to be appendages of the country, nor the country of the town; I want the town to be impregnated with the beauty of the country, and the country with the intelligence and vivid life of the town'. But there is also the question of how such a deconcentration of the current globalized urban could be achieved.

8   The evidence suggests that these bands were actually able to eke out a good living in terms of diet, health and amount of leisure time (Suzman, 2017).

9   That said, architects like Shigeru Ban are trying to come to terms with the new reality of permanent urban disaster by designing housing which can be quickly constructed out of materials to hand or materials that can be quickly imported, are light and cheap.

10 Pigeons tend to retreat to nooks and crannies to die or are predated so that their passing goes unnoticed (Burgess, 2018).

11 London was once 'the city of kites and crows' (Shakespeare, *Coriolanus*).

12 In Madrid, for example, parakeets are regarded as sufficiently 'anti-social' that about 11,000 parakeets are to be exterminated to control what city authorities say has become a threat to public health. In 2005 there were only 1,700 of the birds in Madrid, but by 2019 their number had risen to some 13,000. Many are descended from pets released after their ownership was made illegal (Wilkinson, 2020).

13 In some British cities, feeding gulls is now an offence.

14 The reverse relationship is found with animals like rats, bedbugs, cockroaches and flies. Residents of less well-off areas are more likely to be exposed to pests like these (Biehler, 2013). They are most abundant in the poorest and most crowded areas where neglect and crowding are more likely.

15 We do not know when this process started but it may be that some animals adapted to urban cycles of light and dark quite some time ago (Martinez-Abrain and Jiménez, 2015)

16 As in the case of Manchester.

17 According to one report (Osborne, 2018), China has assigned over 60,000 soldiers to plant trees, chiefly in Hebei province, which encircles Beijing, all as part of China's plan to plant at least 84,000 square kilometres of trees by 2020, so as to increase the forested extent of China from 21 per cent of the total landmass to 23 per cent, with a further aim of getting to 26 per cent by 2035.

18 See treepedia (http://senseable.mit.edu/treepedia [accessed July 2, 2020]) for an estimation of tree cover in over 40 large cities.

19 And it's not just trees. Planting shrubs is important too.

20 Things can change quite rapidly. From the end of the nineteenth century until the 1950s, Detroit was known as 'the city of trees,' with more trees per capita than any other industrialized city in the world. But by 1980, more than half a million trees had died. Of the 20,000 trees marked dead or hazardous in 2014, the city had removed only 2,000 or so. That said, there are now tree-planting programmes in Detroit and in other US cities like Philadelphia.

21 Tree cover in England stands at about 10 per cent, lower than the UK average of 13 per cent of the land area (with England at 10 per cent, Wales at 15 per cent, Northern Ireland

at 8 per cent and Scotland at 19 per cent.) and a long way below the EU average of 38 per cent. But the English figure, for example, is up from 5 per cent nationwide in 1919 and is equivalent to levels of cover during the Middle Ages, which ranged from 15 per cent of England at the time of the Domesday Book in 1086, to somewhere between 6 and 10 per cent by 1300. Cover in Scotland is considerably higher than in medieval times, when only about 4 per cent of the country was wooded.

22   Compared with France at 31 per cent, Germany at 33 per cent and Spain at 37 per cent. Many European countries are, in fact, more forested now than in the past. Across Europe, between 1950 and 2010, amid rapid postwar reconstruction, woods and grasslands grew in area by roughly 150,000 square miles.

23   Gardening is also big business. The American gardening industry alone was worth $47.8 billion in retail sales, according to the US National Gardening Association National Gardening Survey (https://gardenresearch.com/view/national-gardening-survey-2020-edition/ [accessed September 2, 2020). In England, according to Floud (2019), the comparable figure was £11 billion, helped by a boom in the use of allotments. Unfortunately, since the 1950s there has been a 65 per cent reduction in allotment land in the UK, concentrated in the least deprived communities.

24   Indeed, so strong is the gardening imperative that it could be argued that in certain senses the innovations that it stimulated prefigured much wider changes, from central heating, 'developed in the service of plants long before it was applied to people' (Floud, 2019: 288) through steam engines 'used in gardens years before their use in manufacturing industry' (2019: 288) to the use of iron and glass in greenhouses, again used first in the service of plants.

25   One study found an 81.6 per cent decline in aquatic insect abundance between 1969 and 2010 in a German nature reserve.

26   In the United States, homeowners used up to ten times more pesticide than farmers (US Fish and Wildlife Service, 2000).

27   At last count, marine protected areas rose from 0.9 per cent of the ocean to 7.4 per cent in 2020 but many of these are not enforced.

28   Scientists have found a few means of studying what a really quiet ocean would be like, for example in the immediate aftermath of 9/11 around New York and Boston and during the Hindu Nyepi festival in Bali, a day of silence. Coronavirus offers a similar opportunity.

29   Canada's Fatal Light Awareness Program (FLAP), founded in 1993, and its subsidiary program, Birdsafe, are models of what can be achieved. It has lobbied intensively for greater migratory bird protection in Canada which is divided between federal and provincial governments; specifically, Section 32(1) of the Canadian Species at Risk Act (SARA); and Section 14 of the Ontario Environmental Protection Act (EPA), whereby it is now an offence to kill or injure birds as a result of reflective light or windows on buildings. Since a case in 2013, it is now an offence under Ontario's EPA and the federal SARA for a building to emit reflected light that kills or injures birds. For sceptics about the efficacy of these kinds of measures, it is worth mentioning New York's Javits Center. After retrofitting with fritted translucent glass panels and a green roof in 2009, by 2015 bird fatalities had dropped by 90 per cent (Poon, 2019).

30   In 2015, New York State decided to turn off non-essential lights in state-run buildings during periods of peak migration. A number of New York landmark buildings have also signed up to the National Audubon Society's Lights Out programme and turn off their lights in these periods.

31   Additionally, many of the species that people most associate with the countryside (such as hares or partridges) actually depend on a semi-natural agricultural system and could well lose out in a land-sparing system. In Western Europe, a number of schemes are designed to protect species like these and so support sharing rather than sparing. But, whilst effective in some areas, loss of biodiversity still continues.

32   Handley (2016) does not mention that people and animals have often shared sleeping spaces (and still do), even though the cover of her book shows two people, Tobias and Sarah, sleeping peacefully together on their wedding night in a bed that is shared with a sleeping lamb, representing God's protection.

10
Dreaming More Human Cities 2

Three more knots of practices are going to have to be unravelled and retied to get to more human cities. In this chapter, I round off the previous chapter by considering each of them in turn.

Change the Agrilogistic Machine

First, there is *the agrilogistic machine* that keeps cities fed. It needs fundamental change so that it calls a halt to pummelling the land and trawling the sea past any sense. Morton (2016) argues that this errant behaviour is the result of an unconscious algorithm gone mad, a runaway that cannot stop itself from reproducing twilight over and over again. Whether that is the case or not, we are bearing the weight of historical decisions made a very long time ago in the transition to sedentary agriculture (such as corralling the constant labour needed to keep land productive, choosing to invest in just a few possible food sources, especially grains like wheat and rice, and accepting a degree of inequality (see Scott, 2017). The country and the city are now one, bound together by a continual search for productivity for its own sake, which could just as easily be seen as the act of eating gone mad, a kind of urban death drive arising from the reign of an empire of food that has overreached itself.

Changing Agriculture

In a world where so many mammals consist of domesticated livestock human beings keep to eat (Thomas, 2017: Bar-On et al., 2018)[1], this pessimistic diagnosis doesn't seem so very far off the mark. We are literally eating up the world[2], a world which has been turned into a reservoir of land, freshwater and sea whose chief purpose is to feed cities by killing animals in one way (extinction through loss of habitat) or another (farming). The figures speak for themselves. Humans make up just 0.06 per cent of all biomass on the planet (measured in gigatonnes of carbon) but they have caused the loss of 83 per cent of all wild mammals and half of all plants. More than one third of mammals are people, and just 4 per cent are wild animals. Meanwhile, farmed poultry now make up 70 per cent of all birds while livestock make up 60 per cent of all mammals (Bar-On et al., 2018). The rise of this treadmill of slaughter, which, in itself, signals an extraordinary historical change in the make-up of diets, has had a whole series of negative environmental effects, from the destruction of tropical forest for pasture to the growth of water-hungry feed crops (and water-hungry meat products like hamburgers[3]), from serious air pollution (for example, through the effects on emissions via methane – not least when belched from cows) and ground pollution (for example, through the ammonia used in fertilizer) water pollution (via slurry and fertilizer)[4], from threats to health – like new kinds of epizootic disease, microbial resistance and obesity – to extensive soil loss. It is clearly a major factor in climate change – while other industries have been cutting greenhouse gas emissions, emissions from agriculture have been broadly level or actually increasing, fuelled by significant demand growth, projected to be more than 70 per cent between 2005 and 2050, driven by a growing world population, rising affluence – and urbanization (FAO, 2013; Lymbery and Oakeshott, 2014; Renton, 2014). In 2013, emissions from livestock agriculture provided 14.5 per cent of greenhouse gas emissions. Beef and cattle milk production contributed 41 and 20 per cent of the sector's emissions while pig meat and poultry meat and eggs contributed a further 9 and 8 per cent respectively (FAO, 2013). Methane is proving to be a particular problem. More than half of the methane in the atmosphere now arises from anthropogenic sources and, of this, about half arises from agriculture, a figure which is increasing everywhere except in Europe (Jackson et al., 2020).

Intensive livestock agriculture has produced an increasingly sterile countryside, sometimes akin to a death zone, polluted by fertilizers and pesticides, stripped of soil, and using far too much water[5] and antibiotics. It has had a number of malign consequences for human health. And it has activated a blizzard of animal welfare issues resulting from the installation of archipelagos of mechanized death whose ill effects were documented in a previous chapter though it is worth noting that recent advances in slaughter-house design mean that fewer cows and pigs now need to be driven towards their deaths with electric prods (Cavell et al., 2008; Grandin, 2012). It's an advance of sorts.

Practically, this abuse of the environment and other beings cannot go on much longer without causing such malign effects that the very fabric of the urban will start to be undermined. But changing it will not be easy. Though any rational being considering the system we have now as though it were a de novo innovation would think that they had trespassed on a tragicomedy, still it is embedded in many self-supporting ways. Changing it will challenge many different interests which represent settled means of doing things and making profits as well as tackling mistaken or timid government policies and the subsidies that go with them (Paulson Institute, 2020). That means not so much the farmers, many of whom are willing to change course (and in some cases are doing so), as majoritarian interests like the big agricultural combines, finance and banking – the practice of commodity futures was effectively built around the supply of agricultural produce to cities, whether that be hogs or grain – insurance, transport and logistics, engineering and design, and latterly information and biotechnology. All these interests look set to lose from change, at least in the short term, and, as the examples of tobacco and oil show, they will not go quietly into the night.

The sterility of the current urbanized hinterland, otherwise known as 'countryside', can be illustrated through the example of the English countryside. After all, English countryside is popularly represented as a set of green and verdant fields, dotted with picturesque woodland copses, inhabited by solid rural stock, both human and nonhuman, and by birds twittering, bees buzzing and lambs baaing. It is sometimes regarded as the epitome of a domesticated landscape, Blake's 'green and pleasant land', now marketed around the world as a place in which place somehow comes true. But take away the conservation zones and the fact that the British population join wildlife and environmental organizations in their droves (Cocker, 2018), and the bulk of what is left often resembles a particularly brutal factory transforming the land into one in which '99 per cent of flower-rich meadows have been destroyed and 44 million breeding birds have vanished from the countryside' (Cocker, 2018: 287). Those green fields have often become killing fields.

As drivers travel down the motorways of the UK, what they are often seeing is a vista akin to a desert in all but name (Cocker, 2018), one populated in 2017 by over 230 million farm animals (Lang, 2020) (not forgetting that this figure includes animals sequestered in what are, in effect, warehouses), animals that – in most cases – will soon be on their way to a slaughterhouse. Approximately 2.6 million cattle, 14.5 million sheep, 982 million broiler chickens, 50 million boiling fowl (including so-called 'spent' hens), 14 million turkeys, 15 million ducks and geese, and 10 million pigs are slaughtered in any year. The profusion of livestock animals is hardly a surprise: their production dominates UK land use. Even prime cereal land is often used to provide feed for them.

In the UK in 2019, an estimated 17.5 million hectares of land were 'utilized agricultural area', 72 per cent of all land. In all, 10,193,000 hectares were permanent grassland and another 4,714,000 hectares were cropland (DEFRA, 2020). But look at what is happening to this land under a system of agriculture which values increased production (and its correlates, intensification and simplification) above all and has the subsidies to prove it. Like the rivers, only 14 per cent of which are in 'good ecological condition' and all of which have some degree of chemical pollution (Environment Agency, n.d.), the fields are frequently polluted by fertilizers (like nitrogen and phosphates) and slurry, battered by herbicides, fungicides and pesticides (which have had to become stronger to overcome resistance) and beset by questionable land management practices. Nitrogen and phosphate pollution is still extensive, even though it has fallen back, and some of the nitrogen converts into nitrous oxide, a potent greenhouse gas. The topsoil is disappearing too. Perhaps the most extreme example can be found in the peat zone of the English Fenlands where the draining of the land and intensive agriculture has produced a quite extraordinary denudation of the peat layer.

> In 1851 [an iron column] was hammered into the freshly drained peat [...]. [it's top] was level with the ground. Today it stands 13 feet (3.6m) above it. Peat is being lost at the rate of over half an inch (1.5cm) a year, and in some areas is predicted to disappear completely. (Cocker, 2018: 185)

Finally, wildlife is disappearing fast, not surprisingly given that the UK has failed to reach any but three of the 20 UN biodiversity targets agreed on 10 years ago, and on six has actually gone into reverse (RSPB, 2020). *The State of Nature 2019* (Hayhow et al., 2019), a combined report by more than 50 nature conservation and research organizations, describes the toll on terrestrial and freshwater wildlife in Great Britain between 1970 and 2016 in one of 'the most nature depleted countries in the world'. The abundance indicator for 697 terrestrial and freshwater species showed a significant decline in the average level of abundance of 13 per cent. 58 per cent of species showed negative trends, 42 per cent of species showed positive trends. The distribution indicator of 6,654 priority species in the UK declined by 27 per cent. Of 8,431 species that have been assessed against the International Union for Conservation of Nature (IUCN) Regional Red List criteria, 15 per cent of the extant species for which sufficient data are available are classified as threatened and therefore at risk of extinction. What does all of this mean on the ground? Take just mammals. One in five British land mammals now faces extinction (Mathews et al., 2018), even including the fox in countryside areas.

> Over a quarter of all British birds are under threat [...] The hedgehog population is down by over a quarter. Toads are down 68 per cent in 30 years, water voles are no longer found in 94 per cent of the places where they once lived. Likewise, mountain hares are in steep decline, as are rabbits. (Rushby, 2018: 2)

Just as worryingly, the flying insect population has declined precipitously. For example, there was a 50 per cent decline in flying insects hitting cars in Kent between 2004 and 2019 (Tinsley-Marshall et al., 2020). Another report (Powney et al., 2019) also found British insects declining at an alarming rate. Widespread losses of pollinating insects in Britain were reported between 1980 and 2013, with the declines concentrated in rarer species. As importantly, insects form the base of thousands upon thousands of other food chains. In other words, something serious has happened to insects, the result of global warming certainly but, more particularly, the result of intensive farming, which means that insects are starved out or killed by pesticides, high levels of roadkill and general urban growth, which, through light pollution, confuses their nocturnal activity. And the consequences are severe: lack of pollination[6], a declining stock of available food for other wildlife (especially birds – the disappearance of insects is a major reason why Britain's farmland birds have more than halved in number since 1970[7]) and shrinking rates of decomposition among them.

And it is the demands of cities that are the forces behind all of this – through the multiple demands of their populations for heterogenous forms of food, without any sense of the consequences, through a general public ignorance of farming practices that has been engendered over many years now and through supply chains which privilege speedy response to consumer demand over any sense. Of course, all of this could be changed and most of it could be changed rapidly. So, for example, in Britain, farming practices could be altered. At the very least, more land could be given over to different forms of farming which are both more sustainable and more friendly to both domesticated and wild animals, such as certain kinds of wilding which go with the grain of ecological processes rather than continually depleting the land (Tree, 2018) or simply using spring-sown cereals which can benefit farmland wildlife by providing an overwinter stubble. Existing environmental legislation, which has got tighter, could be properly enforced. Subsidies, which are often simply a gift from the taxpayer to the richer farmer, could be repurposed towards doing more environmental good rather than just doing more (Helm, 2019).

The greatest irony in all this is that British cities have become more welcoming to some wildlife than the so-called countryside as monoculture has replaced diversity. They can become, at least partially, substitute environments. And it isn't just foxes, either. Many birds are thriving. In London, for example, between 1900 and 1975, five species were lost but 20 new species colonized the city. The upward trend has continued, to at least 60 species by 2012, though some farmland species and species dependent on niches in buildings are struggling (Woodward et al., 2017). Again, 'it is now commonplace for bumblebee numbers and species diversity to be much greater in suburban and urban areas than in the countryside' (Cocker, 2018: 288). Indeed, a recent paper (Samuelson et al., 2018) argues that bumblebee populations are stronger in British urban than rural areas, partly because bumblebees are less likely to be exposed to pesticides and partly because of the greater availability and variety of flowers in gardens and parks[8].

Whatever the case, the very same urbanization processes are producing many of the same results in radically different environments. Take just the case of Australia, an example of a vast, hot and mainly dry continent whose towns and cities are generally crammed in along the coastline. It might be thought to be close to the polar opposite of the British countryside. But there too, we see the same urban depredations. There too, we see a large fall-off in species diversity and in numbers of wild animals; 10 per cent of Australian land mammals have gone extinct since European settlement. Flannery (2012) argues that we are likely entering a new round of extinctions unless rapid action is taken. In particular, new farming practices are needed to combat pollution, poisoning via pesticides, water shortages and soil loss. But there are solutions. Managing fire by returning to past indigenous practices, cultivating indigenous grains and vegetables, eliminating

Food Waste

Most grotesquely, and to return to a previous point, there is the issue of *food waste*. Food is produced in a cockamamie way, it's true. But then it doesn't even get consumed. About a third of all food – 1.3 billion tonnes – is wasted globally, waste that contributes to climate change through the production of 8 per cent of total anthropogenic greenhouse gas emissions (FAO, n.d.), and is responsible for the multiplication of water shortages, the amplification of food insecurity and hunger, and the instigation of unnecessary animal deaths. By one estimate, reducing global food waste by a relatively modest 250 million tonnes by 2050 would be the 'equivalent of reducing carbon emissions by 600 million [tonnes] annually. Even more encouraging is an associated reduction of 132 million hectares of agricultural land required to feed the population by 2050' (Mandyck and Schulz, 2015: 31). Somewhere between a quarter and a half of all the food produced in the United States is currently wasted (Stuart, 2009; Bloom, 2010; Mandyck and Schulz, 2015). Bloom (2010) estimates that figures like this mean that around 133 billion lb of food is wasted annually – near to half a billion dollars of food waste each day.

> Forty three billion pounds are tossed at retail and 90 billion by the consumer. That's $161.6 billion of losses, with meat, poultry and fish (30 per cent), vegetables (19 per cent) and dairy (30 per cent) leading the way. In a culture that sometimes seems obsessed with calories, Americans discard some 141 trillion annually. (Mandyck and Schulz, 2015: 60)

The situation is less severe but still serious in countries like the UK where it is estimated that 10.2 million tonnes of food is wasted each year of which around 60 per cent is 'avoidable', meaning that it could have been eaten at some point[9]. According to figures from the Department for Environment, Food and Rural Affairs, 1.8 million tonnes of food waste is generated by food manufacturers, about 1 million tonnes by the restaurant trade and 260,000 tonnes by retailers. The bulk though, 7 million tonnes, is generated by households. Much of this food waste ends up in landfill.

Meanwhile, so far as fishing is concerned, the situation is, if anything, worse. Led, in terms of fishing days (Kroodsma et al., 2018), by the Chinese, Taiwanese, Spanish and Italian fleets[10], on one 2018 FAO estimate, 35 per cent of global catches are wasted. The United Nations Environment Programme (UNEP) has claimed that, after excluding discards, spoilage, fishmeal and inedible portions, humans eat barely more than half of all fish caught in the world[11]. The most obvious type of waste in the fishing industry is the 'discards': unwanted by-catch that are too small or of the wrong species are thrown back into the sea. In many fisheries, an estimated 70 to 80 per cent of these fish die in the process.

> Europe wastes more than almost anywhere else in the world: the EC estimates that between 40 and 60 per cent of all fish caught are thrown back into the sea. Greenpeace suggests that of the 186 million fish caught by European fleets, 117 million are thrown back. (Stuart, 2009: 124–5)

But it isn't just discards, which may even have reduced slightly since 2009 (FAO, 2018). They account for a quarter of all losses. The rest of the losses come from either a lack of knowledge or lack of proper equipment like refrigeration or ice-makers, lack of use of devices that can eliminate by-catch (like LEDS to illuminate exits in nets), and losses between landing and consumption, which are very high too. The result of these kinds of practices is clear at least. Three quarters of all marine fish species are on the brink of, or below, sustainable population levels. Only 4 per cent of the world's oceans remain in a pristine state. The rest have been affected to differing degrees by over-fishing, pollution and climate change but shifting ecological baselines mean that we are often not aware of the overall consequence: the oceans are much emptier now than they were two centuries ago.

So far as distribution and retail are concerned, there are all kinds of reasons for this state of food superfluity in the developed world: the promotion of uniformity of size, shape, colour and appearance generally in vegetables, and the lack of labour to pick them, increasing portion sizes (which also prompt overeating), the rise of prepared foods and convenience foods more generally, time-poor cultures, the demise of a culture of consumer thrift and the rise of a culture of spontaneity (with higher margins on goods which make surplus food into a smaller percentage of profit), even increasing plate and refrigerator sizes.

But, whatever the reasons for these levels of waste, the effects are obvious. This is a world in which many animals die in vain: there is not even the excuse that they are going to be food. So far as meat animals are concerned, not only could the cereals fed to them be used to feed far more people directly than can the meat they produce but, in many cases, their flesh will, in effect, rot away for naught, a fact only compounded by the limited use made of many animals' body parts – unlike in the past when the whole animal tended to be used for something.

Though the United States might be one of the most egregious examples of food waste, many other countries are catching up fast. China is one striking instance. There, it is estimated that 17 to 18 million tons of food are being discarded annually, enough wasted food to supply 30 to 50 million people for a year (Huang and Qin, 2020). The Chinese problem is predominantly urban. In Shanghai, 80 per cent of households throw away edible produce, amounting to 12 per cent of all food supplies (Gu, 2019)[12]. The situation in China has become so bad that President Xi Jinping initially supported an internet campaign to persuade people to finish the food on their plates rather than leave a portion of it to go to waste, an action that would be regarded as a matter of courtesy in Chinese culture[13], and has since extended this action with a 'clean plate' campaign that began in 2020.

One counter to food waste is *greater efficiency* of distribution. That efficiency, which requires wholesale adaptation of supply chains, can come from several sources. For example, food recovery systems are concerned with donating surplus food to people who don't have access to the food they need rather than sending it to landfills through various means such as community groups, colleges and universities, through supermarket action and through government legislation. They require massive expansion. Equally, there are more efficient food use systems like LeanPath which use software and comparative data to track and measure food use in commercial systems so as to minimize waste.

Eat Less Meat

But there is another counter to this wayward agrilogistic tendency: cities must learn to live within ecological footprints that are not only proportionate but massively more efficient. It would require a number of steps to achieve but, as Smil (2013) points out, it is undoubtedly a practical possibility. As Derrida (2008: 71) puts it 'perhaps qualitative conditions [can] be changed, together with quantity, the evaluation of quantity, as well as the general organization of the field of food and nourishment'.

In particular, cities need to drastically reduce eating 'meat' or stop eating it altogether. After all, 'industrial agriculture to produce meat is the coal-mining of food production' (Egan, 2019: 12). There is a large literature that mines this theme. It argues that cutting meat production through taxation and promoting a vegan diet is a necessity since 'animal products cause more damage than [producing] construction materials such as sand or cement, plastics or metals. Biomass and crops for animals are as damaging as [burning] fossil fuels' (UNEP International Resource Panel, 2016: 21; see also UNEP, 2010). It gives the lie to Kotkin's (2016) argument that we can find ways to feed any rate of growth in urban population. No doubt we could. But on the current trajectory that will destroy what's left of the planet. We can but hope that the chickens don't come home to roost.

There are many ways a reduction in meat consumption could be achieved. We could know about what we kill, for example. We could take a leaf from the practices of many native peoples who situate killing animals in relationships of accountability and respect, a theme I will return to in the next chapter. We could join the rapidly growing 'eat-what-you-kill' movement that insists on only eating animals that have been dispatched by the hand of the person who carries out the killing (Murphy, 2015). We could stop eating so much meat (indeed, there is a current trend in some Western countries to only eating meat at weekends or other flexitarian variants) or we could turn to vegetarianism or veganism[14].

'Vegetarianism' is a word that was coined in the 1840s, as a result of the founding of the Vegetarian Society in the UK in 1847 and the American

Vegetarian Society in 1850. Of course, vegetarian practices have been an important constant of certain cultures like Buddhism and Hinduism and Jainism for millennia[15]. In Western cultures, these practices have formed an important tradition for many millennia now. For example as Lestel (2016) points out, the classical period had its vegetarian proponents. In Britain, in the seventeenth and eighteenth centuries, the motives for leading such a lifestyle were many and varied (Stuart, 2006). They came from certain kinds of Christian beliefs, especially a prelapsarianism which argued that eating flesh had been unlawful in the Garden of Eden and that it was time to return to a state of harmony free from the carnage of animal death. They came from revolutionary ideals which can be traced at least to some of the participants in the English Revolution and, later, to direct democrats like Oswald and poets and revolutionaries like Shelley who saw meat-eating as a bloodthirsty moment in the obscene cavalcade of luxury (Stuart, 2006). They came from utilitarian demographers who were convinced that meat-eating was a waste of resources which could be better used to feed people in other ways. They came from anatomists, doctors and natural philosophers more generally, including Descartes, Gassendi and Bacon, who believed both that human intestines were not suited to eating meat, and that meat eating caused overstimulation to the body, and who espoused a more general notion of sympathy, an important component of a new moral philosophy. They came from travellers in and builders of Empire who were heavily influenced by the mores of Indian civilization and saw in India a different, healthier and more balanced world whose principles they could venerate. And they came from a general cultural current that extended more compassion to animals. It is no particular surprise, then, that London, for example, had at least two vegetarian restaurants by the turn of the nineteenth century.

In the United States, vegetarianism has a long and complicated history too (see Iacobbo and Iacobbo, 2004) dating from the colonial era, a history which, initially at least, was closely allied with Christian beliefs and a notion of God's covenant with humanity[16]; condemnation of cruelty to animals was a constant amongst a certain kind of Christian preacher. By the beginning of the nineteenth century vegetarianism was firmly established, the result of both this native Christian tradition, growing movements like temperance (the consumption of alcohol was often linked to meat-eating), general disease prevention frequently allied to the promotion of a more healthy lifestyle, and a certain degree of cross-pollination from English radical writers. Still, much of mainstream America remained firmly resistant to vegetarianism until the late twentieth century.

'Veganism' is of more recent origin. As a word, it was only coined in 1944, when a British woodworker instigated a meeting with a number of other non-dairy vegetarians to search out a word that would describe their lifestyle. But it was not until the 1970s that veganism really accelerated as a part of the counter-culture. It remained a minority preoccupation, but, in the last few years, fuelled by health and environmental concerns and boosted by social media, it has become closer to the mainstream (Larsson, 2019; Reynolds, 2019).

In other words, vegetarianism and veganism are no passing fads. They are generally growing in influence in many countries, boosted by the current cultural sheen of veganism. That said, exact figures are difficult to come by. For example, in the UK, according to one recent poll, 5.7 per cent of the population were vegetarians, in another it was 7 per cent but in yet another poll the figure was only 3.5 per cent. One 2016 Ipsos/MORI survey found that there were 542,000 vegans in the UK, an increase from 150,000 in just 10 years. A 2018 study found that 0.2 per cent of the British population had stopped eating meat in the previous year. There are also some concrete sales figures which suggest a substantial increase in the consumption of non-meat products. For example, in the UK between 2013 and 2018 Mintel found that sales of meat-free foods increased by 22 per cent. An Ipsos/MORI poll found that 49 per cent of British consumers would eat a plant-based substitute for meat. All this said, nine out of ten British households still buy red meat.

In the US, at last count, it was estimated that around 3.4 to 5 per cent of Americans were vegetarians, according to which poll you choose, a proportion of the population which has been reasonably stable for some time. Vegans form between 0.4 and and 2 per cent of the population, showing how variable polls can be. Turning to sales figures again, sales of plant-based food are rising by 5 to 8 per cent each year but with many being sold to flexitarians who still eat meat. It's not just meat: cow's milk sales have been declining while plant-based milk sales have been increasing.

Then there is investment in meat substitutes. The global meat substitutes market is expected to register a compound annual growth rate of 7.8 per cent between 2019 and 2026 (Shapiro, 2018; ReportLinker, 2019), boosted by the so-called 'impossible burger' and the many other alternative artificial meats now starting to come on to the market from companies like Beyond Meat, Sweet Earth Natural Foods, Memphis Meats and Finless Foods (Reese, 2018; Little, 2019). It may even be possible to mass produce artificial protein which is palatable, like the recently announced Solein (Boffey, 2019). That would be a game-changer. (At the same time, a search for replacements for what are still widely used animal by-products like the $100 billion business of leather has begun[17].)

Whatever the exact case, the general uptick in non-meat and non-dairy sales and the general downturn in meat and dairy sales in Western countries like the UK and the US is clearly not just an artefact of the rise of vegetarianism and veganism but also arises out of a general flexitarian tendency to eat less meat generally, most often based on health grounds. For example, the EAT-Lancet et al. report on Food in the Anthropocene (2019) argues that, for reasons of both personal and planetary health, a 'best available food' diet rich in plant-based foods like pulses, grains, fruits, vegetables, nuts and seeds, along with fewer animal-based foods is an imperative, a conclusion in line with the work of many authors (e.g. Poore and Nemecek, 2018). By 2050, the report estimated that would require a more than doubling of consumption of plant-based foods worldwide and at least a 50 per cent reduction in meat. In turn, that requires a wholesale shift in food production practices. That won't be easy, given how entrenched are the vested interests in maintaining these practices and how successful they have been at lobbying. It is worth remembering that the equivalent of some $700 billion in agricultural subsidies goes each year mainly to bolster crops like corn and soya, to prop up meat and dairy, and to subsidize the cheap raw materials used in intensive livestock production and for highly processed foods (Food and Land Use Coalition, 2019)[18].

All this said, just stopping or reducing meat consumption might not be quite the environmental panacea it is sometimes portrayed as. For example, White and Hall (2017) considered the impacts of giving up all animal farming in the United States. They found that total greenhouse gas emissions would be reduced but by a more modest amount than sometimes claimed. Plant-only agriculture would produce 23 per cent more food but nutritional deficiencies might increase. In other words, the current system is not geared up to making an overnight switch[19]. Other foods wouldn't be instantly available. Something would have to be done about all of the foods produced for animals (including pets), which are often human-inedible. And so on.

Change Agricultural Practices

An important part of less meat eating would be *new and less obtrusive agricultural systems*. This transition is going to be the most difficult goal to achieve whilst also being the most necessary. There is compelling evidence that numerous urban civilizations have failed or been terminally weakened because the large populations of their cities outstripped their food systems or made them vulnerable to unexpected threats like climate change – Ancient Rome being a case in point (Rose, 2016; Woolf, 2020). Equally, the agricultural footprints of most contemporary cities are unsustainable in their current form and need changing in short order before they begin to fail (Steel, 2009). Meat production isn't just a matter of the industrial exploitation of animals. It has large knock-ons effects on agriculture more generally and on how cities are fed. In particular, around 40 per cent of the world's cereals, equivalent to 700 million tonnes, are fed to farm animals. Another 500 million tonnes of roots, tubers, fishmeal, brans, pulses, oilseeds and oilcakes like soymeal also go to feed farm animals. But we do not get a return. 'Globally, we give more than three times more food to livestock than they give us back in the form of milk, eggs and meat, meaning that on average livestock lose over 70 per cent of their calories in the harvests fed to them' (Stuart, 2009: 139)[20].

But there are clearly ways of reorganizing existing agricultural and food systems by using regenerative farming strategies such as grassland carbon sequestration, growing more appropriate foodstuffs and manure management. One particular example shows what can be done. To counter the worldwide degradation of soil, no-till farming has been growing in popularity (Dang et al., 2020). Dating from the 1940s, no-till farming is one way of growing crops or pasture from year to year without disturbing the soil through tilling it. It has many benefits. For example, it increases the amount of water that infiltrates into the soil and aids both organic matter retention and the cycling of nutrients in the soil. It can help to reduce or even eliminate soil erosion. It also helps to boost the amount and variety of life in and on the soil. The most powerful benefit of no-till farming is an improvement in the soil's biological fertility, making soils more resilient. But a useful by-product is that farming operations are made much more efficient. All this said, some commercialized variants of no-till farming are heavily dependent on general purpose weedkillers like glyphosate to make up for the fact that deep ploughing kills more weeds. This is hardly an advance.

There are many other agricultural techniques which can be deployed to produce better urban agricultural reservoirs and food systems and there is no space to name them all. They have, in any case, been documented again and again (see Hawken, 2017; Food and Land Use Coalition, 2019; Kothari et al., 2019, Lang, 2020; Steel, 2020; or, most recently, the finalists for the Rockefeller Food System Vision Prize). Perhaps the most relevant to this book is making the immediate built-up area of cities into a food-growing resource again via urban agriculture. Nowadays, this form of farming is often associated with a past when agriculture often took place within the city's bounds. For example, in Paris in the second half of the nineteenth century, it is estimated that 8,500 urban farmers were cultivating just under 3,500 acres (1,400 hectares) within the city boundaries (one sixth of the urban area). These small urban farms 'supplied the city year-round with one hundred thousand tons of high-quality, high-value salad and vegetable crops, with enough to export to England. Each 2.5 acre plot (1 hectare) was capable of supplying fifteen Parisians with their caloric needs' (Cockrall-King, 2012: 83).

Here, then, was a high-yield and diverse agricultural system which, when combined with a tendency for many urban dwellers with the means to do so to grow backyard vegetables, meant that cities like Paris could still be significant agricultural producers. Now modern urban agriculture is trying to recreate systems like these – in Paris and elsewhere (Steel, 2009; 2020; Cockrall-King, 2012). Though they often go under the tag of 'local' food systems, and are the subject of a vast literature, the matter of local has to be treated carefully or it can be fetishized, leaving the bulk of the food system unaffected (McLaren and Ageyman, 2015). That said, these urban systems, consisting of mixes of urban farms (some, as we have seen, on roofs), community gardens, school gardens, allotments, apiaries and the intensive use of backyards, are not without impact. And much, much more could be done.

Then, there is vertical farming, which aims to produce quick-growing, high value crops on or near the premises of urban food outlets (Despommier,

2011; Steel, 2020). Though they are difficult to scale, such mainly hydroponic farms have a number of advantages such as: allowing year-round crop production; providing food to areas that lack arable land; giving immunity to weather-related crop failure; enabling re-use of water; using no pesticides, fertilizers or herbicides; drastically reducing dependence on energy; generating no food waste due to shipping or storage; and creating no agricultural runoff.

Population

Second, we need to think about *population growth*. The elephant in the room, as it has so often been described, will continue to be population growth and the demands it makes on the Earth. These are 'inescapable matters' (Haraway, 2018: 74) which are a matter of multispecies – not just one species – reproductive justice. Maybe we can produce a planet which will support 9 or even 12 billion people – the estimates vary wildly depending on the assumptions made about the drivers of population growth[21]. But one thing seems certain under current circumstances: as the world population grows yet more clouds of animal death will loom on the horizon. In other words, we are crowding out much of what allows us room to think about ourselves as something other than ourselves: beings who think and act as visitors rather than conquerors, as a differentiated, multiform humanity able to exist in a mutuality of being (Sahlins, 2013; Haraway, 2016; 2018). The cosmic gas station is not just there to fill up with human beings, in other words.

This is sensitive territory, of course, as the recent debate over the apparently disproportionate size of the effect that having fewer children has on climate change shows only too well (Wynes and Nicholas, 2017; Basshuysen and Brandstedt, 2018; Brandstedt, 2019)[22]. Some commentators (e.g. Murphy, 2018) want to do without the category of population altogether on the grounds that it has been used to justify or even drive a whole series of grim episodes in human history and to power prejudices and inequalities, especially towards women, that still exist. The act of counting itself can often be complicit. Better, then, to put it to one side. I demur from this stance. As Haraway (2018: 86) points out, for all their faults the figures mean something. 'Made is not made up.'

That is not to say that the critics do not have a point, only that they overextend it. True, simply reducing human numbers will never be the answer by itself but, at this point in history, childlessness might well be thought of as a public good without having to imply coercion (Ganesh, 2020: 18). That means rethinking a whole set of other world orders and especially the overaccumulation that feeds – or doesn't feed – population expansion. We need to think of human populations as a part of wider *kin* structures which rely on all manner of forms of symbiogenesis in which the kinfolk live each other's lives and die each other's deaths and we need to think about new practices and expectations of population control which do not just play a blame game but instead express new notions of worth which understand reproduction in very different ways (Murphy, 2017)[23]. It follows that we need to think of cities as equilibrating structures rather than as the vast magnets for population concentration and reproduction that they have become. There is, after all, some evidence that cities do actually slow the rate of population growth overall.

That said, the parts of the world where the population pressures on cities will be at their most extreme (fuelled by population growth and in-migration) – Africa (especially Nigeria), India and China – are also the parts of the world which are under the greatest environmental stress (Simone and Pieterse, 2017). Of these, Africa is the obvious example: 'a simple [...] way to put this is that, at present, 15 per cent of the world's population is African, by 2050 it will be 25 percent, and by 2100 above forty per cent' (Simone and Pieterse, 2017: 33). So far as urban population is concerned, the situation is even starker: African cities will bear the brunt of this increase. In the main, they are ill-prepared for the onslaught of young people, although there are cities like Lagos which are innovating in numerous ways, from floating architecture to urban innovation start-ups (French, 2016; https://urbanchallenge.co/). This innovation is desperately needed. For example, one projection estimates that the population of Lagos could be 88 million by 2100, four times its current size, others that the city could reach between 61 and 100 million people (Hoornweg and Pope, 2016).

But, at risk of labouring the point, reproduction cannot be understood simply as a matter of human welfare. It needs to be thought of as a multispecies affair in which humans aren't the only actors in the tale and where what were formerly regarded as the 'props' have to be given a say in a new version of the extended family, one with the same kinds of affective resonances but laid out on a broader canvas[24]. For this version, 'population' becomes a matter of with rather than and – of a kind of comity, and a heightened affinity that entails new reproductive responsibilities and especially understanding each birth as a kind of collective triangulation with other species rather than as an individual decision[25]. Composition, not accumulation, as Haraway would put it. It's about redefining kinship to include other species. It's not such a bizarre idea as all that. After all, there are already more American homes with companion animals than with children (Brooks, 2020). A number of commentators (e.g. Crist, 2020) have tried to mount a critical high horse by stubbornly misunderstanding Haraway's basic point that it's not just about us humans[26]. Yet what is being suggested is very much in the mould of the contemporary idea of a chosen family (Weston, 1997).

After all, Whitehead (1978 [1929]: 21) claims that the primary purpose of life is not self-preservation but 'rather the origination of conceptual novelty – novelty of appetition', the urge to create. If that is so, sheer human numbers are not the point. Such a view could have some substantial policy consequences – like equilibrating population with a city's environmental footprint. If that footprint is small, the city can have more population[27]. Or there is Haraway's (2016) proposal that each human birth should be linked to an animal symbiont, rather like Phillip Pullman's daemons, but expressed through various minor genetic modifications, so that a kind of relay of care is produced. Whatever the action taken, population can never again be thought of as simply a human category. That would be to miss the point.

The Right to the City

Finally, the *right to the city* needs to be redefined as an inclusive right that can include nonhuman beings. Such a frame of mind is not common, however. For example, when a respected urbanist like Kotkin (2016) argues that dispersion should become an important part of the rationale of modern cities, he refers to the environmental impacts on other beings only rarely. For him, 'urbanism for the rest of us' is firmly marked out as 'for human beings only'. 'The rest of the rest of us' don't figure[28]. They only look on. They are 'environment'[29].

In a more general vein, the problem recurs again and again. For example, Hardt and Negri (2017; 2019) want to refigure democratic organization and make urban space into the commons. But, for all their talk of plurality, the only accredited actors that they seem to allow into the fold are human beings. The multitude is a human multitude. The general intellect is general to humans. Other actors cannot be let close to the important work of politics, lest they pollute the political imagination. But, increasingly, as Wark points out, the multitude includes all kinds of beings in a multispecies muddle: 'the human might not be a unique species but one of many that plays and is open to the world' (2017: 83). After all, cities are places where animals like coyotes and mountain lions and the weasels called fishers can, however uneasily, coexist, and where 'leopards prowl downtown Mumbai and, in 2015, a wolf walked into a Dutch village for the first time in 150 years' (Cheshire and Uberti, 2016: 61).

Yet at the same time, Hardt and Negri (2017) do provide pointers to another kind of approach in their analysis of the forms of social extraction of what is held in common being made over into private property. However, what Hardt and Negri miss from their analysis is the vast network of nonhuman relationships, which in their schema often figure only as passive elements like infrastructure and the built environment and the environment generally conceived, and which are never fully acknowledged as part of a much wider inhuman force. They quite rightly point to the fact that the resource of social cooperation can be used to further progressive causes as well as being used as a fuel in modern capitalism, but cooperation with a planet which in their scheme of things cannot be a social actor remains a concept only, crowded out by a strange kind of economism that acknowledges both the peril the planet is in and the fact that production involves the creation of forms of life but is hesitant to take the next, more radical step.

So we need to think about new forms of political technology that enable cities to begin practising a politics which takes in all its constituent beings and our reciprocal duties to them. Such a fundamental political restructuring will not be easy, to understate the obvious. But there are straws of precedent in the wind. After all, corporations are already treated as legal persons in many countries (Winkler, 2018). And if corporations can have a civil rights movement, why not other entities? In some countries, this movement to endow other than human entities with rights is now taking on a shape which is more than just theoretical. Stone's (1972) classic paper argued that if corporations, joint ventures, municipalities, nation states and even ships could have rights in law, then why not trees, rivers and ecosystems? Throughout legal history, he argued, each successive extension of rights to some new entity has been considered unthinkable – but not for long (Grear, 2012). As if to prove the point, trees, rivers and ecosystems have now been given legal standing in some countries. In the United States, the Lake Erie ecosystem has been given legal standing. In New Zealand, two rivers and a mountain have been given the rights to legal personhood on the grounds that these entities are especially sacred to the Maori. The new status of the rivers and mountain means that if someone abuses or harms them, this amounts to the same situation legally as harming the Maori tribes in that area. In Ecuador, the rights of nature have been written into the country's constitution as a specific chapter[30]. Rather than treating nature as property under the law, the Rights for Nature articles acknowledge that nature in all its diversity has the 'right to exist, persist, maintain and regenerate its vital cycles, structure, functions and its processes in evolution' (GARN, n.d.). Under this constitution, the people have the legal authority to enforce these rights on behalf of ecosystems. In other words, the ecosystem itself can be named as a defendant. In Bolivia, nature also has rights, though on a legal though not a constitutional level. In other words, there are at least some straws in the wind. Perhaps we could move on from these beginnings?

That said, I am not entirely sure that a rights-based discourse will cut the mustard unless it is extended in various ways. Such a discourse tends to cement the idea that nonhuman entitlement can only arise from interests that make the human into the benchmark (Grear, 2019), exactly the bind that it is so important to escape[31]. Other beings deserve their own forms of entitlement which are 'more empirically faithful to what's there' (Grear, 2019: 2)[32]. There are some ways around – not out of – this conundrum, however. One is to call on the so-called 'epistemic injustice' literature (Kidd et al., 2017). Entities are excluded from being known except through epistemic categories owned by others who claim the right of interpreting and testifying to their actions as if that were an unproblematic move. Such cognitive biases have damaging consequences, not least in the case of animals. Another is to consider the so-called 'deep equality' literature (Waldron, 2017). Entities can be sorted into categories which recognize that they are not all are born with the same characteristics whilst recognizing that a principle of basic equality can still apply. Such a principle might be based, as just one instance, on Arendt's notion that every entity is born as a 'newcomer', the spark of life at birth making an entrance into history with 'the capacity of beginning something anew, that is, of acting' (Arendt, 2018: 336). But, of course, it's more complicated than that. How does one institute such an abstract principle in practice? Perhaps by trying to equalize the distribution of misfortune among entities? Perhaps by extending equal respect to all entities? Perhaps....

Each of these literatures – commons, rights, epistemic justice, deep equality – begins with principles that seem to exude clarity but they soon get bogged down in a morass of practical political issues. For animals, so often displaced from the political community, one route out of this political bind might be to institute a new art of political assembly which can rework the prevailing political ecology by refashioning what can count as common ground (Amin and Thrift, 2014), so bringing them back into the land of the living. One particularly relevant example of this art is the nascent political technology which is the so-called 'parliament of things'. By drawing in all manner of quasi-objects, entities that are made up of relations with other entities and which are therefore in constant negotiation, Latour (2015; 2017; 2018) intends to create a party of third parties which, through deliberation, are intended to come out of the parliamentary process as 'well-constructed', that is existing as the result of 'adequate negotiations'. The traditional players (humanity, nature, science, technology) step off the stage or, more precisely, they never existed in the first place. Unified collectives are replaced by a summons to share space (Cohen, 2014). Difference and change occur through acts of continual and unceasing diplomacy which allow every quasi-object both a speaking and a listening role (Simons, 2017). In a sense the parliament is always in session in this middle ground of overlapping authorities, bringing actors into negotiation who have often been excluded, even though they clearly have effects, and so exposing conventional actors like states and corporations to negotiations with the actors that they have most affected but who have never been allowed a say before. The intention is clear, at least, to modify the self-interests of actors and make them willing to cede territory or redefine what they mean by it.

But it is also clear that a parliament of things is not without its issues. For example, there is the issue of its practicability in a world which is populated by state and corporate titans who sometimes seem to have combined the greed of Croesus with his corresponding poverty of imagination. Despite the power of his rallying cries, Latour (2017; 2018) is well aware of the forces that are lined up against him but, for all his talk of a state of war, he seems wary of the kinds of actions that would likely be needed to bring something even remotely like a parliament of things into session as a general political technology. He might be aware that the best argument will not necessarily win, but he seems to many to neglect of more conventional political actions that might promote the institution of some quite conventional structures that would help to give the best argument a better chance.

Another nascent political technology focuses on the future incarnations of not just humans and animals but also the planet itself. How are they to be represented? Surely they should have some sort of come-back? We need to become 'good ancestors', in other words (Krznaric, 2020) instead of allowing future generations to take on our debts. But experiments in intergenerational democracy are taking place. For example, Finland has a parliamentary Commission for the Future that scrutinizes legislation for its impact on future generations. In 2015 Wales passed a Well-being of Future Generations Act, which is intended to make sure that policy decisions can be made which acknowledge future impacts. In Japan, a movement called Future Design aims to conduct citizen assemblies which include groups representing future citizens. Ultimately, it wants a Ministry of the Future set up as part of central government (Krznaric, 2020). This emphasis on forging a better future also provides a note of caution. Scientific advances may muddy the waters, for example through the creation of human/nonhuman chimeras as well as chimeras made up from the cells of different kinds of animals. If this is to be the case, what rights should be ascribed to these hybrids? All of the traditional issues of animal rights are raised by chimeras plus some[33].

To conclude, even if a rights-based discourse which construes moral relations as formal and a priori were to be accepted as legitimate, there is the question of what rights are appropriate for other beings (Puig de la Bellacasa, 2017)? Here, notwithstanding the real problems with his emphasis on individual autonomy and property, Kant gives us an intriguing clue based on a quality of interdependence which could in turn lead to a stance based less on prior entitlements and more on the quality of practical interaction to be found in a particular situation – and the accompanying ability any situation provides to negotiate coexistence. As is well known, Kant makes a distinction between innate and acquired rights. Innate rights are universals that all free and finite beings have 'in virtue of our humanity' (only one is usually acknowledged, freedom) whereas acquired rights are forged under a 'general will' that gives legitimacy to public laws that are valid for everyone, usually enforced by the state and the rule of law. But one right that Kant also mentions briefly is 'the right to be somewhere'[34]. Is this an innate or an acquired right? Kant seems to class it as an acquired right but is this a correct assumption?

> Kant [...] conceive[s] of our own legitimate possession of a place as a 'possession in common' with all others. To think of the earth's surface as possessed in common, that is to say, is an *a priori* necessary condition of the unavoidable act of first acquisition in virtue of one's coming into the world as an embodied agent. While we have a right to be somewhere (otherwise we could not act), we also need to take into account that the piece of space we take up at every particular point in time cannot be taken up by any other person. And

given that, as Kant explains elsewhere, 'originally no one had more right than another to be on a place on the earth', we can do so only by thinking of the earth's surface as commonly owned. Kant thus employs the idea of original common possession of the earth in order to visually express what it means to exist as an embodied moral agent, together with other such agents, within limited space, namely, to acknowledge that the corollary of one's own right to be somewhere is one's acknowledgement of others' equal right. (Huber, 2017: 15 [emphasis in the original])

Perhaps, then, the right to be somewhere can provide a key to the lock that we have placed on the world in that it leads on to notions of hospitable and inhospitable interactions and spaces that both frame and are framed by any situation. After all, 'a relation conceived as "external" is dramatically reconfigured when it is recognized that the terms of the relation ("man", "animal") are intimately caught up in the relation itself' (Wood, 2019: 215).

What is clear in any case is that, rights or not, we need to think about cultivating new kinds of practices that contain within them a different stance to the world. Such mindset-changing doesn't come just from strength of argument or the lessons of catastrophe. It also requires new kinds of embodiment which allow the world to be experienced differently and consequently stir the political juices differently (Sloterdijk, 2015). Old habits and dispositions must be replaced by new ones (D. Wood, 2019). Repetition can be practised differently, we can turn and turn about a delinquent space, we can transform flotsam into valued keepsakes, we can slow down time (Bogost, 2012). Through such practices, we can bring ourselves into new relationships with other entities. By themselves, these practices may not solve things but they can edge us closer to a different place from which we will see and care about different things.

To draw on Sophocles' *Antigone*, we need cities that no longer separate the care of life from the government of the city. We need to consciously plot a peaceable kingdom, the one so beloved of philosophy. There may even be technological fixes to some of these problems. For example, it is already possible to track animals from space. Soon it could be possible to identify each and every one, follow and even 'translate' their behaviour. This development comes with risks, of course. For example, in informationalizing animals, it might be that they become purely informational problems, open to the most reductive forms of calculation, as already happens with some farm animals. In other words, greater visibility does not necessarily equate to less expendability. But, equally, as Gabrys (2016) points out, they might also be thought of as means of lighting up and extending encounters between humans, animals and technical systems in new and interesting ways, such as, for example, by pinpointing grotesque food chains and by alerting watchers to the effects of environmental depredations and untoward detentions[35]. Again, it should also be possible to start defending threatened animals, using all manner of machines like drones[36]. Perhaps in time an urban alliance between humans, animals and machines will come into existence.

Notes

1 Only 32 per cent of vertebrate biomass consists of human beings, and vertebrate wildlife make up a miserable 3 per cent (Bar-On et al., 2018).
2 Ironically, of course, not just us. For example, it is estimated that the 94 million cats in the United States consume 12 million lb of flesh every day, the equivalent of 3 million chickens (Herzog, 2010).
3 It takes 660 gallons of virtual water (3,300 litres) to make a single hamburger, all of the water needed to make the product, equivalent to 4.1 years of drinking water for an average person or a full week of water use by the average US household.
4 Agriculture, particularly meat and dairy production, accounts for 70 per cent of global freshwater consumption, 38 per cent of total land use and 19 per cent of global greenhouse emissions (UNEP, 2010; FAO, 2017).
5 One telling fact is that in the UK tree sparrows have declined by 97 per cent over the last 40 years owing to industrialized agriculture, a figure which uncannily parallels Chairman Mao's attempt to make exactly the same species extinct in China in 1958 (Shapiro, 2001; Lymbery and Oakeshott, 2014).
6 Not just bees are responsible for pollination – so are large numbers of moths and flies and these are threatened too.
7 For example, Denerley et al. (2018) show that cuckoos are declining in number because of the decline in moths whose larvae are their main prey in lowland agricultural landscapes.
8 This is important given that, overall, between 2000 and 2014 the population of 66 bumblebee species fell by 17 per cent in Europe and 46 per cent in North America when compared to a base period of 1901 to 1974 (Soroye et al., 2020).
9 Though, as Stuart (2009) points out, available figures are effectively estimates. So, on one estimate, retailers in the UK produced 1.6 million tonnes of food waste each year. This could be an underestimate. On the other hand, other estimates are lower.
10 Many of the largest fleets are subsidized by their governments.
11 The situation may well be worse since it is almost impossible to estimate numbers of fish wasted onshore, fish killed in the sea by fishing gear (especially abandoned nets), fish that die in trawl nets and fall out of the net before reaching the deck, as well as the deaths of all kinds of sea animals that do not count as fish like jellyfish, coral, sponges, sea-snakes and the like (Stuart, 2009).
12 By contrast, only 2 per cent of food is discarded in rural areas.
13 The increase in meat-eating is not an inevitable result of development, however. The rate of increase in meat-eating in India is much less than that found in China because of that country's vegetarian traditions.
14 For all the talk, overall consumption of vegetables, both in the UK and worldwide, is still small with 74 per cent of the adult UK population not managing to eat five vegetables a day. That is much lower than it was in the 1950s, when freshly cooked daily meals were still something that most people took for granted.
15 India is often pointed to as an example of a viable vegetarian culture. Though it is clearly an important exemplar, recent work by Natrajan and Jacob (2017) suggests that meat-eating may be more widespread than has commonly been thought and that there are much wider variations in its prevalence between location, caste and gender than has often been argued to be the case.
16 It is suggested that at least two Native American tribes practised vegetarianism but the evidence is hazy.
17 It is now becoming possible to grow leather in factories without the need for animals, as in the case of the firm Modern Meadow (Economist, 2017).
18 Additionally, about $5 trillion a year is spent on subsidies for the fossil fuels which industrialized agriculture use so profligately.
19 In the United States, as Foer (2009: 256) points out, 'there isn't enough nonfactory chicken produced [...] to feed the population of Staten Island and not enough nonfactory pork

to serve New York City'. Even though the situation is better now, getting to more ethical eating is going to be challenging.

20   Chickens are the most efficient land animals so far as conversion of feed into meat is concerned (2 kg of grain for every pound of weight), followed by pigs (5 kg of grain for every pound of weight), followed by cattle (10 kg of grain for every pound of weight).

21   So whereas the United Nations argues that there is an 80 per cent probability that the world population will increase to between 9.6 and 12.3 billion people by 2100 with the median at 10.9 billion, the International Institute for Applied Systems Analysis projects that the world population will peak at 9.73 billion in 2064 and then start a slow decline to 8.79 billion by 2100, mainly because of assumptions about fertility and mortality and especially the effects of women's education on fertility (Vollset et al., 2020). Other reports have the peak at 8.7 billion in 2055, or even less (Bricker and Ibbitson, 2019).

22   This debate is conducted almost entirely in terms of human welfare, it should be noted.

23   Murphy quite rightly decries the way in which both the main pressures of population growth and the blame tend to be unequally sheeted home to the poor. But, rather like the equivalent argument around the impacts of climate change, that cannot mean that things should necessarily be left just as they are, even if, there are some signs of a general slowdown in the rate of population growth.

24   In any case, many commentators would argue that the nuclear family has done real damage. It is brittle, bad for children and the elderly, and 'liberates the rich and ravages the working class and the poor' (Brooks, 2020: 14). As the nuclear family has got smaller and single-person households have grown in number these problems have only multiplied. The rich nuclear family buys an extended family by hiring workers to help out. Everyone else sinks or swims.

25   As the bonds of sex and gender have loosened so this insight seems easier to countenance.

26   Typical criticisms arising from this misunderstanding include: 'Neo-Malthusianism', 'A war on poor women and people of colour', We don't know how many people the planet can carry', 'It's all the fault of capitalism anyway', etc. But it's not either/or.

27   Such a stance has obvious problems, however. Many cities in the Global South have small environmental footprints when compared with their counterparts in the Global North, but the last thing that they need is more population.

28   Ironically, one of his inspirations is apparently Aristotle, perhaps the world's first biologist, for whom the natural world was a thing of wonder, which he enjoined us to love and understand (Leroi, 2014).

29   In certain senses, the nonhuman right to occupy urban space is already implicitly recognized, even if only in the most minimal fashion, in some countries' laws. For example, in the UK, a driver is legally required to report running over a dog (as well as horses, cattle, cows, pigs, goats, sheep, donkeys and mules – but not cats).

30   Although this move, part of the ecological sensibility of 'sumac kawsay', is precarious (see Gerlach, 2017).

31   Added to which, rights have often proven to be exclusionary.

32   Other difficulties abound from problems of definition to issues of distortion.

33   As these different experiments pan out, a number of urban institutions exist that could take on some of the load of caring for the future. For example, universities already do some of this work through the actions of their employees and students. Their ability to manoeuvre may have been severely constrained by marketization but they are one of the few institutions generating knowledge and criticism in equal measure. (Thrift, 2016).

34   In some ways, this might be understood as akin to Arendt's notion of the refugee as inhabiting a place called nowhere, displaced from the political community, for whom seeking a place is the first step on the road back, though, in general, Arendt was sceptical of the notion of rights.

A New Settlement

35   Already, the animal sensor tracking database, Movebank (www.movebank.org/cms/movebank-main), is starting to take on some of these functions, especially as smaller and smaller animals, down to swarms of insects, are able to be tracked using new satellite arms and ever smaller sensors, as well as radar.

36   Thus a recent report noted that in the Californian desert small machines that can fire lasers are being used to dissuade kestrels from attacking a threatened species of tortoise – threatened because of large urban landfill sites that have drawn the kestrels out into the desert.

11
There Is Another World But It Is This One[1]

Introduction

Let me turn once more to the issue of a change of mindset that is at the heart of the alter-political project., If we don't want to suffer the ignominy of being the entity that, through ignorance, folly and simple malice, made the horrific into a routine, we have to expand our circle of friends. The alternative is that we will end up destroying each and every signpost to a different model of humanity, one which treasures partial connection and correspondingly a 'we' which both is and isn't. Forging such a model is not going to be easy but neither is it impossible. In the last 200 years or so, for example, many animals in cities have begun to be treated as neighbours, even friends.

The current urban forcings and flailings of the planet may seem to presage naught but woe. It would be easy to declare, Cassandra-like, that winter is here and, every being is becoming a refugee. But that doesn't have to be the case. What we need now is a curve of invention that will finally allow us to announce childhood's end and stop hollowing out the planet. What will that invention actually consist of? I am not sure that the Western staple of appeals to Eastern religions will do it, even though Shinto and some variants of Buddhism do clearly contain grains of wisdom. Nor, by itself, will yet another condemnation of capitalism, even though capitalism is clearly in the thick of it as a means of foreclosing on the planet. Nor will a mass outbreak of vegetarianism (though that would certainly help). Nor will the fantastical mass engineering projects beloved of those who believe that there is a technological fix for everything. Nor will preaching conservation to the Global South when large parts of the Global North's backyard are themselves an ecological desert, as though responsibility lies elsewhere[2]. Nor will declarations of hope that simply sidestep the damage done. Nor, indeed, will a simple acknowledgement of narrow human weaknesses in the face of a planet that 'doth not need Either man's works or his own gifts'[3].

Rather we need to find a point of balance between the scientific and the speculative where a truce can be called and we can throw off beliefs that have been set in concrete in favour of understanding that 'the destruction that presents itself to us cannot be presented' (Colebrook, 2016: 117–18). Unless and until we can find not just matching publics able to apprehend each of the multiple, interacting forces that have brought us to this pass and, equally, a means of redefining publics in the first place so that they include more beings and their modes of existence, we will in large part be preaching into a vacuum. We need to become less ferociously sure about what our place in the world is, and that means taking a collective view or rather collective views which cleave to the Guattari (2000) dictum that we need to become both more united and increasingly different. It is rather like Viveiros de Castro's (2011: 16) apparently inconstant Tupi people who befuddled missionaries by insisting on not insisting on beliefs – or obeisance to rites or idols or priests or sovereign gods: people for whom 'the other was not merely good to think – the other was necessary for thinking'. In other words, we need to learn a new way to speak and think and act, certainly not the usual pessimistic anthropology but rather the embrace of new narrative affects which are less sure of order and more forgiving of the world as a jumble of partial connections, affects which live *relationship to others* and not self-identity and thereby register both injuries we prefer not to see and possibilities we do not entertain. Peoples like Viveiros de Castro's Tupi can give us some clues as to how we might relearn being in the world and how to discover new means of belonging to it.

When Latour calls for new practices of diplomacy, he tends to gloss over the fact that this form of politics also requires new kinds of subjects ready and willing to come to the table. In a world which, on the one side, is prone to affective storms, fake news, industrial-scale gaslighting and the like, and, on the other side, subjects who, precisely at the moment when it has become increasingly apparent that subjects are flat surfaces improvised in the moment, not introspective depths (Chater, 2018), seem to spend more and more of their time in search of a core inner world, this may seem like a stretch. Or perhaps not. One way of understanding this refractory tendency might be as the inculcation of a new phase of the civilizing process laying down fresh modes of *politeness* towards the world which transit to new kinds of moral virtue.

I am not making some grand statement about the absorption of grand moral absolutes here, by the way. Rather, I am suggesting that over time it is possible to inculcate different everyday senses of what is right – what Montaigne (2003) called the ordinary virtues – that fuel interaction with other beings. These ordinary virtues, everyday deportments, lesser moralities, minor conformities – call them what you will – involve the recognition of difference, respect for difference and making common cause with difference in order to precipitate 'a public culture of welcome' (Ignatieff, 2017). The historical record supports our ability to engineer shifts in the perception of moral virtue through public evocation and public cultivation (Ignatieff, 2017) and, as I pointed out above, it is important to acknowledge the strides that have already been made, often in surprisingly short order, in producing senses of tolerance, respect and constraint to others, including animals. So there is reason to think that we can change how we currently inhabit ourselves so that cruelty, arrogance, hatred and contempt for other beings become less and less acceptable. This change would be a return – of a sort – to the original notion of manners as not just the conventions surrounding polite social interaction but, more generally, people's habits, social conventions, morals and general mode of life (Thomas, 2018). In this conception, any kind of greedy or grasping behaviour would be regarded as in bad taste, as an unnecessary vulgarity while cruelty would be shunned. Of course, none of this is to say that struggles over what strategies are necessary to ensure the future of cities and the planet would suddenly come to an end, but it would mean that the backcloth of assumptions that inform everyday interactions and judgements would have been changed.

Take once again the case of the status of animals in Western cultures. Cruelty to animals is now generally looked down upon by many people. Alexander von Humboldt (1829), one of Darwin's inspirations and a powerful critic of colonialism, might famously have written that 'Cruelty to animals is one of the most significant vices of a low and ignoble people. Wherever one notices them, they constitute a sign of ignorance and brutality which cannot be painted over even by all the evidence of wealth and luxury,' but still in his time bad treatment was frequently a norm. This is not to say that cruelty to animals no longer exists, of course, as the circulation of animal abuse videos sadly attests. But many institutions now exist to prevent such abuse, including even a specialized animal police force in the Netherlands, and public attitudes have clearly changed. As Thomas (2017) points out, the use of fur and feathers as decoration has all but died out and in less than a century. Hunting animals for pleasure is now looked on with puzzlement or even downright disgust by a large part of the world's population and has been replaced in their esteem by practices like wildlife conservation, birdwatching, environmental tourism and photography – so much photography! (Lorimer, 2015). Vegetarianism has moved from a small sidebar to Western cultures to becoming a viable nutritional alternative, sometimes, it's true, for health reasons, but often also for ethical reasons. Wild animals are not just declining either. Conservation efforts can and do work. Since 1993, extinction rates would have been three to four times higher without determined efforts at conservation (Bolam et al., 2020). Bears, golden jackals, wolves, lynx and wolverines are busy repopulating Europe. 'The European bison is up from one population to thirty-three; the […] southern chamois has increased five-fold since 1970; there has been a 14,000 per cent increase in European beavers since the 1950s, and deer and wild boar numbers have quadrupled […]'. Meanwhile, in the United States, 'the birth rates of wolves and grizzly bears for the first time in many generations exceed the rates at which humans kill them […]. American bison is off the threatened list' (Thomas, 2017: 49).

But calling for the reconstruction of moral virtue is not enough. What we are also talking about here is the need to rework what the process of subjectification *can be*, not *is*. But whereas Elias, the founder of work on the 'civilizing process', was intent on documenting the way in which the modern state produced a shift in cultural mores, here the aim is to become more in tune with the world, not in some mystical way that instils a false sense of harmony, but as a practical agenda (Thrift, 2011). For example, what would a state intent on fostering rather than regimenting life look like? If states have become biopolitical agents, intent on controlling, grooming and reproducing populations, how can they be changed so that they respond to more convivial ways of being than the broadly economic logics that currently seem to be their stock in trade? Indeed, how can they be changed so that the very notion of population comes under the microscope and can be framed in new ways which respect all kith and kin (Murphy, 2017)? What this shift requires is a new kind of civility, one which is both cognitive and affective and which redraws the boundaries of the human community to include other beings and extends civility to them too.

All People That on Earth Do Dwell

And that point brings us back again to the lives of indigenous peoples like Viveiros de Castro's Tupi people for inspiration about new ways to speak and think others. I am not indulging in some kind of cod nostalgia here, nor am I trying to simply co-opt their ontologies, as if that were possible. But the fact remains that many indigenous peoples (and not a few scientific and philosophical thinkers, it might be added) have never made the distinctions between human and nonhuman that we take for granted[4].

> In the Sundarbans, for example, the people who live in and around the mangrove forest have never doubted that tigers and many other animals possess intelligence and agency. For the first peoples of the Yukon, even glaciers are endowed with moods and feelings, likes and dislikes. Nor would these conceptions have been unthinkable for a scientist like Sir Jagadish Chandra Bose, who attributed elements of consciousness to vegetables and even metals, or for the primatologist Imanishi Kinji who insisted on 'the unity of all elements on the planet earth – living and nonliving'. (Ghosh, 2016: 64)

In referring to the examples provided by indigenous peoples, there is no intention to simply invert the anthropological principle that 'no ontology is better or more truthful in itself than another' (Descola, 2013: 66) by worshipping at their feet or regarding them as the source of a new epistemic Nile. For example, it is at least arguable whether any of them have ever lived in complete harmony with nature, a common trope (Langlitz, 2018). Equally, it is no doubt possible to 'other' indigenous people to a dangerous degree by forgetting, for example, that their ideas about and attitudes towards animals are anchored not just in a different cosmology but also in everyday interactions with animals which they share in common with many other peoples (Hugh-Jones, 2019). Finally, it's not as if indigenous people never kill animals or eat them. In other words, rather than idealizing them, by, for example, projecting our hopes and concerns onto their ways of life, indigenous peoples can give us some sense of the variation that is possible in our relationship with the world, different cosmological schemas which, by demonstrating openness to the emerging worlds around us, suggest different possibilities that might allow us to get to, quite literally, a different place through different origin stories[5], different perceptions of how space and time can appear, and different modes of coexistence (see also Herzfeld, 2016).

Take just as one example the case of Kohn's (2013) forest-dwelling Runa of Peru. They live within a complex system of semiosis which assumes that the forest is a vast ecology of selves in which one must stand as a self in relation to many other kinds of selves, and in which communicating with these other selves always involves at least some degree of becoming with others and also certain configurations of possibility that come and go that Kohn names as form. Equally, as Kohn (2013: 22) makes clear, the forest itself thinks; 'it is because thought extends beyond the human that we can think beyond the human'. Or take the case of the Cree, one of the largest First Nations groups in North America (Berkes, 2012; Ingold, 2012). For the Cree, similarly, all organisms can have points of view so that dealing with nonhuman animals is 'not fundamentally different from dealing with fellow humans' (Ingold, 2012: 47). Therefore, the idea that the human view is literal and the animal view is figurative is alien to the Cree – organisms are not *like* persons, they *are* persons. So it is that, for example, Cree hunters

> notice things about the environment that geese do not, yet by the hunters' own admission, geese also notice things that humans do not. What is certain, however, is that humans figure in the perceptual world of geese just as geese figure in that of humans. It is clearly of vital importance to geese that they should be as attentive to the human presence as to the presence of any other potential predator. On the basis of past experience, they learn to pick up the relevant warning signs and continually adjust their behavior accordingly. And human hunters, for their part, attend to the presence of geese in the knowledge that geese are attending to them. (Ingold, 2012: 49)

The point can be made more broadly: to Cree hunters 'it was quite clear […] that animals, not people or high-powered rifles, controlled the success of the hunt. Bear, beaver and elk would not offer themselves to someone who treated them disrespectfully or failed to distribute their meat in the proper manner' (Weston, 2017: 9).

Examples like these[6] point to a different, perspectival way of conceptualizing worlds: it is possible to think of other species or types of being as 'persons', though persons that see the world in a particular characteristic kind of way which acknowledges many kinds of alterity and metamorphosis. 'Personhood is not added on to the living organism, [it is] implicated in the very condition of being alive' (Ingold, 2012: 45). This is, in other words, a 'cosmos totally impregnated with subjecthood' (Viveiros de Castro, 2015: 182), a cosmos in which 'all humans share the same culture – human culture. What changes is the nature of what they see, according to the body these referential humans possess' (Viveiros de Castro, 2013: 3), with the result that 'all animals and cosmic constituents are intensively and virtually persons, because all of them, no matter which, can reveal to transform themselves into persons' (Viveiros de Castro, 2014: 58). Animist schemas like this in which,

> the object is a particular case of the subject, where every object is a particular case of the subject in potentia [where] instead of the solipsistic formula 'I think therefore I am', the indigenous cogito must be articulated [...] as 'It exists, therefore it thinks' (Viveiros de Castro, 2015: 187)

can be matched up by other schemas like totemism (Descola, 2014), which also opt for what Viveiros de Castro calls 'a sensible materialism'. Unless we take more note of examples like these, and how they make friends or even kin out of others, we will continue to plough a furrow that privileges appetite over good sense and encroachment over enlightenment.

Of course, the inspiration that indigenous peoples provide is not some kind of ready-made solution. After all, as Hamilton (2017: 106) briskly points out, 'it is not patronizing to say that Indigenous peoples do not have the solutions to the Anthropocene. The Anthropocene is as much a shock to them as it is to everyone else. To turn to them for answers shoulders them with an impossible burden.' But where I differ with Hamilton is that it seems clear to me that indigenous peoples' ontologies can provide both hope and inspiration, hope that there *are* other ways of thinking cities which can stimulate 'new kinds of we' (Kohn, 2013: 23)[7] and the inspiration that such signposts can provide to new practices that can change the way that we live in the world. Though there are many things that indigenous peoples do not or cannot know there are some things that they know that we either never knew or have banished to the outer regions of our thinking.

We could, in other words, begin to embrace a kind of 'humanimality', a politics that re-establishes contact with our animality through a pragmatics of mutual inclusion (Abram, 2011; Massumi, 2014; Haraway, 2016). It is a politics of becoming human through challenging accepted norms of what that quality might be. But this is easy to say and, more often than not, exceptionally difficult to do. Currently, there is a gulf between highfaluting statements of philosophical intent and the multiple ways in which these politics are already happening in and through particular dynamic and open-ended situations. Cities can make good a more general link between these antipodes by providing context, concreteness and the kind of everyday cordiality which they are able to generate. They can build new collectives which understand that it is possible to make common cause whilst also realizing that 'one cannot have everything one wants – not only in practice but even in theory' (Berlin, 2017: 3).

Most particularly, I think we need to think about the space and the politics of cities again against the history of dispossession of all and sundry that has come to characterize the planet. In the seventeenth and eighteenth centuries, the oceans became understood as open to the claims of nation and property, able to be segmented and appropriated for ordered forms of mobility. Agriculture has been through many similar revolutions before becoming fixated on the corporatist agrilogistics that currently reigns in which space is simply a moment of production for production's sake. But cities have always had a more chequered history. True, they contain some of the most rigid moments in the history of property demarcation and of the state setting out its reasoning in stone. But, as I pointed out in the previous chapter, they can and do follow other models. At their best, they display something more embedded, something which genuinely un-expects the expected. There is no reason why this kind of space cannot become more general. Latour (2016b) writes about turning lands back into disputed territories but this seems too small a step, a rediscovery of geography rather than a geography of rediscovery (Thrift, 2017). We need new classifications, new scales and legends, new lines and signs that will turn urban space into something more fluid and accommodating of diversity, space that acknowledges that all – all – ecologies are more (or, if you like, less) than human[8]. From figure to field (Waldheim, 2016), in other words. And, correspondingly, from the straitjacket of belief to practices of worlding which approach a problem experimentally rather than either declaring a determinate solution which only needs to be set out and kept to for all to be well or, alternatively, cleaving to very general values like 'flourishing' or 'care' or 'hospitality', which sound so user-friendly that it is assumed that they must somehow exert traction, though how exactly that might be manifested usually remains not just cloudy but indeterminate (Tsing et al., 2017).

Four moves come to mind that might bring such an interdependent vision to pass. One is cultivating the kind of close, custodial attachment to place known as 'country' by indigenous Australians. As already noted, I hesitate to utter thoughts and judgements about the worlds of indigenous peoples because they can so easily be turned into caricatures weighed down with expectations that they were never meant to meet and profundities that are stand-ins for thinking. But, equally, the attachments that many indigenous peoples have to the environment in which they live – for which the word attachment is really too weak a term – offer a model of a rolling way of life, a *process* of inhabitation through paths and trails that is accountable because it is both set within and beholden to a multispecies kin group that *takes nonhumans seriously* – it treats them with respect as partners in an entangled and mutually constituted existence – and equally because it acts as the curator of the knowledge of the land and its inhabitants in which that group sits (Kohn, 2013). And that means we need to think about how we might transform urban space into something akin to country in the indigenous Australian sense where 'I cannot help but think of my country. It cannot help but think of me' (cited in Povinelli, 2016: 79).

This is not to wander down some kind of quasi-Heideggerian route, it should be said straight away. When Heidegger uses the metaphor of the path, for example, he doesn't mean for the path to be going anywhere. His woodpaths are meant to signify 'a confusing path through woods that makes linear progress from one place to another very difficult' (Ellard, 2015: 79). The pull of departure is not for him: 'the ethos of moved Dasein [is] a sojourn in an assigned location within the world' (Sloterdijk, 2017b: 30). The paths all return home, in other words. For Heidegger, that means that city is inaccessible – his thought is determinedly extra-urban. As Sloterdijk puts it:

> In cities, Heidegger expects to find human beings who have run away from necessity, are too free, and have been let loose into arbitrariness, who do not know what they want and should do, and hence for the most part settle for the first available option. In urban forms of life, he senses the irony that is more suspicious and hateful to him than any other kind [...] the temptation to float freely and detach oneself from the Dasein that is anchored in a situation. In irony, subjectivism asserts itself, a subjectivism which is only familiar with contingent, gratuitous devotion to things and persons, together with a correspondingly arbitrary aversion to them. The city engenders forms of life in which everything 'washes together in the uniformly distanceless' into a gathering within the false [...] That the majority in cities are also not merely dispersed but have duties and must face emergencies both privately and publicly – the philosopher of gathering will know nothing of this. (2017b: 29)

It follows that Heidegger's path can actually say very little about the many quintessentially urban activities which rely on movement and interchange, the best as well as the worst. He cannot register 'bricolage, intersection, collation, compromise, the whole spectrum of operations that constitute organized knowledge as a profession and community building as a social plastic art' (Sloterdijk, 2017b: p30)[9]. Heidegger tends to go deep, all the time sacrificing breadth. But this obduracy, which all but deletes cities from consideration, doesn't have to follow on from the notion of a path. There are other ways and other means.

Another move is to think of cities as composites of the trails of all kinds of being which allow those beings to be borne into an active, shared gathering, a quest 'whose function is to insist that our mother country is a foreign land whose language we have not yet earned the right to speak' (Carey, 2018: 357). It is not that the notion of trails is iconic, a kind of key to the universe – as the notion can sometimes be cast in the writing of authors like Ingold on lines (2015). Rather, though trails can unite all kinds of beings in productive crossings, they do so in tentative, interested ways which add up to a time-tested, habitualized means of knowing how to live which provides not only a sense of direction (*to*) but also carries a kind of wisdom played out in use (*through*) (Moor, 2016). They are a means of organizing knowledge which, at the same time, points to different ways of thinking association as knots of trails that not only question but also 'shimmer', that set in motion an ephemeral and iridescent experience of 'being part of a vibrant and vibrating world' (Rose, 2017: 53). They are 'broad sensory affects, cognitive imprints, and material indentations' which are both motion and lure (Povinelli, 2016: 79). It follows that they are also implicitly unruly: false turns can turn out to have value, unexpected things can turn up, the provisional can be honoured as something other than the opposite of the fixed. Trails are not just repetitions, then (though they may well have rhythm). They can access multiple realities. Cities based on a model like this would be patchworks of different combinations, united by their differences, intent on searching out new forms of the human, hands to the tiller, certainly, but allowing the tiller a certain amount of free play.

Such an unsettled model of continuous transformation (including of what transformation can mean) combines with a spookier notion of space. Cities can bend spaces by producing new trails. Recent technological advances have both made this easier to see and driven new forms of trail which have spilled over into more general models of space as incompletion. Thus, we can now see that trails start from the quality of what Barad (2007) calls intra-action as opposed to inter-action, a move intended to undo the implicit understanding of interaction as the meeting between two fully formed 'whole' objects. Each intra-action has at least the potential to generate new symbioses. Equally, we can see that trails are always alterations, no matter how small the alteration might appear. Even the most recondite and nacreous space is in constant churn.

Another move follows on. For some time now, space has been considered to be relative and multidimensional, no longer dealing in the certainty of Euclidean space. But we can now go further by allowing for 'spooky actions at a distance', as Einstein put it. All things are not connected, but those that are connected are connected in ways which challenge conventional conceptions of distance based on simple proximity. Things that are far apart can be more intimately connected than those close to each other just as we now realize that particles on opposite sides of the universe can be connected. The same event can be taking place in widely varying locations. 'In the era of global warming, nothing is really far away' (Ghosh, 2016: 26). The world is non-local as well as local and there are many varieties of both. Space is more like an old frayed rug than a smooth plane and it is constantly emerging. Indeed, on at least one account space is a projection of objects existing in a quite different realm[10]. It is not the basement floor of reality, in other words. This is an uncannily similar notion to that of country in which non-local phenomena can,

> leap out of space; they have no place in its confines. They hint at a level of reality deeper than space, where the concept of distance ceases to apply, where things that appear to lie far apart are actually nearby or perhaps the same thing manifested in more than one place [...]. (Musser, 2015: 168)

Then, one final move. We could think more deeply about cultivating different kinds of urban spatial expertise. A whole archive of such initiatives already exists, after all, from psychogeography through forms of urban exploration like parkour in its various manifestations to the many variants of people's mapping. Or, perhaps more interestingly, we might consider other illicit forms of urban spatial expertise that have a long history but are hidden from general view – like the skills of the professional burglar which is akin to that of many animals in the city.

> People usually focus on what burglars take, but it's how they move that's so [...] interesting. [...] They might not live in a city full of secret passages and trapdoors – but they make it look as if they do. They have their own tools and floor plans, their own ways to get from A to B. [...] They flash in and out of the world like ghosts. (Manaugh, 2016: 22–3)

Lands and Loves and Life: Politics Again

Let me finally turn to politics and alter-politics just once more. In this book, I have tried to point to means for refashioning what cities could be and how we might think about them. After all, taking back sovereignty from the greedy and the distracted and making reparations for the damage we have done requires good government and not just slogans (Lewis, 2018). It requires practical steps that attract the right enemies. It requires signposts that can point away from a Seinfeld city to a more companionable, a more resonant, a more expressive, a more responsible city, a city of gratitude for others' existence, a city of mutual inclusion in which 'personhood and perspectiveness – the capacity to occupy a point of view – is a question of degree, context, and position' (Viveiros de Castro, 2014: 57). This kind of call to arms can sound like way too sentimental a fix, more Disney than Deleuze. But it doesn't have to be that way. New kinds of cooperation, operating through a mix of affects and modes of governance and political technologies that are only half-articulated, as trails rather than as finished structures which produce predictable but limited outcomes, may be the only way forward for cities given the seriousness and urgency of the situation in which we now find ourselves – a world in which we are busily cutting the foundations out from under our feet. We need other ways of speaking city in which we can become a composite, a city which no longer hands out insults to the dignity of others as a matter of course but fashions a community of communities which contains within it new ways of noticing. We need to aim towards cities that act as *massively integrated communities* in which the imprint of events can be felt by all and turned from historical into cellular memory through new relationships of accountability and communicative understanding fostered by multispecies kin groups. Sounds entirely too fancy? Maybe and then again maybe not.

Most particularly, cities could hold out the possibility of becoming a new 'middle ground' (White, 1991). Just as Native Americans and Europeans met in the region around the Great Lakes *pays d'en haut* in the brief period between 1650 and 1815, and, though the two parties regarded the other as virtually nonhuman, were still able to construct a common, mutually comprehensible world which seemed to bring people together rather than force them apart, in part by constructing what were, in effect, kin relationnships using Native American ceremonial structures which had first evolved in the thirteenth century on the Great Plains. Similarly, cities could become a multispecies middle ground in which the human and the nonhuman could become irrevocably mixed and blended into a wider symbiotic humanity through capitalizing on all manner of creative understandings – and misunderstandings – arising out of unclear boundaries. Like the original middle ground, these alliances will not be made up out of mystical affinities but out of elaborate networks of contact, negotiation, mediation, compromise and reconciliation[11]. They will be dependent on gift exchange and on special ceremonies which would be the equivalent of the calumet ceremony, a political ritual of reconciliation which varied from tribe to tribe but which mixed the hard realities of trade with the softer recognition of mutual frailties via several days of ritual feasting, gift-giving, singing and dancing, and the use of the calumet pipe. The calumet ceremony, which was a means of creating multiple significant real or metaphorical kinfolk through what might be considered as an extended process of adoption, has obvious resonances with many of the themes of this book.

In other words, if urban spaces could achieve the goal of becoming more like a country in which kinship relations can be constantly generated, thus occupying a new kind of between in which the continual work of creating humanity becomes a given, then maybe they could stop acting as generators of human creativity which only exist through parasitism rather than symbiosis and instead become 'well-tempered' (Rose, 2016) cradles of urban intercivilization, beckoning towards homes rather than home. Cities would become the new nations. Not the first nations, of course. Certainly not the second nations, which have unleashed war and oppression. Rather, a group of third nations which can act as diplomats and caretakers, never indifferent, never doing things by halves. Then, and only then, might cities be able to point to new horizons which could unleash 'the wildernesses of freedom' humanity patently lacks at present[12]. But this would be a different kind of freedom which includes within its ambit nonhuman forces and systems which have been given no place in a calculus of liberty where being independent of precisely those forces and systems is what has been 'considered one of the defining characteristics of freedom itself' (Ghosh, 2016: 119). Freedom can no longer operate independently of necessity as too often happens now. That stance is not just one-sided, it is suicidal. Instead we need to build a future of freedom to care for the planet by constructing an urban realm whose diverse inhabitants understand deep in their marrow that the future cannot be 'understood nor saved alone' (Midgley, 1978: 138), especially when it is a humanity which has narrowed its options so severely, which has looked in when it should have looked out. Humankind may have become 'anaesthetized, massacred, dishonored' (Stengers, 2015: 156) but it can still act. It is not impotent, even in the face of the elements of humanity who want to keep on taking until the last trump from a planet that cannot hear us but can still exact revenge. It can move towards more hospitable practices which at the same time express a simple gratitude, practices which give humanity – all of humanity – the time to grow enough to both understand what our place in the scheme of things might be and the wherewithal to make the most of what days might be bequeathed to us.

On reflection, perhaps gratitude is the wrong word. Maybe a better word is the word I used in Chapter 1, namely honour[13]: not just the giving and receiving of respect but the need to be worthy of respect, of recognition (Appiah, 2010). Honour is both a shared code and the suite of feelings that go with it: at a minimum, pride, dignity and, most especially, in the current conjuncture, the impulse to extend the dignity of recognition and indeed courtesy to all others by honouring the planet and all its beings. Spenser's bright squadrons are already planted all around us. There is no need to call on the ministry of angels.

Now, of course, like most things, honour can be and has been perverted (Frevert, 2011) but it seems to me that gathering a set of feelings like this is crucial in making a moral leap, as is making its negative correlates feel more and more unworthy, correlates like shame, disgrace, mendacity, slyness and listlessness. Put quite simply, we need to generate a general and pressing sense of a grievous harm being done to the great canopy of the world under which we all shelter, but a harm which can be set to rights. Producing such a revolution in moral behaviour is never going to be easy, but that is what we need. In particular, we need to respond to the world precognitively in very different ways (Thrift, 2006). This requires rebalancing our feelings so that beings that had been considered unequal can be given due respect. In recent times, more and more human beings have been included amongst beings of due weight. It is not perhaps such a big leap as all that to extend that recognition to other beings and, indeed, to the world at large. Rebooting our 'patterning instinct' (Lent, 2017) is never going to be easy but, since it has happened many times already, there is no reason to think that it cannot be achieved again.

Let me put it one more way, by referencing once more Auden's lane to the land of the dead. For this act of honouring is also about the longing for something better, which manifests itself in common human narratives like resurrection. Let me illustrate what I mean. One of the best Stanley Spencer resurrection paintings is reckoned to be *The Resurrection of the Soldiers*. What is important about this painting is that it is an utterly inclusive moment of happiness and joy in a reunion of the dead that brings about a recognition of the worth of all living things. It isn't just the soldiers that are resurrected after no doubt agonizing deaths on a First World War battlefield. The animals get their due too, from the central motif of a pair of fallen mules redux, still harnessed to their wagon, to all of the horses breaking out of the ground along with the humans. Spencer is renowned for the way in which he concentrates on the mundanities of life but, in this version of the resurrection, these mundanities become a kind of transubstantiation, a mysterious and joyous new normality that points to another way, a way measured out in both the utterly quotidian yawn of a young man still in khaki uniform as he returns to life and the buoyancy of the surprise with which the revived mules prick up their ears (Prodger, 2018)[14].

Let's make no mistake about it, we are talking about what would be an equivalent resurrection: a massive political project of levitation that institutes a new kind of normality. This is a project that can never rely on[15], the kinds of Manichean solutions promoted by those who cleave to binary salvation/damnation theories. It is going to be multifarious. But it is also an inclusive project[16]: after all, 'however precarious or small it might be, each achievement matters' (Stengers, 2015: 153). In other words, I remain improbably hopeful. I am still searching for the sunshine. With 7.6 billion people currently alive on the planet, and with many of them based in large cities which tend to be more politically active, there really ought to be room for progress. After all, politics is a matter of addition, not subtraction, and there is enough politics here for everyone to make a contribution[17]. As the climate scientist Robert Somerville puts it, 'we don't need bullets, we need buckshot' (Macfarlane, 2015b). Of course, it is hard to imagine 'a new narrative of biospheric humility gaining traction in a world where selfish and avaricious behaviour is so deeply entrenched […]. But it is similarly hard to see any hope of rebuilding a more sustainable, just, and human world without it' (Weis, 2013: 155). Peak city doesn't have to mean peak killing.

Perhaps precisely because cities are such founts of creativity, their denizens can undermine their own premises and build something that can persevere as more than an occupying force premised on loneliness and the bitter work of mourning and atonement for paths not taken and futures laid waste. They can produce cities that resonate with slow grace and mutual sacrifice rather than cities that just grasp the world and hang it out to dry. They can produce cities which are not just about having as a form of flailing and flensing but rather about cities which understand having as breathing in the world. They can produce cities that aren't just 'ours' but a patchwork of belongings. They can produce the happy warriors we so desperately need that, by inventing new arts of inhabiting the earth, can extract us from under the pile of ashes that we are making. Along the way, these warriors can produce the stories and fables of forms of governance and interaction that give every entity the chance of a role in the common task of inter-relation. And those stories and fables can gradually chip away at our current urban edifices, building something in their stead that will act diplomatically rather than destructively, something in which the world is no longer too small for us[18].

To put it another way: cities have to give up being predators. The carnivore has to be brought under control. The city has to become human.

Notes

1. From Atkinson (1997: 351).
2. 'The pious urgings of so many Australians to citizens of countries far poorer than our own to preserve their rainforests and other instances of biodiversity, while we do so little at home, is increasingly resented. Imagine being a Bangladeshi villager who is encouraged to share their environment with man-eating tigers – by a people so uncaring about their own environment that they can't lift a finger even to protect a small bat or endangered rodent' (Flannery, 2012: 69).
3. Milton, Sonnet 19, *Paradise Lost*.
4. Indeed, Latour has been taken to task for ignoring these resources (see Demos, 2016).
5. As Diski (2010) points out, many cultures strike a much less aggressive pose concerning the differences between humans and animals, for example, positing an origin in which animals and humans are created from the same mould, cleaving to myths and legends in which animals impregnate humans, or sometimes, as in the case of Ancient Egypt, worshipping creatures which have both animal and human characteristics.
6. There are others, of course. Take the practice of Shinto. Whilst not considered as animist as such, it still takes it as read that spirits (kami) manifest in multiple forms: as rocks, trees, rivers, animals, places and people. Spirits and people are not separated. They exist within the same world and share its interrelated complexity. Or take the practices of the Sierra Nevada de Santa Marta peoples of Colombia, who see themselves as the elder brothers of all other humans charged with ensuring the circulation of life (Ulloa, 2006; 2011).
7. In turn, we can see the way that such a position opens up other horizons. The world of immanent humanity is also a world of immanent divinity in which a host of gods inhabit the earth. The link to Tarde's work is obvious.
8. This point of view chimes with modern evolutionary theory and its attention to cases in which convergence can take place in very different environments (Losos, 2017).
9. As has been pointed out many times now, the result is that Heidegger has no real theory of knowledge and an unpolitical notion of the political. Dwelling far from the city, he doesn't really need them.
10. In other words, the question becomes not why non-locality exists, but rather why does locality? Things and their spatial positions are no longer necessarily coincident. Just because things are closer or farther apart doesn't mean that we can necessarily assume that they have a stronger or weaker relation. We might even go further. Space might be thought of as just one state of the universe, just as ice is one of the possible states of water (Musser, 2015).
11. A large literature is developing on conflict and compromise – and on when compromise folds over into complicity (see Lepora and Goodin, 2013). It remembers that morality is action-guiding and that there are many different types of compromise. This is the realm of so-called non-ideal theory, an important part of contemporary moral philosophy.
12. Hughes (1957). I have taken this motif from his poem 'The Jaguar'.
13. Honour has a long history as an object of study taking in Simmel and Bourdieu. It is often now regarded as an emotional leftover, tainted by its misuse, but that doesn't have to be the case.
14. Note that resurrection does not have to imply salvation, though it clearly does for Spencer.
15. Which is not to ignore the unequal sources of ontic power that arise out of late liberalism whose pressing obsessions often act out norms that do untold damage.
16. And it is hardly a new thought either. 'Plato … dreamed that once upon a time humans and other animals spoke together, which is to say that they listened to one another' (Krell, 2013: 5).
17. I do not mean to signal here that this necessarily has to be a disordered or at least decentralized affair. There is pretty good evidence that careful tactical development trumps simple protest politics most of the time (Heller, 2017).
18. The echo of Wordsworth is purposeful.

References

Abrahams, G., Johnson, B. and Gellatly, K. (eds) (2016) *Art + Climate Change*. Melbourne: Melbourne University Press.
Abram, D. (2011) *Becoming Animal*. New York, NY: Vintage.
Ackerman, J. (2016) *The Genius of Birds*. London: Corsair.
Ackerman, J. (2020) *The Bird Way*. London: Corsair.
Adams, C.J. (1990) *The Sexual Politics of Meat. A Feminist-Vegetarian Theory*. London: Bloomsbury.
Aguirre, J.C. (2019) 'Australia is deadly serious about killing millions of cats', *New York Times*, April 25.
Alamgir, M., Campbell, M.J., Sloan, S., Clements, G.R., Mahmoud, M.I. and Laurance, W.F. (2017) 'Economic, socio-political and environmental risks of road development in the tropics', *Current Biology*, 27 (20): R1130–40. https://doi.org/10.1016/j.cub.2017.08.067
Alberti, M. (2015) 'Eco-evolutionary dynamics in an urbanizing planet', *Trends in Ecology and Evolution*, 30. http://dx.doi.org/10.1016/j.tree.2014.11.007
Alberti, M., Marzluff, J. and Hunt, V.M. (2017) 'Urban-driven phenotypic changes: empirical observations and theoretical implications for eco-evolutionary feedback', *Philosophical Transactions of the Royal Society B*, 372. doi.org/10.1098/rstb.2016.0029
Albertin, C.B., Simakov, O., Mitros, T., et al. (2015) 'The octopus genome and the evolution of cephalopod neural and morphological novelties', *Nature*, 524: 220–4.
Allen, S., Allen, D., Phoenix, V.R., Le Roux, G., Jiménez, P.D., Simmonneau, A., Binet, S. and Galop, D. (2019) 'Atmospheric transport and deposition of microplastics in a remote mountain catchment', *Nature Geoscience*. doi.org/10.1038/s41561-019-0335-5
Amati, M., Saunders, A., Boruff, B. and Devereux, D. (2017) 'We're investing heavily in urban greening, so how are our cities doing?', *The Conversation Australia*, September 27. https://theconversation.com/were-investing-heavily-in-urban-greening-so-how-are-our-cities-doing-83354 (accessed July 2, 2020).
Amin, A. and Thrift, N.J. (2002) *Cities*. Cambridge: Polity.
Amin, A. and Thrift, N.J. (2014) *Arts of the Political*. Durham, NC: Duke University Press.
Amin, A. and Thrift, N.J. (2016) *Seeing Like a City*. Cambridge: Polity.
Amodio, P., Boeckle, M., Schnell, A.K., Ostojic, L., Fiorito, G. and Clayton, N. (2018) 'Grow smart and die young: why did cephalopods evolve intelligence?' *Trends in Ecology and Evolution*, 20. doi.org/10.1016/j.tree.2018.10.010
Andermann, T., Faurby, S., Turvey, S.T., Antonelli, A. and Silvestro, D. (2020) 'The past and future human impact on mammalian diversity', *Science Advances*, 6. doi: 10.1126/sciadv.abb2313
Anderson, D. (2015) *Imaginary Cities*. London: Influx Press.
Anderson, K., Broderick, J.F. and Stoddard, I. (2020) 'A factor of two: how the mitigation plans of "climate progressive" nations fall far short of Paris-compliant pathways', *Climate Policy*. doi.org/10.1080/14693062.2020.1728209
Anderson, V.D. (2004) *Creatures of Empire. How Domestic Animals Transformed Early America*. New York, NY: Oxford University Press.
Andrews, K. (2015) *The Animal Mind. An Introduction to the Philosophy of Animal Cognition*. London: Routledge.

References

Andrews, K. (2020) *How to Study Animal Minds*. Cambridge: Cambridge University Press.

Andrews, K. and Monsó, S. (2020) 'Rats are us', *Aeon*, March 2. https://aeon.co/essays/why-dont-rats-get-the-same-ethical-protections-as-primates (accessed June 30, 2020).

Angel, S. (2012) *The Atlas of Urban Expansion*. Cambridge, MA: Lincoln Institute of Land Policy. Updated 2017 at www.atlasofurbanexpansion.org/ (accessed August 10, 2020).

Angier, N. (2017) 'Birds beware: the praying mantis wants your brain', *New York Times*, September 22.

Ansell, D., Gibson, F. and Salt, D. (eds) (2016) *Learning from Agri-environment Schemes in Australia: Investing in Biodiversity and Other Ecosystem Services on Farms*. Canberra: ANU Press.

Ara, K., Kawano, K.M. and Mikami, O.K. (2018) 'Nut-dropping behaviour of carrion crows in Hakodate City, Hokkaido', *Japanese Journal of Ornithology*, 67. doi: 10.3838/jjo.67.243

ASPCA (2019) *Pet Statistics*. New York, NY: American Society for the Prevention of Cruelty to Animals.

Appiah, A. (2010) *The Honor Code. How Moral Revolutions Happen*. New York, NY: Norton.

Arendt, H. (2018) *Thinking Without a Banister. Essays in Human Understanding*. New York, NY: Schocken Books.

Aristotle (1984) *Nichomachean Ethics*. Oxford: Oxford University Press.

Aristotle (2015) *Politics*. Oxford: Oxford University Press.

Armstrong, P. (2016) *Sheep*. London: Reaktion.

Arsenault, C. (2014) 'Only sixty years of farming left if soil degradation continues', *Scientific American*, December 5.

Assael, B. (2018) *The London Restaurant, 1840–1914*. Oxford: Oxford University Press.

Associated Press (2017) 'Nearly 70,000 birds killed in New York in attempt to clear safer path for planes', *The Guardian*, January 14.

Atkins, P. (ed.) (2012) *Animal Cities. Beastly Urban Histories*. Farnham: Ashgate.

Atkinson, K. (1997) *Human Croquet*. London: Doubleday.

Auliya, M., Altherr, S., Ariano-Sanchez, D. et al. (2016) 'Trade in live reptiles, its impact on wild populations, and the role of the European market', *Biological Conservation*, 204 (Part A): 103–19. doi.org/10.1016/j.biocon.2016.05.017

Avery, M. (2019) 'The common pheasant – its status in the UK and the potential impacts of an abundant non-native', *British Birds*. https://britishbirds.co.uk/article/the-common-pheasant-its-status-in-the-uk-and-the-potential-impacts-of-an-abundant-non-native/ (accessed June 30, 2020).

Avital, E. and Jablonka, E. (2000) *Animal Traditions. Behavioural Inheritance in Evolution*. Cambridge: Cambridge University Press.

Baic, G. (2016) *Feeding Gotham. The Political Geography and Economy of Food, 1790–1860*. Princeton, NJ: Princeton University Press.

Balakrishnan, K. (2018) 'The impact of air pollution on deaths, disease burden, and life expectancy across the states of India: The Global Burden of Disease Study 2017', *The Lancet Planetary Health*, 3 (1): E26–39. https://doi.org/10.1016/S2542-5196(18)30261-4

Balcombe, J. (2016) *What a Fish Knows. The Inner Lives of Our Underwater Cousins*. New York, NY: Scientific American/ Farrar, Strauss and Giroux.

Ballard, J.G. (1966) *The Crystal World*. London: Fourth Estate.

Barad, K. (2007) *Meeting the Universe Halfway. Quantum Physics and the Entanglement of Matter and Meaning*. Durham, NC: Duke University Press.

Baraniuk, C. (2018) 'Is this fish self-aware?' *Hakai Magazine*, September 12, 1–3. www.hakaimagazine.com/news/is-this-fish-self-aware/ (accessed June 24, 2020).

Baranov, V., Jourdan, J., Pilotto, F., Wagner, R. and Haase, P. (2020) 'Complex and nonlinear climate-driven changes in freshwater insect communities over 42 years', *Conservation Biology*. doi.org/10.1111/cobi.13477

Barber, B.R. (2017) *Cool Cities. Urban Sovereignty and the Fix for Global Warming*. New Haven, CT: Yale University Press.

Barbier, E. (2019) *The Water Paradox. Overcoming the Global Crisis in Water Management*. New Haven, CT: Yale University Press.

Bar-On, Y., Phillips, R. and Milo, R. (2018) 'The biomass distribution on Earth', *PNAS*, 115 (25): 6506–11. doi.org/10.1073/pnas.1711842115

Barrett, L.P., Stanton, L. and Benson-Amram, S. (2018) 'The cognition of "nuisance" species', *Animal Behaviour*, 30. doi: 10.1016/j.anbehav.2018.05.005

Barron, M., Goldblatt, B., Ho, C. et al. (2016) *Understanding New York City's Food Supply*. New York, NY: New York City Mayor's Office.

Barua, M. and Sinha, A. (2017) 'Animating the urban: an ethological and geographical conversation', *Social and Cultural Geography*, 10: 1160–80.

Barrowclough, G.F., Cracraft, J., Klicka, J. and Zink, R.M. (2016) 'How many kinds of birds are there and why does it matter?' *PLoS ONE*, 11. doi.org/10.1371/journal.pone.0166307

Basshuysen, P.V. and Brandstedt, E. (2018) 'Comment on "The climate mitigation gap: Education and government recommendations miss the most effective individual actions"', *Environmental Research Letters*, 13 (4): #048001. https://iopscience.iop.org/article/10.1088/1748-9326/aab213 (accessed July 6, 2020).

Batty, M. (2018) *Inventing Future Cities*. Cambridge, MA: MIT Press.

Baynes-Rock, M. (2015) *Among the Bone Eaters. Encounters with Hyenas in Harar*. University Park, PA: Pennsylvania State University Press.

Baxter-Gilbert, J.H., Riley, J.L., Neufeld, C.J.H., Litzgus, J.D. and Lesbarrères, J. (2015) 'Road mortality potentially responsible for billions of pollinating insect deaths annually', *Journal of Insect Conservation*, 19: 1029–35.

Beach, T., Luzzadder-Beach, S., Krause, S. et al. (2019) 'Ancient Maya wetland fields revealed under tropical forest canopy from laser scanning and multiproxy evidence', *PNAS*, 116 (43): 21469–77. doi.org/10.1073/pnas.1910553116

Beck, A. (1973) *The Ecology of Stray Dogs, The Ecology of Free-Ranging Urban Animals*. Baltimore, MD: York Press.

Beiser, V. (2018) *The World in a Grain: The Story of Sand and How It Transformed Civilization*. New York, NY: Riverhead.

Benkoff, G., Lubken, U. and Sand, J. (eds) (2012) *Flammable Cities: Urban Conflagration and the Making of the Modern World*. Madison, WI: University of Wisconsin Press.

Bennett, C.E., Thomas, R.J., Williams, M. et al. (2018) 'The broiler chicken as a signal of a human reconfigured biosphere', *Royal Society Open Science*, 5: 1–11. doi.org/10.1098/rsos.180325

Bennie, J.J., Duffy, J.P., Inger, R. and Gaston, J. (2014) 'Biogeography of time partitioning in mammals', *PNAS*, 38: 13727–32.

Benson, E. (2010) *Wired Wilderness. Technologies of Tracking and the Making of Modern Wildlife*. Baltimore, MD: Johns Hopkins University Press.

Benson-Amran, S., Dantzer, B., Stricker, S., Swanson, E.M. and Holekamp, K. (2016) 'Brain size predicts problem-solving ability in mammalian carnivores', PNAS, 113: 2532–57.

Berger, J. (2008) *The Better to Eat You With. Fear in the Animal World*. Chicago, IL: Chicago University Press.

Berger, J. (2009 [1980]) *Why Look at Animals?* London: Penguin.

Berkes, F. (2012) *Sacred Ecology*. New York, NY: Routledge.

Berlin, I. (2017) 'A message to the 21st century', *New York Review of Books*. www.nybooks.com/articles/2014/10/23/message-21st-century/ (accessed July 8, 2020).

References

Berlin, J. (2019) 'Beloved symbol becomes a pest', *National Geographic*, February, 126–43.

Bernardino, J., Bevanger, K., Barrientos, R. et al. (2018) 'Bird collisions with power lines: state of the art and priority areas for research', *Biological Conservation*, 222: 1–13. doi.org/10.1016/j.biocon.2018.02.029

Berns, G. (2018) *What It's Like to be a Dog. And Other Adventures in Animal Neuroscience*. London: Oneworld.

Bernstein, M., Narayan, T., Cornier, L. and Bourgeois, A. (2019) 'Context-specific tool use by Sus Cebifrons', *Mammalian Biology*, 98. doi.org/10.1016/j.mambio.2019.08.003

Berwald, J. (2018) *Spineless. The Science of Jellyfish and the Art of Growing a Backbone*. New York, NY: Riverhead Books.

Bessire, L. and Bond, D. (2014) 'Ontological anthropology and the deferral of critique', *American Ethnologist*, 41: 440–56. doi.org/10.1111/amet.12083

Biehler, D.D. (2013) *Pests in the City. Flies, Bedbugs, Cockroaches, and Rats*. Seattle, WA: University of Washington Press.

Bisceglio, P. (2018) 'Are cities making animals smarter?', *The Atlantic*, August 19. www.theatlantic.com/science/archive/2018/08/cities-animal-intelligence-fishing-cats/567538/ (accessed July 1, 2020).

Blanchette, A. (2020) *Porkopolis. American Animality, Standardized Life, and the Factory Farm*. Durham, NC: Duke University Press.

Bloom, J. (2010) *American Wasteland. How America Throws Away Nearly Half of its Food (And What We Can Do About It)*. Cambridge, MA: Da Capo Press.

Bloomfield, L.S.P., McIntosh, T.L. and Lambin, E.F. (2020) 'Habitat fragmentation, livelihood behaviors, and contact between people and nonhuman primates in Africa', *Landscape Ecology*, 35: 985–1000. doi.org/10.1007/s10980-020-00995-w

Blum, J. (2016) *Green Infrastructure: Socio-Ecological Perspectives*. New York, NY: Apple.

Boffey, D. (2019) 'Plan to sell 50m meals made from electricity, water and air', *The Guardian*, June 29.

Bogaard, A. Fochesato, M. and Bowles, S., (2019) 'The farming-inequality nexus: new methods and evidence from Western Eurasia', *Antiquity*, 93 (371): 1129–43. doi.org/10.15184/aqy.2019.105

Bogost, I. (2012) *Alien Phenomenology, Or What It's Like to Be a Thing*. Minneapolis, MN: University of Minnesota Press.

Bolam, F.C., Mair, L., Angelico, M. et al. (2020) 'How many bird and mammal extinctions has recent conservation action prevented?', *Conservation Letters*. doi.org/10.1111/conl.12762

Bond-Lamberty, B., Bailey, V.L., Chen, M., Gough, C.M. and Vargas, R. (2018) 'Globally rising heterotrophic respiration over recent decades', *Nature*, 560: 80–3.

Bonebrake, T.C. and Cooper, D.S. (2014) 'A Hollywood drama of butterfly extirpation and persistence over a century of urbanization', *Journal of Insect Conservation*, 18: 683–92.

Bonham, C. (2019) *Green Spaces in Residential Gardens*. ONS Data Science Campus. https://datasciencecampus.ons.gov.uk/projects/green-spaces-in-residential-gardens/ (accessed July 2, 2020).

Bonnett, A. (2014) *Unruly Places. Lost Spaces, Secret Cities, and Other Inscrutable Geographies*. Boston, MA: Houghton Mifflin Harcourt.

Borda-de-Água, L., Barrientos, R., Beja, P. and Pereira, H. (eds) (2017) *Railway Ecology*. Berlin: Springer.

Borgonie, G. and Lau, M. (2017) 'Life goes deeper', *Aeon*. https://aeon.co/essays/deep-beneath-the-earths-surface-life-is-weird-and-wonderful (accessed July 9, 2020).

Bowles, S. and Choi, J.-K. (2020) 'The Neolithic agricultural revolution and the origin of private property', *Journal of Political Economy*, 127 (5). www.journals.uchicago.edu/doi/abs/10.1086/701789 (accessed June 25, 2020).
Bradshaw, J. (2017) *The Animals Among Us. The New Science of Anthrozoology*. London: Allen Lane.
Brady, S.P. and Richardson, J.L. (2017) 'Road ecology: shifting gears toward evolutionary perspectives', *Frontiers in Ecology and the Environment*, 15 (2): 91–8. doi.org/10.1002/fee.1458
Bramwell, L. (2016) *Wilderburbs. Communities on Nature's Edge*. Seattle, WA: University of Washington Press.
Brand, A. (2019) *The Hidden World of the Fox*. London: Collins.
Brandstedt, E. (2019) 'Reproductive choices and climate change Part 2: Should individuals have fewer children to mitigate climate change?', *LSE Blog*. www.lse.ac.uk/philosophy/blog/2018/04/18/reproductive-choices-and-climate-change-2/ (accessed July 6, 2020).
Brans, K.I. and Meester, L. (2018) 'City life on fast lanes: urbanization induces an evolutionary shift towards a faster lifestyle in the water flea *Daphnia*', *Functional Ecology*, 32. doi.org/10.1111/1365-2435.13184
Bremner, R. (2020) 'Sardines shrink to half their size in a decade as the seas get warmer', *The Times*, February 7.
Brennan, J. (2017) *Against Democracy*. Princeton, NJ: Princeton University Press.
Brenner, N. (ed.) (2014) *Implosions/Explosions. Towards a Study of Planetary Urbanization*. Berlin: Jovis.
Brenner, N. (2018) 'Debating planetary urbanization: for an engaged pluralism', *Environment and Planning D. Society and Space*, 36: 570–90.
Brenner, N. and Schmid, C. (2013) 'The urban age in question', *International Journal of Urban and Regional Research*, 38 (3). doi.org/10.1111/1468-2427.12115
Brenner, N. and Schmid, C. (2015) 'Towards a new epistemology of the urban', *City*, 19 (2–3): 151–82.
Bricker, D. and Ibbitson, J. (2019) 'What goes up: are predictions of a global population crisis wrong?', *The Guardian*, January 27.
Brighter Green (2011) *Skillful Means. The Challenges of China's Encounter with Factory Farming*. New York, NY: Brighter Green.
Brook, R. and Dunn, N. (2013) *Urban Maps*. Farnham: Ashgate.
Brooks, D. (2020) 'The nuclear family was a mistake', *The Atlantic*, March. www.theatlantic.com/magazine/archive/2020/03/the-nuclear-family-was-a-mistake/605536/ (accessed July 6, 2020).
Brown, F.L. (2016) *The City Is More Than Human. An Animal History of Seattle*. Seattle, WA: University of Washington Press.
Buchanan, B. (2008) *Onto-Ethologies. The Animal Environments of Uexkull, Heidegger, Merleau-Ponty, and Deleuze*. Albany, NY: State University of New York Press.
Buchanan, B. (2012) 'Being-with animals: reconsidering Heidegger's animal ontology', in A. Vallely and A. Gross (eds) *Animals and the Human Imagination*. New York, NY: Columbia University Press.
Buczkowski, G. (2010) 'Extreme life: history plasticity and the evolution of invasive characteristics in a native ant', *Biological Invasions*, 12: 3343–9.
Buehler, J. (2109) 'City crows may have high cholesterol because they eat fast food', *New Scientist*, August 26.
Bullard, N. (2020) 'Peak beef is better climate news than you thought', *Bloomberg Green*, February 27. www.bloomberg.com/news/articles/2020-02-27/peak-beef-is-better-climate-news-than-you-thought?sref=JMv1OWqN (accessed August 24, 2020).
Bulkeley, H.A. (2012) *Cities and Climate Change*. London: Routledge.

References

Bull, J., Holmberg, T. and Asberg, C. (eds) (2017) *Animal Places: Lively Cartographies of Human-Animal Relations*. London: Routledge.

Bulliet, R.W. (2005) *Hunters, Herders, and Hamburgers. The Past and Future of Human-Animal Relationships*. New York, NY: Columbia University Press.

Burgen, S. (2018) 'Fears for environment in Spain as pigs outnumber people', *The Guardian*, August 19.

Burgess, K. (2018) 'Mystery of missing dead pigeons solved', *The Times*, June 30.

Burt, J. (2005) 'John Berger's "Why Look at Animals?": a close reading', *Worldviews*, 9: 203–18.

Byrne, D. (2013) *How Music Works*. London: Canongate.

Cabannes, Y. and Marocchino, C. (eds) (2018) *Integrating Food into Urban Planning*. London: UCL Press.

Cairns, S. and Jacobs, J. (2014) *Buildings Must Die*. Cambridge, MA: MIT Press.

Calarco, M. (2008) *Zoographies. The Question of the Animal from Heidegger to Derrida*. New York, NY: Columbia University Press.

Calthorpe, P. and Walters, J. (2017) 'Autonomous vehicles: hype and potential', *Urban Land*, March 1. https://urbanland.uli.org/industry-sectors/infrastructure-transit/autonomous-vehicles-hype-potential/ (accessed June 22, 2020).

Calvino, U. (2010) *Invisible Cities*. New York, NY: Vintage.

Campbell, C. (2013) *Bonzo's War. Animals Under Fire, 1939–1945*. London: Constable.

Campbell, C. and Park, A. (2020) 'Inside the global quest to trace the origins of COVID-19 – and predict where it will go next', *Time*, July 23.

Candea, M. (ed.) (2012) *The Social After Gabriel Tarde*. London: Routledge.

Carey, P. (2018) *A Long Way from Home*. London: Faber.

Carlen, E. and Munshi-South, J. (2020) 'Widespread genetic connectivity of feral pigeons across the Northeastern megacity', *Evolutionary Applications*. doi.org/10.1111/eva.12972

Carrington, D. (2019) 'Light pollution is a key bringer of insect apocalypse', *The Guardian*, November 22.

Carrington, D., Duncan, P. and Barkham, P. (2019) 'Watchdog permits 170,000 wild bird killings in five years', *The Guardian*, February 22.

Caron, C. (2018) 'Montreal turns to coyote hazing after 18 people are bitten', *New York Times*, December 14.

Carson, R. (1950) *The Sea Around Us*. New York, NY: Oxford University Press.

Cartwright, N. (1992) *The Dappled World. A Study of the Boundaries of Science*. Cambridge: Cambridge University Press.

Casewell, N. and Ainsworth, S. (2019) 'Why are so many people still dying from snake bites?', *BBC News*, January 21. www.bbc.co.uk/news/world-45332002 (accessed June 30, 2020).

Cavell, S., Diamond, C., McDowell, J., Hacking, I. and Wolfe, C. (2008) *Philosophy and Animal Life*. New York, NY: Columbia University Press.

Chakrabarty, D. (2014) 'Climate and capital: conjoined histories', *Critical Inquiry*, 41: 1–23.

Chakrabarty, D. (2015) *The Human Condition in the Anthropocene*. The Tanner Lectures in Human Values. Yale University, February 18–19. https://tannerlectures.utah.edu/Chakrabarty%20manuscript.pdf (accessed June 19, 2020).

Chatelain, M., Gasparini, J. Jacquin, L. and Frantz, A. (2014) 'The adaptive function of melanin-based plumage colouration to trace metals', *Biology Letters*, 10. doi.org/10.1098/rsbl.2014.0164

Chater, N. (2018) *The Mind is Flat. The Illusion of Mental Depth and the Improvised Mind*. London: Allen Lane.

Cheng, L., Abraham, J., Hausfather, Z. and Trenberth, K.T. (2018) 'How fast are the oceans warming?' *Science*, 363 (6423): 128–9.

Cheshire, J. and Uberti, O. (2016) *Where the Animals Go. Tracking Wildlife with Technology in 50 Maps and Graphics*. London: Particular Books.
Chester, M., Fraser, A., Matute, J., Flower, C. and Pendyala, R. (2015). 'Parking infrastructure: a constraint on or opportunity for urban redevelopment? A study of Los Angeles County parking supply and growth', *Journal of the American Planning Association*, 4: 268–86. doi.org/10.1080/01944363.2015.1092879
Chez, K.W. (2017) *Victorian Dogs, Victorian Men. Affect and Animals in Nineteenth-Century Literature and Culture*. Columbus, OH: Ohio State University Press.
Chiang, T. (2019) *Exhalation*. London: Picador.
Chinese Academy of Sciences (2015) 'Maps reveal extent of China's antibiotics pollution'. http://english.cas.cn/newsroom/archive/news_archive/nu2015/201507/t20150715_150362.shtml (accessed August 18, 2020).
Chittka, L. and Wilson, C. (2018) 'Bee-brained', *Aeon*, https://aeon.co/essays/inside-the-mind-of-a-bee-is-a-hive-of-sensory-activity (accessed September 20, 2020).
Chittka., L. and Wilson, C. (2019) 'Expanding consciousness', *American Scientist*, 107. www.americanscientist.org/article/expanding-consciousness (accessed September 18, 2020).
Clark, T.J. (2017) 'Picasso and tragedy', *London Review of Books*, August 17: 33–8.
Clarke, S.C., McAllister, M.K., Milner-Gulland, E.J. et al. (2006) 'Global estimates of shark catches using trade records from commercial markets', *Ecology Letters*, 9. doi.org/10.1111/j.1461-0248.2006.00968.x
Cocker, M. (2018) *Our Place. Can We Save Britain's Wildlife Before It Is Too Late?* London: Cape.
Cockrall-King, J. (2012) *Food and the City. Urban Agriculture and the New Food Revolution*. New York, NY: Prometheus Books.
Cocozza, P. (2017) *How to Be Human*. London: Hutchinson.
Coetzee, J.M. (1999) *The Lives of Animals*. Princeton, NJ: Princeton University Press.
Cohen, J.J. (ed.) (2014) *Inhuman Nature*. Washington, DC: Oliphaunt.
Cohen, N. and Reynolds, K. (2016) *Beyond the Kale: Urban Agriculture and Social Justice Activism in New York City*. Athens, GA: University of Georgia Press.
Colebrook, C. (2016) 'What is the anthro-political?' in T. Cohen, C. Colebrook and J.H. Miller, *Twilight of the Anthropocene Idols*. London: Open Humanities Press, pp. 81–125.
Colebrook, C. (2017) 'Sex and the (Anthropocene) city', *Theory Culture & Society*, 34: 39–60.
Colley, C. and Wasley, A. (2020) 'Industrial-sized pig and chicken farming continuing to rise in UK', *The Guardian*, April 7.
Collingham, L. (2012) *The Taste of War. World War II and the Battle for Food*. New York, NY: Penguin.
Collingham, L. (2017) *The Hungry Empire. How Britain's Quest for Food Shaped the Modern World*. London: Bodley Head.
Comaroff, J. (2016) 'Built on sand: Singapore and the new state of risk', *Harvard Design Magazine*, 39: 1–8.
Coombs, M., Puckett, M., Richardson, J., Mims, D. and Munshi-South, J. (2018) 'Spatial population genomics of the brown rat (*Rattus norvegicus*) in New York City', *Molecular Ecology*, 27 (1): 83–98. doi.org/10.1111/mec.14437
Connolly, W. (2017) *Facing the Planetary. Entangled Humanism and the Politics of Swarming*. Durham, NC: Duke University Press.
Conty, A.F. (2018) 'The politics of nature: new materialist responses to the Anthropocene', *Theory Culture & Society*, 35, Annual Review: 73–96.
Coppinger, R. and Coppinger, L. (2016) *What Is a Dog?* Chicago, IL: University of Chicago Press.

References

Courland, R. (2011) *Concrete Planet. The Strange and Fascinating Story of the World's Most Common Man-Made Material*. Amherst, NY: Prometheus Books.
Corkery, M and Yaffe-Bellany, D. (2020a) 'The food chain's weakest link: slaughterhouses', *New York Times*, April 18.
Corkery, M. and Yaffe-Bellany, D. (2020b) 'Meat plant closures mean pigs are gassed or shot instead', *New York Times*, May 14.
CPRE (2019) *Night Blight. Mapping England's Light Pollution and Dark Skies*. London: Campaign to Protect Rural England.
Creed, B. (2017) *Stray. Human-Animal Ethics in the Anthropocene*. Sydney: Power Publications.
Criado Perez, C. (2019) *Invisible Women. Exposing Data Bias in a World Designed for Men*. London: Chatto and Windus.
Crist, M. (2020) 'Is it OK to have a child?', *London Review of Books*, 45 (5), February 5.
Cronin, B. (2015) 'Island life: Crossrail Wallasea Wild Coast Project', *New Civil Engineer*, July 24: 15–19.
Crowley, S.L., Hinchliffe, S. and McDonald, R.A. (2018) 'Killing squirrels. Exploring motives and practices of lethal wildlife management', *Environment and Planning E. Nature and Space*. doi.org/10.1177/2514848617747831
Curry, H.A., Jardine, N., Secord, J.A. and Spary, E.C. (eds) (2018) *Worlds of Natural History*. Cambridge: Cambridge University Press.
Danahy, M.A. and Morse, D.D. (eds) (2017) *Victorian Animal Dreams. Representations of Animals in Victorian Literature and Culture*. London: Routledge.
Dang, Y.P., Dalal, R.C. and Menzies, R.C. (eds) (2020) *No-Till Farming Systems for Sustainable Agriculture: Challenges and Opportunities*. Berlin: Springer.
Danowski, D. and Viveiros de Castro, E. (2017) *The Ends of the World*. Cambridge: Polity.
Dargis, M. (2020) '"Dolittle" review: Baa, humbug', *New York Times*, January 15.
Daskin, J.H. and Pringle, R.M. (2018) 'Warfare and wildlife declines in Africa's protected areas', *Nature*, 553: 328–32.
Daston, L. (2019) *Against Nature*. Cambridge, MA: MIT Press.
Daston, L. and Mitman, G. (eds) (2005) *Thinking with Animals. New Perspectives on Anthropomorphism*. New York, NY: Columbia University Press.
Davis, H. and Turpin, E. (eds) (2015) *Art in the Anthropocene. Encounters Among Aesthetics, Politics, Environments and Epistemologies*. Ann Arbor, MI: Open Humanities Press.
Davis, M. (2010) 'Who will build the ark?', *New Left Review*, 61. https://newleftreview.org/issues/II61/articles/mike-davis-who-will-build-the-ark (accessed July 9, 2020).
Davis, M. (2016) 'The coming desert. Kropotkin, Mars and the pulse of Asia', *New Left Review*, 97: 23–43.
Davis, M. (2017) 'El diablo in wine country', *London Review of Books*, November 21: 14. www.lrb.co.uk/blog/2017/october/el-diablo-in-wine-country (accessed June 22, 2020).
Dawson, A. (2016) *Extinction. A Radical History*. New York, NY: OR Books.
Dawson, A. (2017) *Extreme Cities. The Peril and Promise of Urban Life in the Age of Climate Change*. London: Verso.
Day, L. (2007) *Field Guide to the Natural World of New York City*. Baltimore, MD: Johns Hopkins University Press.
Debaise, D. (2017a) *Speculative Empiricism. Revisiting Whitehead*. Edinburgh: Edinburgh University Press.
Debaise, D. (2017b) *Nature as Event. The Lure of the Possible*. Durham, NC: Duke University Press.
DEFRA (2020) *Agriculture in the United Kingdom 2019*. London: Department for Environment, Food and Rural Affairs.
de la Cadena, M. (2015) *Earth Beings. Ecologies of Practice Across Andean Worlds*. Durham, NC: Duke University Press.

Deleuze, G. and Parnet, C. (2007) *Dialogues II*. New York, NY: Columbia University Press.
Demos, T.J. (2016) *Decolonizing Nature. Contemporary Art and the Politics of Ecology*. Berlin: Sternberg Press.
Denerley, C, Redpath, S.M., van der Wal, R., Newson, S., Chapman, J.W. and Wilson, J.D. (2018) 'Breeding ground correlates of the distribution and decline of the common cuckoo *Cuculus Canorus* at two spatial scales', *Ibis*. doi.org/10.1111/ibi.12612
Derrida, J. (2008) *The Animal That Therefore I Am*. New York, NY: Fordham University Press.
Derrida, J. (2017) *Of Spirit. Heidegger and the Question*. Chicago, IL: University of Chicago Press.
Derryberry, E., Phillips, J.N., Derryberry, G.E., Blum, M.J. and Luther, D. (2020) 'Singing in a silent spring: birds respond to a half-century soundscape reversion during the COVID-19 shutdown', *Science*, doi: 10.1126/science.abd5777
Descola, P. (1986) *La Nature Domestique: Symbolisme et Praxis Dans L'Écologie des Achuar*. Paris: Maison des Sciences de l'Homme.
Descola, P. (2013) *The Ecology of Others*. Chicago, IL: Prickly Paradigm Press.
Descola, P. (2014) *Beyond Nature and Culture*. Chicago, IL: University of Chicago Press.
Despommier, D. (2011) *The Vertical Farm. Feeding the World in the 21st Century*. London: Picador.
Despret, V. (2016) *What Would Animals Say if We Asked the Right Questions?* Minneapolis, MN: University of Minnesota Press.
DeStefano, S. (2011) *Coyote at the Kitchen Door. Living with Wildlife in Suburbia*. Cambridge, MA: Harvard University Press.
Dickens, C. (1862) 'Two dog-shows', *All the Year Round*, 171 (2): 493–7.
Dickey, C. (2012) 'On the trail of the elusive vampire squid from hell', *Los Angeles Review of Books*, October 21.
Dickman, C. (2020) 'Update on number of animals killed in Australian bushfires'. *University of Sydney News blog*, January 8. www.sydney.edu.au/news-opinion/news/2020/01/08/australian-bushfires-more-than-one-billion-animals-impacted.html (accessed June 30, 2020).
Dickman, C., Van Eeden, L., Nimmo, D. et al. (2020) *Australia's 2019–2020 Bushfires. The Wildlife Toll (Interim Report)*. Sydney: World Wildlife Fund.
Diehl, R.H. (2013) 'The airspace is habitat', *Trends in Ecology and Evolution*, 28: 377–9.
Dinerstein, E.R., Vynne, C., Sala, E. et al. (2019) 'A global deal for nature: guiding principles, milestones and targets', *Science Advances*, 5. doi:10.1126/sciadv.aaw2869
Dinerstein, E.R., Joshi, A.R., Vynne, C. et al. (2020) 'A global "safety net" to reverse biodiversity loss and stabilize Earth's climate', *Science Advances*, 6. doi:10.1126/sciadv.abb2824
Diski, J. (2010) *What I Don't Know About Animals*. London: Virago.
De Waal, F. (2016) *Are We Smart Enough to Know How Smart Animals Are?* New York, NY: WW Norton.
Dogs Trust (2017) *Stray Dogs Survey Report 2017*. London: Dogs Trust. www.dogstrust.org.uk/news-events/news/stray%20dogs%20report_v4.pdf (accessed June 29, 2020).
Dolgin, E. (2019) 'The secret social lives of viruses', *Nature*, June 18. www.nature.com/articles/d41586-019-01880-6 (accessed June 23, 2020).
Domanska, R. (2017) 'Animal history', *History and Theory*, 56: 267–87.
Donovan, T. (2015) *Feral Cities. Adventures with Animals in the Urban Jungle*. Chicago, IL: Chicago Review Press.
Douglas, A.E. (2010) *The Symbiotic Habit*. Princeton, NJ: Princeton University Press.

References

Dover, J.W. (2015) *Green Infrastructure. Incorporating Plants and Enhancing Biodiversity in Buildings and Urban Environments*. London: Routledge.

Duarte, C.M., Agusti, S., Barbier, E. et al. (2020) 'Rebuilding marine life', *Nature*, 580: 39–51. doi.org/10.1038/s41586-020-2146-7

Ducatez, S., Sol, D., Sayol, F. and Lefebvre, L. (2020) 'Behavioral plasticity is associated with reduced extinction risk in birds', *Nature Ecology and Evolution*, 4: 788–93. doi.org/10.1038/s41559-020-1168-8

Dunn, R. (2019) *Never Home Alone: From Microbes to Millipedes, Camel Crickets and Honeybees, the Natural History of Where We Live*. New York, NY: Basic Books.

DCRPC (2010) *Greater Philadelphia Food System Study*. Philadelphia, PA: Delaware Valley Regional Planning Commission.

EAT-Lancet, Willett, W., Rockström, J. et al. (2019) *Food in the Anthropocene: the EAT-Lancet Commission on Healthy Diets from Sustainable Food Systems*. thelancet.com/commissions/EAT (accessed July 3, 2020).

Eckert, J., Racokzy, H., Call, J., Herrmann, E. and Hanus, D. (2018) 'Chimpanzees consider humans psychological states when drawing statistical inferences', *Current Biology*, 28: 1959–63.

Economist (2016) 'Why British dogs are getting smaller', *The Economist*, August 11.

Economist (2017) 'More skin in the game', *The Economist*, August 26.

Edgerton, D. (2006) *The Shock of the Old*. London: Profile.

Edwards, P.N. (2010) *A Vast Machine. Computer Models, Climate Data, and the Politics of Global Warming*. Cambridge, MA: MIT Press.

Egan, T. (2019) 'Fake meat will save us', *New York Times*, June 21.

Einhorn, B. (2019) 'China's selling genetically-modified mice for $17,000 a pair', *Bloomberg Prognosis*, April 1. www.bloomberg.com/news/articles/2019-04-01/china-s-demand-for-17-000-gene-altered-lab-mice-is-skyrocketing (accessed July 10, 2020).

Ekwurzel, B., Boneham, J. Dalton, M.W., Heede, R., Mera, R.J., Allen, M.R. and Frumhoff, P.C. (2017) 'The rise in global atmospheric CO_2, surface temperature, and sea level from emissions traced to major carbon producers, *Climatic Change*, 144: 579–90.

Elden, S. (2006) 'Heidegger's animals', *Continental Philosophy Review*, 19: 273–91.

Ellard, C. (2015) *Places of the Heart. The Psychogeography of Everyday Life*. New York, NY: Bellevue Press.

Ellis, E.C. (2018) *Anthropocene. A Very Short Introduction*. Oxford: Oxford University Press.

Emery, J. (2016) *Bird Brain. An Exploration of Avian Intelligence*. Lewes: Ivy Press.

Emmett, R. and Lekan, T. (eds) (2016) *Whose Anthropocene? Revisiting Dipesh Chakrabarty's 'Four Theses'*. Munich: Rachel Carson Center for Environment and Society.

Environment Agency (n.d.) 'Catchment data search'. https://environment.data.gov.uk/catchment-planning/ (accessed November 17, 2020).

Erickson, J. (2019) 'Nocturnal flight calls increase building collisions among migrating birds', *The University of Michigan Record*, April 4.

Escobar, A. (2017) *Designs for the Pluriverse. Radical Interdependence, Autonomy, and the Making of Worlds*. Durham, NC: Duke University Press.

Esponda, F. and Gordon, D.M. (2015) 'Distributed nestmate recognition in ants', *Proceedings of the Royal Society Series B*, 282: 20142838.

European Environment Agency (2013) 'Populations of grassland butterflies decline almost 50 per cent over two decades', *European Environment Agency News*, July 17. www.eea.europa.eu/highlights/populations-of-grassland-butterflies-decline (accessed July 10, 2020).

Fa, J., Seymour, S., Dupain, J., Amin. R., Albrechtsen, L. and Macdonald, D. (2006) 'Getting to grips with the magnitude of exploitation: bushmeat in the Cross–Sanaga rivers region, Nigeria and Cameroon', *Biological Conservation*, 129 (4): 497–510.

Fagan, B. (2017) *Fishing. How the Sea Fed Civilization*. New Haven, CT: Yale University Press.

Faith, J.T., Rowan, J., Du, A. and Koch, P.L. (2018) 'Plio-Pleistocene decline of African megaherbivores: no evidence for ancient hominin impacts', *Science*, 362 (6417): 938–41. doi.org/10.1126/science.aau2728

FAO (n.d.) Food Wastage Footprint and Climate Change. Rome: Food and Agriculture Organization of the United Nations. www.fao.org/3/a-bb144e.pdf (accessed November 17, 2020).

FAO (2013) *Tackling Climate Change Through Livestock. A Global Assessment of Emissions and Mitigation Opportunities*. Rome: Food and Agriculture Organization of the United Nations. www.fao.org/3/a-i3437e.pdf (accessed July 3, 2020).

FAO (2016) *State of the World's Forests*. Rome: Food and Agriculture Organization.

FAO (2017a) *Global Land Outlook*. Rome: Food and Agriculture Organization of the United Nations/ Convention to Combat Desertification.

FAO (2017b) *Water for Sustainable Food and Agriculture*. www.fao.org/3/a-i7959e.pdf (accessed September 8, 2020).

FAO (2018) *The State of World Fisheries and Aquaculture 2018 – Meeting the Sustainable Development Goals*. Rome: Food and Agriculture Organization of the United Nations. www.fao.org/3/i9540en/i9540en.pdf (accessed June 29, 2020).

FAO (2020) *Food Outlook. Biannual Report on Global Food Markets*. Rome: Food and Agriculture Organization of the United Nations. www.fao.org/3/ca9509en/CA9509EN.pdf (accessed August 24, 2020).

Farley, P. and Roberts, S. (2011) *Edgelands. Journeys into England's True Wilderness*. London: Vintage.

FarmingUK (2018) 'Larger poultry farms needed to keep the UK supplied with chicken'. www.farminguk.com/news/larger-poultry-farms-needed-to-keep-uk-supplied-with-chicken_49689.html (accessed August 17).

Favini, J. (2020) 'What if competition isn't as "natural" as we think?', *Slate*, January 23. https://slate.com/technology/2020/01/darwin-competition-collaboration-evolutionary-biology-climate-change (accessed June 23, 2020).

Feinstein, J. (2011) *Field Guide to Urban Wildlife*. Mechanicsburg, PA: Stackpole Books.

Fiddes, N. (1991) *Meat. A Natural Symbol*. London: Routledge.

Fitzgerald, A.J. (2015) *Animals as Food. (Re)connecting Production, Processing, Consumption, and Impacts*. East Lansing, MN: Michigan State University Press.

Fitzhugh, T.W. and Richter, B.D. (2004) 'Quenching urban thirst: growing cities and their impacts on freshwater ecosystems', *BioScience*, 54: 741–54.

Flannery, T. (2012) 'After the future. Australia's new extinction crisis', *Quarterly Essay*, (49): 1–80.

Fleming, A. (2018) 'Pet food is an environmental disaster – are vegan dogs the answer?', *The Guardian*, June 26.

Flores, D. (2016) *Coyote America. A Natural and Supernatural History*. New York, NY: Basic Books.

Floud, R. (2019) *An Economic History of the English Garden*. London: Allen Lane.

Flusser, V. (1992 [1987]) *Vampyrotheuthis Infernalis*. New York, NY: Atropos.

Fochesato, M., Bogaard, A. and Bowles, S. (2019) 'Measuring ancient inequality: The challenges of comparability, bias, and precision', *Antiquity*, 93 (370): 853–69. doi.org/10.15184/aqy.2019.106

Foer, J.S. (2009) *Eating Animals. Should We Stop?* London: Penguin.

Foer, J.S. (2019) *We Are the Weather*. London: Hamish Hamilton.

Foer, J.S., Thuras, D. and Morton, E. (2016) *Atlas Obscura. An Explorer's Guide to the World's Hidden Wonders*. New York, NY: Workman.

Food and Land Use Coalition (2019) *Growing Better. Ten Critical Transitions to Transform Food and Land Use*. www.foodandlandusecoalition.org/global-report/ (accessed November 18, 2020).

References

Forbes, D.K and Thrift, N.J. (2006) *The Price of War. Urbanization in Vietnam, 1954–1985*. London: George Allen and Unwin.

Forbes, P. (2018) 'We are heading for a new Cretaceous, not for a new normal', *Aeon*, October 29.

Forman, R.T.T. and Alexander, L.E. (1998) 'Roads and their major ecological effects', *Annual Review of Ecological Systems*, 29: 207–31.

Forrest, S. (2016) *The Age of the Horse. An Equine Journey through Human History*. London: Atlantic Books.

Forty, A. (2012) *Concrete and Culture. A Material History*. London: Reaktion.

Found, R. (2017) 'Interactions between cleaner birds and ungulates are personality dependent', *Biology Letters*, 13. doi.org/10.1098/rsbl.2017.0536

Fossil Fuel Report (2019) *Banking on Climate Change*. New York: Rainforest Action Network.

Foster, C. (2016) *Being a Beast*. London: Profile Books.

Foster, J.B. and Burkett, P. (2016) *Marx and The Earth. An Anti-Critique*. Leiden: Brill.

Franklin, S. (2007) *Dolly Mixtures. The Remaking of Genealogy*. Durham, NC: Duke University Press.

Freire, K.M.F., Belhabib, D., Espedido, J.C. et al. (2020) 'Estimating global catches of marine recreational fisheries', *Frontiers in Marine Science*. doi.org/10.3389/fmars.2020.00012

French, H.W. (2016) 'How Africa's new urban centers are shifting its old colonial boundaries', *The Atlantic*, July 1.

Frevert, U. (2011) *Emotions in History – Lost and Found*. Budapest: Central European University Press.

Frost, S. (2016) *Biocultural Creatures. Toward a New Theory of the Human*. Durham, NC: Duke University Press.

Frutos, R., Lopez Roig, M., Serra-Cobo, J. and Devaux, C.A. (2020) 'COVID-19: the conjunction of events leading to the coronavirus pandemic and lessons to learn for future threats', *Frontiers in Medicine*, 7. doi.org/10.3389/fmed.2020.00223

Fry, T. (2014) *City Futures in the Age of a Changing Climate*. London: Routledge.

Fry, T. (2017) *City Remaking. An Introduction to Urban Metrofitting*. London: Bloomsbury.

Fudge, E. (2002a) 'A left-handed blow: writing the history of animals', in E. Fudge and N. Rothfels (eds) *A Left-Handed Blow. Writing the History of Animals*. Bloomington: Indiana University Press, pp. 1–18.

Fudge, E. (2002b) *Animal*. London: Reaktion Books.

Fudge, E. (2008) *Pets*. Stocksfield: Acumen.

Fuentes, A. (2007) 'Monkey and human interconnections: the wild, the captive, and the in-between', in R. Cassidy and M. Mullin (eds) *Where the Wild Things are Now. Domestication Reconsidered*. New York, NY: Berg, pp. 123–45.

Fuentes, A. (2009) *Evolution of Human Behavior*. New York, NY: Oxford University Press.

Fuller, M., Goriunova, O. (2020) *Bleak Joys. Aesthetics of Ecology and Impossibility*. Minneapolis, MN: University of Minnesota Press.

Fuller, R.A., Tratalos, J. and Gaston, K.J. (2009) 'How many birds are there in a city of half a million people?', *Diversity and Distributions*, 15. doi.org/10.1111/j.1472-4642.2008.00537.x

Fullerton, J. (2019) 'Mugged by macaques: the urban monkey gangs of Kuala Lumpur', *The Guardian*, January 28.

Gabrys, J. (2016) *Program Earth. Environmental Sensing Technology and the Makings of a Computational Planet*. Minneapolis, MN: University of Minnesota Press.

Gallagher, J. (2018) 'More than half your body is not human', *BBC News*, April 22. www.bbc.co.uk/news/health-43674270 (accessed June 23, 2020).

Ganesh, J. (2020) 'The climate case for childlessness', *Financial Times*, February 1: 18.

GARN (n.d.) 'Rights of nature articles in Ecuador's constitution'. https://therightsofnature.org/wp-content/uploads/pdfs/Rights-for-Nature-Articles-in-Ecuadors-Constitution.pdf (accessed November 17, 2020).

Garrett, B.L. (2018) 'Who owns the space under cities? The attempt to map the ground beneath our feet', *The Guardian*, July 10.

Gaynor, K.M., Fiorella, K.J., Gregory, G.H., Kurz, D.J., Seto, K.L., Withey, L.S. and Brashares, J.S. (2016) 'War and wildlife: linking armed conflict to conservation', *Frontiers in Ecology and the Environment*, 14. doi.org/10.1002/fee.1433

Gaynor, K.M., Hojnowski, C.E., Carter, N.M. and Brashares, J. (2018) 'The influence of human disturbance on wildlife nocturnality', *Science*, 360: 1232–5. doi.org/10.1126/science.aar7121

Gaynor, K.M., Brown, J.S., Middleton, A.D., Power, M.E. and Brashares, J.S. (2019) 'Landscapes of fear: spatial patterns of risk perception and response', *Trends in Ecology & Evolution*, 34 (4): 355–68.

Gee, H. (2013) *The Accidental Species. Misunderstandings of Human Evolution*. Chicago, IL: University of Chicago Press.

Gehrt, S.D., Riley, S.D. and Cypher, B.L. (eds) (2010) *Urban Carnivores. Ecology, Conflict and Conservation*. Baltimore, MD: Johns Hopkins University Press.

Georgescu, M., Morefield, P., Bierwagen, B.G. and Weaver, C.P. (2014) 'Urban adaptation can roll back warming of emerging metropolitan regions', *PNAS*, 111: 2909–14.

Gerlach, J. (2017) 'Ecuador's experiment in living well: Sumak kawsay, Spinoza and the inadequacy of ideas', *Environment and Planning A*, 49: 2241–6.

Geyer, R., Jambecki, J.R. and Law, K.L. (2017) 'Production, use, and fate, of all plastics ever made', *Science Advances*, 3. doi:10.1126/sciadv.1700782

Ghosh, A. (2016) *The Great Derangement. Climate Change and the Unthinkable*. Chicago, IL: University of Chicago Press.

Gibbens, S. (2019) 'Wild bees are building their homes from plastic – and scientists aren't sure why', *National Geographic*, June 5. www.nationalgeographic.co.uk/animals/2019/06/wild-bees-are-building-their-homes-plastic-and-scientists-arent-sure-why (accessed July 1, 2020).

Gibson, K, Rose, D.B. and Fincher, R. (eds) (2015) *Manifesto for Living in the Anthropocene*. New York, NY: Punctum.

Gilbert, S.F., Sapp, J., and Tauber, A.I. (2012) 'A symbiotic view of life: we have never been individuals', *The Quarterly Review of Biology*, 87: 325–41.

Gill, V. (2019) 'Early ocean plastic litter traced to 1960s', *BBC News*, April 16. www.bbc.co.uk/news/science-environment-47914580#:~:text=Old%2D fashioned%20metal%20boxes%20that,coast%20of%20Ireland%20in%201965 (accessed November 18, 2020).

Gillespie, K. (2018) *The Cow with Ear Tag #1389*. Chicago, IL: University of Chicago Press.

Ginn, F. (2014) 'Sticky lives: slugs, detachment and more-than-human ethics in the garden', *Transactions of the Institute of British Geographers*, 39: 532–544.

Ginn, F., Beisel, U. and Barua, M. (2014) 'Living with awkward creatures: vulnerability, togetherness, killing', *Environmental Humanities*, 4: 113–23.

Gintis, H., van Schaik, C. and Boeham, C. (2015) 'Zoon politikon. The evolutionary origins of human political systems', *Cultural Anthropology*, 56 (3): 327–53.

Ginsburg, S. and Jablonka, E. (2019) *The Evolution of the Sensitive Soul. Learning and the Origins of Consciousness*. Cambridge, MA: MIT Press.

Glendinning, S. (2000) 'From animal life to city life', *Angelaki*, 5: 19–30.

Glendinning, S. (2015) 'A time after Copernicus', in K. Nagai, C. Rooney, D. Landry, M. Mattfeld, C. Sleigh and K. Jones (eds) *Cosmopolitan Animals*. London: Palgrave Macmillan, pp. 14–28.

Glick, M. (2019) *Infrahumanisms. Science, Culture and the Making of Modern Personhood*. Durham, NC: Duke University Press.

Godfrey-Smith, P. (2018) *Other Minds. The Octopus and the Evolution of Intelligent Life*. London: Collins.

Goodwin, D. (2017) *The Urban Tree*. London: Routledge.

References

Gordon, D.M (2018) 'An ant colony has memories that its individual members don't have', *Aeon*, December 11. https://aeon.co/ideas/an-ant-colony-has-memories-that-its-individual-members-dont-have (accessed June 24, 2020).

Gorman, J. (2019) 'Rise of the golden jackal', *New York Times*, January 14.

Gottlieb, R. and Ng, S. (2017) *Global Cities. Urban Environments in Los Angeles, Hong Kong, and China*. Cambridge, MA: MIT Press.

Goulson, D. (2019) *The Garden Jungle or Gardening to Save the Planet*. London: Cape.

Goulson, D. (2020) *Insect Declines and Why They Matter*. Maidstone: Kent Wildlife Trust/ South West Wildlife Trust.

Graham, S. (2017) *Vertical City. The City from Satellites to Bunkers*. London: Verso.

Graham, S. (2020) *Cities Under Siege. The New Military Urbanism*. London: Verso.

Grandin, T. (2012) 'Making slaughterhouses more humane for cattle, pigs, and sheep'. www.grandin.com/references/making.slaughterhouses.more.humane.html (accessed September 3, 2020).

Gray, J. (2017) 'Walking backwards into the future', *New Statesman*, December 8, 88–91.

Gravel, R. (2016) *Where We Want to Live. Reclaiming Infrastructure for a New Generation of Cities*. New York, NY: St Martin's Press.

Grear, A. (ed.) (2012) Special Issue on Should Trees Have Standing? 40 Years On. *Journal of Human Rights and the Environment*, 3 (0).

Grear, A. (2019) 'It's wrongheaded to protect nature with human-style rights', *Aeon*, March 19. https://aeon.co/ideas/its-wrongheaded-to-protect-nature-with-human-style-rights (accessed July 6, 2020).

Greed, C. (2017) *Stray: Human-Animal Ethics in the Anthropocene*. Sydney: Power Publications.

Greenberg, J.R. and Holekamp, K.E. (2017) 'Human disturbance affects personality development in a wild carnivore', *Animal Behaviour*, 132. doi: 10.1016/j.anbehav.2017.08.023

Greenberg, P. (2010) *Four Fish. The Future of the Last Wild Food*. New York, NY: Penguin.

Greenberg, P. (2014) *American Catch. The Fight for Our Local Seafood*. New York, NY: Penguin.

Greenwood, V. (2019) 'Happy as a crab that just finished a maze', *New York Times*, October 24.

Gregory, A.C., Zayed, A.A., Conceição-Neto, N. et al. (2019) 'Marine DNA viral macro- and microdiversity from pole to pole', *Cell*, 177 (5): 1109–1123.e14. doi.org/10.1016/j.cell.2019.03.040

Grosz, E. (2017) *The Incorporeal. Ontology, Ethics, and the Limits of Materialism*. New York, NY: Columbia University Press.

Grove, M., Cadenasso, M., Pickett, S.T.A., Machlis, G. and Burch, W.R. (2015) *The Baltimore School of Urban Ecology. Space, Scale and Time for the Study of Cities*. Baltimore, MD: Johns Hopkins University Press.

Gruber, R., Schiestl, M., Boeckle, M, Frohnweiser, A., Miller, R., Gray, R.D., Clayton, N.S. and Taylor, A.H. (2019) 'New Caledonian crows use mental representations to solve metatool problems', *Current Biology*, 29. doi.org/10.1016/j.cub.2019.01.008

Gu, B. (2019) 'Four steps to food security for swelling cities', *Nature*: 566: 31–3.

Guattari, F. (2000) *The Three Ecologies*. London: Continuum.

Gutierrez, M., Daniels, M., Jobbins, G., Almazor, G.G. and Montenegro, C. (2020) *China's Distant-Water Fishing Fleet: Scale, Impact and Governance*. London: Overseas Development Institute.

Guo, Y., Gasparrini, A., Li, S. et al.(2018) 'Quantifying excess deaths related to heatwaves under climate change scenarios: a multicountry time series modelling study', *PLoS Medicine*. doi.org/10.1371/journal.pmed.1002629

Haddad, N.M., Brudvig, L.A., Clobert, J., Davies, K.F., Gonzalez, A., Holt, R.D. and Lovejoy, T.E. (2015) 'Habitat fragmentation and its lasting impact on Earth's ecosystems', *Science Advances*, 1. doi.org/10.1126/sciadv.1500052

Hage, G. (2015) *Alter-Politics. Critical Anthropology and the Radical Imagination*. Carlton: Melbourne University Press.

Haines, A., Hanson, C. and Ranganathan, J. (2018) 'Planetary Health Watch: integrated monitoring in the Anthropocene epoch', *The Lancet Planetary Health*, 2. doi.org/10.1016/S2542-5196(18)300047-0

Hallmann, C.A., Sorg, M., Jongejans, E. et al. (2017) 'More than 75 percent decline over 27 years in total flying insect biomass in protected areas', *PLoS ONE*. doi.org/10.1371/journal.pone.0185809

Hamilton, C. (2017) *Defiant Earth. The Fate of Humans in the Anthropocene*. Cambridge: Polity.

Handley, S. (2016) *Sleep in Early Modern England*. New Haven, CT: Yale University Press.

Hanson, T. (2019) 'Biodiversity conservation and armed conflict: a warfare ecology perspective', *Annals of the New York Academy of Science*, 1429: 50–65.

Hanson T., Brooks T.M., Da Fonseca G.A. et al. (2009) 'Warfare in biodiversity hotspots', *Conservation Biology*, 23: 578–87. doi.org/10.1111/j.1523-1739.2009.01166.x

Haraway, D. (2003) *The Companion Species Manifesto. Dogs, People, and Significant Otherness*. Chicago, IL: Prickly Paradigm Press.

Haraway, D. (2008) *When Species Meet*. Minneapolis, MN: University of Minnesota Press.

Haraway, D. (2016) *Staying with the Trouble. Making Kin in the Cthulucene*. Durham, NC: Duke University Press.

Haraway, D. (2018) 'Making kin in the cthulucene: reproducing multispecies justice', in A.E. Clarke, and D. Haraway (eds) *Making Kin, Not Population*. Chicago, IL: Prickly Paradigm Press, pp. 67–100.

Hardt, M. and Negri, A. (2017) *Assembly*. New York, NY: Oxford University Press.

Hardt, M. and Negri, A. (2019) 'Empire, twenty years on', *New Left Review*, 120: 67–92.

Harman, G. (2012) *Weird Realism. Lovecraft and Philosophy*. Winchester: Zero Books.

Harman, G. (2016) *Dante's Broken Hammer*. London: Repeater.

Harman, G. (2018) *Object-Oriented Ontology. A New Theory of Everything*. London: Pelican.

Harwatt, H. (2019) 'Including animal to plant protein shifts in climate change mitigation policy: a proposed three step policy', *Climate Policy*, 19: 533–41.

Harwatt, H., Ripple, W.J., Chaudhary, A., Betts, M.G. and Hayek, M.N. (2019) 'Scientists call for renewed Paris pledges to transform agriculture', *Lancet Planetary Health*. doi.org/10.1016/S2542-5196(19)30245-1

Harrison, M. (2020) 'Our magical barn owls are in danger of disappearing', *The Times*, February 29.

Hartocollis, A. (2019) 'It's horses vs. motors in Senegal', *New York Times*, September 10.

Hassall, C. (2014) 'The ecology and diversity of urban ponds', *Water*, 1: 187–206.

Hauser, C. (2020) 'Nearly 2 million chickens killed as poultry workers are sidelined', *New York Times*, April 28.

Hawken, P. (ed.) (2017) *Drawdown: The Most Comprehensive Plan Ever Proposed to Reverse Global Warming*. London: Penguin.

Hayhow, D.B., Eaton, M.A., Stanbury, A.J. et al. (2019) *The State of Nature 2019*. London: The State of Nature Partnership. https://nbn.org.uk/wp-content/uploads/2019/09/State-of-Nature-2019-UK-full-report.pdf (accessed July 3, 2020).

Heald, O.J.N., Fraticelli, C., Cox, S.E., Stevens, M.C.A., Faulkner, S.C., Blackburn, T.C. and Le Comber, S. (2019) 'Understanding the origins of the ring-necked parakeet in the UK', *Journal of Zoology*. doi.org/10.1111/jzo.12753

Hedden, W.P. (1929) *How Great Cities are Fed*. Boston, MA: D.C. Heath.

References

Heede, R. (2014) 'Tracing anthropogenic carbon dioxide and methane emissions to fossil fuel and cement producers, 1854–2010', *Climatic Change*, 122: 229–41.
Heller, N. (2017) 'Out of action. Do protests work?', *The New Yorker*, August 21.
Hellen, N. (2020) 'Built-up Britain: green land gobbled up by urban sprawl', *The Times*, January 5.
Helm, D. (2019) *Green and Prosperous Land*. London, Collins.
Helmreich, S. (2016) *Sounding the Limits of Life. Essays in the Anthropology of Life and Beyond*. Princeton, NJ: Princeton University Press.
Hennan, M. and Macnamara, P. (2017) *The Peregrine Returns. The Art and Architecture of an Urban Raptor Recovery*. Chicago, IL: University of Chicago Press.
Heppenheimer, E., Brzeski, K.E., Hinton, J.W. et al. (2018) 'High genomic diversity and candidate genes under selection associated with range expansion in eastern coyores (*Canis iatrans*) populations', *Ecology and Evolution*, 24. doi.org/10.1002/ece3.4688
Herculano-Houzel, S. (2020) 'Birds do have a brain cortex – and think', *Science*, 369. doi:10.1126/science.abe0536
Herzfeld, C. (2016) *Wattana. An Orangutan in Paris*. Chicago, IL: University of Chicago Press.
Herzog, H. (2010) *Some We Love, Some We Hate, Some We Eat*. New York, NY: HarperCollins.
Heyes, C. (2018) *Cognitive Gadgets. The Cultural Evolution of Thinking*. Cambridge, MA: Harvard University Press.
Hewitt, K. (1983) 'Place annihilation: area bombing and the fate of urban places', *Annals of the Association of American Geographers*, 73, 257–84.
Higgins, P. (2015) *Eradicating Ecocide. Laws and Governance to Stop the Destruction of the Planet* (2nd edition). London: Shepheard-Walwyn.
Hill, J.E., DeVault, T., Belant, T. (2019) 'Cause-specific mortality of the world's terrestrial vertebrates', *Global Biogeography and Ecology*, 28: 680–89.
Hinchliffe, S., Bingham, N., Allen, J. and Carter, J. (2016) *Pathological Lives. Disease, Space and Biopolitics*. Chichester: Wiley Blackwell.
Hoddle, M. (2019) 'Quagga and zebra mussels', Center for Invasive Species, UC Riverside. https://cisr.ucr.edu/invasive-species/quagga-zebra-mussels#:~:text=Zebra%20mussels%20were%20found%20at,they%20filter%20feed%20year%20round. (accessed August 8, 2020).
Hodgetts, T. and Lorimer, J. (2018) 'Animals' mobilities', *Progress in Human Geography*, 44: 4–26.
Holbraad, M., Pedersen, M.A. and Viveiros de Castro, E. (2014) 'The politics of ontology: anthropological positions', *Theorizing the Contemporary, Fieldsights*. https://culanth.org/fieldsights/the-politics-of-ontology-anthropological-positions (accessed June 19, 2020).
Hoornweg, D. and Pope, K. (2016) 'Population predictions for the world's largest cities in the 21st century', *Environment and Urbanization*, 29(1): 195–216. https://journals.sagepub.com/doi/pdf/10.1177/0956247816663557 (accessed July 6, 2020).
Horowitz, A. (2016) *Being a Dog. Following the Dog into a World of Smell*. New York, NY: Scribner.
Horowitz, A. (2019) 'Dogs are not here for our convenience', *New York Times*, 3 September.
Horst, M. and Gaolach, B. (2015). 'The potential of local food systems in North America: a review of foodshed analyses', *Renewable Agriculture and Food Systems*, 30: 399–407.
Horton, B.P., Khan, N.S., Cahill, N. et al. (2020) 'Estimating global mean sea-level rise and its uncertainties by 2100 and 2300 from an expert survey', *Climate and Atmospheric Science*, 3, doi.org/10.1038/s41612-020-0121-5

Horton, K.G., Nilsson, C., Vann Doren, B., La Sorte, F.A., Dokter, A.M. and Farnsworth, A. (2019) 'Bright lights in the big cities: migratory birds' exposure to artificial light', *Frontiers in Ecology and Environment*, 17 (4). doi.org/10.1002/fee.2029

Howard, S.R., Avarguès-Weber, A., Garcia, J.E., Greentree, A.D. and Dyer, A.G. (2019) 'Numerical cognition in honeybees enables addition and subtraction', *Science Advances*, 5 (2): doi.org/10.1126/sciadv.aav0961

Howell, P. (2015a) *At Home and Astray. The Domestic Dog in Victorian Britain*. Charlottesville, VA: University of Virginia Press.

Howell, P. (2015b) 'Mary Tealby and the Battersea Dogs and Cats Home', *Journal of Victorian Culture Online*. http://jvc.oup.com/2015/10/05/philip-howell-mary-tealby-and-the-battersea-dogs-and-cats-home/ (accessed June 29, 2020).

Howes, D. (2018) 'Preface', in V. Henshaw, K. McLean, D. Medway, C. Perkins and G. Warnaby (eds) *Designing with Smell. Practices, Techniques and Challenges*. London: Routledge.

Hu, W. (2019) 'Rats are taking over New York City', *New York Times*, May 22.

Huang, A. and Qin, J. (2020) 'Xi declares war on food waste, and China races to tighten its belt', *New York Times*, August 21.

Huber, J. (2017) 'Cosmopolitanism for Earth dwellers: Kant on the right to be somewhere', *Kantian Review*, 17: 1–25.

Hughes, T. (1957) *The Hawk in the Rain*. London: Faber and Faber.

Hugh-Jones, S. (2019) 'Rhetorical antinomies and radical othering: recent reflections on responses to an old paper concerning human-animal relations in Amazonia', *HAU. Journal of Ethnographic Theory*, 9: 162–71.

Hume, D. (2010) *The Theory of Moral Sentiments*. London: Penguin.

Hunt, N. (2019) *The Parakeeting of London*. London: Paradise Road.

Iacobbo, K. and Iacobbo, M. (2004) *Vegetarian America: A History*. New York, NY: Praeger.

Ibisch, P.L., Hoffmann, M.T., Kreft, S. et al. (2016) 'A global map of roadless areas and their conservation status', *Science* 354: 1423–7. doi.org/10.1126/science.aaf7166

IBPES (2019) *Global Assessment Report on Biodiversity and Ecosystem Services*. Bonn: Intergovernmental Science Policy Platform on Biodiversity and Ecosystem Services.

Ignatieff, M. (2017) *The Ordinary Virtues. Moral Order in a Divided World*. Cambridge, MA: Harvard University Press.

Im, E., Pal, J.S. and Eltahir, E.A.B. (2017) 'Deadly heat waves predicted in the densely populated agricultural regions of South Asia', *Science Advances*. doi:10.1126/sciadv.1603322

Imachi, H., Nobu, M.K., Nakahara, N. et al. (2020) 'Isolation of an archaeon at the prokaryote–eukaryote interface', *Nature*, 577: 519–25. doi.org/10.1038/s41586-019-1916-6

Ingold, T. (2011) *Being Alive. Essays on Movement, Knowledge and Description*. London: Routledge.

Ingold, T. (2012) 'Looking for lines in nature', *Earthlines Magazine*, 3: 48–51.

Ingold, T. (2015) *The Life of Lines*. London: Routledge.

Jablonka, E. and Lamb, M.J. (2014) *Evolution in Four Dimensions. Genetic, Epigenetic, Behavioral, and Symbolic Variation in the History of Life*. Cambridge, MA: MIT Press.

Jackson, R.B., Saunois, M., Bousquet, P. et al. (2020) 'Increasing anthropogenic methane emissions arise equally from agricultural and fossil fuel sources', *Environmental Research Letters*, 15, iopscience.iop.org/article/10.1088/1748-9326/ab9ed2

James, S. P. (2009) 'Phenomenology and the problem of animal minds', *Environmental Values*, 18: 33–49.

References

Jardine, N. (ed.) (1996) *Cultures of Natural History*. Cambridge: Cambridge University Press.

Jarvis, B. (2019) 'Climate change could destroy his home in Peru. So he sued an energy company in Germany', *New York Times Magazine*, April 9: 23–36.

Jemisin, N.K. (2016) 'The city born great', *Tor.com*. www.tor.com/2016/09/28/the-city-born-great/ (accessed July 10, 2020).

Jensen, L. (2009) *The Rapture*. London: Bloomsbury.

Johnson C.K., Hitchens P.L., Pandit P.S., Rushmore J., Evans T.S., Young C.C.W. and Doyle M.M. (2020) 'Global shifts in mammalian population trends reveal key predictors of virus spillover risk', *Proceedings of the Royal Society, Series B*, 287. doi.org/10.1098/rspb.2019.2736

Johnson, D. (2017) *Fen*. London: Vintage.

Johnson, M.T.J. and Munshi-South, J. (2017) 'Evolution of life in urban environments', *Science*, 358 (6363). doi.10.1126/science.aam8327

Johnson-Ulrich, L., Lehmann, K.D.S., Turner, J.W., Holekamp, K.E. (2018) 'Testing cognition in the *Umwelt* of the spotted hyena', in N. Bueno-Guerra and F. Amici. (eds) *The Experimental Umwelt: A Practical Guide to Animal Cognition*. Cambridge: Cambridge University Press, pp. 244–65.

Johnston, M. (2015) *Trees in Towns and Cities. A History of British Urban Arboriculture*. Oxford: Windgather Press.

Johnston, M. (2017) *Street Trees in Britain: A History*. Oxford: Windgather Press.

Jones, K.A., Venter, O., Fuller, R.A., Allan, J.R., Maxwell, S.L. and James, P.N. (2018) 'One-third of global land is under intense human pressure', *Science*, 360: 788–91.

Jones, K.R., Klein, C.J., Halpern, B.S. et al. (2018) 'The location and protection status of Earth's diminishing marine wilderness', *Current Biology*, 15: P2506–2512.E3. doi.org/10.1016/j.cub.2018.06.010

Jones, M. (2019) 'Ocean uproar: saving marine life from a barrage of noise', *Nature*, 568: 158–61.

Joppa, L.N., Loarie, S.R. and Pimm, S.L. (2008) 'On the protection of "protected areas"', *PNAS*, 105: doi.org/10.1073/pnas.0802471105

Kalof, J. (ed.) (2017) *The Oxford Handbook of Animal Studies*. Oxford, Oxford University Press.

Kang, S. and Eltahir, E.A.B. (2018) 'North China Plain threatened by deadly heatwaves due to climate change and irrigation', *Nature Communications*, 9: Article #2894.

Kant, I. (1997) *Lectures on Ethics*. Cambridge: Cambridge University Press.

Kant, I. (2006) *Anthroplogy From a Pragmatic Point of View*. Cambridge: Cambridge University Press.

Kean, H. (2017) *The Great Cat and Dog Massacre: The Real Story of World War Two's Unknown Tragedy*. Chicago, IL: University of Chicago Press.

Kean, H. and Howell, P. (eds) (2018) *The Routledge Companion to Animal-Human History*. London: Routledge.

Keegan, M. (2018) 'Another outbreak is a certainty: are we ready for a superbug epidemic', *The Guardian*, June 26.

Keim, R. (2016) 'What is she thinking? The new anthropomorphism', *The Chronicle Review*, October 7: B4–B9.

Kennedy, M. and Matias, D. (2019) 'Spotted: a swarm of ladybugs so huge it showed up on national weather service radar', *NPR*, June 6. www.npr.org/2019/06/06/730254007/spotted-a-swarm-of-ladybugs-so-huge-it-showed-up-on-national-weather-service-rad?t=1597424819864 (accessed November 18, 2020).

Kevany, S. (2020a) 'Millions of US farm animals to be culled by suffocation, drowning and shooting', *The Guardian*, May 19.

Kevany, S. (2020b) 'Hundreds of thousands of chickens to be culled after Covid disruption', *The Guardian*, August 31.

Kidd, I.J. Medina, J. and Pohlhaus, G. (eds) (2017) *The Routledge Handbook of Epistemic Injustice*. London: Routledge.
Kingsolver, B. (2012) *Flight Behavior*. London: Faber and Faber.
Kingsolver, B. (2019) 'Great Barrier', *Time*, September 23: 104.
Kirksey, E. (2016) *Emergent Ecologies*. Durham, NC: Duke University Press.
Klein, R. (2017) 'Partners in the wilderness', *Deccan Herald*, December 12.
Klein, J. (2018) 'Coyotes conquered North America. Now they're heading South', *New York Times*, May 24.
Klem, D. (2009) 'Avian mortality at windows: the second largest human source of bird mortality on earth', *The Condor*, 113 (2): 470–71.
Klem, D., Farmer, C.J., Delacratez, N., Gelg, Y. and Saenger, P.G. (2009) 'Architectural and landscape risk factors associated with bird-glass collisions in an urban environment', *The Wilson Journal of Ornithology*, 121: 126–34.
Klinenberg, E. (ed.) (2016) 'Climate change and the future of cities', *Public Culture*, 79 (Special Issue): 187–441.
Koch, A., Brierley, C., Maslin, M.M. and Lewis, S.L. (2019) 'Earth system impacts of the European arrival and Great Dying in the Americas after 1492', *Quaternary Science Reviews*, 207: 13–36. www.sciencedirect.com/science/article/pii/S0277379118307261 (accessed June 22, 2020).
Kodas, M. (2017) *Megafire. The Race to Extinguish a Deadly Epidemic of Flame*. New York, NY: Houghton Mifflin Harcourt.
Kofalk, H. (2000) *No Woman Tenderfoot: Florence Merriam Bailey, Pioneer Naturalist*. College Station, TX: Texas A&M University Press.
Kohn, E. (2013) *How Forests Think. Toward an Anthropology Beyond the Human*. Berkeley, CA: University of California Press.
Korsgaard, C.M. (2018) *Fellow Creatures. Our Obligations to the Other Animals*. Oxford: Oxford University Press.
Kothari, A., Salleh, A., Escobar, A., Demaria, F. and Acosta, A. (eds) (2019) *Pluriverse. A Post-Development Dictionary*. New Delhi: Tulika.
Kotkin, J. (2016) *The Human City. Urbanism for the Rest of Us*. Chicago, IL: Agate.
Kreling, S., Gaynor, K.M. and Coon, C. (2019) 'Roadkill distribution at the wildland-urban interface', *Journal of Wildlife Management*, 83 (6). doi.org/10.1002/jwmg.21692
Krell, D. (2013) *Derrida and Our Animal Others. Derrida's Final Seminar, 'The Beast and the Sovereign'*. Bloomington, IN: Indiana University Press.
Kroll, G. (2018) 'Snarge', *Aeon*, March 31. https://aeon.co/essays/what-roadkill-says-about-the-insatiability-of-human-speed (accessed June 30, 2020).
Kroodsma, D.A., Mayorga, J., Hochberg, T., Miller, N.A., Boerder, K. and Ferretti, F. (2018) 'Tracking the global footprint of fisheries', *Science*, 359: doi: 10.1126/science.aao5646
Krznaric, R. (2020) *The Good Ancestor. How to Think Long-Term in a Short-Term World*. London: W H Allen.
Kuhn, J. (2019) 'Classify viruses – the gain is worth the pain', *Nature*, February 20. www.nature.com/articles/d41586-019-00599-8 (accessed June 23, 2020).
Kulp, S.A. and Strauss, B.H. (2019) 'New elevation data triple estimates of global vulnerability to sea-level rise and coastal flooding', *Nature Communications*, 10: Article #4884.
Kuper, A. (2017) 'Why humanity's luck may be running out', *Financial Times Magazine*. www.ft.com/content/778c7678-a312-11e7-9e4f-7f5e6a7c98a2 (accessed June 26, 2020).
Kurgan, L. (2013) *Close Up at Distance. Mapping, Technology and Politics*. New York, NY: Zone Books.
Kurlansky, M. (2020) *Salmon. A Fish, the Earth, and the History of a Common Fate*. New York, NY: Random House.

References

Kyba, C.C.M., Kuester, T., Sánchez de Miguel, A. et al. (2017) 'Artificially lit surface of Earth at night increasing in radiance and extent', *Science Advances*, 3 (11): e1701528. doi.org/10.1126/sciadv.1701528

Laffoley, D. and Baxter, J.M. (2019) *Ocean Deoxygenation: Everyone's Problem*. Gland: International Union for the Conservation of Nature.

Laland, K. (2017) *Darwin's Unfinished Symphony. How Culture Made the Human Mind*. Princeton, NJ: Princeton University Press.

Lamb, V., Marschke, M. and Rigg, J. (2019) 'Trading sand, undermining lives: omitted livelihoods in the global trade in sand', *Annals of the Association of American Geographers*, 109. doi.org/10.1080/24694452.2018.1541401

Lang, T. (2020) *Feeding Britain. Our Food Problems and How to Solve Them*. London: Pelican.

Langlitz, N. (2018) 'Salvage and self-loathing. Cultural primatology and the spiritual malaise of the Anthropocene', *Anthropology Today*, 34 (6): 16–20.

Langlitz, N. (2019) 'Primatology science: on the birth of actor-network theory from Baboon field observations', *Theory Culture & Society*, 36: 83–105.

Larsson, N (2019) 'Which is the world's most vegan city?', *The Guardian*, January 17.

Latour, B. (2004) *Politics Without Nature. How to Bring the Sciences into Democracy*. Cambridge, MA: Harvard University Press.

Latour, B. (2012) 'Love your monsters', *Breakthrough Journal*, 2. https://the breakthrough.org/journal/issue-2/love-your-monsters (accessed June 19, 2020).

Latour, B. (2015) '… counter a metaphysical machine with a bigger metaphysical machine'. Does *An Inquiry into Modes of Existence* have a system?' (trans. S. Muecke; originally *Les Temps Modernes*, 682: 72–85). www.bruno-latour.fr/sites/de fault/files/downloads/140-MANIGLIER-SYSTEME-GB.pdf (accessed July 6, 2020).

Latour, B. (ed.) (2016a) *Reset Modernity!* Cambridge, MA: MIT Press.

Latour, B. (2016b) '*Onus Orbis Terrarum*: About a possible shift in the definition of sovereignty', *Millennium*, 44: 305–20.

Latour, B. (2017) *Facing Gaia. Eight Lectures on the New Climatic Regime*. Cambridge: Polity.

Latour, B. (2018) *Down to Earth. Politics in the New Climatic Regime*. Cambridge: Polity.

Laurance, W.F., Peletier-Jellema, A., Geenen, B. et al. (2015) 'Reducing the global environmental impacts of rapid infrastructure expansion', *Current Biology*, 25 (7): R255–68.

Laville, S. (2019) 'Governments and firms in 28 countries sued over climate crisis', *The Guardian*, July 4.

Lawler, A. (2015) *Why Did the Chicken Cross the World? The Epic Saga of the Bird That Powers Civilization*. London: Duckworth Overlook.

Laybourn-Langton, L., Rankin, L. and Baxter, D. (2019) *This is a Crisis. Facing Up to the Age of Environmental Breakdown*. London: Institute for Public Policy Research.

Layton, G. (2019) 'Cheese meltdown', *New Scientist*, February 16: 30–5.

Le Blond, J. (2018) 'World's first no-kill eggs go on sale in Berlin', *The Guardian*, December 22.

Lent, J. (2017) *The Patterning Instinct. A Cultural History of Humanity's Search for Meaning*. London: Prometheus.

Leroi, A.M. (2014) *The Lagoon. How Aristotle Invented Science*. London: Bloomsbury.

Leist, A. (2010) *J.M. Coetzee and Ethics. Philosophical Perspectives on Literature*. New York, NY: Columbia University Press.

Lepora, C. and Goodin, R.E. (2013) *On Complicity and Compromise*. Oxford: Oxford University Press.

Lesté-Lasserre, C. (2020) 'Octopuses taste their food when they touch it with their arms', *New Scientist*, 29 October.
Lestel, D. (2016) *Eat This Book. A Carnivore's Manifesto*. New York, NY: Columbia Press.
Levy, A. (2019) 'How evolution builds genes from scratch', *Nature*, 574: 314–16.
Lewis, M. (2018) *The Fifth Risk. Undoing Democracy*. London: Penguin.
Lewis, S.L. and Maslin, M. (2018) *The Human Planet. How We Created the Anthropocene*. London: Pelican.
Lewis, S.L., Wheeler, Mitchard, E. and Koch, A. (2019) 'Restoring natural forests is the best way to remove atmospheric carbon', *Nature*, 568: 25–8.
Li, P. (2018) 'China's voice for the voiceless'. Nottingham: China Policy Institute.
Lindeque, P., Cole, M., Coppock, R.L. et al. (2020) 'Are we underestimating microplastic abundance in the marine environment? A comparison of microplastic capture with nets of different mesh-size', *Environmental Pollution*. doi.org/10.1016/j.envpol.2020.114721
Linshi, J. (2015) 'The temperature in this Iranian city just hit 164 degrees', *Time*, August 2: https://time.com/3981478/iran-heatwave-bandar-mahsahr/ (accessed November 18, 2020).
Lister, B.C. and Garcia, A. (2018) 'Climate-driven declines in arthropod abundance restructure a rainforest food web', *PNAS*. doi.org/10.1073/pnas.1722477115
Little, A. (2019) *The Fate of Food. What We'll Eat in a Bigger, Hotter, Smarter World*. London: Oneworld.
Longcore, T., Rich, C., Mineau, P. et al. (2012) 'An estimate of avian mortality at Communication Towers in the United States and Canada', *PLoS ONE*, 7. doi.org/10.1371/journal.pone.0034025
Loram, A., Tratalos, J., Warren, P.H. and Gaston, K.J. (2007) 'Urban domestic gardens: the extent and structure of the resource in five major cities', *Landscape Ecology*, 22: 601–15.
Lorimer, J. (2015) *Wildlife in the Anthropocene. Conservation After Nature*. Minneapolis, MN: University of Minnesota Press.
Lorimer, J. (2016) 'Gut Buddies: multispecies studies and the microbiome', *Environmental Humanities*, 8: 57–76
Lorimer, J. (2017) 'Parasites, ghosts and mutualists: a relational geography of microbes for global health', *Transactions of the Institute of British Geographers*, 42, 544–58.
Lorimer, J., Hodgetts, T. and Barua, M. (2017) 'Animal's atmospheres', *Progress in Human Geography*, 43: 26–45.
Lorimer, J., Hodgetts, T., Grenyer, R., Greenhough, B., McLeod, C. and Dwyer, A. (2019) 'Making the microbiome public: participatory experiments with DNA sequencing in domestic kitchens', *Transactions of the Institute of British Geographers*, 4: 524–41.
Losos, J.B. (2017) *Improbable Destinies. Fate, Chance, and the Future of Evolution*. New York, NY: Riverhead Books.
Loss, S.R., Will, T. and Marra, P.P. (2013a) 'The impact of free-ranging domestic cats on wildlife of the United States', *Nature Communications*, 4. doi:10.1038/ncomms2380
Loss, S.R., Will, T., Marra and P.P. (2013b) 'Estimates of bird collision mortality at wind facilities in the United States', *Biological Conservation*, 168: 201–9.
Loss, S.R., Will, T. and Marra, P.P. (2014) 'Refining estimates of bird collision and electrocution mortality at power lines in the United States', *PLoS ONE*. doi.org/10.1371/journal.pone.0101565
Loss, SR., Will, T. and Marra, P.P. (2015) 'Direct mortality of birds from anthropogenic causes', *Annual Review of Ecology, Evolution, and Systematics*, 46. doi.org/10.1146/annurev-ecolsys-112414-054133

References

Loss, S.R., Will, T., Loss, S.S. and Marra, P.P. (2018) 'Bird-building collisions in the United States: estimates of annual mortality and species vulnerability', *The Condor*, 116: 8–24.
Lovegrove, R. (2008) *Silent Fields. The Long Decline of a Nation's Wildlife*. Oxford: Oxford University Press.
Lubow, A. (2003) 'The secret of The Black Paintings', *New York Times*, July 27.
Lush (2014) *A Global View of Animal Experiments 2014*. Manchester: Lush Cosmetics, Ethical Consumer Research Programme.
Lymbery, P. and Oakeshott, I. (2014) *Farmageddon. The True Cost of Cheap Meat*. London: Bloomsbury.
Lynas, M. (2020) *Our Final Warning. Six Degrees of Climate Warming*. London: Fourth Estate.
Macdonald, H. (2014) *H is for Hawk*. New York, NY: Grove Press.
Macdonald, H. (2020) *Vesper Flights*. London: Cape.
Macfarlane, R. (2015a) *Landmarks*. London: Penguin Books.
Macfarlane, R. (2015b) 'Why we need nature writing', *New Statesman*, September 2.
MacInnes, M. (2020) *Gathering Evidence*. London, Atlantic.
McDonald, C. (2013) 'How many birds are killed by windows?', *BBC News*, May 4.
McAlister, E. (2017) *The Secret Life of Flies*. London: Natural History Museum.
McLaren, D. and Ageyman, J. (2015) *Sharing Cities. A Case for Truly Smart and Sustainable Cities*. Cambridge, MA: MIT Press.
McShane, C. and Tarr, J.A. (2007) *The Horse in the City. Living Machines in the Nineteenth Century*. Baltimore, MA: Johns Hopkins University Press.
Mabey, R. (2010 [1973]) *The Unofficial Countryside*. Toller Fratrum: Little Toller.
Machlis, G.E., Hanson, T., Špirić, Z. and McKendry, J.E. (eds) (2011) *Warfare Ecology: A New Synthesis for Peace and Security*. Berlin: Springer Verlag.
Machtans, C. A., Wedeles, C.R. and Bayne, E.M. (2013) 'A first estimate for Canada of the number of birds killed by colliding with building windows', *Avian Conservation and Ecology*, 8, 6.
Mackall, J.W. (1922) *The Life of William Morris*. New York, NY: Dover.
Mathews, F., Kubaszewicz, L., Gunnell, J., Harrower, C., McDonald, R.A. and Shore, R.F. (2018) *A Review of the Population and Conservation Status of British Mammals*. London: Mammal Society.
Manaugh, G. (2016) *A Burglar's Guide to the City*. New York, NY: Farrar, Strauss and Giroux.
Mandyck, J.M. and Schulz, E.B. (2015) *Food Foolish. The Hidden Connection Between Food Waste, Hunger and Climate Change*. New York, NY: Carrier Corporation.
Manne, K. (2017) *Down Girl: The Logic of Misogyny*. Oxford: Oxford University Press.
Manning, E. (2013) *Always More Than One. Individuation's Dance*. Durham, NC: Duke University Press.
Margulis, L. (1998) *The Symbiotic Planet. A New Look at Evolution*. London: Weidenfeld and Nicolson.
Marohn, C.L. (2020) *Strong Towns*. Hoboken, NJ: John Wiley.
Marra, P.P. and Santella, C. (2016) *Cat Wars: The Devastating Consequences of a Cuddly Killer*. Princeton, NJ: Princeton University Press.
Marris, E. (2011) *Rambunctious Garden. Saving Nature in a Post-Wild World*. New York, NY: Bloomsbury.
Martinez-Abrain, A. and Jiménez, J. (2015) 'Anthropogenic areas as incidental substitutes for original habitats', *Conservation Biology*, 30. doi.org/10.1111/cobi.12644
Marx, K. (1867) *Capital. Critique of Political Economy*. Volume 1. Harmondsworth: Penguin.
Marzluff, J.M. (2014) *Welcome to Subirdia. Sharing Our Neighbourhood with Wrens, Robins, Woodpeckers and Other Wildlife*. New Haven, CT: Yale University Press.

Marzluff, J.M. and Angell, T. (2012) *Gifts of the Crow. How Perception, Emotion, and Thought Allow Smart Birds to Behave Like Humans*. New York, NY: Atria.
Massumi, B. (2014) *What Animals Teach Us about Politics*. Durham, NC: Duke University Press.
Mather, J.A., Anderson, R.C. and Wood, J.B. (2010) *Octopus. The Ocean's Intelligent Invertebrate*. Portland, OR: Timber Press.
Mattern, S. (2017) *Code and Clay, Data and Dirt. Five Thousand Years of Urban Media*. Minneapolis, MN: University of Minnesota Press.
Maxwell, S.L., Evans, T., Watson, J.E.M., Morel, A., Grantham, H. and Duncan, A. (2019) 'Degradation and forgone removals increase the carbon impact of intact forest loss by 626%', *Science Advances*, 5. doi:10.1126/sciadv.aax2546
May, R., Nygard, T., Falkdalen, U., Astrom, J., Hamre, O. and Stokke, B.G. (2020) 'Paint it black: efficacy of increased wind turbine rotor blade visibility to reduce avian fatalities', *Ecology and Evolution*, 10. doi.org/10.1002/ece3.6592
Mbembe, A. (2019) *Necropolitics*. Durham, NC: Duke University Press.
Meager, D. (2016) 'A new report says some British dairy cows have never seen sunlight', *Vice*, June 7.
Melville, E.G.F. (1997) *A Plague of Sheep. Environmental Consequences of the Conquest of Mexico*. Cambridge: Cambridge University Press.
Merleau-Ponty, M. (1964) *The Primacy of Perception*. Evanston, IL: Northwestern University Press.
Merrill, D. and Leatherby, L. (2018) 'Here's how America uses its land', *Bloomberg*, July 31.
Michaelson, R. and van der Zee, B. (2020) 'How the Middle East's water shortage drives demand for live animal imports', *The Guardian*, January 23.
Midgley, M. (1978) *Beast and Man*. Ithaca, NY: Cornell University Press.
Mietkiewicz, N., Balch, J.K., Schoenagel, T., Leyk, S., St Denis, L.A. and Bradley, B.A. (2020) 'In the line of fire. Consequences of human-ignited wildfires to homes in the U.S. (1992–2015)', *Fire*, 3. doi.org/10.3390/fire3030050
Miles, L., Johnson, J.C., Dyer, R.L. and Verrelli, B.C. (2018) 'Urbanization as a facilitator of gene flow in a human health pest', *Molecular Ecology*, 27 (16): 3219–30. doi.org/10.1111/mec.14783
Milner, G. (2016) *Pinpoint. How GPS Is Changing Our World*. London: Granta.
Milks, A., Parker, D. and Pope, M. (2019) 'External ballistics of Pleistocene hand-thrown spears: experimental performance data and implications for human evolution', *Scientific Reports*, 9: Article #820. www.nature.com/articles/s41598-018-37904-w (accessed June 26, 2020).
Millman, O. (2016) 'FAA aims to save millions of birds by changing static red airport lights', *The Guardian*, March 24.
Mitman, G., Armiero, M. and Emmett, R.S. (eds) (2018) *Future Remains. A Cabinet of Curiosities for the Anthropocene*. Chicago, IL: University of Chicago Press.
Moch, S. (2020) 'From farm to factory: the unstoppable rise of American chicken', *The Guardian*, August 17.
Møller, A.P. (2019) 'Parallel declines in abundance of insects and insectivorous birds in Denmark over 22 years', *Ecology and Evolution*, 9 (11): 6581–7. doi.org/10.1002/ece3.5236
Monbiot, G. (2019) 'The destruction of the Earth is a crime: it should be prosecuted', *The Guardian*, March 28.
Montaigne, M. (2003) *The Complete Works*. London: Everyman.
Montgomery, D.R. and Bikle, A. (2016) *The Hidden Half of Nature. The Microbial Roots of Life and Heath*. New York, NY: Norton.
Montgomery, S. (2015) *The Soul of an Octopus. A Surprising Exploration into the World of Consciousness*. New York, NY: Atria.
Moor, R. (2016) *On Trails. An Exploration*. London: Aurum.
Moore, R. (2016) *Slow Burn City*. London: Picador.

References

Mora, C., Tittensor, D.P., Adl, S., Simpson, A.G.B. and Worm, B. (2011) 'How many species are there on Earth and in the ocean?' *PLoS Biology*, 9. https://doi.org/10.1371/journal.pbio.1001127

Moran, D., Kanemoto, K., Jiborn, M., Wood, R., Tobben, J. and Seto, K. (2020) 'Carbon footprints of 13000 cities', *Environmental Research Letters*, 13 (6). https://iopscience.iop.org/article/10.1088/1748-9326/aac72a/pdf (accessed June 22, 2020).

Morgan, K. (2009) 'Feeding the city: the challenge of urban food planning', *International Planning Studies*, 14: 341–8.

Morgan, K. (2014) 'Nourishing the city: the rise of the urban food question in the Global North', *Urban Studies*, 52. doi.org/10.1177/0042098014534902

Morgan, K. and Sonnino, R. (2010) 'The urban foodscape: world cities and the new food equation', *Cambridge Journal of Regions, Economy and Society*, 3. doi.org/10.1093/cjres/rsq007

Morris, S. (2020) 'Bristol declares an ecological emergency over loss of wildlife', *The Guardian*, February 4.

Morton, O. (2009) *Eating the Sun. How Plants Power the Planet*. London: Fourth Estate.

Morton, T. (2016) *Dark Ecology. For a Logic of Future Coexistence*. New York, NY: Columbia University Press.

Morton, T. (2017) *Humankind. Solidarity with Nonhuman People*. London: Verso.

Morton, T. (2018) *Being Ecological*. London: Pelican.

Mostafavi, M. and Doherty, G. (eds) (2015) *Ecological Urbanism*. Zurich: Lars Muller.

Muir, J. (2011 [1911]) *My First Summer in the Sierra*. Boston, MA: Houghton-Mifflin.

Mukherjee, S. (2017) 'Cancer's invasion equation', *The New Yorker*, September 4.

Murphy, K. (2015) 'Blessed be my freshly slaughtered dinner', *New York Times Sunday Review*, September 5.

Murphy, M. (2017) *The Economization of Life*. Durham, NC: Duke University Press.

Murphy, M. (2018) 'Against population, towards alterlife', in A.E. Clarke and D. Haraway (eds) *Making Kin, Not Population*. Chicago, IL: Prickly Paradigm, pp. 101–24.

Musser, G. (2015) *Spooky Action at a Distance*. New York, NY: Scientific American/Farrar, Strauss and Giroux.

Nance, S. (ed.) (2015) *The Historical Animal*. Syracuse, NY: Syracuse University Press.

Natrajan, B. and Jacob, S. (2017) 'Provincialising vegetarianism', *Economic and Political Weekly*, 53 (9). www.epw.in/journal/2018/9/special-articles/provincialising-vegetarianism.html (accessed July 3, 2020).

Neff, E.P. (2018) 'What is a lab animal?' *Lab Animal*, 47: 223–7.

Netz, R. (2009) *Barbed Wire. An Ecology of Modernity*. Middletown, CT: Wesleyan University Press.

NESCent Working Group, Martin, L.J., Adams, R.I. et al. (2015) 'Evolution of the indoor biome', *Trends in Ecology & Evolution*, 30 (4): 223–32.

Newkey-Burden, C. (2019) 'How can we say we love our pets when we treat them so badly?', *The Guardian*, May 25.

Nicholls, E. and de Ibarra, N.H. (2017) 'Assessment of pollen rewards by foraging bees', *Functional Ecology*, 31: 76–87.

Nicol, S. (2018) *The Curious Life of Krill. A Conservation Story from the Bottom of the World*. Washington, DC: Island.

Nicolson, A. (2017) *The Seabird's Cry: The Lives and Loves of Puffins, Gannets and Other Ocean Voyagers*. London: Collins.

Nieder, A., Wagener, L. and Rinnert, P. (2020) 'A neural correlate of sensory consciousness in a corvid bird', *Science*, 369: doi:10.1126/science.abb1447

Nijhuis, M. (2015) 'What roads have wrought', *The New Yorker*, March 20: 15–16.

Nijman V, Htun, O.O. and Shwe, N.M. (2017) 'Assessing the illegal bear trade in Myanmar through conversations with poachers: topology, perceptions, and trade links to China', *Human Dimensions of Wildlife*, 22: 172–82.
Nimmo, D., Bennett, A. and Clarke, M. (2014) 'Over-burning could be damaging Australia's wildlife for 100 years', *The Ecologist*, August 29.
Nimmo D.G., Avitabile, S., Banks, S.C., Bliege Bird, R., Callister, K. and Clarke, M. (2018) 'Animal movements in fire-prone landscapes', *Biological Reviews*, 94: 981–98.
Nordhaus, T. (2018) 'The Earth's carrying capacity for human life is not fixed', *Aeon*, July 6. https://aeon.co/ideas/the-earths-carrying-capacity-for-human-life-is-not-fixed (accessed July 22, 2020).
Nowak, D.J. and Greenfield, E.J. (2018) 'Declining urban and community tree cover in the United States', *Urban Forestry and Urban Greening*, 32: 32–55.
Nuwer, R. (2019) 'A rising threat to wildlife: electrocution', *New York Times*, January 1.
O'Connor, T. (2013) *Animals as Neighbors. The Past and Present of Commensal Species*. East Lansing, MI: Michigan State Uiversity Press.
O'Neill, D.W., Fanning, A.L., Lamb, W.F. and Steinberger, J.K. (2018) 'A good life for all within planetary boundaries', *Nature Sustainability*, 1: 88–95.
O'Rourke, K. (2013) *Walking and Mapping. Artists as Cartographers*. Cambridge, MA: MIT Press.
Okin, G.S. (2017) 'Environmental impacts of food consumption by dogs and cats', *PLoS ONE*. doi.org/10.1371/journal.pone.0181301
Oliver, K. (2009) *Animal Lessons. How They Teach Us to Be Human*. New York, NY: Columbia University Press.
Orros, M. and Fellowes, M. (2014) 'Supplementary feeding of the reintroduced red kite *Milvus milvus* in UK gardens', *Bird Study*, 61: 260–3.
Orros, M. and Fellowes, M. (2015) 'Wild bird feeding in a large UK urban area: characteristics and estimates of energy input and individuals supported', *Acta Ornithologica*, 50: 43–58.
Osborne, H. and van der Zee, B. (2020) 'Live export: animals at risk in giant global industry', *The Guardian*, January 20.
Osborne, S. (2018) 'China reassigns 60,000 soldiers to plant trees in bid to fight pollution', *The Independent*, February 15.
Oswald, A. (ed.) (2014) *A Ted Hughes Bestiary. Poems*. New York, NY: Farrar, Straus and Giroux.
Oswald, Y., Owen, A. and Steinberger, J.K. (2020) 'Large inequality in international and intranational energy footprints between income groups and across consumption categories', *Nature Energy*, 5: 231–9.
Otto, S.P. (2018) 'Adaptation, speciation and extinction in the Anthropocene', *Proceedings of the Royal Society, Series B*, 285. doi.org/10.1098/rspb.2018.2047
Owens, A, Cochard, P., Durrant, J., Perkin, E.K. and Seymoure, B. (2019) 'Light pollution is a driver of insect declines', *Biological Conservation*. doi.org/10.2139/ssrn.3378835
O'Rourke, K. (2013) *Walking and Mapping. Artists as Cartographers*. Cambridge, MA: MIT Press.
Pachirat, T. (2011) *Every Twelve Seconds. Industrialized Slaughter and the Politics of Sight*. New Haven, CT: Yale University Press.
Pacyga, D.A. (2015) *Slaughterhouse. Chicago's Union Stock Yard and the World It Made*. Chicago, IL: Chicago University Press.
Parfit, D. (1984) *Reasons and Persons*. Oxford: Oxford University Press.
Parkes, D.N. and Thrift, N.J. (1980) *Times, Spaces, Places. A Chronogeographic Perspective*. Chichester: Wiley.
Paulson Institute (2020) *Financing Nature: Closing the Global Biodiversity Financing Gap*. Chicago: Paulson Institute.

References

Pauly, D. and Zeller, D. (2016) 'Catch reconstructions reveal that global marine fisheries catches are higher than reported and declining', *Nature Communications*, 7: #10244. www.nature.com/articles/ncomms10244 (accessed June 29, 2020).

Pearlmutter, D., Sanesi, D. and O'Brien, L. (eds) (2017) *The Urban Forest. Cultivating Green Infrastructure for People and the Environment*. Berlin: Springer.

Phys.org (2020) 'Almost 2 million acres of Great Britain grassland lost as woodland and urban areas expand'. https://phys.org/news/2020-07-million-acres-great-britain-grassland.html (accessed August 8, 2020).

Pierre-Louis, K. and Popovich, N. (2018) 'Nights are warming faster than days. Here's why that's dangerous', *New York Times*, July 11.

Pimm, S.L. and Joppa, L.N. (2015) 'How many plant species are there, where are they, and at what rate are they going extinct?', *Annals of the Missouri Botanical Garden*, 100. doi: 10.3417/2012018

Pinker, S. (2012) *The Better Angels of Our Nature. A History of Violence and Humanity*. London: Penguin.

Plummer, K.E., Risely, K., Toms, M.P. and Siriwardena, G. (2019) 'The composition of British bird communities is associated with long-term garden bird feeding', *Nature Communications*, 10: article #2088. doi.org/10.1038/s41467-019-10111-5

Poon, L. (2019) 'New York City will require bird-friendly glass on buildings', *Bloomberg CityLab*, December 13th. www.bloomberg.com/news/articles/2019-12-13/nyc-is-making-its-buildings-bird-friendly (accessed August 31, 2020).

Poore, J. and Nemecek, R. (2018) 'Reducing food's environmental impacts through producers and consumers', *Science*, 360: 987–92.

Poppick, L. (2019) 'The glowing squid that illuminates the strangeness of nature', *The Atlantic*, February 24.

Potapov, P., Hansen, M.C., Laestadius, L., Turubanova, S., Yaroshenko, A. and Thies, C. (2017) 'The last frontiers of wilderness: tracking loss of intact forest landscapes from 2000 to 2013', *Science Advances*, 3. doi: 10.1126/sciadv.1600821

Powney, G.D., Carvell, C., Edwards, M., Morris, R.K., Roy, H.E., Woodcock, B.A. and Isaac, N.J.B. (2019) 'Widespread losses of pollinating insects in Britain', *Nature Communications*, 10. doi.org/10.1038/s41467-019-08974-9

Potts, A. (2012) *Chicken*. London: Reaktion.

Povinelli, E.A. (2016) *Geontologies. A Requiem to Late Liberalism*. Durham, NC: Duke University Press.

Powers, R. (2018) *The Overstory*. London: Heinemann.

Preston, E. (2018) 'A classic test of animals' minds has a fish problem', *The Atlantic*, December 17. www.theatlantic.com/health/archive/2018/12/fish-mirror-test/578197/ (accessed June 24, 2020).

Pringle, R., Wilson, M., Calladine, J. and Siriwardena, G. (2019) 'Associations between gamebird releases and generalist predators', *Journal of Applied Ecology*, 21: 1–12.

Probyn, E. (2016) *Eating the Ocean*. Durham, NC: Duke University Press.

Probyn, E. (2020) *Sustaining Seas. Oceanic Space and the Politics of Care*. Lanham, MD: Roman and Littlefield.

Prodger, M. (2018) 'After the bullets, the brushes: how the First World War transformed art', *New Statesman*, August 15.

Proctor, L. (2019) 'Priorities for the next 10 years of human microbiome research', *Nature*, 563: 623–5.

Prum, R.O. (2017) *The Evolution of Beauty. How Darwin's Forgotten Theory of Mate Choice Shapes the Animal World – and Us*. New York, NY: Doubleday.

Puig de la Bellacasa, M. (2017) *Matters of Care. Speculative Ethics in More Than Human Worlds*. Minneapolis, MN: University of Minnesota Press.

Pyne, S. (2015) *Fire. Nature and Culture*. London: Reaktion.

Quammen, D. (2012) *Spillover. Animal Infections and the Next Human Pandemic*. New York, NY: Vintage.

Rai, T.S., Valdesolo, P. and Graham, J. (2017) 'Dehumanization increases instrumental violence, but not moral violence', *PNAS*, 114 (32): 8511–16. www.pnas.org/content/114/32/8511 (accessed July 10, 2020).
Rail Safety and Standards Board (2014) *Analysis of the Risk from Animals on the Line.* London: RSSB.
Raftery, A.E., Zimmer, A. Frierson, D.M.W., Startz, R. and Liu, P. (2017) 'Less than 2 °C warming by 2100 unlikely', *Nature Climate Change*, 7: 637–41.
Ratti, C. and Claudel, M. (2016) *The City of Tomorrow. Sensors, Networks, and the Future of Urban Life.* New Haven, CT: Yale University Press.
Raulff, U. (2017) *Farewell to the Horse. The Final Century of Our Relationship.* London: Allen Lane.
Raymond, C., Matthews, T. and Horton, R.M. (2020) 'The emergence of heat and humidity too severe for human tolerance', *Science Advances*, 6 (19): eaaw1838. doi.org/10.1126/sciadv.aaw1838
Rees, A. (2018) 'Animal agents', *Aeon*. https://aeon.co/essays/can-animals-shape-their-own-lives-or-the-course-of-history (accessed July 1, 2020).
Reese, J. (2018) *The End of Animal Farming.* Boston, MA: Beacon Press.
Reiter, S., Holsdunk P., Woo, T. et al. (2018) 'Elucidating the control and development of skin patterning in cuttlefish', *Nature*, 562: 361–6.
Renton, A. (2014) *Planet Carnivore. Why Cheap Meat Costs the Earth.* London: Guardian.
Rentokil (2018) *The Rentokil Pest Control Report 2018. Insights from Pest Control Markets across the World.* Camberley: Rentokil.
ReportLinker (2019) 'Meat substitute market by product, source, category: global opportunity analysis'. www.reportlinker.com/p05563944/Meat-Substitute-Market-by-Product-Type-Source-Category-Global-Opportunity-Analysis-and-Industry-Forecast.html?utm_source=GNW (accessed September 5, 2020).
Reticker-Flynn, N. and Englemann, E.G. (2019) 'A gut punch fights cancer and infection', *Nature*, 23 January. www.nature.com/articles/d41586-019-00133-w (accessed June 23, 2020).
Reynolds, G. (2019) 'Why do people hate vegans?', *The Guardian*, October 25.
Richards, E. (2017) *Darwin and the Making of Sexual Selection.* Chicago, IL: University of Chicago Press.
Richtel, M. (2019) *An Elegant Defense. The Extraordinary New Science of the Immune System.* New York, NY: William Morrow.
Richtel, M. and Jacobs, A. (2019) 'A mysterious infection, spanning the globe in a climate of secrecy', *New York Times*, April 6.
Riede, T., Eliason, C.M., Miller, E.H., Goller, F. and Clarke, J.A. (2016) 'Coos, booms and hoots: the evolution of closed-mouth vocal behaviour in birds', *Evolution*, 70. doi.org/10.1111/evo.12988
Rifkin, H. (2015) 'In U.S., more say animals should have same rights as people', *Gallup News*, May 18. https://news.gallup.com/poll/183275/say-animals-rights-people.aspx (accessed June 27, 2020).
Ripple, W.J., Abernethy, K., Betts, M.G. et al. (2016) 'Bushmeat hunting and extinction risk to the world's mammals', *Royal Society Open Science*, 3. doi.org/10.1098/rsos.160498
Riskin, J. (2018) *The Restless Clock: A History of the Centuries-Long Argument Over What Makes Living Things Tick.* Chicago, IL: University of Chicago Press.
Ritchie, H. and Roser, M. (2019) 'Meat and dairy production'. Our World in Data. Oxford Martin School. https://ourworldindata.org/meat-production (accessed November 18, 2020).
Ritvo, H. (1987) *The Animal Estate. The English and Other Creatures in the Victorian Age.* Cambridge, MA: Harvard University Press.
Robbins, J.A., Roberts, C., Weary, D.M., Franks, B. and von Keyserlingk, M.A.G. (2019) 'Factors influencing public support for dairy tie stall housing in the US', *PLoS ONE*, 14: doi.org/10.1371/journal.pone.0216544

References

Roberts, A. (2017) *Tamed. Ten Species That Changed Our World*. London: Hutchinson.
Roberts, T. (2016) 'We spend 90% of our time indoors. Says who?', *Building Green*. www.buildinggreen.com/blog/we-spend-90-our-time-indoors-says-who (accessed June 25, 2020).
Rocha, J.C., Peterson, G., Bodin, O. and Levin, S. (2018) 'Cascading regime shifts within and across scales', *Science*, 362: 1379–83.
Rochard, J.B.A. and Horton, N. (1980) 'Birds killed by aircraft in the United Kingdom, 1966–76', *Bird Study*, 27: 227–234.
Roden, D. (2014) *Dark Phenomenology. Philosophy at the Edge of the Human*. London: Routledge.
Rodgers, L. (2018) 'Climate change: the massive carbon dioxide emitter you may not know about', *BBC News*. www.bbc.co.uk/news/science-environment-46455844 (accessed June 22, 2020).
Romanes, G.J. (2016 [1892]) *Intelligence of Ants*. Middletown: LM Publishers.
Romero, S. (2017) 'Coyotes are colonizing cities. Step forward the urban hunter', *New York Times*, December 26.
Rose, D.B. (2011) *Wild Dog Dreaming. Love and Extinction*. Charlottesville, VA: University of Virginia Press.
Rose, D.B. (2017) in T. Van Dooren, U. Munster, E. Kirksey, D.B. Rose, M. Chrulew, and A.L. Tsing, 'Lively ethnography: storying animist worlds', *Multispecies Studies*, pp. 77–94. Durham, NC: Duke University Press.
Rose, J.F.P. (2016) *The Well-Tempered City. What Modern Science, Ancient Civilizations, and Human Nature Teach Us About the Future of Urban Life*. New York, NY: Harper Books.
Ross, C. (2017) *Ecology and Power in the Age of Empire*. Oxford: Oxford University Press.
Rowan, A. and Kartal, T. (2018) 'Dog population and dog sheltering trends in the United States of America', *Animals*, 8 (5): 68. doi.org/10.3390/ani8050068
Roxburgh, H. (2018) 'Is Chongqing's "horizontal skyscraper" the answer to overcrowded cities?', *The Guardian*, June 4.
RSPB (2020) *A Lost Decade for Nature*. London: Royal Society for the Protection of Birds.
Rushby, K. (2018) 'The British countryside is being killed by herbicides and insecticides – can anything save it?', *The Guardian*, May 31.
Ruskin, J. (1884) *The Storm-Cloud of the Nineteenth Century*. London: London Institution.
Rutz, C., Loretto, M.-C., Bates, A. et al. (2020) 'COVID-19 lockdown allows researchers to quantify the effects of human activity on wildlife', *Nature Ecology and Evolution*. doi.org/10.1038/s41559-020-1237-z
Ruyer, R. (2016) *Neofinalism*. Minneapolis, MN: University of Minnesota Press.
Samaan, M. and Spencer, R. (2020) 'Dog lovers fight to protect Cairo strays', *The Times*, February 22.
Safina, C. (2016) *Beyond Words. What Animals Think and Feel*. New York, NY: Henry Holt.
Safina, C. (2020) *Becoming Wild. How Animals Learn to Be Animals*. London: Oneworld.
Sahlins, M. (2013) *What Kinship Is – and Is Not*. Chicago, IL: University of Chicago Press.
Samuelson, A.E., Gill, R.J., Brown, M.J.F. and Leadbeater, E. (2018) 'Lower bumblebee colony reproductive success in agricultural compared with urban environments', *Proceedings of the Royal Society, Series B*. https://doi.org/10.1098/rspb.2018.0807
Sánchez-Bayo, F. and Wyckhuys, K.A.G. (2019) 'Worldwide decline of the entomofauna: a review of its drivers', *Biological Conservation*, 232: 8–27.
Santlofer, J. (2016) *Food City. Four Centuries of Food-Making in New York*. New York, NY: W.W. Norton.

Saunders, G. (2018) *Fox 8*. London: Bloomsbury.
Sax, B. (2000) *Animals in the Third Reich. Pets, Scapegoats and the Holocaust*. London: Continuum.
Sax, B. (2003) *Crow*. London: Reaktion.
Scales, H. (2018) *Eye of the Shoal. A Fishwatcher's Guide to Life, the Ocean and Everything*. London: Bloomsbury.
Scheel, D., Chancellor, S., Hing, M., Lawrence, M., Linquist, S. and Godfrey Smith, P. (2017) 'A second site occupied by *Octopus tetris* at high densities, with notes on their ecology and density', *Marine and Freshwater Behavior and Physiology*, 50. doi.org/10.1080/10236244.2017.1369851
Scheffers, B.R., Oliveira, B.F., Lamb, I. and Edwards, D.P. (2019) 'Global wildlife trade across the tree of life', *Science*, 366 (6461): 71–6. doi.org/10.1126/science.aav5327
Schilthuizen, M. (2018) *Darwin Comes to Town. How the Urban Jungle Drives Evolution*. London: Quercus.
Schmitz, O.J. (2017) *The New Ecology. Rethinking A Science for the Anthropocene*. Princeton, NJ: Princeton University Press.
Schwartz, A.L.W., Shilling, F.M. and Perkins, S.E. (2020) 'The value of monitoring wildlife roadkill', *European Journal of Wildlife Research*, 66: #18. doi.org/10.1007/s10344-019-1357-4
Schweid, R. (2014) *Octopus*. London: Reaktion.
Scott, A.C. (2018) *Burning Planet. The Story of Fire Through Time*. Oxford: Oxford University Press.
Scott, D. (2014) *Gilbert Simondon's Psychic and Collective Individuation*. Edinburgh: Edinburgh University Press.
Scott, J.C. (2017) *Against the Grain. A Deep History of the Earliest States*. New Haven, CT: Yale University Press.
Seas at Risk (2019) *The Multi-issue Mitigation Potential of Reducing Ship Speeds*. London: GL Reynolds.
Sengers, F., Turnheim, B. and Berkhout, F. (2020) 'Beyond experiments: embedding outcomes in climate governance', *Environment and Planning C: Politics and Space*, 38: 1–32.
Senivaratne, S, Roegli, J., Séférian, R. et al. (2019) 'The many possible climates from the Paris Agreement's aim of 1.5 °C warming', *Nature*, 558: 41–49.
Shapiro, J. (2001) *Mao's War Against Nature. Politics and the Environment in Revolutionary China*. Cambridge: Cambridge University Press.
Shapiro, J.A. (2011) *Evolution. A View From the 21st Century*. New York, NY: Prentice Hall.
Shapiro, P. (2018) *Clean Meat. How Growing Meat Without Animals Will Revolutionize Dinner and the World*. London: Gallery Books.
Shaviro, S. (2015) *Discognition*. London: Repeater Books.
Shaw, A. (2016) *The Trees*. London: Bloomsbury.
Shaw, D.G. (2013) 'A way with animals. Preparing history for animals', *History and Theory*, 52: 1–12.
Shochat, E., Warren, P.S., Faeth, S.H., McIntyre, N.E. and Hope, D. (2006) 'From patterns to emerging processes in mechanistic urban ecology', *Trends in Ecology &. Evolution*, 21. doi:10.1016/j.tree.2005.11.019
Simondon, G. (2012) *Two Lessons on Animal and Man*. Minneapolis: University of Minnesota Press.
Simone, A. and Pieterse, E. (2017) *New Urban Worlds. Inhabiting Dissonant Times*. Cambridge: Polity.
Simons, M. (2017) 'The parliament of things and the Anthropocene. How to listen to quasi-objects', *Techne. Research in Philosophy and Technology*, 21: 1–25.
Sinclair, I. (2010) 'Introduction' in R. Mabey, *The Unofficial Countryside*. Toller Fratrum: Little Toller, pp. 7–13.

References

Sloterdijk, P. (2012) 'Voices for animals: a fantasy on animal representation', in G.G. Smulewicz-Zucker (ed.) *Strangers to Nature. Animal Lives and Human Ethics.* Lanham, MD: Lexington Books, pp. 121–36.
Sloterdijk, P. (2015) *You Must Change Your Life.* Cambridge: Polity.
Sloterdijk, P. (2017a) *The Aesthetic Imperative.* Cambridge: Polity.
Sloterdijk, P. (2017b) *Not Saved. Essays After Heidegger.* Cambridge: Polity.
Sloterdijk, P. (2018) *What Happened in the 20th Century?* Cambridge: Polity.
Smalley, A.L. (2017) *Wild by Nature. North American Animals Confront Colonization.* Baltimore, MD: Johns Hopkins University Press.
Smil, V. (2013) *Should We Eat Meat? Evolution and Consequences of Modern Carnivory.* Oxford: Wiley-Blackwell.
Smil, V. (2019) *Growth. From Microorganisms to Megacities.* Cambridge, MA: MIT Press.
Smith, M. (2011) *Against Ecological Sovereignty. Ethics, Biopolitics, and Saving the Natural World.* Minneapolis, MN: University of Minnesota Press.
Soroye, P., Newbold, T. and Kerr, J. (2020) 'Climate change contributes to widespread declines among bumble bees across continents', *Science,* 367 (6478): 685–8. doi.org/10.1126/science.aax8591
Sparrow, T. (2014) *The End of Phenomenology. Metaphysics and the New Realism.* Edinburgh: Edinburgh University Press.
Specht, J. (2019) *Red Meat Republic. A Hoof-to-Table History of How Beef Changed America.* Princeton, NJ: Princeton University Press.
Spelt, A., Williamson, C., Shamoun-Baranes, J., Shepard, E.L.C., Rock, P. and Windsor, S. (2019) 'Habitat use of urban-nesting lesser black backed gulls during the breeding season', *Scientific Reports,* 9. doi:10.1038/s41598-019-46890-6
Srinavasan, L. (2013) 'The biopolitics of animal being and welfare: dog control and care in the UK and India', *Transactions of the Institute of British Geographers,* 38 (1): 116–19.
Staaf, D. (2017) *Squid Empire. The Rise and Fall of the Cephalopods.* Lebanon, NH: ForeEdge.
Stacho, M., Herold, C., Rook, N., Wagner, H., Axer, M. and. Amunts, K. (2020) 'A cortex-like canonical circuit in the avian forebrain', *Science,* 369. doi: 10.1126/science.abc5534
Stafford, K. (2019) 'Chained and neglected: Detroit's dog problem persists despite child deaths', *Detroit Free Press,* December 15.
Standaert, M. (2020) 'Coronavirus closures reveal vast scale of China's secretive wildlife farm industry', *The Guardian,* February 25.
Steel, C. (2009) *Hungry City. How Food Shapes Our Lives.* London: Vintage.
Steel, C. (2020) *Sitopia. How Food Can Save the World.* London: Penguin.
Steele, E.J., Al-Mufti, S., Augustyn, K.A. et al. (2018) 'Cause of Cambrian explosion – terrestrial or cosmic?', *Progress in Biophysics and Molecular Biology,* 136: 3–23.
Steffen, W., Broadgate, W., Deutsch, L., Gaffney, O. and Ludwig, C. (2015) 'The trajectory of the Anthropocene: the Great Acceleration', *The Anthropocene Review,* 2: 81–98.
Steffen, W., Rockström, J., Richardson, K. et al. (2018) 'Trajectories of the Earth System in the Anthropocene' *PNAS,* 115 (33): 8252–9. doi.org/10.1073/pnas.1810141115
Stengers, I. (2013) 'Matters of cosmopolitics: on the provocations of Gaia. Isabelle Stengers in conversation with Heather Davis and Etienne Turpin,' in E. Turpin (ed.) *Architecture in the Anthropocene. Encounters Among Design, Deep Time, Science and Philosophy.* Ann Arbor, MI: Open Humanities Press, pp. 171–82.
Stengers, I. (2015) *In Catastrophic Times. Resisting the Coming Barbarism.* Chicago, IL: Open Humanities Press.

Stengers, I. (2017) 'Preface', in D. Debaise (ed.) *Speculative Empiricism. Revisiting Whitehead*. Edinburgh: Edinburgh University Press, pp. xii–xix.

Stephens, L., Fuller, D., Boivin, N. et al. (2019) 'Archaeological assessment reveals Earth's early transformation through land use', *Science*, 365 (6456): 897–902. doi.org/10.1126/science.aax1192

Stephens, L., Ellis, E. and Fuller, D. (2020) 'The deep Anthropocene', *Aeon*, October 1.

Stokstad, E. (2020) 'The pandemic stilled human activity. What did this "anthropause" mean for wildlife?', *Science*, August 13. www.sciencemag.org/news/2020/08/pandemic-stilled-human-activity-what-did-anthropause-mean-wildlife# (accessed August 28, 2020).

Stone, C. (1972) 'Should trees have standing – toward legal rights for natural objects', *Southern California Law Review*, 45: 450–501.

Strassburg, B.N, Iribarrem, A., Beyer, H.L. and Visconti, P. (2020) 'Global priority areas for ecosystem restoration', *Nature*, 586. doi.org/10.1038/s41586-020-2784-9.

Striffler, S. (2005) *Chicken. The Dangerous Transformation of America's Favorite Food*. New Haven, CT: Yale University Press.

Stroud, J.L. (2019) 'Soil health pilot study in England: outcomes from an on-farm earthworm survey', *PLoS ONE*, 14. doi.org/10.1371/journal.pone.0203909

Struzik, E. (2017) *Firestorm. How Wildfire Will Shape Our Future*. New York, NY: Island Press.

Stuart, T. (2006) *The Bloodless Revolution. Radical Vegetarians and the Discovery of India*. London: Harper Collins.

Stuart, T. (2009) *Waste. Uncovering the Global Food Scandal*. London: Penguin.

Subramanian, S. (2017) 'How Singapore is creating more land for itself', *New York Times*, April 20.

Sueur, J., Krause, B. and Farina, A. (2019) 'Climate change is breaking Earth's beat', *Trends in Ecology & Evolution*, 34: 971–3. doi.org/10.1016/j.tree.2019.07.014

Sullivan, H. (2020) 'Some of Australia's smallest species could be lost to wildfires', *New York Times*, January 13.

Suzman, J. (2017) *Affluence Without Abundance. The Disappearing World of the Bushmen*. London: Bloomsbury.

Sverdrup-Thygeson, A. (2019) *Extraordinary Insects*. London: Mudlark.

Swart, S. (2010) *Riding High: Horses, Humans and History in South Africa*. Johannesburg: Wits University Press.

Taft, D. (2016) 'The raven, the original goth, makes a home in New York', *New York Times*, February 10.

Tague, I.H. (2015) *Animal Companions. Pets and Social Change in Eighteenth-Century Britain*. University Park, PA: Pennsylvania State University Press.

Tahir, T. (2017) 'Pets on the rise as world grows richer', *The Guardian*, August 29.

Tang, D. (2019) 'Babies? We'd prefer to look after a pet, say Chinese', *The Times*, December 6.

Tarr, J.A. and McShane, C. (2008) 'The horse as an urban technology', *Journal of Urban Technology*, 15: 5–17.

Taussig, M. (2019) *Palma Africana*. Chicago, IL: Chicago University Press.

Tawada, Y. (2014) *Memoirs of a Polar Bear*. New York, NY: New Directions.

Taylor, K. (2009) *Cruelty*. Oxford: Oxford University Press.

Taylor, M. and Watts, J. (2019) 'Revealed: The 20 firms behind a third of all carbon emissions', *The Guardian*, October 9.

Taylor, K., Gordon, N., Langley, G. and Higgins, W. (2008) 'Estimates for worldwide laboratory animal use in 2005', *ATLA*, 36: 327–42.

Tennessen, J., Parks, S.E., Swierk, L., Reinert, L.K., Holden, W.M., Rollins-Smith, L., Walsh, K.A. and Langkilde, T. (2018) 'Frogs adapt to physiologically costly anthropogenic noise', *Proceedings of the Royal Society, Series B*, 285. doi.org/10.1098/rspb.2018.2194

References

Tews, J., Bert, D.G. and Mineau, D. (2013) 'Estimated mortality of selected migratory bird species from mowing and other mechanical operations in agriculture', *Avian Conservation and Ecology*, 8 (2): 8. doi.org/10.5751/ACE-00559-080208

Thomas, C. (2017) *Inheritors of the Earth. How Nature is Thriving in an Age of Extinction*. London: Allen Lane.

Thomas, K. (1983) *Man and the Natural World. Changing Attitudes in England 1500–1800*. London: Allen Lane.

Thomas, K. (2018) *In Pursuit of Civility. Manners and Civilization in Early Modern England*. New Haven, CT: Yale University Press.

Thompson, K. (2018) *Darwin's Most Wonderful Plants. Darwin's Botany Today*. London: Profile.

Thornton, A. (2019) *'This is how many animals we eat each year'* World Economic Forum, February 8, www.weforum.org/agenda/2019/02/chart-of-the-day-this-is-how-many-animals-we-eat-each-year/ (accessed August 24, 2020).

Thrift, N.J. (1990) 'Transport and communication, 1730–1914', in R.L. Dodgshon and R. Butlin (eds) *A New Historical Geography of England and Wales*. London: Academic Press (Second edition), pp. 453–86.

Thrift, N.J. (2005) 'But malice aforethought: cities and the natural history of hatred', *Transactions of the Institute of British Geographers*, NS30: 133–50.

Thrift, N.J. (2006) *Non-Representational Theory*. London: Routledge.

Thrift, N.J. (2011) 'Lifeworld, Inc. – and what to do about it', *Environment and Planning D. Society and Space*, 29: 5–26.

Thrift, N.J. (2014) 'The "sentient" city and what it may portend', *Big Data and Society*, 2: 1–21.

Thrift, N.J. (2016) 'The university of life', *New Literary History*, 47: 389–417.

Thrift, N. J. (2017) 'Space', in Richardson, D. (ed.) *The International Encyclopedia of Geography: People, the Earth, Environment, and Technology*. New York, NY: Wiley: pp. 123–38.

Tibbets, E.A., Agudelo J., Pandit, S. and Riojas, J. (2019) 'Transitive inference in *Polistes* paper wasps', *Biology Letters*, 15. doi.org/10.1098/rsbl.2019.0015

Tinsley-Marshall, P., Skilbeck, A. and Riggs, A. (2020) 'Monitoring of ecosystem function at landscape scale demonstrates temporal difference in invertebrate abundance in Kent and South–East England', Kent Wildlife Trust. Draft Report. www.kentwildlifetrust.org.uk/sites/default/files/2020-02/Bugs%20Matter%20report%20website%20version_0.pdf (accessed July 13, 2020).

Toomey, D. (2014) *Weird Life. The Search for Life that Is Very Different from Our Own*. New York, NY: Norton.

Tree, I. (2018) *Wilding. The Return of Nature to a British Farm*. London: Picador.

Trotter, S. (2019a) 'Birds behaving badly: the regulation of seagulls and the construction of public space', *Journal of Law and Society*, 46: 1–28.

Trotter, S. (2019b) 'The regulation of urban gulls across the UK: a study of control measures', *British Birds*, May 9. https://britishbirds.co.uk/article/the-regulation-of-urban-gulls-across-the-uk-a-study-of-control-measures/ (accessed July 2, 2020).

Tsing, A., Swanson, H., Gan, E. and Bubandt, N. (eds) (2017) *Arts of Living on a Damaged Planet*. Minneapolis, MN: University of Minnesota Press.

TUC (2018) 'Number of people working night shifts up by more than 150,000 in 5 years', www.tuc.org.uk/news/number-people-working-night-shifts-more-150000-5-years (accessed November 18, 2020).

Turner, W.R., Nakamura, T. and Dinetti, M. (2004) 'Global urbanization and the separation of humans from nature', *BioScience*, 54: 585–90.

Turpin, E. (ed.) (2013) *Architecture in the Anthropocene. Encounters Among Design, Deep Time, Science and Philosophy*. Ann Arbor, MI: Open Humanities Press.

Twilley, N. (2019) 'Home smog', *New York Times*, April 8.

UITP (2018) *World Metro Figures 2018*. Brussels: International Association of Public Transport.
Ulloa, A. (2006) *The Ecological Native. Indigenous Peoples' Movements and Eco-Governmentality in Colombia*. New York, NY: Routledge.
Ulloa, A. (2011) 'The politics of autonomy of indigenous peoples of the Sierra Nevada de Santa Marta, Colombia', *Latin American and Caribbean Ethnic Studies*, 6: 79–107.
UNEP (2010) *Assessing the Environmental Impacts of Production and Consumption. Priority Products and Materials*. Geneva: United Nations Environment Programme. www.unep.fr/shared/publications/pdf/dtix1262xpa-priorityproductsandmaterials_report.pdf (accessed July 3, 2020).
UNEP International Resource Panel (2016) *Global Material Flows and Resource Productivity*. Paris: United Nations Environment Programme.
United Nations (2019) *World Population Prospects 2019*. New York, NY: United Nations.
United States Fish and Wildlife Service (2016) *National Survey of Fishing, Hunting and Wildlife-Associated Recreation*. Washington, DC: Department of the Interior.
Urban Climate Change Network (2015) *Climate Change and Cities. Summary for City Leaders*. New York, NY: Earth Institute, Columbia University.
US Fish and Wildlife Service (2000) *Homeowner's Guide to Protecting Frogs*. Arlington, VA: US Fish and Wildlife Service.
USDA (2019) 'Livestock slaughter'. NASS. www.nass.usda.gov/Publications/Todays_Reports/reports/lstk0619.pdf (accessed November 18, 2020).
Valles-Colomer, M., Falony, G., Darzi, Y. et al. (2019) 'The neuroactive potential of the human gut microbiota in quality of life and depression', *Nature Microbiology*, 623–32. doi.org/10.1038/s41564-018-0337-x
van der Ree, R., Smith, D.J. and Grilo, C. (2015) *Handbook of Road Ecology*. London: Wiley-Blackwell.
van Dooren, T. (2014) *Flight Ways. Life and Loss at the Edge of Extinction*. New York, NY: Columbia University Press.
van Dooren, T. (2020) *The Wake of Crows. Living and Dying in Shared Worlds*. New York, NY: Columbia University Press.
van Dooren and Rose, D.B. (2012) 'Storied places in a multispecies city', *Humanimalia*, 3 (2): 1–27.
Van Heezik, Y., Smyth, A., Adams, A. and Gordon, J. (2010) 'Do domestic cats impose an unsustainable harvest on urban bird populations?', *Biological Conservation*, 143: 121–30.
Van Klink, R., Bowler, D.E., Gongalsky, K.B., Swengel, A.B., Gentile, A. and Chase, J.M. (2020) 'Meta-analysis reveals declines in terrestrial but increases in freshwater insect abundances', *Science*, 368 (6489): 417–20. https://science.sciencemag.org/content/368/6489/417 (accessed June 24, 2020).
Velten, H. (2007) *Cow*. London: Reaktion.
Velten, H. (2013) *Beastly London. A History of Animals in the City*. London: Reaktion.
Verghis, S. (2019) 'Black Saturday. The bushfire that shocked Australia', *BBC News*, February 7. www.bbc.co.uk/news/world-australia-47038202 (accessed August 28, 2020).
Vialles, C. (1994) *Animal to Edible*. Cambridge: Cambridge University Press.
Viveiros de Castro, E. (2011) *The Inconstancy of the Indian Mind. The Encounter of Catholics and Cannibals in 16th Century Brazil*. Chicago, IL: Prickly Paradigm.
Viveiros de Castro, E. (2013) 'Some reflections on the notion of species in history and anthropology', *Bio/Zoo*, 10: 1–4.
Viveiros de Castro, E. (2014) *Cannibal Metaphysics. For a Post-Structural Anthropology*. Minneapolis, MN: Univocal.

References

Viveiros de Castro, E. (2015) *The Relative Native. Essays on Indigenous Conceptual Worlds*. Chicago, IL: Hau.
Vogel, G. (2017) 'Where have all the insects gone?', *Science*, 356: 576–9.
Vollset, S.E., Goren, E., Yuan, C., Cao, J., Smith, A.E. and Hsiao, T.S. (2020) 'Fertility, mortality, migration, and population scenarios for 195 countries and territories from 2017 to 2100: a forecasting analysis for the Global Burden of Disease Study', *The Lancet*, 396. doi.org/10.1016/S0140-6736(20)30677-2
Von Humboldt, A. (1829) *Personal Narrative of Travels to the Equinoctial Regions of the New Continent, During the Years 1799–1804*. London: Longman, Hurst, Rees, Orme and Brown.
Waldheim, C. (2016) *Landscape as Urbanism*. Princeton, NJ: Princeton University Press.
Waldron, J. (2017) *One Another's Equals. The Basis of Human Equality*. Cambridge, MA: Belknap Press.
Walker, E. (2008) *Horse*. London: Reaktion.
Wallace-Wells, D. (2019) *The Uninhabitable Earth. A Story of the Future*. London: Allen Lane.
Walling, P. (2018) *Till the Cows Come Home. The Story of Our Eternal Dependence*. London: Atlantic.
Wang, H., Shao, J., Luo, X., Chuai, Z., Xu, S., Mingxia, G. and Zhouyi, G. (2020) 'Wildlife consumption ban is insufficient', *Science*, 367. doi: 10.1126/science.abb6463
Warde, P., Robin, L. and Sorlin, S. (2018) *The Environment. A History of an Idea*. Baltimore, MD: Johns Hopkins University Press.
Wark, M. (2017) *General Intellects. Twenty-One Thinkers for the Twentieth Century*. New York, NY: Verso.
Warren, M. (2019) 'Sharks squeezed out by longline fishing vessels', *Nature*, July 24. https://www.nature.com/articles/d41586-019-02265-5 (accessed June 29, 2020).
Webster, B. (2018) 'Fishermen accused over illegal catches', *The Times*, April 12.
Webster, B. (2020) 'Honey trap as city hives leave wild bees at risk', *The Times*, September 30.
Weintraub, K. (2019) 'These whales are seranaders of the seas: it's quite a racket', *New York Times*, January 7.
Weis, T. (2013) *The Ecological Hoofprint. The Global Burden of Industrial Livestock*. London: Zed Books.
Welti, E.A.R., Roeder, K.A., de Beurs, K.M., Joern, A. and Kaspari, A. (2020) 'Nutrient dilution and climate cycles underlie declines in a dominant insect herbivore', *PNAS*, 117: 7271–5.
Westerhold, T., Marwan, N., Drury, A. et al. (2020) 'An astronomically-dated record of Earth's climate and its predictability over the last 66 million years', *Science*, 369. doi: 10.1126/science.aba6853
Weston, K. (2009) *Families We Choose. Lesbians, Gays, Kinship*. Durham, NC: Duke University Press.
Weston, K. (2017) *Animate Planet. Making Visceral Sense of Living in a High-Tech Ecologically Damaged World*. Durham, NC: Duke University Press.
Westling, L. (2014) *The Logos of the Living World. Merleau-Ponty, Animals, and Language*. New York, NY: Fordham University Press.
White, R. (1991) *The Middle Ground. Indians, Empires, and Republics in the Great Lakes Region, 1650–1815*. Cambridge: Cambridge University Press.
White, R.R. and Hall, M.B. (2017) 'Nutritional and greenhouse gas impacts of removing animals from US agriculture', *PNAS*, 114 (48): E10301–8. doi.org/10.1073/pnas.1707322114
Whitehead, A.N. (1929) *The Aims of Education and Other Essays*. New York, NY: Free Press.

Whitehead, A.N. (1968) *Modes of Thought*. New York, NY: Free Press.
Whitehead, A.N. (1978 [1929]) *Process and Reality*. New York, NY: Free Press.
Whitehead, A.N. (1985) *Symbolism. Its Meaning and Effect*. New York, NY: Fordham University Press.
Whitehead, A.N. (2015 [1920]) *The Concept of Nature*. Cambridge: Cambridge University Press.
Whitehead, H. and Rendell, L. (2015) *The Cultural Lives of Whales and Dolphins*. Chicago, IL: Chicago University Press.
Wilkinson, I. (2020) 'Madrid to cull 11,000 pesky parakeets as health danger', *The Times*, February 17.
Willes, M. (2017) *The Curious World of Samuel Pepys and John Evelyn*. New Haven, CT: Yale University Press.
Williams, P. (2020) *Jellyfish*. London: Reaktion.
Wilson, E.O. (2015) *Half-Earth. Our Planet's Fight for Life*. New York, NY: Norton.
Winder, R. (2017) *The Last Wolf. Hidden Springs of Englishness*. London: Abacus.
Winkler, A. (2018) *We the Corporations. How American Businesses Won Their Civil Rights*. New York, NY: Liveright Publishing.
Wischermann, C., Steinbrecher, A. and Howell, P. (eds) (2018) *Animal History in the Modern City. Exploring Liminality*. London: Bloomsbury.
Woinarski, J.C.Z., Burbidge, A.A. and Harrison, P. (2015) 'Ongoing unraveling of a continental fauna: decline and extinction of Australian mammals since European settlement', *PNAS*,112: 4531–40.
Woinarski, J., Legge, S., Dickman, C. (2019) *Cats in Australia. Companion and Killer*. Clayton: CSIRO.
Wolfe, C. (2003) *Zoontologies. The Question of the Animal*. Minneapolis: University of Minnesota Press.
Wolfe, C. (2015) *Animal Rites. American Culture, the Discourse of Species, and Posthumanist Theory*. Chicago, IL: University of Chicago Press.
Wood, D. (2019) *Reoccupy Earth. Notes Toward an Other Beginning*. New York, NY: Fordham University Press.
Wood, P. (2019) *London is a Forest*. London, Quadrille.
Woodruff, M. (2020) 'The face of the fish', *Aeon*, July 3. https://aeon.co/essays/fish-are-nothing-like-us-except-that-they-are-sentient-beings (Accessed August 12, 2020).
Woodward, I., Arnold, R. and Smith, N. (2017) *The London Bird Atlas*. London: John Beaufoy/London Natural History Society.
Woolf, G. (2020) *The Life and Death of Ancient Cities. A Natural History*. Oxford: Oxford University Press.
Woolf, V. (1998 [1933]) *Flush*. Oxford: Oxford University Press.
Wong, A.C., Holmes, A., Ponton, F., Lihoreau, M, Wilson, K., Raubenheimer, D. and Simpson, S.J. (2015) 'Behavioral microbiomics: a multidimensional approach to microbial influence on behavior', *Frontiers in Microbiology*. doi.org/10.3389/fmicb.2015.01359
World Meteorological Organization (2019) *The Global Climate in 2015–2019*. Geneva: World Meteorological Organization.
World Wildlife Fund/Institute of Zoology (2020) *Living Planet Report 2020. Bending the Curve of Biodiversity Loss*. Gland: World Wildlife Fund.
Wotton, K.R., Gao, B., Myles H.M. et al. (2019) 'Mass seasonal migrations of hoverflies provide extensive pollination and crop protection services', *Current Biology*, doi.org/10.1016/j.cub.2019.05.036
Wright, J. (2016) *A Natural History of the Hedgerow*. London: Profile Books.
Wróbel, S. (2015) 'Domesticating animals: a description of a certain disturbance', in S. Wróbel, *The Animals in Us – We in Animals*. Frankfurt: Peter Lang, pp. 219–38.
Wynes, S. and Nicholas, K.A. (2017) 'The climate mitigation gap: education and government recommendations miss the most effective individual actions',

Environmental Research Letters, 12 (7): #074024. https://iopscience.iop.org/article/10.1088/1748-9326/aa7541 (accessed July 6, 2020).

Xi Jinping (2015) *Full text from President Xi Jinping's Speech in Seattle*. Washington, DC: National Committee on United States-China Relations. www.ncuscr.org/content/full-text-president-xi-jinpings-speech (accessed July 2, 2020).

Xu, C., Kohler, T.A., Lenton, T.M., Svenning, J. and Scheffer, M. (2020) 'Future of the human climate niche', *PNAS*, 117 (21): 11350–5. doi.org/10.1073/pnas.1910114117

Yawada, Y. (2014) *Memoirs of a Polar Bear*. New York, NY: New Directions.

Yearwood, L. and McKibben, B. (2020) 'Want to do something about climate change? Follow the money', *New York Times*, January 11.

Yong, E. (2018) 'When humans war, animals die', *The Atlantic*, January 10.

Young, E. (2005) 'Swordfish heat their eyes for the hunt', *New Scientist*, January 10.

Young, R. (2017 [2003]) *The Secret Life of Cows*. London: Faber.

Zagorsky, J.L. (2017) 'Are catastrophic disasters striking more often?' *The Conversation*, September 8. https://theconversation.com/are-catastrophic-disasters-striking-more-often-83599 (accessed November 18, 2020).

Zhang, P., Wei, J., Zhao, C., Zhang, Y., Li, C., Liu, S., Dicke, M., Yu, X. and Turlings, T.C.J. (2019) 'Airborne host–plant manipulation by whiteflies via an inducible blend of plant volatiles', *PNAS*, 116: 7387–96.

Zhang, S. (2020) 'Rats have not changed. We have', *Science*, June 8.

Zhong, R. and Tang, A. (2019) 'A vicious, untreatable killer leaves China guessing', *New York Times*, April 22.

Zielinska-Dabkowska, K. and Xavia, K. (2019) 'Protect our right to light', *Nature*, 568: 451–3. www.nature.com/articles/d41586-019-01238-y (accessed July 6, 2020).

Zielinski, S. and Zachos, E. (2018) 'What do wild animals do in wildfires?', *National Geographic*, July 31.

Zimmer, C. (2017) 'Ancient viruses are buried in your DNA', *New York Times*, October 4.

Zimmer, C. (2019a) 'Germs in your gut are talking to your brain. Scientists want to know what they're saying', *New York Times*, January 29.

Zimmer, C. (2019b) 'These mice sing to one another – politely', *New York Times*, February 28.

Index

Ackerman, J. 56
'adopters' 72
affects (feelings) 48–9
Africa
  population growth 180
  war and animal deaths 92
African swine fever 88, 147
aggregate 26–7
agricultural subsidies 171, 177
agriculture
  changing 167–72
  changing practices 177–9
  and half-Earth 162
  systemic defects 29
  use of horses 78
agrilogistic machine 167–79, 195
air pollution 28, 136, 158, 168
alter-politics 8, 10, 50, 198–201
animal agency 72–5
  differential, in interactions with cities 75–87
animal culture 133–4
  cities, and impoverishment 139
  transmission 138–9
animal deaths and killings
  and animal agency 74–5
  caused by other animals 127–8
  in and because of cities 1, 7–8, 31, 69–70, 80, 92–128
  and climate change 124–5
  COVID-related 123
  for fashion 95–6
  for food 1, 77, 83–7, 101–12, 167–8, 169
  and habitat loss 160
  pest eradication 95, 117–18
  to preserve other animals 128
  quandaries 127–8
  for science and medicine 116–17
  for sport 116
  stopping unnecessary 126–7
  and trafficking 117
  and urban infrastructure 8, 119–22
  in war 79, 92
animal ethology 133–4
animal rights
  vs 'the greater human good' 126
  hard-line discourse 128
animal/non-human thinking 2, 7, 53–68, 95
  approaching on its own terms 49–50
  and centres of experience 48–9
  cities as reservoirs of 15–16
  examples 55–63
  humans as gauge for 53–4, 55
  and recasting human thinking 4
  and science 53, 54–5
animal welfare 168
animals
  adaptation to cities 8, 130–41, 154–6, 157–8, 171
  building cities to accommodate 153–4, 156–7, 159–64
  common characteristics 39
  cruelty to 93, 96–7
  cruelty distained 191
  dictionary definition 39
  differential separation 94, 96–102
  as food for thought 4
  impact of climate change 124–5
  impact of urban habits 31
  individuation 137, 139–40
  innovation 138, 140
  as neighbours and friends 189
  number of species 39
  and 'parliament of things' 183
  personhood 9, 41–2, 193–4
  in philosophy and social theory 7, 39–43
  relationship to cities 70–2
  in science 54–5
  in Spencer's *Resurrection* 200–1

Index

subjective experiencing 139–40
symbiosis 43–50
symbolic factors 140–1
treatment 9
as urban nuisance 82, 155
violence towards 94
viral diseases 123
what is an animal? 95–6
see also companion animals; livestock
Annales School 87
'anthropause' 123–4
Anthropocene 6, 16–20, 87, 194
anti-politics 10
antibiotic resistance 88
antibiotics 16, 88
Antigone 185
ants 61
archaea 45, 46, 71
Arendt, H. 183, 187 n.34
Aristotle 11 n.10, 32, 187 n.28
art 152
arthropods 61, 64, 71
atanthropes 72
attachment to place 195–6
Auden, W. H. 200
Australia 101
  animal fire deaths 124–5
  animals killed by feral cats 127–8
  impact of sheep on land 77
  sheep export deaths 77
  urban depredation 171–2
  urban tree loss 158–9

bacteria 45–6
  and disease 122
  in houses 71
  human microbiome 46–7
bacteriophages 46
Ballard, J. G. 5, 153
Bank of America 19
Barad, K. 197
barbed wire 74
Barber, B. R. 149
barn owls, roadkill 120
basement living 24
bats 3, 110, 122
  and pandemics 123
Battersea Dogs Home 100
Baynes-Rock, M. 72
beavers 118, 191

bees 132, 159, 171
  thinking 61–2
behavioural adaptation 131–4
behavioural plasticity 53, 56, 61, 132
Beijing 34 n.17, 34 n.18, 99, 117
  basement living 24
  stray cats 101
biocultural diversity 134
biodiversity 22, 64, 92, 128, 156, 161, 170
  cities 70, 158, 171
bird feeding 130–1, 155–6, 160
  and changes in beaks 135
bird strike (on aircraft) 121
birds 4, 55–6, 117
  adaptation to cities 70, 135, 138, 154–5, 171
  aesthetic dimension of mate attraction 141
  communication tower collisions 156–7
  decline in farmland 170
  designing cities for 160
  killed by cats 127, 128
  migrant population decline 161
  and the millinery trade 95–6
  power line collisions 119
  railway deaths 121
  roadkill 120
  thinking 56
  window collisions 119, 161
  see also game shoots
birdwatching 96
bison, conservation 191
black widow spiders 135–6
blackbirds 135
Bloom, J. 172
bobcats 136
Bolivia 182
Bonham, C. 159
Bristol 20
Britain *see* United Kingdom
British Empire 77
brownfield sites 130
Buddhism 189
Bulliet, R. W. 107
bushmeat 109–10
butterfly extirpation 122
Byrne 24

240

Cabannes, Y. 87
calumet ceremony 199
camel crickets 71
camels 79, 89 n.15
Canada 19
  bird communication tower collisions 157
  bird power line collisions 119
  bird window collisions 119, 161
  migratory bird protection 166 n.29
  roadkill 120
Canada geese 3, 70, 82, 89 n.3
capitalism 10, 189
carbon dioxide
  impact of high levels 18
  ocean absorption 57
  removal by trees 158
carbon dioxide emissions 10, 127
  cement industry 27
  cities 17, 19–20, 21, 25, 26
  corporations 18, 19
  meat production 109
  and soil degradation 29
Carson, R. 25–6
Cartwright, N. 43
cats 70, 71, 79, 82, 92, 118, 186 n.2
  animals killed by 125, 127–8
  as pets 98, 99
  roadkill 120
  strays 101
cells 44, 45, 46
cement manufacturers 18
cephalopods 116
  thinking 58–61
Charles River Laboratories 117
cheese 106
Chicago 82, 104, 118, 161
  'yards' 104
chickens 75–6, 83–7, 126
  battery hens 86
  broiler production 84–6
  cognitive abilities 85
  COVID-related killing 123
  grain-to-meat conversion 187 n.20
  intensively farmed 106
  numbers slaughtered 105, 108, 169
  rise in consumption 108, 198
  slaughterhouse cruelty 86–7
chimeras 184

chimpanzees 64 n.2, 64 n.10, 132, 133–4, 142
China 89 n.13, 180
  agricultural antibiotics 88
  animal testing 117
  cement use 27
  climate change effects, North China Plain 35 n.45
  and COVID-19 123
  distant water fishing 111
  dredging for sand 23
  food security issues 88–9
  food waste 173
  land sparing 162
  meat-eating 147
  metro expansion 24
  pet ownership 98–9, 127
  tree planting 165 n.17
  wildlife farms 117
chloroplasts 45
Citibank 19
cities 15–36
  agricultural footprints 177
  animal adaptation to 8, 130–41, 154–6, 157–8, 171
  animal deaths in or because of 1, 7–8, 31, 69–70, 80, 92–28
  and/of the Anthropocene 16–17
  anthropogenic vs. anthropomorphic 151
  and attachment to place 195–6
  bacteria and viruses 45, 46
  beneficial aspects 26
  and 'better' ecologies 70
  building differently 153–66
  change, possibilities of 8, 16, 20, 32, 147–87, 194–201
  and climate change 17–18, 19–20
  as commons 69, 181
  complexity 48
  as composites of trails 196–7
  damage done by 1–2, 6, 25–30, 31
  differential engagement with animal agency 75–87
  as evolutionary forcing agents 134–5
  excessive hygiene effects 47
  expansion in four dimensions 21–4
  food and food systems 87–9, 107–8
  and human cultural evolution 142
  'humanifyng' 151

241

Index

and 'humanimality' 194
inclusive nonhuman rights to 181–5
infrastructure, and animal death 8, 119–22
and innovation 140
as massively integrated communities 198
as 'middle ground' 198–9
as multiplicities of beings 69–70
myriad habitats 130–1
need for reduction in meat-eating 174
and population growth 20–1, 180
and redefined humanity 2–3, 5–6
relationship to animals 70–2
re-presentation 151–3
as reservoirs of non-human thinking 15–16
'safety structures' 31–2
'sentient' 15
sequestration of food animals 94, 102–7
as symbiont organisations 69
as third nations 199
and violence 92–4
what needs to be done? 148–51
and zoonotic diseases 122–4
cliff swallows 135
climate change 25, 118, 177, 179
and agriculture 168
cities and 17–18, 19–20
culpability for 18–20
impact on animals 64, 124–5
inter-urban knowledge transfer 149
see also global warming
coal companies 18–19
cochineal 115 n.46
Cocker, M. 170
cockroaches 71, 117
Cocozza, P. 11 n.15
cod 57
Coetzee, J. M. 83–4
cognitive buffer hypothesis 89 n.10
cognitive ecology 132
Colebrook, C. 32
commensal animals 72
commodity futures 168
companion animals (pets) 97–9
see also pet food industry
concentrated animal feeding operations (CAFOs) 106

concrete 27
conservation 124, 161, 162, 189, 191
cormorants 138
corporate culpability for climate change 18–19
Council of Tall Buildings and Urban Habitat 22
countryside
sterility of urbanized 168, 169
urbanization 25
COVID-19 123–4
cows/cattle 60, 88, 122, 126, 138
and capital 11 n.17
dairy 106–7, 126
exiled from cities 103, 104
grain-to-meat conversion 187 n.20
intensively farmed 106
interaction with the human world 73
numbers slaughtered 104, 105, 108, 169
and slaughterhouse advances 168
water needs 125
coyotes 75, 81–3, 154, 155
Cree people 193
Cretaceous period 18
crows (corvus genus) 55, 70, 120, 155
intelligence 64 n.7, 132, 133,
Cruel Treatment of Cattle Act (1822) 97
cruelty to animals 93, 96–7
broilers and battery hens 86–7
deliberate ignorance of 126
distained 191
Cruelty to Animals Act (1835) 97
cultural evolution 142–3
curlews 121
cuttlefish 65 n.13

dairy industry 106–7
inefficiency 109
Dante 7
Darwin, C. 113 n.4, 136, 141, 151, 191
Darwinism 95
Daston, L. 42, 61
Davis, M. 32 n.3
Dawkins, R. 48, 143 n.12
De Waal, F. 54
Debaise, D. 49
deep biosphere 34 n.28

Index

deep equality 183
deforestation 30
Deleuze, G. 5, 44, 139
Department for Environment, Food and Rural Affairs 172
Derrida, J. 40, 42, 84, 174
Descartes, R. 54
Descola, P. 5
Despret, V. 102
Detroit 100–1, 165 n.20
diplomacy 8–9, 190
disasters
  natural 28
  standardized 148
diseases 30, 122–4
DNA 134, 136, 139, 140
dogs 1, 2, 48, 53, 70, 71, 79, 92, 122
  as pets 98, 99
  railway deaths 121
  roadkill 120
  strays 81, 99–101
dolphins 55, 64 n.2
domesticated animals
  colonization of North America 74
  and increased inequality 72
  and zoonotic diseases 122
  see also companion animals; livestock
Domran, Josh 152
donkeys 90 n.19, 114 n.33
dual inheritance theory 134
Ducatez, S. 138
Dunn, R. 71

EAT-Lancet Commission 88, 176
Ebola infection 123
ecocide 19
ecological domino effect 148
ecological emergency 20
ecological imperialism 77
ecology without nature 69
ecosystem rights 182
Ecuador 182
Egypt, street dogs 100
Einstein, A. 197
elevators 22
Elias, N. 191
end of times 50–1 n.3
energy generation by humans 26

England
  change in attitudes to companion animals 97
  curlew destruction 121
  factory farming 86
  meat-eating 101–2
  sheep 76
  sterile 'countryside' 169
  tree cover 165–6 n.21
entanglement 44–8
environment
  damage by cities 25
  effects of agriculture 168
  effects of road and rail construction 22
  importance of insects 62–3
  of living beings 49
epigenetics 134, 136, 140
epistemic injustice 182
eugenics movement 112 n.2
evolution 136–43
  'extended' 140
  human cultural 142–3
  individuation and innovation 137–40
  and symbiosis 141
  symbolic factors 140–1
extinction 31, 110, 125, 170, 171
extirpation 122

factory farming 86, 111, 126
Fagan, B. 110, 111
fall armyworms 89
FAO 29, 30, 109, 111, 172
farm animals *see* livestock
Federal Aviation Administration 156
Federal Migratory Bird Treaty Act (1918) 96
Feinstein, J. 71
fertilizers 169
financiers, culpability for climate change 19
Finland 184
fires 11 n.13, 124–5
First World War 79, 85
fish
  impact of climate change 125
  thinking 57–8
fish farming 111–12

243

Index

fishing 110–11
  peak 'capture' 110
  unsustainable 'harvesting' 29
  waste 172–3
fission-fusion 81
Flannery, T. 171, 202 n.2
flexitarianism 174, 176
flies 62–3, 112, 118
floods 27, 124
Flusser, V. 59–61
food 87–9
  postdomestic systems 107–8
food recovery systems 174
food security 88–7, 125
food waste 172–4
foodsheds 107–8
Forbes, D. K.
Ford, Henry 105
fossil fuel financing 19
Foster, C. 1
foxes 95, 117, 120, 125
  intra-species variation 131
  rural extinction threat 170
  urban 71, 72, 154, 155
freedom, re-configured 199
Frumhoff 19
Fry, T.
fulmars 56
fungi 45, 46, 51 n.4
  in houses 71
Future Design, Japan 184

G20 summit (2019) 22
Gabrys, J. 185
game shoots 116
garden ponds 159
gardens 159
gas companies 18–19
geckos 72
Gee, H. 53
gene-culture co-evolution 55, 140, 142
genetic adaptation 134–6
genetic drift 140
genetics, basics challenged 140
geology, re-working 23
Germany 63, 156
  Nazi 113 n.8
Ghosh, A. 192
Gilbert, S. F. 47

Global North 110, 118, 189
Global South 88, 110, 189
global warming 17–18, 28, 63, 64, 170
  see also climate change
glyphosates 178
Godfrey-Smith, P. 58, 59
golden jackals 90 n.26
Gorongosa National Park, Mozambique 92
governmental culpability for climate change 18–19
Great Lakes 73
great-tailed grackles 132
greenhouse gas emissions
  agriculture 168
  animal farming 177
  food waste 172
  see also carbon dioxide emissions; methane emissions
grizzly bears 191
Guangzhou 163
Guattari, F. 190
gulls 154–5

H7N7 avian flu pandemic 123
habitat fragmentation 22, 122, 136
habitat loss 160
Hacking, I. 134
Hage 11 n.12
half-Earth 162–3
Hall, M. B. 177
Hamilton, C. 194
Handley, S. 166 n.32
Haraway, D. 45, 127, 134, 179, 180, 181
Hardt, M. 181
Harman, G. 42
Harwatt, H. 109
heat waves 35 n.44
hedgehogs 95, 120, 170
hedgerows 154
Heede, R. 18, 19
Heidegger, M. 7, 39–41, 195–6
Hewitt, K. 92
Heyes, C. 142
HIV/AIDS epidemic 123
Hogarth, W. 96–7
Holocene interglacial 16
homelessness 30

homocentrism 43
honour 200
Hopkins, G. 43
horses 60, 64 n.7, 75, 78–81, 138, 200
   exiled from cities 80–1, 103
'Hothouse Earth' 17
house-dwelling species 71
house finches 135
housing problems 30
Houston 163
hoverflies 62–3
Howell, P. 100
Hoyle-Wickramasinghe hypothesis
   65 n.17
human–animal dualism 15
human–animal interagency 72–5
human body
   coevolutionary symbiosis 46–7
   effects of urban habits 30
human evolution 142–3
human exceptionalism 7, 127
human speciesism 1, 2
humanimality 194
humanity
   as 'horde of inhumanity' 2
   'human' category unsettled 1
   killing spree 108–9
   moving towards honour 199–200
   as multi-species community 20, 50,
      154, 189, 199
   redefining 2–6
   treatment of those 'outside' 3–4, 9,
      93–4
humans
   contrasted with animals in philosophy
      39–43
   cruelty 93
   dangers of animals on roads 120
   multiple and centralized centres of
      perception 49
   percentage of biomass 167
   road deaths 120
   thinking, as gauge for animal thinking
      53–4, 55
   violence 92–4
   zoonotic diseases 122–3
humble ants 140
hunting
   Cree attitudes 193
   disgust at 191
   industrialized 109–12
Hurricane Florence 124
hyenas 92, 89 n.10

immune system 46, 47, 134
India 180
   meat eating 186 n.15
   rhesus-macaque monkeys 132–3
   street dogs 100
   urban air pollution 35 n.47
indigenous Australians 195
indigenous peoples 192–4
Ingold, T. 151, 193
insects
   'control' as pests 117
   farming 112
   and gardens 159
   genetic adaption to cities 135
   population decline 63–4, 170
   roadkill 120
   thinking 61–3
instincts
   and animal inferiority 39, 94
   containing behavioural
      plasticity 53
intelligence
   and brain size and complexity 138
   cephalopods 58, 59
   different evolutionary roads to 53
   increase in city-dwelling animals 132
   rats 118
   swarm 61
intensive farming 106, 168, 170
inter-species breeding 141
interdependence 184
intergenerational democracy 184
International Energy Agency 22

Jackson Laboratory 116
Jakarta 35 n.43, 36 n.55
James, S. P. 41
Japan 98 n.13, 184
Jeffries, R. 5
jellyfish 57–8
Jensen, L. 5
Johnson, D. 5
Jones, M. 122
JPMorgan Chase 19

Index

kangaroos 120
Kant, I. 39, 42, 50 n.1, 184–5
Kingsolver, B. 5
Klem, D. 119
Knutson, R. 120
Kohn, E. 193
Korsgaard, C. M. 9, 43
Koselleck, R. 78, 81
Kotkin, J. 174, 181
Kroll, G. 160
Kyba, C. C. M. 29

Lacey Act (1900) 96
Lack, D. 137
ladybird migration 66 n.31
Lagos 180
Laland, K. 138
land reclamation 23
land sharing 160–1
  in time 163
land sparing 161–2
landfill 23
Lang, T. 87
language 40, 42
Latour, B. 149, 154, 183, 190, 195
LeanPath 174
Leopold, A. 124
Lestel, D. 126, 175
Levi-Strauss, C. 4
light pollution 28–9, 156–7, 170
Linnaeus 3
livestock (farm animals, meat animals) 101–2
  antibiotic dosing 88
  de-animalization 102
  evolutionary bonanza 136–7
  innovation prevented 140
  live exports 125
  as percentage of mammals 167
  restricted lives 126
  sequestration from cities 94, 102–7
  UK numbers 169
  see also chickens; cows/cattle; pigs; sheep
lizards 135
London 110, 118, 130, 159, 164, 175
  beehives 159
  bird species 171
  food outlets 108
  horses 79–80
  livestock 101, 114 n.29
  pigeons 155
  rooftops 157
  slaughterhouses 103
  stray dogs 100, 101
looping effect 134
Los Angeles 36 n.51, 82, 118, 136, 157
  trees 156, 158
Lovegrove, R. 7
Lyme disease 122

Mabey, R. 130, 153
Macdonald, H. 1
Macfarlane, R. 1
MacInnes, M. 5
Manaugh, G. 198
Mandyck, J. M. 172
manners 190–1
Mao Zedong 98
Maori peoples 182
maps and mapping 152–3
Marc, Franz 4
Margulis, L. 45, 48
marmalade hoverfly 62–3
Marocchino, C. 87
Marris, E. 159
Marx, K. 32–3 n.3, 76, 165 n.7
Marzluff, J. M. 133, 155–6
meat animals *see* livestock
meat-eating 101–2
meat-free diets 109 *see also* vegetarianism; veganism
meat production
  and 'de-animalization' 107
  environmental impact 109, 174
  global scale 108–9
  inefficiency 109
  knock-ons to agriculture 177
  and pet industry 127
  removal from meat consumption 107–8
  sequestration of farm animals from cities 94, 102–7
  and waste 173
meat substitutes 176
  China 147
  England 101–2
  as evolutionary impulse 126

246

Index

Middle East 125
  stopping or reducing 174–7
megacities 24
Mehretu, Julie 152
Merleau-Ponty, M. 40, 42
Merriam, Clinton Hart 113 n.6
Merriam-Bailey, Florence 95–6
methane emissions 10, 18, 19, 26, 168
metrofitting 164
Mexico 76–7
mice 130
  'control' as pests 117, 118
  gene-altered 116
microbiome 46–7
microplastics 27, 33 n.10
Middle East Respiratory Virus (Mers) 123
Milan Urban Food Pact 87
Millet, L. 5
mindset change 9, 20, 150–1, 189–92
miner birds 132
mirror test 53
mitochondria 45
Montaigne, M. 190
Moore, R. 164
moral virtue, reconstruction 190–1
Morgan, K. 87
Morris, W. 7
Morton, T. 167
mosquitos 135
Movebank 188 n.35
mussels (quagga and zebra) 73
Musser, G. 197

Native/First Nation Americans 186 n.16, 193, 198–9
nature writing 1
  and environmental apocalypse 5
Negri, A. 181
Nemecek, R. 109
New Caledonian crows 55
New York 110, 130, 158, 161
  bird building collisions 119
  Central Park ecology 143 n.3
  coyotes 82
  crows and ravens 155
  food shed 107
  insect conservation 159
  lights out programmes 166 n.30

pet numbers 98
post-bird strike killing of birds 121
rats 118
rooftops 157
slaughterhouses 103–4
stray dog drowning 114 n.20
New Zealand 101, 138
  animals killed by cats 128
  nonhuman rights 182
  sheep population 77
Nicolson 56
night-time industry and culture 24
Nipah virus 123
nitrogen pollution 169
nitrous oxide 25, 169
noise pollution 28, 121, 132
  oceans 121–2, 160
non-ideal theory 202 n.11
North America
  bird communication tower collisions 156–7
  colonization by domestic animals 74
  food origins 108
  house-dwelling species 71
  urban animal species 70–1
  urban coyotes 81–2, 155
  whale deaths by shipstrike 121
no-till farming 178
nuclear family 187 n.24
nutrient pollution 125, 169

oceans fish
  acidity 17
  changes to benefit wildlife 159–60
  emptiness 173
  impact of climate change 125
  life in 57
  link to cities 25–6
  noise pollution 121–2, 160
  plastic pollution 25, 27
  segmentation and appropriation 194–5
  see also fishing
O'Connor, T. 72
octopuses 54, 58–9, 116
oil companies 18–19
ontological emergency 8
oppression 4, 9, 199
Our Children's Trust 19

247

Index

Pachirat, T. 105
Pacyga, D. A. 104
pandemics 30, 70, 123–4
paper wasps 62
parakeets 155, 165 n.12 *see also* ring-necked parakeets
Parfit, D. 18
Paris 110, 157, 178
Paris Agreement 17, 19
Paris Commune 91 n.41
parliament of things 149, 183–4
partial connection ('disjunctive synthesis') 44
peak car 33 n.15
'peak pasture' 109
peat depletion 169–70
People's Dispensary for Sick Animals 96
peppered moth 135
peregrine falcons 138
personhood, encompassing all beings 9, 42–3, 193–4
pest eradication 117–18
pesticides 136, 169, 170, 171
pet food industry 127
pets *see* companion animals
pheasant shooting 116
Phillipson, Heather 4
phosphate pollution 169
pigeons 64 n.7, 70, 79, 154
　adaptation to cities 130, 131, 132, 135
　London population 155
pigs 106, 122, 126
　African swine fever 88, 147
　Chinese pork demand 147
　COVID-related killing 123
　exiled from cities 103, 104
　grain-to-meat conversion 187 n.20
　intensively farmed 106
　numbers slaughtered 105, 108, 169
　rise in consumption 108, 109
　and slaughterhouse advances 168
　and swine flu 100, 123
plants
　as 'democracies' of experience 48–9
　see also trees
plastic 25, 27
Pleistocene 83
political will 20, 30–1,

politics 9–10, 149–51, 198–201
　of imagination 152
pollution 28–9, 168, 169
　oceans 25, 27, 121–2, 160, 173
　see also specific forms
Poore, J. 109
population 179–81
　size, and past extinctions 31
power line collisions 119, 157
praying mantises 62
Preservation of Grain Act (Vermin Acts) (1532, 1566) 95
Probyn, E. 75
prokaryotes *see* archaea; bacteria
protists 45
Prum, R. O. 141
Pullman, P. 181

raccoons 71, 89 n.7
railways, and animal deaths 121
Rankin, Jessica 152
rats 54, 72, 82, 124, 128, 130
　'control' as pests 117, 118
　evolutionary clusters 136
　intelligence 62, 118
　killed for research 116
Raulff, U. 80
ravens 155
red kites 154, 155
reforestation 158
relationalism 44
Remy 102
Resurrection of the Soldiers, The (Spencer) 200–1
rhesus-macaque monkeys 132–3
rights
　innate vs. acquired 184–5
　for nonhuman beings 182, 184–5
Rights for Nature 182
ring-necked parakeets 3, 89 n.4
Ritvo, H. 93
road and rail expansion 22
roadkill 120, 135
Rockefeller Food System Vision Prize 178
rodents 82, 118, 130 *see also* mice; rats; squirrels
Romanes, G. 61
Rome 101

Rome, Ancient 114 n.23, 177
rooftop transformation 157
Roridula 51 n.11
Royal Society for the Protection of
    Animals 96
Royal Society for the Protection of
    Birds 96
Runa people of Peru 193
Rushby, K. 170

sand 23, 27
Santlofer, J. 103–4
Sapp, J. 47
sardines 125
Schulz, E. B. 172
science, and animal thinking 53, 54–5
seabed mining 115 n.40
sea level rise 17, 27–8
Seattle Underground 34 n.32
Second World War 79, 92
selfish gene hypothesis 143 n.12
sense of self 53, 54
serotonin 47
severe acute respiratory syndrome
    (Sars) 123
sharks 112
Shaw, A. 5
sheep 74, 75, 76–8, 88, 122, 138
    exile from cities 104
    numbers slaughtered 105, 108, 169
Shelley, Percy Bysshe 175
Shinto 189, 202 n.6
shipstrike 121, 160
Sinclair, I. 153
Singapore, land reclamation 23
slaughterhouses 86, 102, 103–6, 107, 123
    new kinds (from 1870s) 104–6
    modern industrialized (from 1950s)
    recent advances 168
sleep 163
Sloterdijk, P. 8, 17, 18, 31–2, 40, 196
smell, knowing through 53–4
Smil, V. 174
snakes 71, 89 n.8, 117, 128 n.1, 129 n.16
Snyder, G. 69
soil degradation 29–30 see also no-till
    farming 178
solein 176
Somerville, R. 201

sound, knowing through 54
space, new conceptions 197
Spain 76, 164 n.2
'Spanish flu' pandemic (1918) 123
sparrows 132 see also tree sparrows
Spencer, Stanley 200–1
spiders
    black widow 135–6
    in homes 71
'spooky action at a distance' 197
squid 45, 116 see also vampire squid
squirrels 117, 118, 128, 132, 143 n.3
starlings 135
State of Nature (2019) 170
states, shift required 191–2
Stengers, I. 6
Stone, C. 182
strays 81, 99–101
Stuart, T. 173
swine flu epidemic (2009) 100, 123
symbiosis 7, 43–50, 141, 148
    and cities 69
    and personality 51 n.13
synanthropes 72 see also coyotes; strays

Tauber, A. I. 47
Taussig, M. 59
Taylor, M. 19
thinking
    animal/non-human 2, 4, 7, 15–16,
        48–9, 49–50, 53–68, 95
    and centres of experience 48–9
    cities as grounds for common
        thought 69
    different manifestation of 3
    and human-animal dualism 15–16
    and human exceptionalism 7, 42–3
    human as gauge for animal 53–4, 55
    limits of understanding about 1
    magical 148 10
    necessity of the other for 190
    as a practice of sense-making 51 n.8
    and reciprocal modifications of the
        other 4–5
    as a verb 7
Thomas, C. 137, 191
Thomas, K. 97
Thrift, N. J. 92
Tinbergen, N 137

249

Index

Toronto Green Standard 161
totemism 194
toxic masculinity 11 n.11
traffic accidents 30 *see also* roadkill
traffic noise 28, 121–2
trafficking animals 117
transit ecology 157
tree sparrows 186 n.5
trees, in cities
  and environmental justice 156
  threats to 158–9
Trump, D. 96
tunneling 23–4
Tupi people 190, 192

underground pipes and cables 23
undersea cables 34 n.25
UNEP 172
United Kingdom (Britain, UK) 71, 77, 84
  agriculture 169–71
  animal protection 96
  bird feeding 130–1
  birds and animals in cities 154–5, 171
  companion animals 98
  COVID-related animal killings 123
  food labour force 108
  food waste 172
  foot and mouth culls 123
  garden acreage 159
  insect farms 112
  light pollution 29
  mega-farms 106
  railway deaths 121
  roadkill 120
  slaughterhouses 86–7
  urban expansion 21
  urban tree cover decline 158
  vegetarianism and veganism 175, 176
United States (US) 71, 97, 103, 182
  animal testing statistics 116
  animals' genetic adaptation to cities 135–6
  animals killed by feral cats 127
  biological/ecological wealth imbalance 156
  bird power line collisions 119
  bird protection and birdwatching 96
  bird strike (aircraft) 121
  bird window collisions 119
  broiler production 85–6
  climate suit against government 19
  concentrated animal feeding operations (CAFOs) 106
  conservation 191
  COVID-related animal killings 123
  dairy industry 106–7
  dog and cat euthanasia 99
  food waste 172
  horses in cities, 1900 78, 79
  livestock antibiotics 88
  main fish species eaten 110–11
  natural disasters 28
  nonfactory meat challenges 187 n.19
  pet dogs and cats 98
  roadkill 120
  shift work 24
  slaughterhouses 86, 105
  stray dog curbing of 81
  urban expansion 21
  urban tree cover decline 158
  vegetarianism and veganism 175, 176
  'wilderburbs' 131
universities 187 n.33
urban agriculture 178

vampire squid (vampyroteuthis infernalis) 59–61
VanderMeer, J. 5
veganism 175–6
vegetarianism 174–5, 176, 189, 191
velvet worms 65 n.27
vermin 95, 117–18
vertical farming 178–9
violence
  to animals 94
  in cities 92–4
viruses 45, 46, 122
  as genetic forcing agents 134
vision, assumed primacy 53
Viveiros de Castro, E. 5, 190, 192, 193–4
von Humboldt, A. 191

Wales 184
war, animal casualties 79, 92
war horses 78–9
warfare ecology 92
Wark, M. 181

waste
  urban production 21, 27
  see also food waste
water flea (*daphnia magna*) 135
water
  and cities 27, 122
  needs of exported animals 125
water pollution 28, 168
Watts, J. 19
wealthiest 10 per cent, culpability for climate change 19
Well-being of Future Generations Act (2015), Wales 184
Wells Fargo 19
whales 55, 65 n.11, 65 n.12, 160
  breeding between species 141
  shipstrike 121, 160
White, R. R. 177
whitefly 63
Whitehead, A. N. 44, 48–9, 50, 180
wild animals
  in cities 72, 122–3, 123–4, 154
  fire deaths, Australia 154
  see also bushmeat; coyotes

wilding 171
wildlife corridors 131, 157
wildlife depletion, UK 170
wildlife markets 117
Wilson, E, O. 162
wind turbine deaths 129 n.13
Winder 76
window bird collisions 119, 161
witchiness 31–2
Wittgenstein, L. 10
wolves 74, 82, 118, 181, 191
wool production 76
Woolf, V. 99
World War II 85
Wotton, K. R. 62, 63

Xenophanes of Colophon 60
Xi Jinping 147, 173

Younger Dryas cooling 83

zoecentricism 43
zoonotic diseases 30, 122–4

www.ingramcontent.com/pod-product-compliance
Lightning Source LLC
Chambersburg PA
CBHW052018070526
44584CB00016B/1800